85.

115

SCHOOL AND COMMUNITY

Second Edition

SCHOOL

and

CONTRIBUTORS

JULIAN C. ALDRICH
Professor of Education, New York University

LOIS M. CLARK
Rural Education Division, National Education Association

MARGARET KOOPMAN JOY
Formerly Professor of Social Science
Central Michigan College of Education

ELDON W. MASON
Midwest Director, American Junior Red Cross

CARSON McGUIRE
Professor of Education, University of Texas

MORRIS R. MITCHELL
President, Putney Graduate School of Teacher Education

EDWARD G. OLSEN
Education Director, Chicago Region
National Conference of Christians and Jews
Formerly Director of School and Community Relations
Washington State Office of Public Instruction

ALVIN B. ROBERTS
Director, Department of Audio-Visual Education
Western Illinois State College

JOHN ROTHSCHILD
Executive Director, The Open Road, Inc.

JULIAN W. SMITH
Associate Professor of Education, Michigan State College

CHARLES UGER
Principal, Public School 5, New York City

COMMUNITY

Second Edition

EDWARD G. OLSEN

Editor and Chief Author

PRENTICE-HALL, INC.

Englewood Cliffs, N. J.

First printing .... *June, 1954*
Second printing ...... *June, 1955*
Third printing ..... *January, 1957*
Fourth printing ... *February, 1958*
Fifth printing .... *June, 1960*
Sixth printing .... *June, 1961*
Seventh printing .... *March, 1965*

370.19
05252

PRINTED IN THE UNITED STATES OF AMERICA
79226-C

Preface

In recent years, and especially during the past decade, American educational thinking and practice have moved steadily toward ever-closer and more effective cooperation between schools and their supporting communities. School people everywhere are coming to see that all life is educative; that the democratic school must become definitely concerned with the improvement of community and social living; that functional education requires active participation in constructive community activities; that the community can be utilized as a living laboratory for learning; that the school plant should be a center for community activity; that the major areas and problems of life should give direction to the curriculum; that lay participation in school policy-planning builds public support as well as better school programs; that the school must lead in coordinating community effort for better education and must practice and promote democracy; and that in the Nuclear Air Age the community must be defined in local, regional, national, and even world-wide terms.

Now the school-community movement is coming of age. Even its critics no longer dismiss it as merely the latest in a series of educational fads. On the contrary, this trend to vitalize education by relating the school program to community living may represent the most significant and potentially far-reaching educational development of our century.

This volume, which represents a substantial revision and expansion of the earlier edition, offers a compact overview of the community education movement, with special attention to the community school as an idea and in practice. It outlines basic techniques of community analysis, provides detailed suggestions for using "seven doors" to community understanding and improvement, and presents tested ways of organizing a community resources and study program and securing strong public support in the very process of developing a sound community school. The book is designed to meet the widespread demand for valid "know-how" in community study and service at all school levels from kindergarten through adult education, and in all teaching fields from art to zoology. Students preparing to teach, experienced teachers in elementary and secondary schools, instructors in colleges and universities, workers in adult education, school directors and administrators, parent-teacher association members, and many others should find this volume both rewarding and stimulating. It should prove especially useful in conjunction with the editor's *School and Community Programs* (Prentice-Hall, 1949), a volume of actual case studies illustrating the principles and practices described here.

Thanks are due to all the contributing authors, whose names appear in the front of the book and on the first page of their respective chapters. Each of them approved the final draft of the material contributed by him, but is in no way responsible for any of the other sections. The over-all planning for this revision, its organization, structure, and major emphases, and the extensive editorial work—including criticism, quotations, and nearly all the suggested learning activities and bibliographies—represent the joint effort of the editor and his wife, Pauline Walsh Olsen, formerly director of the Instructional Materials Bureau and Elementary School Coordinator for the Bremerton, Washington, public schools.

Thanks are extended also to the many users of the first edition who made helpful suggestions for this revision and to Maurice Seay, who reviewed the entire manuscript and greatly stimulated its general improvement. Special acknowledgment is made to the many writers and publishers who generously authorized the use of quotations from copyrighted materials. Their contributions have added much and are individually credited within the text itself.

EDWARD G. OLSEN

Table of Contents

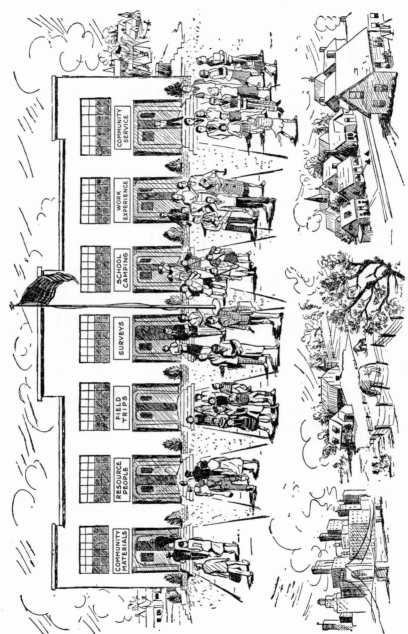

DOORS TO COMMUNITY LEARNING

Part **I**

RELATING
OUR SCHOOLS
TO LIFE

In recent years we have come to realize, however slowly or even reluctantly, that the "community school" is no passing educational fad, no momentary fancy of eccentric theorists. On the contrary, it represents a fruitful and essential extension of accepted educational thinking and practice. We know now that school instruction and guidance must be far more closely related to community life processes and needs than it has been in the past. If this is not done, there is little hope of strengthening American and world democracy through education. But since we are highly resolved to nourish, to invigorate, and to extend democracy, we recognize that community study and service through school education is here to stay. This movement is the most significant single development of its kind in our generation, and it seems destined to grow greatly with continuing sound experimentation at all school levels, in all teaching fields, with all types of students, and in all community areas: local, regional, national, and international.

Chapters in This Section

1. Schools in Transition
2. Learning and Teaching

1

EDUCATIONAL PIONEERS SPEAK FOR THEMSELVES

JOHN AMOS COMENIUS
Moravian, 1592-1670

What has to be done must be done by practice. Artisans do not detail their apprentices with theories, but set them to do practical work at an early stage; thus they learn to forge by forging, to carve by carving, to paint by painting, and to dance by dancing. In schools, therefore, let the students learn to write by writing, to talk by talking, to sing by singing, and to reason by reasoning. In this way schools will become workshops humming with work.

JEAN JACQUES ROUSSEAU
French, 1712-1778

You wish to teach this child geography—and you provide him with globes, spheres, and maps. What elaborate preparations! What is the use of all these symbols; why not begin by showing him the real thing so that he may at least know what you are talking about?

JOHANN HEINRICH PESTALOZZI
Swiss, 1746-1827

Either we lead the children through knowledge of names to that of things, or else through knowledge of things to that of names. The second method is mine. I wish always to let sense impression precede the word, and definite knowledge the judgement. . . . Not until after the foundation of human knowledge (sense impressions of Nature) has been fairly laid and secure would I begin the dull, abstract work of studying from books.

FRIEDRICH WILHELM FROEBEL
German, 1782-1852

We do not feel the meaning of what we say, for our speech is made up of memorized ideas, based neither on perception nor on productive effort. Therefore, it does not lead to perception, production, life; it has not proceeded, it does not proceed, from life. . . . For this reason, and only for this, our inward and outward life, as well as the life of our children, is so poor, because our speech is not born from a life, rich inwardly and outwardly, in seeing and doing; because our speech, our word, is not based on the perception of the thing it designates. Therefore, we hear the sound, it is true, but we fail to get the image; we hear the noise but see no movement.

HERBERT SPENCER
English, 1820-1903

How to live?—that is the essential question for us. Not how to live in the mere material sense only, but in the widest sense. . . . And this being the great thing needful for us to learn is, by consequence, the great thing which education has to teach. To prepare us for complete living is the function which education has to discharge; and the only rational mode of judging an educational course is to judge in what degree it discharges such function.

JOHN DEWEY
American, 1859-1952

Taken literally, the maxim "Teach things, not words," or "Teach things before words" would be the negation of education; it would reduce mental life to mere physical and sensible adjustments. Learning, in the proper sense, is not learning things, but the meanings of things, and this process involves the use of signs, or language in its generic sense. In like fashion, the warfare of some educational reformers against symbols, if pushed to extremes, involves the destruction of intellectual life, since this lives, moves, and has its being in those processes of definition, abstraction, generalization, and classification that are made possible by symbols alone. Nevertheless, these contentions of educational reformers have been needed. The liability of a thing to abuse is in proportion to the value of its right use.

JOSEPH K. HART
American, 1876-1949

The Community is the true educational institution. Within the community there is work that educates and provides for life; within the community are the roots of the cosmopolitanism that marks the truly educated man; within the community there is room for a noble and dignified culture and leisure for all. . . . The democratic problem in education is not primarily a problem of training children; it is the problem of making a community within which children cannot help growing up to be democratic, intelligent, disciplined to freedom, reverent of the goods of life, and eager to share in the tasks of the age. A school cannot produce this result; nothing but a community can do so.

2

CHAPTER **1**

Schools in Transition

Every period of great human conflict is also a time when educational workers begin to re-examine basic philosophies, question current school practices, plan new and better programs of instruction. Our times demand educational advance and reconstruction of a high quality. But what kind of education is most likely to meet the imperative needs of our generation in this atomic air age—human needs that are individual and social, needs that are moral and spiritual as well as emotional and intellectual, needs that are local, national, and worldwide in scope? In which direction and for what basic purpose shall we seek to move? Is not this the overwhelming educational challenge of our times?

Some years ago John R. Tunis wrote a book in which he described what had happened to the thinking of his university classmates since they had graduated twenty-five years before. His final summary went like this: "The lamp of learning, first lighted by the ancient Greeks, tended by the Church through the Dark Ages, blown white and high in the medieval universities, and handed down to us in direct line through Paris, Oxford and Cambridge, has at last produced a group of men whose chief ambitions, if their record tells the truth, is to vote the Republican ticket, to keep out of the bread line, and

---

This chapter is by EDWARD G. OLSEN.

to break 100 at golf. Enviable ambitions? Yes, but does one need to go to college to have such aspirations?" [1]

No, the old education will not do today. Literacy, culture, financial success, social status, getting ahead—these are not enough. The imperative necessity of our time is for the conquest of ignorance, greed, cynicism, and fear through moral and spiritual education of a high order. Youth must understand the social lag of our civilization, must realize that economic depression swept the world during the 1930's because the financial arrangements of that period could not sufficiently distribute the relative abundance the farms and factories could produce; that the Axis terrorized the world in the 1940's because aggressive nationalism was the outlet for totalitarian states in a technological age; and that the free world-communist conflict of the 1950's is at heart a struggle between two opposed value-systems for the minds and loyalties of men. But understanding is not enough. Youth must also become convinced that the responsibility and the opportunity of their generation is to develop in practice better patterns in human relationships, so that the present threat of the Nuclear Air Age may become instead the realization of its glorious promise.

Today, as never before in all human history, the essential study of mankind is man—his individual perplexities, his group relations, his social problems and resources for solving them. Education for more effective democratic living within a schizoid culture is our first responsibility. For as the Educational Policies Commission has aptly said, "The problem of making the democratic spirit prevail in these dark days of hostility and uncertainty falls chiefly to education. The reformer may cry that it is a social problem, the financier may hold that it is an economic problem, the politician may claim that it is a problem of statecraft, and the escapist may fold his hands and murmur resignedly that it is a problem which can be solved only by the inexorable march of destiny. But the

[1] *Was College Worth While?*, pp. 232-234. New York: Harcourt, Brace and Co., Inc., 1936.

basic problem, underneath its social, economic, political masks is forever and always, simply and completely, the problem of modifying human behavior by the method of education. A would-be democracy which fails in time to grasp this principle and to act upon it intelligently and decisively is doomed. Its back is against the wall, the bandage of self-imposed ignorance is over its eyes, and the fingers of invited autocracy are tightened on the triggers of the firing squad." [2]

Our Problem

How can our modern schools—the American people's chief formal agency for education—best help all our children and youth to participate effectively and with personal satisfaction in the enduring processes of human living? How can we, earnest teachers of these needy youth, sensitize them to the intolerable disparities of human circumstance, stimulate in them a deep feeling of personal responsibility for remedying the evils they perceive, give them the knowledge and skills necessary for intelligent judgment and action, acquaint them with the difficulties of arriving at truth in the social field, inculcate respect for honest differences in opinion, give them practice in willing, cooperative group activity, and finally develop in them an unswerving loyalty to democratic ideals and practices? How may teachers best aid these young people to put down deep roots of personal responsibility for group welfare, of realistic social understanding, of intelligent civic loyalties whereby they may flexibly anchor their lives against the surging tides of social barbarism at home as well as abroad? Is not *this* the educational problem of our generation?

The inescapable social fact of this century is that with the progress of industrialization and urbanization, human activities and relationships become steadily more specialized, more complex, more interdependent; yet at the very same time, less familiar and less personalized. Most children of two genera-

[2] *Learning the Ways of Democracy*, p. 40. Washington, D.C.: National Education Association, 1940.

tions ago shared directly and constantly in the elementary experiences of humanity. They learned through early personal experience to till the soil, to tend animals, to make the bread, to care for younger children, to perform successfully the numerous necessary tasks of the household. Being held responsible for carrying farm or home responsibilities, they soon learned to accept personal responsibility, to execute assignments promptly, to work in sustained fashion even at distasteful tasks. Meanwhile, they learned about politics from the arguments of their elders, they participated in the recreational activities of the local community, and they developed their ethical codes in home, church, and community where deeply conflicting patterns of moral behavior usually did not exist. And since they lived close to Nature, they often shared in the mating, birth-process, and death-watch of living things.

These are elementary experiences of humanity—aiding life and battling death, growing food and building a home, governing and worshipping, educating and playing, doctoring and wondering—and it was through sharing intimately in basic human experiences such as these that children of a former day matured emotionally, developed personal character, and attached their emerging, larger loyalties to personalized human values.

Under such conditions children learned to do by doing; the processes in which they shared were consciously cooperative in nature; and the results of their work were significant to themselves as well as to the adults of their own communities. No wonder, then, that the role of the common school, in their day, could be largely that of promoting simple literacy through intensive drill, and transmitting some of the social heritage through memorization of classic book-learning.

But what of our children today, especially those in the cities —where live over half of America's total population? Are they not the children of a "spiritual proletariat," crowded together and drifting aimlessly?

"All over the world, but most particularly in the countries where civilization is supposed to be most advanced, there are collected in great cities huge masses of people who have lost their roots in the earth beneath them and their knowledge of the fixed stars in the heavens above them. They are the crowds that drift with all the winds that blow, and are caught up at last in the great hurricanes.

They are the people who eat but no longer know how their food is grown; who work and no longer see what they help to produce; who hear all the latest news and all the latest opinions but have no philosophy by which they can distinguish the true from the false, the credible from the incredible, the good from the bad.

Is it surprising that as civilization has become more streamlined, democracy has become more unworkable? For these masses without roots, these crowds without convictions, are the spiritual proletariat of the modern age, and the eruption of their volcanic and hysterical energy is the revolution that is shaking the world. They are the chaos in which the new Caesars are born.

. . . This feeling, which pervades the great urban centers, that all things are relative and impermanent and of no real importance, is merely the reflection of their own separation from the elementary experiences of humanity." [3]

These are the children who are indeed dispossessed, for they help to grow no food, they rarely care for pets, their recreation is predominantly passive—through movies, radio, and television—they have no real work experience even in adolescence, they are little concerned about political affairs, they remain largely shut away from the mysterious processes of birth and death. Whether they exist in squalid tenements or reside in luxurious apartments, their lifelong separation from many elementary human experiences is precisely the same. Mistaking money for happiness, street address for success, and "getting by" for true achievement, they live their lives on the periphery of basic human experience rather than at its heart.

The city crowds people together physically even as it renders their wider associations less personalized. Meanwhile, school talk about things increasingly supplants real community

[3] Walter Lippmann, in a syndicated article in the public press under date of Nov. 3, 1938. By permission of the *New York Herald-Tribune*.

experience with things. Just here lies one of the great challenges to education today: to seek in every possible way to counteract the unfortunate effects of urbanization by offering wider opportunities for direct experience with life processes. This same challenge, although in somewhat different form, confronts rural education also— *Why do we teach what we teach?*

How Have Our Schools Responded?

Three major answers are commonly offered as solution to this basic problem of education today. It is noteworthy that each of these three answers reflects not only a different philosophic orientation with consequent varied educational program, but also constitutes a definite stage along the road from the school of yesterday to the school of tomorrow. Let's see how these three outlooks have been interpreted and expressed in our schools. To insure clear contrast, we shall sketch these viewpoints starkly, recognizing as we do that no school now exemplifies in full degree any one of these orientations.

The Academic School

An unforgettable portrait of the traditional schoolmaster is presented in Dickens' story, *Hard Times*. Here is pictured Professor Gradgrind, a teacher of the old school, an educational traditionalist to the core of his being. When the new girl, daughter of a horse trainer, appeared in his class for the first time, Gradgrind fixed her with an accusing eye and demanded that she define a horse. Define a horse? The girl was confused, stammering, unable to reply. To be sure, she had lived around horses all her life and she well knew how to manage and care for horses. But *defining* horses was something she had never before been asked to do, and so she hung her head in shame while the star pupil completed that assignment to the master's entire satisfaction:

"Horse: Quadruped. Graminiverous. Forty teeth, namely, twenty-four grinders, four eye-teeth and twelve incisive. Sheds coat in spring; in marshy country sheds hoofs, too. Hoofs hard, but requiring to be shod with iron. Age known by marks in mouth."

"Now, girl number twenty," said Mr. Gradgrind, "you know what a horse is." And so she did—in terms of the academic school's demand that pupils define, classify, construe, bound, tabulate, systematize, memorize, verbalize!

Although perhaps typical in Dickens' day, this satirical description is merely a caricature of what we now term the "traditional" school. Nevertheless, the fundamental orientation of that school has not basically changed; emphasis still falls primarily upon verbalistic learnings, logically organized, and imposed upon pupils with little real concern for individual differences in backgrounds, needs, or personal interests. For the children it is still fundamentally a process of sitting, memorizing, reciting, and daydreaming. This is true even though recent advances in teacher preparation, together with a slowly changing philosophy and practice of education, have done much to improve traditional schooling during the past third of a century.

The Progressive School

In course of time a new conception of education emerged, largely in reaction against the academic character and repressive discipline of the academic school. This new conception found practical expression in the child-centered "progressive" school, and became for many educators a real crusade. Some of the new devotees even proved themselves as doctrinaire and as fanatical as were any of the traditionalists against whose works they were in utter revolt. Define a horse? What nonsense! Here we try to help children who are interested in horses to comprehend horses, and to express fully their emotional reactions toward horses. We want our children to grow and grow in their conceptions and feelings about horses, until the basic horsiness of horses becomes a living, throbbing, vital aspect of their deepest beings!

Do not distort this emphasis. Progressive education long

since proved itself the most stimulating, most constructive educational development of the past generation. Its basic emphases
upon the emotional needs of the individual, upon learning by
doing, creative self-expression, pupil interests as avenues of
continued educational growth, cooperative planning and problem-solving will remain as permanent major contributions to
all our schools. But *comprehension* and *self-expression* are not
sufficient for children who must live out their lives in this
troubled twentieth century. These young people need to define and to comprehend, of course, but they must learn also
how to *utilize* resources for improved human welfare if they
hope to become competent, well-rounded, and tolerably civilized adults.

The Community School

Now American education is coming of age. The Great Depression, World War II, and the bitter struggle between the
free world and its communist enemies have forced a growing
realization that life is real, life is urgent; life is not all sweet-
ness and light in this best of all possible worlds—it is rather a
towering problem of precarious existence within an unstable
social order. American educators are generally now well aware
that the educational isolation of the school from its community
is as indefensible and as truly impractical as is political isolationism for the nation. And today we know that:

•   The schools of any free nation will fail their primary function
unless they consciously promote social progress in the future as well
as they preserve the culture of the past and prepare the individual
for effective participation in the present.
•   Democratic group progress, like individual adjustment, can
occur in maximum degree only as children and young people become
responsible, effective, contributing members of their communities—
communities that are conceived in local, regional, national, and
world-wide terms.
•   Young people will become responsible participants in community life only as they experience emotionally satisfying, socially
creative, and intellectually stimulating activity in those communities during their formative years.

Our growing awareness of these basic propositions has helped lead us during the past half century through the three fairly distinct stages in thinking which we have already noted. In the first of these stages (Traditional School), education was largely limited to a *subject-matter* approach. Discipline was severe and the interests of the child were rather narrowly conceived. The school was like a castle surrounded by a moat and usually the community beyond was ignored. At the close of the day the drawbridge was let down again and the child went back into the community, generally failing to notice the relation of the discipline and the school subject studied to the actual processes and problems of living there. After the first World War there was a pronounced shift of emphasis into the second stage (Progressive School), much of the reason being the psychological studies in the field of child and adolescent growth and development. *Child interests* now became widely recognized as being educationally significant for the learning process itself. There was a relaxation in formal discipline, an emphasis upon pupil-teacher planning, a strong concern for personality development. The curriculum centered about the interests of the child, and the needs of adulthood were often ignored. The community was studied and its resources utilized rather incidentally. Now, within the past few years, emphasis has shifted again; the emergence of the Community School concept has brought us into the third stage. *Human needs* have come to the fore, and the community is now regarded as a great, living laboratory in which the students of all ages may observe and participate, under guidance, in community enterprises which are educative in nature and designed to be socially constructive. The community school seeks to improve the quality of human living, includes lay people in school policy and program planning, organizes the required core of the curriculum around the major processes and problems of living, makes the school plant a community center for people of all ages, leads in community coordination of educational effort, and practices and promotes democracy in all human relationships.

The accompanying chart presents an attempted summary of this fundamental development in our educational thinking during the past half century or so. Two cautions are in order as you examine it:

• It is over-simplified. Very few schools today can actually be classified exclusively in any one of the three school-type categories. All dates and thumbnail descriptions must be taken to indicate major emphases rather than definitive positions.

• It portrays generally accepted theory, not actual practice in all schools or by most teachers. There is always a time lag between even widespread acceptance of any philosophy and its consistent

PHILOSOPHIC TREND IN AMERICAN SCHOOL EDUCATION
First Half of the Twentieth Century

TYPE OF SCHOOL	TRADITIONAL SCHOOL	PROGRESSIVE SCHOOL	COMMUNITY SCHOOL
DOMINANT PERIOD (of theory)	Until about 1910	About 1920–1930	Since about 1940
ORIENTATION	Book-centered	Child-centered	Life-centered
ULTIMATE AIM	Literacy and "culture"	Personality development	Improvement of living
CURRICULUM PATTERN	Academic subjects	Interest activities	Social processes and problems (core)
FUNDAMENTAL METHOD	Exposition, explanation, memorization	Problem-solving to satisfy personal interests	Problem-solving to meet personal and social needs
LEARNING VALUES	All deferred	All immediate	Both immediate and deferred
KEYNOTE OF DISCIPLINE	Repressive control	Freedom from restraint	Cooperative responsibility
WAYS OF RELATING SCHOOL AND COMMUNITY	Study the community Community materials	Study the community Community materials Use the community Resource people Field trips Surveys Camping	Study the community Community materials Use the community Resource people Field trips Surveys Camping Work experience Serve the community Improvement projects School a community center Involve the community Lay participation Community coordination

application in general practice. Although most American educators now accept the philosophy of the life-centered community school, it is probable that most schools and most teachers are still predominantly traditional in their daily teaching.

Now, as never before, doors must be opened between school and community—two-way doors, so that students and adults alike may study and serve the community by bringing the community into the school, and by taking the school into the community. Our youth must be led to study community affairs, to participate actively in community affairs, and to work with adults to improve community affairs. Surely our schools must help children, youth, and adults to face life's many personal and social problems frankly, and to know and use all available resources for solving or enduring them. Certainly we must educate people to live their lives fully, effectively, creatively, and as joyously as may be possible. Any school which stands aloof from the real problems of living today and tomorrow defeats its own primary function in a free society. It gives only a hothouse learning, sending out from its portals young men and women fundamentally unready to grapple with the insistent issues of this second half of the twentieth century. That is precisely why any practical approach to improved living through education must be a fundamental one, must involve speedy development of the *community-type* school and college, which stand in sharp contrast to the conventional institutions we know so well.

Thus American education stands today upon the very threshold of a wider and far more fruitful orientation than it has ever known: that of the life-centered community school.

What Is a Community School? [4]

Just what is meant, you may ask, by a "community" school or college? Is this some new legal entity, established as such by law or by administrative fiat? Not at all. Is it, then, a novel

[4] This analysis of community school characteristics was first presented in an address before the 1951 Chicago convention of the North Central Association and published in the *North Central Association Quarterly* 26:174-180; October, 1951.

type of building, expressly designed for adult use as well as child education? Not necessarily. Well then, is this merely the latest name for any school in a rural region, or in a small community? Certainly not. Neither is a community school just any school in a larger city which serves exclusively its own neighborhood as one city seems to have assumed when it announced that it would "convert" its elementary and high schools into community schools. All such seizures of the term "community school" distort and confuse the real meaning of our generation's most significant development in school education: the concept and practice of the life-centered community school.

What, then, is this "community school," and how does it go about its educational task? At least seven distinct characteristics of such a school are now evident. Unless a given school has most of these characteristics in high degree and all of them in some, it has no right to be termed a "community school." Such, at least, is the judgment of the *Encyclopedia of Educational Research* and of the National Conference of Professors of Educational Administration, to mention only two sources which cannot lightly be disregarded.[5]

Each of these characteristics is actually a professional "venture-area" into which we can now move with increasing speed, enthusiasm, confidence, and skill. In that very process we shall find that we are also developing the community school, whether it be elementary, secondary, collegiate, or adult in nature.

1. The Community School Improves the Quality of Living Here and Now

The basic function of the modern school is to improve the quality of human living—child living, youth living, adult living—in the area served by the school. Because the school

---

[5] See *Encyclopedia of Educational Research*, p. 1075; also reports of the National Conference of Professors of Educational Administration, Madison, Wisconsin, 1948.

exists in the community, the people there should be better people, physically and emotionally healthier, more understanding of those different from themselves, more competent workers, parents, citizens. Intergroup relationships should also be improved as a direct result of the school's efforts—better labor relations, lessened racial, religious, and nationality tensions. Low standards of cultural and material living, the divorce and crime rates, the increasing extent of mental illness, crippling labor-management struggles, dangerous interracial and interfaith tensions, international fears and conflicts—all of these demand that the modern school's basic and direct concern be that of educating better persons for better living in a better world.

2. The Community School Uses the Community as a Laboratory for Learning

Schooling cannot be realistic if it is confined to the four walls of the classroom, library, shop, or laboratory. If young people are to develop the understandings, concerns, and skills essential to the real improvement of human living, they must have every opportunity to learn about that living through extensive, first-hand, problem-solving experience. Books and visual materials are highly important, but alone they are simply not sufficient. That is why the community school opens doors for experience between school and community—through the wise use of resource people, field trips, community surveys, work experiences, and service projects. Factories and farms, social agencies and museums, council sessions and union meetings—these along with books and pictures are the instructional materials of the community school.

3. The Community School Makes the School Plant a Community Center

This modern school or college provides comfortable, homelike rooms and facilities where people can come together in neighborly fashion to study, work, and play. Open to all through appropriate arrangements are the library, shops, laboratories, gymnasium, auditorium, cafeteria, health center, and class-rooms. Equally available are the playing fields, the picnic grove with its barbecue pit, the demonstration farm, and the school camp. For this school is also an adult center where people gather to hear a speaker or to plan an activity, where parents discuss children's problems, business men keep fit on the volley-ball court, farmers repair machinery, home-makers share new ideas, young couples square dance, factory workers make ceramics, citizens question candidates for public office. The community school is a *used* school, used by adults as well as by children and adolescents, used evenings and daytimes, used week-ends and week-days, used summers and winters. It is the school of all the people, designed and used by them all according to their needs.

4. The Community School Organizes the Curriculum Around the Fundamental Processes and Problems of Living

In planning the community school's curriculum we begin with the admonition of Alexander Pope: "The proper study of mankind is man!" So we center the curriculum "subjects" in the fundamental processes and problems of living yesterday, today, and tomorrow; we seek out and study the stuff of life and not its trappings only; we leave behind our traditional patchwork pro-cedure in curriculum making and begin anew with basic human needs and relationships as the very heart of the new curriculum. That learning program thus comes to focus upon basic indi-vidual and group needs in relation to the culture's dominant values, processes, problems, and potentialities. This means, more specifically, that the required or "core" part of the modern school's program is organized directly around the persisting processes and related problems of human living here and now, today and tomorrow—such as utilizing the natural environment, adjusting to people, exchanging ideas, making a living, sharing in citizenship, maintaining health, improving family living, finding a life philosophy, and the like. Far from "lowering standards," this life-centered curriculum pattern serves to raise the student's own standards of work by making his learning experiences realistic, vital, and personally meaningful. The person who finds a direct and definite relationship between his school studies and the demands of modern life upon him discovers valid purpose in the school program and sees more clearly his own emerging place in school and community life.

5. The Community School Includes Lay People in School Policy and Program Planning

In a real sense the community school is a community-wide enterprise. The community as a whole, not merely the Board of Education and the P.T.A., feels that it has a stake in its school and shares responsibility for that school's success or failure. In the community school its broad policies and program are cooperatively discussed and even planned by civic, business, farm, labor, and professional leaders; by representatives of government, welfare, recreation, religion, and other local institutions; by all citizens who are concerned about education and the quality of living in their community.

6. The Community School Leads in Community Coordination

The community school works closely with all other agencies seeking to improve the quality of living. More than that, it accepts its responsibility to help bring those agencies together in close and continuous cooperation toward that goal. For the school realizes that the local community where people live, and move, and have their being in face-to-face relationships is both matrix and fountainhead of democracy.

It knows that neither the school nor any other agency working alone can ever hope to solve such problems as those involved in reducing racial, religious, and international tensions, providing adequate recreational facilities and guided work experiences, improving standards of living and of taste. In many communities, however, startling success is won when education is conceived as guided experience for better living, when the whole community's responsibility for providing that experience is widely recognized, and when school and other community agencies coordinate their planning and their efforts accordingly.

7. The Community School Practices and Promotes Democracy in All Human Relationships

All our schools stress in many ways the real meaning of democracy: its values and ideals; its foundations, history, advances and defeats; its resources and its obstacles; its manifold complexities and its glorious promise. But the community school goes beyond *information* about democracy, and even beyond *attitudes* of loyalty to democracy; the community school provides *also* ever-widening personal experience in positive community *action* for democracy. This school and its community are therefore living laboratories in which young Americans study and experience democracy as both goal and process, and where they continuously learn the specific skills of effective democratic participation.

Toward Vital Education

Although one or more of these seven characteristics may be found in many conventional schools, it is only the community school which is sufficiently functional and versatile to incorporate them all in a balanced manner. This it does because its supporters realize that education is basically a social process; that educational forms and functions must respond to the changing needs of human beings; that democratic education must be able as well as willing to honor its fundamental obligation of helping people to live more effectively and happily, both as individuals and as members of interdependent social groups.

The community school does not calmly assume, as does the traditional school of the past, that transmission of the Western world's cultural heritage, plus some civic and vocational training, is its chief concern. Neither does the community school make personality development through free expression of individual interests its major goal, as did many of the child-centered or progressive schools of the 1920's and 1930's. The real values of both organized knowledge and individual development are fully recognized by the community school, but primary emphasis always falls upon human-needs-to-be-met as the major purpose.

Historically viewed, the great virtue of the traditional school lies in its systematic organization of subject matter; that of the progressive school is its driving concern for the all-around development of the individual child; that of the emergent community school appears to be its emphasis upon the improvement of human living through cooperative effort democratically organized. *All three* emphases must be maintained in the new school of tomorrow. Not otherwise are the twin goals of individual self-development and democratic community improvement likely to be achieved.

Nor is this emphasis upon life-centered education necessarily a narrow or a provincial one. Visionless, indeed, is he who fails to perceive that in our time the local community is inextricably bound up with the regional, national, and world communities, and must be both studied and improved accordingly. Far from being provincial, therefore, the community school which begins its operation in the service area of the school is ultimately as broad as the earth in its developing concerns and services. The local community is the intellectual starting point and the social service area, but it is always a point of departure, not the final goal.

It should be noted, too, that this community school is never content with *study about* the community, however realistic and vital such study may be. This school also organizes many activities in which students and teachers together actually *participate in* community programs and, beyond that, constructively *contribute toward* practical solutions of community problems.

Democracy is learned—*built into daily behavior*—in the
community school as people of all ages gain experience in
identifying community needs and problems, in analyzing issues
clearly, in planning best probable solutions, in choosing leaders,
organizing working committees for research and reports, evaluating proposals made, carrying out plans, appraising results.
Frank discussion, respect for differences of opinion, imaginative planning, zealous effort, sober judgment, further discussion, planning, action—these are the basic elements of the
democratic process, and these are the firsthand experiences in
group activity shared by all students in the community school.
Ever alert to violations of democracy's principles in school
or community life, these young citizens build the democratic
faith and process into their daily patterns of behavior, the only
reservoir in which democracy can ever be contained. Thus they
lay deep the foundations for a better school and community
today, and, with them, a better world tomorrow. There is no
surer basis than this for improving the quality of living in
both school and community life.

First Five Decades of Our Century

Thus our professional sense of values and direction
has changed: the *traditional school,* with its insistence
upon book-knowledge-set-out-to-be-learned, gave way
to the *progressive school* with its emphasis upon child-interests-to-be-expressed, which now in turn yields to
the *community school* with its stress upon a human-needs-to-be-met purpose. From book-centered,
through child-centered, and into life-centered schools
—this has been the progress of our dominant educational thinking and experience during the first five
decades of our twentieth century.

Learning Activities

Socio-drama

Stage a situation in which several people are discussing modern education. This is a group of neighbors who have just heard a broadcast in which the speaker vehemently demanded that the schools "get back to fundamentals." These roles might be assigned:

1. A defender of modern education
2. A critic of "fads and frills"
3. A confused but open-minded parent
4. A teacher in a community school

Discussion Topics

1. Is the community school a passing fad, or a basic trend?
2. Does the community school idea threaten liberal education?
3. Is a community-oriented school likely to become a provincial one?
4. What do you consider to be the chief weaknesses of the community school? Which of these are defects of theory and which of practical difficulty?
5. How, now, will you define "progressive education"?

Group Projects

1. Take a class census to discover what elements of the academic, progressive, and community schools each member recalls from his own high school experience.
2. Do the same for their college class experiences.
3. Arrange a film forum to show and evaluate several of the motion pictures suggested for this chapter.
4. Set up class committees to study, and recommend in detail, ways of making this course more "life-centered."

Individual Activities

1. State and defend your personal analysis of what makes a good school.
2. Read several of the articles listed, find three or four more similar articles in more recent literature, and contrast the basic ideas expressed.
3. Which of the seven characteristics of the community school are you most willing to accept as valid? About which ones do you have personal doubts or misgivings? On what grounds?

4. Examine some of the more forward-looking curriculums, and evaluate them in terms of the seven characteristics of the community school listed in this chapter.
5. Assume that you are going to spend several days visiting a school which claims to be a community school. How would you go about examining the validity of this claim? List your standards in what you think to be the order of their evaluative significance.

Learning Materials

The lag of the school behind life-needs has been delightfully satirized by Harold Benjamin in his *Saber-Tooth Curriculum* (McGraw-Hill, 1939). Joseph K. Hart's *Education in the Humane Community* (Harper, 1951) dramatizes the deep cleavage that today exists between the confining conditions of school education in big cities and the fine conditions that can flourish in rural areas. George S. Counts' *Education and Civilization in America* (Teachers College, Columbia, 1952) outlines in its first chapter a stark, concise picture of the deeply troubled times in which we live, drawn in terms of basic social trends, current challenges, and our obligation to develop an education equal to these great tasks. Baker Brownell's *The College and the Community* (Harper, 1952) is a critical analysis of the typical college's failure to relate itself to community life and needs, and hence of its failure to educate youth for the modern, cooperative, interdependent world. For a popular overview of the momentous changes which have in 50 years literally transformed America, see Frederick Lewis Allen's *The Big Change* (Harper, 1952).

Progressive education at its best can be sampled through many volumes. Harold Rugg and Ann Shumaker's frankly *Child-Centered School* (World Book, 1928) described in great detail the teaching methods and school organization oriented around children's interests. Two decades later Rugg traced in his *Foundations for American Education* (World Book, 1947) the development of progressive education (Chapter 17), and went on to demonstrate that education must include also a society-centered orientation. John Dewey's small book, *Experience and Education* (Macmillan, 1938), is his critical evaluation of progressive education. Its highlights the pitfalls of newer practices while stressing the importance of learning through those kinds of experiences which lead to more and richer experience. More recently, Carleton W. Washburne's *What Is Progressive Education?* (John Day, 1952) has explained what is properly meant by the term, and describes a good progressive school and the results that should be secured from it.

The community school concept and practice is presented analytically in *The Community School*, edited by Maurice Seay for the National Society for the Study of Education (University of Chicago Press, 1953), and in *The Modern Community School*, edited for the Association for Supervision and Curriculum Development of the National Education

Association by Edward G. Olsen (Appleton-Century-Crofts, 1953). The NSSE yearbook examines the concept of the community school, reports varying practice in the United States and abroad, and evaluates progress and problems in community school development. The ASCD volume uses fictional and actual case studies from which are abstracted basic operating principles upon which some schools have been working toward the community school orientation; it also summarizes the philosophic framework involved. An older book, *The Community School* edited by Samuel Everett (Appleton-Century, 1938), describes the programs of nine community schools in both urban and rural regions, and lists fundamental differences between traditional and community school thinking.

How two rural schools developed comprehensive programs based on their communities' needs and resources is told by Elsie Clapp in her *Community Schools in Action* (Viking Press, 1939) and her later *The Use of Resources in Education* (Harper, 1952). William K. McCharen's *Selected Community School Programs in the South* (George Peabody College, 1948) scrutinizes the community concept in education, describes 22 specific school programs, and evaluates each in terms of community school theory. Challenging examples of what some other community schools are doing to improve their communities' food habits, housing, and clothing selection and care are presented in *School-Community Cooperation for Better Living*, by Charles Durrance and others (University of Florida, 1947). The interrelationships between rural life and school education in a Northern county have been described by Lorene K. Fox, whose *Rural Community and the School* (King's Crown Press, 1948) proposes ways of using school education to improve daily living. The National Society for the Study of Education's Fifty-first Yearbook, Part II, *Education in Rural Communities* (University of Chicago Press, 1952) stresses throughout the interrelationships of school and community, and the responsibility of the school for community improvement.

The Educational Policies Commission's two reports, *Education for All American Children* (1948) and *Education for All American Youth: A Further Look* (1952) describe in comprehensive fashion the kinds of life-centered community schools everywhere needed today. An analysis of American community life as it bears upon all aspects of school practice and community relations is the contribution of Lloyd and Elaine Cook's *Sociological Approach to Education* (McGraw-Hill, 1950). Edward G. Olsen's *School and Community Programs* (Prentice-Hall, 1949) presents over 150 actual case studies of successful community study and service practice at all academic levels and in many teaching fields. *The Community College* (McGraw-Hill, 1950) by Jesse P. Bogue describes the philosophy, role, and campus-community programs of higher institutions which do attempt to meet the life needs of the people of their areas. William H. Kilpatrick's excellent statements of the basic philosophy underlying the whole school-community movement appeared as the Introductions to two older volumes: *Youth Serves the Community*, by Paul Hanna and Research Staff (Appleton-Century, 1936), and Everett's *The Community School* (Appleton-Century, 1938).

The School That Built a Town by Walter Hines Page (Harper, 1952), is a fascinating modern account of a community school that operated as such half a century ago.

Professional journals sometimes devote entire issues to selected aspects of the school-community area. Among such special treatments are these:

THEME	JOURNAL	DATE
"Education for Improved Community Life"	*Bulletin of the National Association of Secondary-School Principals*	May 1946
"Education Helps Build a Region"	*High School Journal*	May 1946
"Secondary Schools and the Community"	*California Journal of Secondary Education*	December 15, 1946
"Teacher in the Community"	*Journal of Educational Sociology*	January 1947
"School and Community Resources"	*School Executive*	January 1948
"Children Need Experiences"	*Childhood Education*	October 1948
"Community Organizations"	*Journal of Educational Sociology*	November 1949
"Toward Community Improvement"	*Journal of Educational Sociology*	November 1952
"Schools and Community Improvement"	*School Executive*	January 1953

Evaluative summaries of significant research in the field of school and community relationships are published at intervals by the *Review of Educational Research*. See, for example, these articles:

TITLE	AUTHOR	ISSUE DATE
"The Community and the School"	Edward G. Olsen	February 1946
"Intergroup Education"	Lloyd Allen Cook	October 1947
"Planning the School Building for Community Use"	Don L. Essex	February 1948
'School-Community Relationships"	Shirley Cooper	October 1949
"Education for Work"	Leonard M. Miller	October 1950
"Design and Pattern of the Curriculum"	Arthur W. Gilbert	June 1951
"Social Effects and Correlates of Education"	Carson McGuire	February 1952
"Adult Education and Community Development"	Ralph D. Spence and Max Wolff	June 1953
"Human Relations and Programs of Action"	William Van Til	October 1953

Other Outstanding Magazine Articles

(Chronological listing—you add later items)

"What Is a School?" William D. Boutwell. Practical discussion of how the older, narrow concept of "school" is broadening into a community-wide concept. *National Parent Teacher* 39:20-21; October 1944.

"The Community School," Maurice F. Seay. Defines a community school and describes the educational experiences it sponsors. Concludes that a community school is democracy in action. *Childhood Education* 24:126-219; November 1947.

"The Community Is the School's Classroom," L. D. Haskew. The school is obligated to help people of all ages meet the genuine life needs they face now. It cannot confine itself to "let's pretend" activities. It is a trustee for social advance. It must cooperate in or lead community coordination for full effectiveness. *School Executive* 67:30-32; January 1948.

"Secondary School as Community School," Clyde M. Campbell. Discerns and discusses four basic trends in school-community relations for the future. *School Executive* 67:60-61; February 1948.

"Developing a Community School in Floodwood," L. E. Harris. A rural community's effective school program is described. *North Central Association Quarterly* 23:334-38; April 1949.

"Community School and its Two-Way Bridges," Will Hayes. Philosophy and historic development of the community school. *Clearing House* 23:457-61; April 1949.

"Shaping the Curriculum of Youth," Paul R. Pierce. The story of the Wells High School in Chicago. *North Central Association Quarterly* 23:339-44; April 1949.

"The School and the Culture, and the Individual," Robert W. Clopton. Analyzes the concepts of education as transmission of culture and as development of the individual. Concludes that the cultural heritage can be transmitted only as it is used and constantly renewed, in the very process of developing individuals. *Educational Record* 31:157-67; April 1950.

"The Community Elementary School," N. T. Edwards. Outlines factors involved in developing a community school through effective two-way flow of ideas between the school and the community. *National Education Association Journal* 39:270; April 1950.

"Challenge to Social Education," Ernest O. Melby. We have depended too heavily on mere knowledge, neglected emotional zeal, and failed to mobilize our community resources. *Educational Leadership* 8:134-38; December 1950.

"Bases for Integration of School-Community Effort," Milosh Muntyan. Explores several concepts underlying school-community programs, and urges full partnership between school and community as a whole. *Educational Leadership* 8:266-70; February 1951.

"The School That Brought a Town to Life," George Laycock. How a rural school revitalized its entire community life by making education realistic in local terms. *The Country Gentleman;* April 1951

"The School That Built a Town," Walter Hines Page. Dramatic description of a community school, as first told in 1901. *Phi Delta Kappan* 34:163-66; February 1953.

"A Community School in a Complex Urban Center," Edith S. Luckman. How a large Philadelphia high school transformed itself by winning faculty support of the community-school idea, organizing for action, winning community support, and arousing school spirit. *American Unity* 12:11-14; November-December 1953.

Motion Pictures

And So They Live. Presents a dramatic, documentary record of home, school, and community in a section of the rural South. Shows the struggle to live where the soil is depleted and where the school curriculum is far removed from the needs of the people. New York University Film Service, 1940, 25 minutes.

Children Must Learn. Shows the life of a poor family trying to subsist on worn-out soil, and suggests the part the school has played in the lives of such people and the kind of curriculum needed instead. New York University Film Service, 1940, 13 minutes.

Wilson Dam School. The democratic planning of teachers and children together, and the use of the community as a laboratory for learning, help point the way to better elementary schools. Tennessee Valley Authority, 1942, 25 minutes.

Lessons in Living. Shows how a school project revitalized a community by giving the children an active part cooperating with parents in changing the school environment and in opening up recreational activities. Brandon, 1945, 22 minutes.

Near Home. A class and teacher study their own community, demonstrating the strength of a learning process which begins with immediate interests and expands outward to the world and backward into the past. International Film Bureau, 1946, 25 minutes.

School in Centerville. Shows how education in rural schools can be geared to the problems of learning to live in the community. Students are seen at work on projects which relate both to their need for knowledge and to the future roles they will have. The three R's are not neglected, but are integrated into meaningful study and activity. National Education Association, 1950, color and black and white, 20 minutes.

School and the Community. How the school and the community can be drawn into a working partnership to which each contributes and from which each draws its share of mutual benefits. McGraw-Hill, 1952, color, 14 minutes.

CHAPTER 2

Learning and Teaching

Traditional notions of how to make a school program are changing. Many teachers are literally reversing their conventional ways of thinking about this tremendous problem. In the past, they have usually thought somewhat along this line: *How can I teach my subject-field more effectively? What can I do to motivate interest in the things I teach?* But now, under the challenge of modern psychology and the impact of this critical era in human history, they are beginning to ask instead: *What abilities and motives must people acquire in order to become well-rounded, efficient, and ethical participators in the ongoing life of a democratic society? How can 1 help people develop those necessary abilities?* This is indeed a reversal in basic orientation—precisely because its point of departure is the discovery of essential child, youth, and adult needs, rather than a projective defense of some logically organized academic field of knowledge. This new educational orientation values subject matter quite as much as does the old, but it insists that appropriate subject matter be used as a tool for more effective living (including deepest appreciations), not merely mastered as an exercise in mental discipline or in academic learning.

Thus it is evident that life-centered education is not just another device for enriching the traditional curriculum, for motivating the slothful student, or for making the teacher's job

This chapter is by EDWARD G. OLSEN.

more interesting. Although any well-managed program of community study and participation achieves these values in large measure, its primary purpose is far more significant. It aims at nothing less than eventual organization of the entire school program around the basic concept of the life-centered, community school. This broad concept, we should note, springs directly from the best we know about the fundamental principles of effective learning at any age level and in any field of study. Let us see how this can be.

How Do We Learn?

By way of illustration, consider the newborn child. Here is an infant with no ideas, no skills, no attitudes, no appreciations, no viewpoints. He is just an egocentric organism utterly unable to deal with his environment. Yet within a few short years this helpless child must develop at least minimum adjustment patterns of behavior. How will he learn to meet his needs? What approaches to environmental realities will he find worth-while? What instructional procedures should we, his teachers and parents, accordingly expect to use? Perhaps reference to the chart on page 29 may help to clarify our thinking about this central problem of effective learning, and hence of desirable teaching method.

Avenues of learning experience—and types of teaching materials—may be classified in four categories or levels. The chart presents them in ascending order according to the degree of reality each one intrinsically represents to the learner.

The first and psychologically basic learning avenue is that of *community experiences:* firsthand learning through immediate sensory contacts with the surrounding environment. Here the community is utilized as a great learning laboratory to be explored, studied, and improved.

The second level is also characterized by direct experience on the part of the learner: *expressive activities.* Now the student expresses through personally created forms his own interpretation of his experiences, ideas, appreciations, and insights.

The third major learning avenue and level is that of *audio-visual materials:* vicarious experience through mechanical

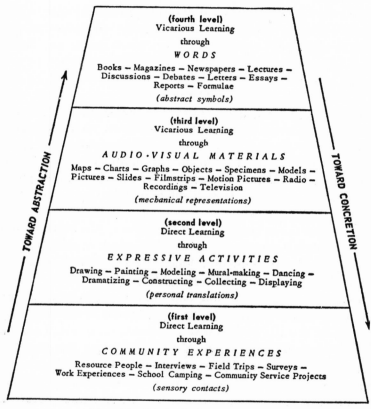

(fourth level)
Vicarious Learning
through
W O R D S
Books — Magazines — Newspapers — Lectures —
Discussions — Debates — Letters — Essays —
Reports — Formulae
(abstract symbols)

(third level)
Vicarious Learning
through
A U D I O · V I S U A L   M A T E R I A L S
Maps — Charts — Graphs — Objects — Specimens — Models —
Pictures — Slides — Filmstrips — Motion Pictures — Radio —
Recordings — Television
(mechanical representations)

(second level)
Direct Learning
through
E X P R E S S I V E   A C T I V I T I E S
Drawing — Painting — Modeling — Mural-making — Dancing —
Dramatizing — Constructing — Collecting — Displaying
(personal translations)

(first level)
Direct Learning
through
C O M M U N I T Y   E X P E R I E N C E S
Resource People — Interviews — Field Trips — Surveys —
Work Experiences — School Camping — Community Service Projects
(sensory contacts)

TOWARD ABSTRACTION

TOWARD CONCRETION

How Good Schools Promote Learning

representations of reality. Such materials can greatly help the learner to transcend his inevitable space and time limitations.

The final learning channel is that of *words:* words written and words spoken. Although words are highly abstract symbols of reality, they are man's finest shorthand way of transmitting, sharing, and criticizing experience.

You will note that the first two "avenues of learning" provide personal, firsthand experiences with the realities of the learner's physical, biological, and social environments, while the latter two approaches offer indirect, or vicarious, experiences. Talking, reading, and simple visual aids far antedate expressive activities and field experiences in the school program. Perhaps that is why these newer teaching approaches are sometimes still regarded merely as fads—as being, even at best, only supplementary to the "real" process of teaching through words and simple visual imagery. Yet it is undeniable that the more direct the learner's constructive experience with reality, the better he develops a practical basis for making his words meaningful, and the more he makes intelligent use of books, discussions, and other secondary sources of experience because they now appear more significant and hence more necessary to him.

Let's go back for a moment to the young child. One of life's realities which he needs to know about is that of fire. How can he best be taught about fire? One way would be to *tell* him, or have him *read* about it. We could say that fire is a reddish-yellowish thing which is hot, will hurt him if it touches him, is man's friend when it cooks his food, but is an enemy when it gets out of control and destroys property and lives. Another approach would be to *show* the child some photographs of fires, perhaps colored motion pictures of leaping flames complete with sound effects. A third way would be to let him *make* a small fire, watch how quickly it can consume paper and wood, and perhaps even thrust his own finger momentarily into the flame. Yet a fourth teaching approach would be that of taking him into the community the next time the fire siren blows, so that he may *see, hear, feel, understand and appreciate* the menace which an uncontrolled fire can become. Such are the four learning approaches to that physical-social reality called fire—through words (abstract symbols), through pictures (mechanical representations), through fire-making (personal translation), and through a community experience (full sensory contact). Is it not obvious that *all four* approaches should be taken if we expect the most effective learning about fire to occur—and that no one, two, or three of these approaches can be adequate alone?

As further illustration, consider the older adolescent. One reality of life about which he should become deeply concerned is that of slum-housing. Realizing this need, a high-school class took a field trip to investigate slums in a nearby metropolis. That trip had been preceded by several weeks of classroom study about the housing problem in general. Those students had already read books about slums and had seen many pictures of slum conditions. But now they actually stood in an "old-law" tenement, officially condemned as unfit for human habitation a half-century previously, but typical of many still occupied in that city. Suddenly two of the students turned to their trip leader and excitedly said, "We've read all about slums—we've seen plenty of pictures of slum housing—we've made charts and graphs—but we didn't dream it was anything like this! Why doesn't somebody *do* something about it?" Through that one vital, direct experience had come a sense of social realism, together with an emotionalized conviction of social need, which had not been achieved through either the symbols or the representations of slum-housing conditions.

Many of us have rightly protested against verbalism in teaching, but let's not be content with our partial success. We still have far to go. In terms of the learning chart, our own thinking and school practice need to move both horizontally (within each charted category) and vertically (into other categories). If we have been concentrating unduly upon the motion picture, for example, we might well explore the audio-visual possibilities of local community photographs, colored slides, museum specimens, and radio transcriptions. Similarly, if we have been using field trips exclusively as a form of community experience, we should certainly look into the uses of resource people in the classroom, student interviews in the field, committee surveys of local conditions, community service project possibilities, and the like. Finally, if we have been concentrating upon books and discussion, or upon audio-visual and expressive activities, or upon community experiences as learning approaches, let's henceforth make balanced use of all four avenues in every unit, every course, every teaching program.

The point should be stressed that every type of learning material and experience is valuable under appropriate circumstances. There is no approach that is "best" under all conditions. In general, though, we must emphasize the fact that direct experience is foundational to all other, even for adults, and that firsthand experiencing, the starting point in realistic education, nevertheless requires interpretation and evaluation through reading and discussion if valid concepts are to be formed. Personal experience without interpretation through words and other symbols is mere sensation, not education; conversely, mastery of words without experiential context to give them meaning is merely verbalization, not functional learning. Education that is meaningful and effective, and thus worthwhile, always requires thoughtful, verbal expression of adequate personal experiences, as well as appropriate channels for personal growth and community improvement through constructive social action.

That is why our professional conception of instructional materials and experiences has broadened enormously in recent years. Today we recognize the equal importance of firsthand, audio-visual, self-expressive, and symbolic experiences in education, and we agree with the National Education Association when it asserts that "the community should be freely used as a laboratory for suitable pupil experiences under school supervision." [1] The need for greatly extended direct experience with community life is likewise emphasized by the Commission on Teacher Education of the American Council on Education. That influential commission reports that "the circumstances of our time make it imperative that the schools should offer chil-

[1] *Proposals for Public Education in Post-War America*, p. 15, 1944.

dren more than book learning in the classrooms. It must, indeed, make use of all the community's resources for providing children with direct and valuable contacts with environmental reality." [2] Likewise the American Association of School Administrators: "The range and depth of firsthand experiences in community living should be increased through the school program. A first essential in teaching youth to live together should be a great extension under school guidance of the range of community experiences for youth. The present practice of making 'school studies' come first and community experiences second should be reversed." [3]

Accordingly, we now stress the appropriate school use of resource people, field trips, community surveys, work experiences, community service projects, and school camping, as well as greatly increased use of constructing activities, audio-visual and written materials, and verbal reports, discussions, plans. Such teaching procedures—carefully developed, coordinated, and evaluated—are the essential tools for learning in the modern school.

Community action and child study are twin foundations for modern curriculum building. Effective learning experiences cannot be planned without sympathetic understanding of individual needs, interests, problems, behavior patternings, and potentialities, on the one hand, and of group expectations, prejudices, tensions, histories, and resources for cooperative effort on the other.

To understand individual behavior, we must take full account of the cultural pressures which do so much to mould it. To improve the quality of community living—and thereby the very nature of those educating influences—school people need to work as closely as possible with the many educative resources of the community: churches, youth organizations, civic agencies, service and fraternal clubs, professional associations; business, industrial and labor groups; press, radio, television; human relations agencies, and the like.

[2] *Teachers for Our Times,* p. 136, 1944.
[3] Twenty-fifth Yearbook, *Schools for a New World,* p. 101, 1947.

That is why real community understanding is essential to effective teaching, and why forward-looking school systems all over the nation are establishing systematic programs of community field study, including participation for their teachers as well as for students. Such firsthand experiences with community life outside the school's four walls bring fresh insights, new zest for living, and a vital background for teaching which enriches the teacher's personality even as it broadens his educational base.

In recent decades, dominant American school theory and resultant practice have moved steadily in one direction—toward ever closer and more cooperative relationship with the supporting community. In this progression, at least five definite stages of development can be noted: (a) school indifference to the community, (b) classroom study about the community, (c) student field observation in the community, (d) occasional direct student participation in community projects, and (e) sustained student-faculty-layman contribution to the improvement of community living. Although some educators neither accept nor approve this expanding conception of what the schools should do, the basic trend is nevertheless marked and is not likely to be reversed or diverted. The "community study and service" idea now begins to permeate school practice at all levels from kindergarten through university, and in many such special fields as curriculum, guidance, methods of teaching, supervision, and administration. In terms of general school acceptance, then, we may say that the school-community movement became noticeable during the 1930's, grew steadily in extent and prestige in the 1940's, and seems likely in the 1950's to achieve common acceptance in the clearly emerging community-school pattern.

How Shall We Teach?

There is close relationship between the basic principles of democratic teaching and their daily expression in the community school. The following contrasts demonstrate that fact.

| BASIC PRINCIPLES OF SUCCESSFUL TEACHING AT ANY ACADEMIC LEVEL | HOW COMMUNITY SCHOOL PROGRAMS UTILIZE THESE PRINCIPLES |

Educate the whole child. The child is not just a mind to be instructed: he is a physically, socially, emotionally, ethically, *and* intellectually growing person. If his powers are to develop in proper harmony, he needs learning activities which challenge his emerging interests and abilities in all the areas of his growth.

(1) **Integrated learning occurs.** Well-planned community study projects necessarily involve not only intellectual understanding but, simultaneously, social poise, emotional control, physical activity, aesthetic response, and bodily skills. Pupils who explore a tenement house or a coal mine, for instance, develop all these aspects of the personality in unconscious integration.

Keep the program informal, flexible, and democratic. Children are restless and need confidence in their own powers and achievements. They therefore need every chance to ask questions freely, confer with other children informally, share in planning their individual and group activities, carry personal responsibility for group projects, help to judge critically the results of their efforts. This requires that the entire classroom atmosphere be friendly and democratic as well as informal and flexible, and that children not be held in unfair competition with standards of performance beyond their possible ability to achieve.

(2) **Informality, flexibility, and democracy are essentials of any program.** Field trips, interviews, surveys, service projects, work experiences, and school camping cannot be standardized from pupil to pupil, from class to class, or from year to year. Every child who participates can discover facts and report findings valuable to the group, and hence, builds confidence in himself as he knowingly contributes to the advancement of the project. Group planning, shared responsibility, and mutual evaluation are possible in the highest degree.

Capitalize upon present pupil interests. It is of utmost importance that the teacher first discover what interests and purposes his students already have, and then use these drives as springboards to further desirable learning. Thus, limited interests may develop into wider interests, undesirable purposes into praiseworthy purposes, and the child's educational growth be best promoted.

(3) **Every child is interested in his own community.** He may not be much concerned with irregular verbs or with the life cycle of *bacillus typhosis,* but he is considerably interested in telling friends about his next-door playmate who is ill with typhoid fever. Beginning with these immediate interests, it is not hard for the alert teacher to stimulate class concern about the fact that the city does not inspect the milk supply, and that well-written letters of protest might be sent to the health commissioner and to the editor of the local newspaper.

Let motivation be intrinsic. Most learners find few desirable incentives in the traditional system of school marks, honors, and penalties. Their most moving incentives are those of real life itself: to explore the new and the interesting, to associate actively with other people, to manipulate and construct things, to compare opinions about matters which seem important, and to express one's self artistically.

(4) **The keynote is—"Let's find out!"** Let's find out where that frog lives . . . what a police reporter does . . . how to interview an employer . . . Life-centered projects, such as these, which actually develop out of students' interests, concerns, and needs, require little artificial stimulation for their initiation and development. The operating incentives are those which are natural in people's lives and fundamental in their interests; they are definitely not artificial or academic.

Make learning experiences vivid and direct. Generalizations will be mere verbalisms unless they are based upon meaningful personal experiences. That is why children need constant opportunity for motion pictures, radio programs, excursions, interviews, service projects, work experience, and the like. Through such media the children receive more concrete, interesting, and meaningful educational experiences than they are likely to receive through the printed page alone.

(5) **Firsthand contact is ultimate realism.** "We read all about traffic accidents," remarked one high school student as the class left the morgue after having seen what a drunken driver could do to himself, "and we had several safety films, too. But the horror of that bloody, smashed body—I'll sure be *mighty* careful about my own driving from now on!" Strong medicine for adolescents? Yes—but not too strong, and many of them need such unforgettable firsthand experiences as vivid lessons that will really sink in.

Stress problem-solving, the basis of functional learning. Real education comes about when children intelligently attack real problems, think them through, and then do something to solve them. Every chance should therefore be given for pupils to discover, define, attack, solve, and interpret both personal and social problems within the limitations of their own present abilities, interests, and needs.

(6) **Real life abounds in problems.** These problems may be vast or trivial, personal or social, intimate or remote, but all of them are important to some people in some degree. Pupils who visit a public health clinic to learn the truth about the symptoms, detection, and treatment of tuberculosis are gaining valuable experience in problem-solving; so also are those who climb to the roof to visualize better the local village's transit development.

BASIC PRINCIPLES OF SUCCESSFUL TEACHING AT ANY ACADEMIC LEVEL	HOW COMMUNITY SCHOOL PROGRAMS UTILIZE THESE PRINCIPLES
Provide for the achievement of lasting pupil satisfactions. Students who dislike their work learn little from it, and retain that little briefly. Every effort should therefore be made to maintain learning situations wherein children will achieve genuine success, find personal satisfaction therein, and thus grow intellectually, emotionally, socially.	(7) **Possible satisfactions are many and varied.** Children who discover for themselves how an elevator works, who aid in constructing a health exhibit for the county fair, or who help a neighboring farmer terrace his hillside can experience deep emotional satisfaction as well as increased intellectual understanding. Such projects bring feelings of success; success is satisfying; satisfaction brings increased enthusiasm; enthusiasm leads to further activity of the similarly creative and hence basically satisfying nature.
Let the curriculum mirror the community. Learning situations must reflect life in the pupil's own community if they are to be most effective. Since little transfer of training between diverse situations can be expected, it is essential that the core of the required curriculum directly reflect the basic social processes and problems of the community, rather than the logical subject areas of the traditional school, or the socially insignificant interest-units of many activity schools. Not otherwise will the curriculum relate functionally to the personal interests, experiences, and needs of young people today.	(8) **The community is used as a living laboratory.** Within every community, large or small, urban or rural, go on the basic social processes of getting a living, preserving health, sharing in citizenship, rearing children, seeking amusement, expressing religious impulses, and the like. When pupils study familiar though actually unknown processes, develop intellectual perspectives, improve emotional outlooks and serviceable personal skills as they observe and participate in these processes, they are discovering for themselves not only the problems they face, but also the resources they can utilize in attacking those problems. Thus life, as well as the school, becomes truly educative in their eyes.

Such are some broad, fundamental principles of successful democratic teaching. Is it not clear that vital study of one's own community relates education to life in concrete fashion, providing not only a living laboratory, but also the nearly perfect springboard of interest into the larger world? And is it not even more evident that teachers must themselves become acquainted with the community laboratory before they can direct others in its use? Surely this means that those of us who teach, or who plan to do so, must know our communities; not casually, merely as sightseers, but as critical participants who come through a wide range of thoughtful personal experiences to know intimately the communities in which we live and work. Beyond that we must also go. We must develop the ability to understand and to work with any community, large or small, in terms of its social structure, its needs, problems, and resources, both physical and human. If we hope to help our pupils learn to live more abundantly in this "big, blooming, buzzing confusion" we call modern civilization, we must become untiring students of the community and its myriad relationships.

How Can Teachers Develop Community-Competence?

Do you really know the community in which you grew up, or in which you now live? Have you worked actively with others to improve the quality of living, of human relations, in that community? Can you point to personally satisfying and creative experiences with varied geographic, historical, and human factors which shape our living today? *Do you know your community?*

It is increasingly expected that teachers in all fields will know how to utilize varied community resources for classroom purposes, and will be skilled in developing school activities devoted to community betterment. It is, therefore, essential that you become familiar with the community as a functioning unit in American life; that you acquire basic knowledge of community structure and function; growing insight concerning the nature of society and its values, aspirations, and struggles; a reasonable objectivity toward problems of community improvement and social reconstruction; and some degree of skill and facility in the human relations of community living. All of this requires that you actually and continually combine your understanding of community life with your conscientious participation in the life of a real community. *Knowledge about* and direct *experience with* your community must be deliberately planned and developed as twin parts of one learning process.

You haven't time, you say? But how can you expect to develop community competence if you do not actually participate in a variety of community activities and responsibilities? And if you yourself do not have a "sense of community," how can you hope to develop such concern in children and young people?

Teachers cannot be adequately prepared for their widening community responsibilities unless they themselves experience, throughout the training program, many aspects of community and regional life which have educative significance. That is why professional courses should serve to produce or strengthen in all candidates these essential backgrounds and abilities:

• **Firsthand, thoughtful acquaintance** with the natural environment and with industry, commerce, labor, government, social agencies, regional history, promotional organizations— with the community's life in its many aspects.

• **Clear understanding** of the community-study, service, and leadership movement in the United States and abroad, in terms of its purposes, trends, and influence.

• **Demonstrated competence** in planning, developing, and evaluating curricular use of community documents, local audio-visual materials, resource people, field trips, surveys, work experience, community service projects, and school camping.

• **Growing ability** to work with lay individuals and community organizations in ways that are genuinely democratic, cooperative, and effective.

• **Professional outlook** which conceives of education as a guided process of growth through which the individual progressively reconstructs his experience toward more intelligent and ethical action to improve the quality of human living.

Professional abilities like those just listed cannot be developed solely within classroom walls and libraries. Many of us teachers are people who went to school and never quite got out. Probably we liked to read, received good marks in college, were interested in ideas, enjoyed working with younger people, were facile with words, had presentable personalities, desired institutional security—and so, in due time, extended our role of book-minded student to that of book-minded teacher. We thus exchanged several classrooms of other teachers for one we called our own, but we still were dominantly inclined to "transmit the book" within the sheltered schoolroom. Immersed in an ocean of words, we were typically not even aware of our own indifference to the community's structure and forces, processes and problems, needs and resources. Yet these are the living social factors which daily mould our lives and those of our students. We were not ready, then, to recognize the fact that realistic, firsthand studies of the community and of the child are the twin foundations of any functional professional program in teacher education. We are beginning now to accept that premise in our practice.

In the last analysis, real ability to function in a community-school situation will develop through growing experience in working cooperatively, for the solution of common problems, with boys and girls, parents, community leaders, welfare organizations, pressure groups, and so forth, from day to day. The following suggestions are offered to the teacher who desires to fit himself for more effective educational leadership. These pointers are equally valid for prospective teachers and for those already teaching.

•   **Widen your friendships.** Deliberately cultivate personal friendships with people of different backgrounds but of common civic and social concerns. Recognize human differences as normal, desirable, and personally enriching. Make a wide variety of social contacts with people of different races, nationalities, classes, and political, economic, and religious beliefs. Visit pupils in their homes, enter into their recreational life, observe them in public places and in their work situations. Utilize your experiences to enter sympathetically into the lives of people in your present community. Help lessen the social distance between teachers and other occupational groups. Be friendly with people!

• **Know your community.** If you understand the ongoing life of your community, its customs and mores, needs and values, problems and resources, you can teach more surely while sharing in community leadership and making intelligent personal adjustments. It is well to know community "causes" and their leaders, the important political, labor, and business figures, the occupations and prejudices of school board members, causes of any previous frictions between town and school, the community blocks which support purposes similar and antagonistic to the purposes of the school, and the like. Study your community!

• **Work with community groups.** Be sure to get acquainted with your community agencies and their leaders, and demonstrate your interest in cooperating with them. Every teacher should understand the work of such useful agencies as the city, county, and state health and welfare departments, county agricultural offices, municipal recreation agencies, private charitable organizations, church and religious societies, settlement houses, farm and labor organizations, and human relations organizations such as the National Conference of Christians and Jews, the American Friends Service Committee, the Urban League, the Anti-Defamation League of B'nai B'rith, the Catholic Interracial Council, and the like. You will often need to contact such groups about community and school problems, and should therefore resolutely break down the inertia or reticence which may have kept you from visiting them. Invariably these face-to-face meetings with leaders of community organizations prove both interesting and stimulating, and lead you to increase the breadth of your own experience. Then you are ready to participate with others in studying community needs and attacking community problems, particularly those which bear upon the non-school education of boys and girls. Remember that you are more interested in helping groups formulate and achieve civic purposes than you are in getting personal or school publicity. Be sure also to attend public meetings in the community, talk with people there, introduce yourself, express your appreciation for what others do for community welfare. Work with others!

• **Use community resources in your teaching.** If you want your teaching to be really vital, stimulating, and useful, you will have to plan for curricular use of varied community resources in any teaching field and in nearly every unit of work. In so doing, you will utilize a rich variety of resource people, field trips, student surveys, work and camping experiences, and community service projects, each closely correlated with appropriate printed and audio-visual materials and with other classroom pupil activities. Utilize your resources!

• **Be an active citizen.** Be sure to become a legal resident of your teaching area, and to vote in all local, state, and national elections. Understand local community problems and issues; be prepared to exert your influence as well as to vote ethically. Learn the techniques and practice the handling of controversial issues in your community as well as in your classroom. Make yourself competent in the art of scientific thinking, so that you can remain objective but not detached. Live your patriotism!

An Imperative Task

Teacher-educating institutions—whether public or private, large or small, urban or rural—are now confronted by a new and serious professional responsibility: to train professional workers in education to be as community-conscious as they are school-conscious, as aware of civic needs as they are of child development, as competent in community building as in curriculum construction. Certainly this is no easy task, but clearly it is an imperative one, and it is imperative now.

Learning Activities

Socio-drama

After a P.T.A. meeting, two parents begin to argue about how children really learn. They appeal for help to the following:

1. An elderly parent who remembers a teacher "battle-axe" of his generation and is confused by present methods
2. A young teacher who knows the scientific findings about the learning process
3. A teacher of 30 years' experience who is somewhat contemptuous of modern theories
4. An educational psychologist.

Assign these roles and play them to the full; then discuss the assumptions of each position taken and their validity in terms of present scientific knowledge.

Discussion Topics

1. How far should a teacher be responsible for "putting roots down" into the community where he teaches?
2. List 15 community problems a teacher beginning work in a new community might encounter. Choose several of these for intensive analysis.
3. What other principles of successful teaching should be added to the list presented on pages 35-37?
4. How can we best prepare public-school teachers for the growing emphasis on moral and spiritual values in education?

Group Projects

1. Present a skit to show the difference between "verbalistic" and "experiential" approaches in teaching.
2. Examine curriculum guides, courses of study, and units of work to determine the extent to which they imply the experience-approach to learning.
3. Analyze the validity of the learning chart on page 29 in terms of your own experiences in and out of school.
4. Spell out the specific ways in which members of your class can improve their community competencies during the next six months.
5. In a symposium, review and contrast the major points made by Dewey in his *Experience and Education* and by Kelly in his *Education for What Is Real*.

Individual Activities

1. Write out for yourself a specific plan for improving your own community understanding and leadership abilities during the next year.
2. Outline a unit of work of interest to you, utilizing all four "levels of learning" as charted on page 29.
3. Propose a rating scale by which to judge professional competence for community school teaching. Present this to the class for critical discussion and refinement.

Learning Materials

The role of experience in education should be considered in terms of scientific psychological findings. Arthur Gates and others in Chapter 13 of their *Educational Psychology* (Macmillan, 1942) analyze the development of meanings, and show the necessity of having a perceptual basis for generalizing. Ernest Horn's *Methods of Instruction in the Social Studies* (Scribner's, 1937) deals in Chapters 4 and 5 with the problem of meaning, the symbolic character of language, and the relation of experience to reading. Anderson and Gates in Chapter 1 of the National Society for the Study of Education's *Learning and Instruction* (1950) point out that "It is only through experience that we learn" and then clarify the importance of the quality of experience in relation to the quality of learning. William H. Kilpatrick's monograph, *Modern Education: Its Proper Work* (Hinds, Hayden & Eldredge, 1949) explains similarly the nature of the basic learning-through-experience theory which underlies the practice and program of the modern school. John Dewey's little book, *Experience and Education* (Macmillan, 1938) is a readable analysis of this philosophy of learning and, hence, of teaching. Laboratory validation for this philosophy is reported by Earl C. Kelly in his *Education for What Is Real* (Harper, 1947), in which he analyzes the findings of the Hanover Institute in the field of vision, and the nature of perception and knowing, as experimental basis for a reconstructed theory of education. He concludes that education for what is real is not cold-storage information; it is direct and continuous remaking of the world in which the individual lives. *They Learn What They Live* by Helen Trager and M. R. Yarrow (Harper, 1952) is a constructive appraisal of a pioneer experiment in intergroup education at the primary school level. Helpful material can also be found in the following magazine articles:

"The Importance of Perceptual Learning," Stephen M. Corey. An intensive analysis showing that true learning must be based upon examined perception of events experienced. *Educational Screen* 24: 394-97, 404; Nov. 1945: *Education Digest* 11:1-5; January 1946.

"Community and Child Development," Dan W. Dodson. The community is society in microcosm and must be studied as such if we are to understand children. *Journal of Educational Sociology* 20:264-71; January 1947.

"We Learn What We Live," William H. Kilpatrick. How learning comes out of experience, how learning means growth, and how learning shapes experience and gives it fuller, richer content. *Childhood Education* 25:53-56; October 1948.

"Experiences to Meet Goals," J. Cecil Parker. Analyzes the relationships between direct and vicarious experiences in the learning situation, and concludes that both types are essential in terms of achieving student purposes. *Educational Leadership* 6:199-203; January 1949.

"Depth of Meaning," Edward W. Dolch. Analyzes two kinds of meaning in word-symbols, extent and depth, and suggests that depth comes through years of life activities, travel, and imaginative living. *Education* 69:562-66; May 1949.

"Vision Takes the Lead in the Experience Curriculum," Glenna E. Bullis. Explains how child development occurs best through direct-experience observations in the community. *Nation's Schools* 46:60-61; November 1950.

"Clarifying the Role of the School," W. N. Featherstone. The school's distinctive function is that of symbolizing and rationalizing experience. The functional nature of meaning is discussed in terms of education for work, for civic participation, and for insight. *Educational Leadership* 8:198-202; January 1951.

"Community Resources for Intergroup Education," Edward G. Olsen. Offers practical suggestions for learnng about human relations through the use of resource people, field trips, surveys, and social living. *Educational Outlook* 27:147-53; May 1953; *Education Digest* 19:47-49; October 1953.

Community competencies teachers need are of two basic kinds: professional (as teachers) and civic (as citizens). Both kinds have been indicated in many references suggested throughout this volume. Now we mention only two volumes which, taken together, will give you a clearer notion of needed abilities. *The Cultivation of Community Leaders* by William W. Biddle (Harper, 1953) is an excellent guide showing how citizens, teachers, and students can cooperate to develop effective leadership for community action. *The Modern Community School*, edited by Edward G. Olsen (Appleton-Century-Crofts, 1953), stresses by implication the professional responsibilities of the teacher toward and in the community. *How Children Use the Community for Learning* by Effie G. Bathurst (U. S. Office of Education Bulletin 1953, No. 6; U. S. Government Printing Office, Washington 25, D.C.) indicates many specific abilities needed by teachers who want to develop a program that is meaningful to children and also promises to lead to better living. In addition, you should find these articles worthwhile and intrinsically interesting:

"Teacher as Community Engineer," Howard Y. McClusky. Teacher education should make the teacher well-acquainted with his community, including its class structure, and should stimulate him to act as community catalyst or coordinator. *Michigan Education Journal* 23:197ff.; December 1945.

"Training Teachers for Active Participation in Solving Community Problems," Paul B. Gillen. Reports findings of a nation-wide survey and outlines a suggested program. *Teachers College Record* 47:323-30; February 1946.

"Gear the Curriculum to Your Community," Geoffrey Graham. Describes an extension course in community study taken by a group of teachers, with emphasis upon objectives, procedure, and committee findings. *Educational Leadership* 5:97-101; November 1947.

"Preparing Teachers for Community Living," Harley Holmes and Troy L. Stearns. Describes a 12-week internship program in community-mindedness and leadership for prospective teachers. *Nation's Schools* 42:28-30; September 1948.

"A Functional Workshop," Harold S. Tuttle. Describes a teacher-education summer workshop in which students spend full time in a neighboring local community making surveys of needs and resources, and reporting their findings directly to local lay groups. *Teachers College Record* 52:181-87; December 1950.

"Community Resources Publications and Workshops by State Departments of Education," Edward G. Olsen. Reports a research study showing to what extent and through what means the 48 state departments of public instruction were providing leadership in the broad field of community resources, and their use in the school's instructional program. *School and Society* 74:24-26; July 14, 1951.

"Promoting Community Study Programs in Washington State," Edward G. Olsen. Illustrates a state-wide program carried on over a five-year period, with suggestions for next steps in such a development. *School Executive* 58-60; September 1951.

"Teacher and a Community Service Program," Hollis A. Moore. Examines various explanations offered in the literature to account for the typical role of the teacher in the community. Concludes that community service programs cannot develop without better teacher selection, improved in-service education, and relaxation of community controls over personal behavior of teachers. *Junior College Journal* 22:283-92; January 1952.

"Sharing the Reservoir of School Staff Resources" (in the *School Executive* 72:42-65; January 1953) documents many ways in which school personnel help improve the community in a score of areas from coast to coast.

"Community Participation in Teacher Education," Gladyce H. Bradley. Explains the procedures through which active participation in the work of selected community agencies was made an integral part of a "Principles of Teaching in Secondary Schools" college course. *Educational Administration and Supervision* 39:218-24; April 1953.

Motion Pictures

Learning Democracy Through School-Community Projects. Elementary and high-school students participate in school councils, a rural field day, safety patrols, clean-up campaign, Red Cross work, parent-teacher-student meetings, a community council, and a youth center. Locke Films, 1947, black and white or color, 20 minutes.

Learning Through Cooperative Planning. A project of concern and interest to children and the community is skillfully developed to provide real experience in planning together. Teachers College, Columbia University, 1948, 20 minutes.

We Plan Together. The entrance of a new boy into a high-school "core" class gives opportunity to illustrate how the class operates democratically in its group activity. Teachers College, Columbia University, 1948, 20 minutes.

Part II

UNDERSTANDING THE COMMUNITY

If you want to be an effective teacher or other educational leader you must know your community, and know it
intimately. You need to know the people and the forces
that play upon and influence them. What are their traditions? Their customs? Their human interrelationships?
Through what basic social processes do they carry on their
life activities? What kinds of problems result?

More than casual knowledge is required. The learning
that comes from the human experience of living in communities must be extended and enriched. It must be fitted
into a comprehensive picture that makes clear the unity
and the complexity, the universality and the individuality
of "the community." Personal involvement is needed to
enrich and give validity to observation and study. Until
you understand the modern community—in terms of its
physical setting, its people, its social organization, its basic
processes and related problems, its evolvement, and its
social-status climate—you are not competent as an educator in the community school. Your observations and analysis, developed together and referred again and again to
an ordered overview of community patterning, will help
you achieve that kind of personal competence.

Chapters in This Section

IN LIFE-CENTERED EDUCATION

COMMUNITY LIFE AND ITS NEEDS

COMMUNITY STRUCTURE and	SOCIAL CLIMATE
Physical Setting — People — Organization	Culture Patterns — Life-styles — Social Statuses

Operating in four areas, through twelve social processes, and on three levels

COMMUNITY AREAS	SOCIAL PROCESSES AND PROBLEMS												COMMUNITY LEVELS
	1	2	3	4	5	6	7	8	9	10	11	12	
Local	Improving Material Conditions	Appreciating the Past	Adjusting to People	Exchanging Ideas	Getting a Living	Sharing in Citizenship	Protecting Life and Health	Improving Family Living	Securing Education	Meeting Religious Needs	Enjoying Beauty	Engaging in Recreation	Psychological Institutional Material
Regional													Psychological Institutional Material
National													Psychological Institutional Material
International													Psychological Institutional Material

Become the "Core" of General Education

Using Seven "Doors"   to Effective Learning

COMMUNITY MATERIALS	RESOURCE PERSONS	FIELD TRIPS	SURVEYS	WORK EXPERIENCES	SERVICE PROJECTS	SCHOOL CAMPING

To Help the Student Attain Personal and Community Competence

In Successful Living

Thus Stimulating Constant Improvement in Social-process Operation and Thereby

Strengthening Democracy, the Civilized Way of Life

CHAPTER 3

Community Setting

"Community" seems a nebulous term, yet it is a tangible concept; it can be defined for useful purposes. Derived from the same roots as "common" and "communal," it suggests a sharing in common. People in a community associate naturally in the everyday affairs of life. They share experiences in common, a common lot. A strong sense of "belonging" develops when many activities are shared by the same people in a setting which is also shared; this feeling we often call "unity," "love of country," or "civic pride."

This sense of the community as a setting and process for life-sharing is clarified by Lloyd Allen and Elaine Forsyth Cook's analysis.[1] They describe the community as "(1) a population aggregate, (2) inhabiting a delimitable, contiguous territory, (3) sharing an historical heritage, (4) possessing a set of basic service institutions, (5) participating in a common mode of life, (6) conscious of its unity, and (7) able to act in a corporate way." A community occupies a delimitable space. It is composed of people who have a sense of belonging together as a community. It is served by institutions and agencies. It can act in a cohesive way to meet crises or problems which arise. These basic elements of the community interact in infinite

---

This chapter is by Lois M. Clark. Chart on page 50 by E. G. Olsen.

[1] *A Sociological Approach to Education*, pp. 48-49. New York: McGraw-Hill, 1950.

variety, evolving communities that are varied and individual. Yet the common elements recur. By understanding these elements as they operate in actual communities we may come to understand both the universal and the individual community.

Community Structure

Where is the community located with respect to natural features? Climatic conditions? In relation to other communities? How is it arranged on the earth's surface? Who are its people? What are their backgrounds? Why are they here? How have they organized to live together and meet their common problems? Such are questions to be considered in studying the three chief elements of the community: (1) its physical setting, (2) its people, and (3) its social organization.

The Physical Setting

Every community has its geographic setting, its base on the land. This setting has a direct and often far-reaching bearing on the nature of the community. The composite of physical factors which underlie various communities will vary. But certain factors are universal and basic.

• **Climate** influences the community in many ways. Temperature range affects agricultural production, may determine the chief community enterprises. Length of the frost-free season largely determines what crops may be grown. Amount and seasonal distribution of precipitation is of great significance, as many communities will attest. Wind velocity and direction must be considered, especially in areas where storms are frequent or may reach hurricane proportions. Recreational activities will respond to climatic differences; so may the "zest" of the people.

• **Size** is significant, whether the community be a city, a compact village, a town-centered rural area, or a sprawling open-country region. Face-to-face relationships are affected by size; so also is the ability of the community to provide services to its people. Community cohesion—the sense of belonging—is affected by size.

• **Topography** may make the community easy or difficult of access, thereby influencing the morés and customs of the people. For instance, isolation from the outer world has helped to preserve customs of an earlier day in many a southern Appalachian community. Occupations may vary, as may recreation, with differing topography.

• **Soil type and fertility** have special significance in communities whose economy is linked to agriculture. Soil drainage is of concern to both city and countryside. Note, for example, the influence of a high water table in New Orleans, of a lowering water table in California. Note, too, the swampy wastelands, the eroded soils, the damage of uncontrolled floodwaters in great areas.

• **Water resources** must serve household and civic needs and provide for industrial use and, in some instances, irrigation. Transportation and shipping may be affected, as may recreational activities of the community.

• **Mineral resources** may have been a major factor in the first location of a community. Its major occupations, even its wealth, may be affected. Availability of building rock may determine community architecture.

• **Forest resources,** including wild game, have been a major factor in the early history of many communities and in some are still a vital factor.

Climate, size, topography, natural resources—these may be regarded as the natural inheritance of a particular community. But the picture of the community's geographic setting is not complete until we see what has been done with this inheritance. Has it been used wisely? Have natural resources been exploited or judiciously managed? Has full advantage been taken of location and size? A few city-communities have been guided by careful planning as they grew into their spatial patterns. In most places, little thought was given to land use or to over-all planning. Increasingly, though, established communities are evolving patterns to gradually correct poor land use and prevent it in the future.

The zoning plans of a city- or town-community area might be studied in connection with this problem. Effort should be made to visualize clearly and in some detail such elements as the spatial location of the community's typical business and facilities, the relation of these to natural features, and their interrelatedness with each other. A social-base map, such as is described in Chapter 6, should be used to indicate the various types of land use.

When these various types of land-use have been "spotted" on the map, it will be fruitful to study it further. How are the community's shape and land-use pattern related to site and topography? How are the various land-use areas related to each other? For example, where is the poorer residential area in elation to the manufactural area? How are the locations of the waterfront or railroad and the commercial area related? What relationship exists between land values and the use made of the land? These are typical of the relationships within the community which warrant exploration. Comparable relationships of the community with other communities and areas should likewise be explored.

People of the Community

Communities with similar geographic settings may and do vary widely in their over-all patterns. Such differences are traceable in part to differences in the people who inhabit the communities. To understand a community we must therefore learn about its people—who and what they are.

•   **Population number** is significant, especially in relation to such factors as land area occupied, the size and nature of neighboring communities, the community's past and its possible future. A population of 1,200 in the sparsely populated Southwest, for example, has different meaning from the same number in a closely knit New England town, or in the suburb of a major city. A town of 10,000 which looks back to days of greater size and stature differs greatly from the area of 10,000 —not yet cohesive enough to be a community—which five years ago was an open field and in another year or two will have redoubled its numbers.

• **Age and sex composition** may profoundly affect a community's organized life. Where the proportion of the very young and the very old is high, leaving relatively fewer people in their productive years, many obligations are placed on the community. In the past few decades, concern with this problem has brought most communities into new relationships with state and national agencies. Proportion of men and women in a community may affect community pattern and problems. Wartime and postwar developments have brought the evolution of new communities predominantly of young people. They present characteristic problems, both now and for future years. In any community, the age of the leadership group, those whose actions and decisions carry most weight, has great significance.

• **Educational status** of its people greatly affects a community's personality and its well-being. The attitudes with which they face situations, how they go about solving problems—these are a general reflection of the community's educational status. The level of formal education and the extent and causes of illiteracy, where it still exists, are important to note. Perhaps even more important are school "dropouts." How many young people are leaving school before completing the schooling from which they could benefit? Why are they leaving?

• **Occupational status,** that is, the ways in which its residents make their livings, colors the community picture. The aspirations of the people for their children are also important. Do they see in the local community suitable vocational opportunities? Or do they feel that their only hope lies elsewhere? How people earn their living may influence their general outlook, determine the general "tone" of the community. A mining town, a prosperous agricultural community, an Oak Ridge or a Los Alamos are far different communities. The difference may arise, not alone from the occupations engaged in, but in part as a by-product of them. For in some occupations people develop social skills and attitudes of a high order; in others these are, at best, irrelevant.

• Ethnic and nationality composition of the community may be important. Some communities are composed almost entirely of "native stock"; that is, of white people from certain specified national backgrounds whose ancestors have lived there for several generations. In other communities two or more different ethnic or nationality groups make up the community. Where this is so, it will be important to learn the extent to which people from the various groups enter into the mainstream of community life. Studies of a Midwest county, for example, show the divergent groups centering many activities around their churches, but in other ways entering freely into general community activities.[2] In other situations considerable isolation or even segregation continues to exist. Sometimes, though the differing group continues to stand apart, its special cultural contributions are recognized by the community in some special way. The possibilities to be explored in this area of human differences are numerous.

• Status relationships within communities vary greatly. Some communities appear to be almost classless. In others caste and class are powerful forces, affecting the lives of individual citizens in diverse ways, and leaving their imprint on the community as a whole. These relationships are treated in detail in Chapter 4.

All of these factors must be investigated if we are to understand the people of any community. It will not be enough to look at each factor singly. No person reacts solely in terms of his age status, or the number of years of his schooling, or the

[2] Frank D. Alexander, and Lowry Nelson, *Rural Social Organization in Goodhue County, Minnesota*. Bulletin 401, Agricultural Experiment Station, University of Minnesota. St. Paul: The University, February 1949.

work he does, or the race or nationality of his ancestors. He is, for instance, Ole Swenson, aged forty, graduate of the local high school, third-generation American of Swedish descent, living in and reacting to a whole set of circumstances that involve other people, the physical setting in which they live, and the organized pattern of their community and the larger world.

Social Organization

"The community is made up not merely of people as people but also of a complex pattern of social units, agencies, organizations, institutions, and informal groups with different backgrounds, with varying and often conflicting objectives and values. . . . Moreover, when studied, each such group assumes meaning as a part of the total social unit—the community."[3] These are the means through which the people of the community take action to meet their problems and satisfy their needs. This web of organizations must be explored to complete the picture of the community's structure. Social organization of the community may be studied through exploration of the following types of groups:[4]

• **Institutions.** Institutionalized organizations have a high degree of permanency and are widely recognized. Major institutions to be identified and studied are: the family, the church, the school, and government in its various aspects. All of these are undergoing changes which need to be recognized and understood in relation to the conditions which affect them.

• **Formally organized groups.** Every community has within it groups which have distinct objectives, elect or appoint officers, have a fairly definite membership, hold meetings and carry on programs of activities, and function according to prescribed rules. A comprehensive summary of these, even for a

[3] Edmund deS. Brunner, "The Administrator and Society." *Teachers College Record*, 53:299-306; March 1952.

[4] See Alexander and Nelson, *op. cit.*, for a helpful organizational analysis of a Midwest county.

small community, would be extensive. The following partial list suggests their scope and variety: business and professional organizations (Chamber of Commerce, manufacturers' association, Business and Professional Women's Club, and so forth); civic groups (Community Chest, service clubs, League of Women Voters, and the like); farm organizations, both general and specific; labor organizations; lodges; school patrons' groups (P.T.A., band parents); sports and hobby clubs; adult study clubs; veterans' organizations; welfare groups (mutual insurance company, safety council, volunteer fire department, W.C.T.U.); youth organizations (Boy and Girl Scouts, Campfire Girls, 4-H Clubs).

• **Agencies.** These are formally constituted groups set up to perform certain specific services. They may be private or public, depending on their source of authority and support; public agencies are increasingly superseding private agencies in meeting many major community needs. Some typical agencies: the library association; county health service; welfare service; state employment service; veterans' service office; agricultural agencies (Extension Service, Production and Marketing Administration; Soil Conservation Service), and human relations agencies such as the Catholic Youth Organization, the National Conference of Christians and Jews, and the Urban League.

• **Private enterprise**—organizations established primarily for profit-making—may be individual enterprises, partnerships, cooperatives, or corporations. Illustrations: Joe's peanut stand, independently owned and operated retail store, doctor or dentist, law partnership, farmer cooperative, chain store, manufacturing company, newspaper, mining corporation, railroad.

• **Informal groups** are declining in relative importance but are still vital to community well-being. They include informal social clubs, recreational get-togethers, work rings (in farming communities), and other similar groups.

An organization may have been created to perform one simple and clear-cut service, or it may offer many and varied services. Some gather to themselves new responsibilities as they grow and develop, eventually functioning in areas far beyond those originally envisoned. They may develop feelings of "vested rights" within a particular field, with characteristic unwillingness to abandon them, even though their service is no longer needed or could be better provided by another group. The actual functions performed by an agency, as well as its interrelationships with other organizations, must therefore be known if the community picture is to be a complete and accurate one.

Agencies and organizations vary in the areas they serve. Government agencies serve the political areas by and for which they were created; they may be local, county-wide, state-wide, nation-wide, or international in scope. Organizations—formal or informal, commercial or non-commercial—may serve areas as small as a neighborhood or as large as the whole world. Some which offer a nation-wide or international service do so only generally through their national organizations. Others serve through units or subdivisions in the region, state, and local community.

Hayes suggests the great range of maturity which may exist in the social organization of a community.[5] Where a high degree of individualization exists, social groups other than families are non-existent. At the height of community development there are "efficient social organizations, with clear purposes, adequate coverage, planned and co-ordinated division of labor, accompanied by enthusiastic participation of the members." But the community may disintegrate into a state of conflict. It will then be characterized by "numerous, conflicting and inefficient social organizations. Most of them are not only struggling to survive but are marked by lack of coordination and division of labor and [by] an atmosphere of exclusiveness."

---

[5] Wayland J. Hayes, *The Small Community Looks Ahead*, pp. 9-16. New York: Harcourt, Brace and Company, Inc., 1947. (Quoted material from pages 13 and 14.)

In a society as complex as ours, deliberate public planning is essential if a satisfactory level of living is to be maintained for all people. While community planning is in a sense a civic obligation, many private agencies share in the responsibility. In a study of the community's social organization it is important, therefore, to discover what is being done to coordinate all community activities directed toward improving the general welfare. This should include exploration of the leadership-load carried by individuals in the community.

Community Process and Problems

In our definition of the community it was made clear that more is involved than a place, some people, and their social organization. The community is active—people participate, they are able to act together. Community activities are carried on by people in order to fulfill their basic human needs. The *social processes* which make up the ongoing life of the community reflect these needs; they are, in fact, maintained to satisfy them. When the social processes fail to function effectively, *social problems* result. To understand the functioning community, we must comprehend the social processes at work. We must also recognize the problems which emerge from their failure.

Twelve aspects of community functioning are suggested for study and exploration. Involved are: (a) social processes (adjustment: positive) and (b) social problems, which indicate some type of failure in the process (maladjustment: negative). Each of the twelve basic processes is described briefly, each is then followed by a still briefer portrayal of typical malfunctionings of the process and of the problems which result.

Improving Material Conditions

The natural environment provides the foundation for making a living. If the community has access to adequate resources, either in the immediate environment or through effective communication with outside sources, a good life is possible for all.

However, people find different ways of adjusting to quite similar environments. This may flow from the uniqueness of human personality; often it is for reasons arising out of differing backgrounds and ideals. One group of people move into a locality and become share-croppers in a one-crop farming program; they remain ill-fed, ill-housed, and ill-clothed. Another group settle on similar land nearby and become farm-owners, practicing diversified farming, preserving their own foodstuffs, enjoying reasonable prosperity. Why? The geographic setting for the two communities is similar, but the ways of adjusting to that setting are markedly different. This suggests that attention should be given to two factors: what the community has as a natural inheritance, and what it has made of that inheritance.

The kinds of homes that are built, the "sky line" of a city, how the people distribute themselves in relation to the natural features of the community such as rivers or hills, what use they make of land features, location, and natural resources in developing ways of making a living—these are a few among many possible evidences of how people utilize the environment. Adjustment to the natural environment involves a nice blend of mastering and submitting to that environment. A satisfactory community adjustment implies that natural resources are fully developed and used; that future as well as present needs are considered; and that the interrelatedness of the local community with the region, the nation, and the world is recognized.

Inadequate Improvement of Material Conditions

• **Failure to develop resources** may doom the community to a subsistence level of living and, under our present economy, to poverty and related low standards in meeting other needs.

• **Exploitation,** aimed at immediate profit without regard for the future, is evidenced by eroded soils, floods, destruction of forests, depleted mineral resources, and similar conditions. The eventual result is a decline in agriculture or other industry and in general standards of living.

Appreciating the Past

Human beings need to have roots, to feel that they "belong." This need is met in part through the day-to-day group life of the community; in part through psychological identification with family and community traditions. A community's present outlook, its values and ideals, are themselves outgrowths of tradition; hence, a community can be better understood when its essential history is known. How long has it existed? How did it come into being? Who settled it? Why? What institutions and enterprises were established? What ideals were upheld? Who were the leaders? What common crises arose?

Does the community take pride in its past achievements? Does it feel a responsibility to meet present needs on a high level? Is there a strong sense of community loyalty? Is recognition given for outstanding contributions to the community's achievements? Affirmative answers to such questions indicate that appreciation of the past operates on a high level. Negative answers may be expected from some "communities," among them ones which have mushroomed near industrial centers. What problems arise from lack of community roots?

Improper Appreciation of the Past Brings Social Problems

• "Ancestor worship," arising from over-exalted regard for the past, may lead to social stagnation. Unreadiness to give proper weight to new conditions brings unrealistic answers; overvaluation of one's own ideas breeds intolerance. Where unreality and intolerance are widespread, the community becomes progressively less able to solve its problems. If "ancestor worship" is limited to a segment of the community—even though a powerful group—opposing viewpoints may emerge and eventually correct the problem.

• Indifference to the past may characterize the community too new to be aware of common roots or the community that, through repeated failure to meet its people's needs, no longer seems worthy of their pride. The emerging community will acquire a past. The decaying community may no longer be a true community because circumstances have changed. Or it may be in need of new and vital leadership to reverse its downward trend.

Adjusting to People

Relationships among people of a community, as people, influence the whole pattern of community living. Such factors as the community's physical setting, its human composition, its social organization affect interpersonal and intergroup adjustments. In a scattered community, contacts may be limited. Where the population is homogeneous, adjustments vary chiefly with the abilities of individuals to "get along" with each other. In more heterogeneous communities it comes about less simply. "Status" and mutual distrust may enter in. The presence in the community of different racial or nationality groups or of divergent occupational groups, the movement of new groups into areas where old residents have long held leadership—these and other factors may divide the people seriously. Vivid illustrations may currently be drawn from leisurely paced rural or suburban areas suddenly "invaded," as they feel, by newcomers who want changes made quickly to provide the good life they envision.

The presence of difference within a community is not, in itself, undesirable. On the contrary, it may stimulate and lead to the enrichment of personal and community life. Deepseated differences may, however, seriously disrupt effective community living. It is important, therefore, to identify the divisive factors in the population pattern, and to discover what organizations deliberately or unwittingly promote group conflict. Many recent attacks on the public schools, for example, have arisen out of an honest concern for what the schools should teach—but this purpose has been distorted by groups deliberately seeking to spread confusion. Often local groups have innocently abetted these efforts. On the other hand, organizations and agencies are at work which deliberately seek to decrease conflict and strengthen wholesome inter-group adjustments. These also should be known and their cooperation sought.

Failure to Adjust to People Brings Social Problems

•   **Personality conflicts** may affect community life in limited, personal ways or, where personal status conflicts between leaders are involved, have far-reaching consequences. Official or semi-official action, or failure to act, may reflect the conflict.

•   **Intergroup tensions** create an atmosphere of distrust, suspicion, and jealousy which discourages wholehearted participation in well-coordinated community activities. Groups may align themselves in relation to all sorts of differences (racial, religious, economic, class status, and the like).

Exchanging Ideas

Communication is basic to the effective functioning of all social processes. How well the people of a community understand each other is vitally important to the community's development. The effectiveness with which they exchange ideas, the mutual stimulation of study and thought as a basis for action, will be reflected in the decisions they make as a community.

Language is, of course, our basic means of exchanging ideas. It is desirable, therefore, to know the community's status in the use of both oral and written language. Is it a one-language community, or is a second language habitual to some of its members? If so, is there adequate communication among all the residents of the community? Irrespective of the language spoken, how literate are the people? Do they use reliable sources of information to reach understanding of matters which concern them? What are these sources of information? The student of the community will wish to explore the availability and use made of such means of exchanging ideas and information as newspapers, magazines, books, pamphlets, telephone and telegraph, movies, radio, and television.

Communication, the exchange of ideas, is the means by which public opinion is formed. And public opinion is extremely potent in determining what individuals or groups within the community think and do. "Public opinion" is in reality a crystallization of the ideas and values which the dominant groups accept and uphold. In part, it is the product of many informal and unorganized influences, some of which are the cultural traditions of the community, its economic interests, and the informal interchange of ideas among its people. In part, it may be the product of carefully organized efforts by special interest groups, who seek converts to altruistic ideals or who wish to exploit the people for personal gain. The dominant groups may not comprise a majority. History is filled with instances of minorities as dominant groups. Sometimes this occurs through failure of citizens to assume their civic responsibilities. Often the majority becomes a tool of the smaller group through use of the means of communication in ways that confuse rather than clarify issues. Sometimes "status" in the community gives a group dominance in determining public opinion.

A complete study of a community thus requires attention to the significant elements of its public opinion. It seeks to discover what forces or agencies—pulpit, press, business interests, political groups, labor organizations, patriotic associations, and so forth—are creating or influencing that opinion.

Malfunctioning in the Exchange of Ideas Brings Social Problems

• **Ineffective communication** may lead to community disintegration through failure to bring pertinent information to bear on vital problems, or through inability to act cohesively on those problems. The community which habitually fails to act, or acts unwisely through inaccurate assessment of conditions, fails its citizens. Continuing failure to meet people's needs is a prime cause of community decay.

• **Distorted use** of the means of communication, and failure of the community to take this into account, may lead to misinformation and misunderstanding and to consequent wrong action. Since pressure groups and propaganda are a recognized part of modern life, measures taken to equip the citizen to deal with them intelligently should be explored.

Making a Living

The physical needs of all people for food, clothing, and shelter must be met and such additional goods and services provided as are considered desirable by the community group in question. In a primitive community, these needs are met directly by each individual or family unit, or, at most, by the clan. Today the work a man does may be many stages removed from the actual feeding, clothing, and sheltering of his family. The process of "making a living" has come to involve many intricately interrelated aspects of community life. Whatever relates to the production, distribution, or consumption of economic goods is a part of it. A study of how a community makes its living should include such various items as the following:

The Community's Basic Economy

The good community has a sound economic base; that is, the means of a good livelihood are available to all able-bodied persons. For the community as a whole this implies that basic resources and the means of developing them are available; that manpower is to be had and is suited to the need; and that there is a market for the product or service. The community's economy may involve a great diversity of enterprise or it may be highly specialized. Agriculture, manufacturing, mining, services to tourists may be its base—the possibilities are many when the essential resources are available in the community or close at hand. For the individual citizen, the good community is one where there is work to be done that is suited to his abilities and where he can be assured of a reasonable return for his labor under satisfactory working conditions. A first look at the community's general economy will give a helpful basis for considering specific aspects of making a living.

The "Good Life" People Want

The things that the people of a community want—the goals they set for themselves—also influence what is done about making a living. With the desire for a moderately high standard of living must go the income to provide it. Hence an adequate and reasonably well-distributed income is important. In exploring the standard of living desired by the people of a specific community, it is important not to use arbitrary criteria. The tendency to measure a community by the percentage of families having bathtubs or telephones, for example, may overlook entirely the relative importance of the two in an isolated area as contrasted to town or city.

Business and Industry

Many people in most communities make their living through some aspect of business or industry. The enterprise may produce raw materials or basic resources: agriculture, fishing, mining, for example. It may process raw materials, be involved in financing other enterprise, transport or distribute goods, and the like. The business or industry may be carried on by an individual or a partnership, through a cooperative organization, or through a corporation, which are all private enterprises.[6] The individual owner or partners may manage their business or hire others to do so; the corporation or cooperative must delegate management. Ownership may reside in the community or elsewhere. Absentee ownership may be accompanied by active interest in the community or by exploitation of it.

Such factors may make an important difference in the life of the community. Note, for example, differences between owner-operated and tenant-operated farming communities. Note, too, the effect on community life of industrialized agriculture and of suburban shopping centers.

The Worker in Business and Industry

Communities where business and industry are diversified offer many levels of work: skilled, semi-skilled, or unskilled

[6] See *How We Organize to Do Business in America*. Washington, D. C.: The Department of Rural Education, National Education Association, and The American Institute of Cooperation, 1952. 34 pages.

labor; managerial work, perhaps self-employment. Where one industry or type of business is dominant, the range of opportunities may be narrower. The worker, at whatever level, needs to be assured of an adequate wage-return from his labor. He is concerned with such matters as hours of work, sanitation, safety practices, compensation for injury and unemployment, regularity of employment, and fringe benefits such as group hospitalization and medical care. In exploring these factors it is important to know the regulations established by law and the extent to which local conditions conform to them, the role played by labor organizations, labor-industry relations, and conditions of work in nearby areas which may affect local standards or the availability of workers.

Service Occupations and the Professions

Many functions need to be performed in the community, whatever the basis of its economy. Houses must be built, decorated, heated, lighted, the plumbing serviced, waste carried away. Families require dental and medical care, must be barbered and manicured, have their laundry done, their cars serviced. Mail must be collected and delivered, streets built and maintained. People must be educated, their religious needs met. The number and variety of services necessary to a good life seem endless. The occupational opportunities thus provided might be explored in relation to the various forms of social organization. What opportunities for making a living are offered by the community's basic institutions: family, church, school, and government? By public and private agencies? By organizations which maintain staffs to assist in their work? By private enterprises not classed as business and industry?

What specialized abilities are called for in these occupations and professions? Is technical or professional preparation needed? On the other hand, are services needed in the community for which suitably trained workers are not available? The unmet demand for certain types of occupational or professional skills might be greatly increased if provision were made for supplying such services.

"The Right Man for the Right Job"

The community and the larger society have work that needs to be done. The worker wants to use his abilities in ways that will insure a good living to him and his family. How, in our complex economy, can the best interests of the individual and society be served? Three aspects of community life have bearing on this question: What provisions are made for pre-employment and on-the-job education or training? What provisions are made to assist in job placement? Are people free to choose work without restrictions as to sex, race, color, religion, or other factor not related to ability to perform the work? Educational institutions, the employing industries, and the community as a whole share in responsibility for these. What is each doing to help? What regulations or policies are in effect? How closely do actual practices in hiring conform to the avowed policies?

The Community's Concern for All Its People

The good community is concerned with the well-being of *all* its people. It therefore develops ways of insuring at least a minimum well-being to persons temporarily or permanently handicapped or in need. Increasingly services to these people are channelled through community agencies, but represent the direct concern of county, state, or federal government—or all of them—for its citizens. Unemployment insurance, old-age benefits, widows' pensions, and mothers' assistance illustrate this trend. The community also looks after its people in more informal ways. Recent gains in employment of the handicapped and the aging depend in no small degree on the will of the people to meet the problems they present. Policies are adopted which transcend legal requirements. Some communities also concern themselves actively with the welfare of the businesses on which the community's living depends. As technological trends bring changes, the sense of mutual responsibility shared by the community, its basic enterprises, and its people becomes more and more important.

The process of making a living is so vital and so affected by change that many crucial problems relate to it. A number of these are noted below without attempt to relate them to the specific aspects of making a living discussed in this section.

Malfunctioning with Respect to Making a Living Brings Social Problems

• **An unsound economic base** may underlie failure in making a living. The community's basic resources may be depleted and no constructive effort made to develop new ones, or failure to advance with new technology may place the community at a disadvantage in competing with other communities. Sporadic employment or low wages, or both, are likely results with accompanying low standards of living. Movement away in search of better opportunity often drains the community of its ablest people, especially its promising youth.

• **Gross inequalities in the distribution of wealth** may exist. Where there is great poverty, the limited purchasing power of individuals and families brings low standards of living for them and a low demand in the community for the products of business and industry and the services of others. Apathy, disgruntledness, "class" rivalry and distrust often characterize such communities.

• **Exploitation, draining away of the rewards from its labor,** has depleted the economy of many a community where absentee ownership of major industry has not been accompanied by a sense of responsibility to the community.

• **Paternalism, dependence on "Mr. Big" to solve problems,** may accompany the concentration in a single person or corporation of power over the means of production. A low citizenship-quotient and low valuation of human growth and development are frequent by-products of paternalism.

• **Unsatisfactory employer-employee relationships** may reflect restrictions by employer or organized labor, or exploitation of labor where there is not a free labor market. Dissatisfied workers, "the slow-down," lack of pride in work (regarding it merely as a commodity for sale) are often accompanied by inefficiency and conflict in community affairs.

• A laissez-faire community attitude with respect to its responsibilities may underlie failure in making a living. Failure to take a long view with respect to use of basic resources; failure to provide assistance in job placement or to insure appropriate educational and training opportunities; failure to attract to or hold in the community suitable industries—these may be serious failures of the community in meeting the needs of its people. They leave to chance and to the private concern of individual citizens and business interests what should be a matter of corporate concern and action.

Sharing in Citizenship

Citizenship is a matter of participation, of sharing, of working *with* people for the common good. The good citizen meets his responsibilities of daily living, gets along with his neighbors, helps to maintain community services. At times he gives leadership; at times he works with others who lead. Citizenship is also a more formal matter of participation in the political life of the community—being an active member of a political party, campaigning, demanding representation, voting, holding office. Both aspects of citizenship are important, and each affects the other.

Government (political citizenship) fulfills its purpose when it helps the community to achieve its highest aims and hopes. In most communities, several "layers" of government operate simultaneously: municipal, town or township, county, state, and federal. School districts, water districts, and the like may operate as additional political units. Often local political boundaries segment the community, making it difficult to function in a corporate way in meeting common problems. The community's ability to fulfill its functions is thereby limited. In studying the community's political structure, note should be made of the ways that have been developed to bridge political boundaries in taking community-wide action, and in providing coordinated, efficient services. Relationships of the larger governmental units to the community should be noted also.

Our nation is founded upon the belief that the greatest good for the most people can be achieved through the democratic process. Every American community shares responsibility for understanding that process more thoroughly, for using it better, for applying it to new and changing conditions. Intelligent, creative leadership is required—leadership that is shared and rotated, that takes in all segments and ages of the population. In this sense, sharing in citizenship permeates every human relationship in the community, whether in family, in school, in business, or in other aspects of daily living.

Inadequate Sharing in Citizenship Brings Social Problems

• **Apathy in respect to political citizenship** at local, state, and national levels invites corruption, boss rule, failure to make government the positive tool for corporate community action.

• **Self-interest of leaders,** evidenced by their major concern with retaining their own positions and powers, brings special privilege for those who support the leader and failure to meet many basic community needs which conflict with the self-interests of those who have power to control leadership.

• **Crime, corruption, and alliance with the underworld** are tangible symptoms of failure of citizens to work positively and effectively enough at their job of citizenship. Communities so large that interpersonal relationships are weak face special problems of this type.

Protecting Life and Health

The community's health status is reflected by statistics on infant and maternal mortality, incidence of disease, number of deaths from various diseases, average length of life, the accident rate, the insanity rate, and the like. General health status may be affected by occupational diseases, by the economic status of the people and standards of living maintained, and by provisions made by the community to safeguard and improve public health.

Corporate action is usually necessary to maintain a safe water supply, safe standards of purity in the milk and food supply, satisfactory housing conditions, adequate sewage and refuse disposal, protection against many hazards to life and safety, and to prevent the spread of communicable disease. Community provision is also needed for health service and medical care, including hospitals, clinics, and dispensaries. Also needed are physicians, dentists, and other such medical specialists; registered and practical nurses; and some type of general community health program. What hospital services are available, how they are organized and administered, how competently they are staffed, what services they offer, and to whom their services are available should be known to the community investigator. The role of group hospitalization plans in making services available should be noted.

The general program of public health should be studied. What is its scope both as to services included and persons reached? What is its program of health education for children and for the adult population? Is nutrition education included? Services to the physically and mentally handicapped should be explored. The incidence of mental illness, mental defectiveness, blindness, deafness, and physical crippling are all factors to be investigated. Provisions for the care and special treatment of such handicapped persons, and for their education in the public schools or by other means, should be studied.

Provisions for the public safety to be studied include police protection, traffic supervision, fire prevention and control, accident prevention, and first-aid facilities. Communities will differ markedly in their provisions for public safety, as they do in all other aspects of community life.

Inadequate Protection of Life and Health Brings Social Problems

• **Human erosion**—maintaining life at a level seriously below effective standards of physical well-being—claims a heavy toll in community life. Both efficiency in production and normal association in group activities are reduced. Its chief causes: preventable illness and substandard housing.

• **High mortality rates** due to disease and to accidental causes reflect community failure to take effective corporate action in establishing safe and healthful conditions. Inadequate education for healthful and safe living and lack of hospital and medical services may also be reflected.

• **Mental illness** is likely to have its basis partly in the malfunctioning of other social processes as well as in the maintenance of physical health. A high incidence of emotional instability as well as outmoded methods of treating the mentally ill are evidences of community malfunctioning.

Improving Family Living

Earlier in this chapter the family was designated as a major institution. It was so classed because it is one of the most universal and permanent forms of social organization. Despite this permanence, the family today is subject to great stresses and strains which are resulting in significant changes. These need to be understood for their effect on the family's role in community life and the community responsibilities they imply.

Two significant changes should be noted. One has to do with size of the family unit. In simpler, less mobile societies, the conjugal family—parents and their children—is reinforced by the larger family or kinship group. In many American communities, the conjugal family lives far from its kinfolk. It tends to depend on a closer emotional relationship within the small, tightly knit group. Yet its members may be pulled in many directions by the divisive organization of the modern community. The other great change is from the patriarchial family, the "father knows best" pattern of authority, toward the egalitarian or democratic family in which all share responsibility.

Effort should be made to discover the status of the community with respect to these two trends. In many smaller communities, including rural areas, the larger kinship group continues to be vital, and the practice of doing things as a family group often persists strongly. Elsewhere some parents, sensing the need to do things as families, are deliberately planning family projects and activities. These should be noted. It is also important to become aware of the community's provisions to reinforce and strengthen the family and to alleviate the difficulties which arise when family stresses and strains become too great.

Failure in Promoting Family Living Brings Social Problems

• **High rate of divorce,** illegitimacy, and prostitution are manifestations of the family's disorganization. Perhaps equally important is the community's attitudes toward these practices.

• **Delinquency and other non-social behavior** by children may, in part, be due to their confusion as to their place in the changing family. Family break-down may be the source, because of failure to understand what is happening, or children may be in rebellion against too rigid family discipline. It should be understood that other factors also incite delinquency.

• **Community apathy to its responsibilities to the family** may be found. Where church, school, government, or special agencies fail to give intelligent support to the family, the community fails in an important role.

Securing Education

Many institutions and agencies share responsibility for helping the community's citizens to secure education. The public schools have, of course, special responsibility for the education of youth; in many instances they also help to provide adult education. In some communities private schools play an important supplementary role. At a time when conflict over the purposes, the content, and the methods of education is widespread, there is special need and value in assessing educational opportunities in the community.

What viewpoint with respect to the nature and purpose of education is dominant? Is it the memorization of an established body of knowledge? Or is emphasis on ability to adapt in a changing society? How is the prevailing viewpoint reflected in the schools? What is the status of the teacher in the community? How is this reflected in working conditions, salaries, and the like? Inquiry should be directed also to the qualifications and methods of selection of school board members; and to the methods of selection, qualifications, salaries, tenure, and so forth, of the superintendent of schools, principals, and other professional staff members. The grade progress of pupils, the extent of pupil "dropouts," the scheduling of school activities (including the so-called "extra-curricular") in relation to the needs of all the children should be explored. It is especially important to learn how the school's curriculum is adapted to the needs of children in this particular community.

Information concerning the educational needs of people beyond school age and what is being done to provide for them will be important, for on them the quality of life in the community depends. How much schooling they have is less important than the way in which they go about solving problems, along with the provisions the community has made for helping them to remain alert and growing. What is being done through agricultural extension service, community libraries, and other agencies and organizations to serve this need? The special role of colleges and universities in adult education and in helping communities meet their problems also warrants exploration.

Failure in Providing Education Brings Social Problems

•   **Widespread illiteracy,** especially among people capable of a moderately high level of learning, continues to be a problem in some localities. This and functional illiteracy were brought to light by selective service tests.

•   **Sterility of much available education**—that is, lack of vital relatedness to the problems of living—is widespread, as numerous surveys and other studies have shown.

•   **A non-rational approach to community problems** is perhaps one of the most telling evidences that much is yet to be done in making education effective. All too typically, the approach to community problems, or other social problems within the community, is on an emotional, biased, non-thinking basis.

Meeting Religious Needs

Man's need to identify himself with his God, and thereby give higher meaning to his relationships with his fellow men, is a deep-rooted one. Often in our American society, where freedom of religious choice prevails and government gives official sanction to no one sect or faith, religion may help to unite a community—or it may prove divisive. Where community life is at its best, intelligent religious guidance reinforces social unity.

The tangible aspects of the community's religious life include its organized churches and missions and various social-religious agencies. In exploring the religious functioning of the community, such questions as these may be asked: What faiths or denominations are represented? Whom do they serve? What programs of religious education and of personal counseling and guidance do they offer? What professional preparation do church leaders and teachers receive? How adequately is the total population of the community being reached? What factors may account for the failure to serve certain groups? What efforts are made by the various churches and faiths to work together and to reinforce each other's programs?

Malfunctioning or Inadequacy in Religious Activities Brings Social Problems

• **Indifference to religion,** with cynicism or atheism widespread, reflects attitudes that may be destructive of community unity and strength.

• **Conflict among denominations and sects** may hamper the full exchange of ideas, of getting along with people.

• **Over-emphasis on traditional values** which have become associated with religion but are not inherent in it, sometimes creates gulfs between the older generation and the younger, to whom the traditions seem less significant.

• **Association of certain "status" factors** with a particular church may shut out those who do not conform. Many long-established churches have tended to grow away from those they once served, thus opening the way for the growth of new sects.

Enjoying Beauty

Beauty is something to be enjoyed day after day. It also provides special experiences which enrich our lives and give them greater meaning. The good community therefore is pleasant to look at and be in. Its concern for beauty shows in its homes, its roads and streets, its public buildings and its parks—everywhere. It is also evidenced in the opportunities provided for asthetic expression along many lines and in various mediums. A Western community has for years held an annual art show to which able artists from throughout the nation are invited to send their paintings. The reflection of this may be seen in the schools and in the churches, in the homes of the community, in the conversations of the people, even now and then in the vocational choice of some young person who has grown up in an environment which values creative expression.

Failure to Appreciate Beauty Brings Social Problems

• **Civic ugliness** often reflects lack of planning and perhaps a lack of civic pride. Ugliness, dirt, haphazard arrangement, treeless streets are typical of the community which fails to appreciate beauty.

• **Absence of esthetic expression** or opportunity to develop it deprives people of enriching, releasing experiences much needed to give balance to living when there are many forces which promote conflict and tension.

Engaging in Recreation

The good community shows many evidences of enriching variety in the lives of its people. They enjoy games, have social celebrations, participate in festivals, develop their esthetic interests and talents. Much of this recreational activity is informal, developed in the family, among friends, in informal social groups. Some of it, particularly reading, may be largely individual. The play activities of children, listening to the radio, viewing television, taking a hike, or going on a picnic, gathering at the drug store for a coke, are all recreational activities which demand little special community planning.

But planned recreation is needed. Churches, lodges, and

other social groups will make a contribution to this, especially for their own affiliates. Special interest groups will devote time and effort to the development of the community theatre, or a symphony orchestra, or other organized program which gives opportunity for esthetic expression and development. The corporate community may provide parks and public playgrounds. The schools will help to develop recreational skills through adult classes as well as for children and youth. Scout organizations, 4-H Clubs, and other youth groups provide for this aspect of children's interests, too. For some of its recreation the community will turn to commercial sources, making certain that desirable standards are met.

The purpose of all this is two-fold: to enable people to express themselves in creative ways, and to relieve tensions which arise from daily living. In exploring how the community engages in recreation, thought should be given to the effectiveness with which these purposes are served. And the adequacy of the provisions for recreation must take into account the availability of the various types to various segments of the community.

Undesirable or Inadequate Recreation Brings Social Problems

• **Inadequate facilities,** over-emphasis on commercial sources, may characterize the community's provisions for recreation. Undesirable social behavior, sometimes becoming delinquency, frequently results, especially among young people.

• **Escape from emotional tension through drugs, drink, or other non-creative and sometimes directly harmful means,** is too often substituted for wholesome recreation.

Such are the twelve fundamental social processes which go on in some form or another in every community—large or small, urban or rural, near or remote, historic or contemporary. Such also are some among the typical social problems which emerge in contemporary American communities as these basic social processes fail to function with full effectiveness.

Community Evolvement

The community has a living quality that connotes capacity to grow, to maintain existence over a period of time, and to fade or die. Failure of the community to evolve—to develop, to open out—in response to changing circumstances means almost inevitable eclipse. Along with this viability, the community observer will have noted a quality of relativeness. He will sense the "here" of the sociological or corporate community in relation to the world beyond; the "now" in relation to what has been and what may be. And he will be aware of the interplay of the several levels of the community's culture.

The Community in the Larger World

The community, as defined in this chapter, is inextricably bound up with the world beyond. As organizational contacts are extended, as friends and kinfolk scatter, and as the means of making a living become more and more dependent on the outer world, citizens of the community become increasingly aware of this relationship. Residents of the local community may come to have a genuine sense of belonging to one or more larger social groupings. In this sense, we might truly say that they are citizens of a *regional community,* the *national community,* and, increasingly, of a *world community.*

Clearly it is important for today's citizens to understand their involvement in these broader communities, for they are inevitably affected by it. Not only is this true for the individual or the family as it meets its daily needs; the community as community is affected. Hayes points out the impact on institutions and social processes. He says, "Community forms which have existed for some time (religious, educational, political and property forms) will tend to remain relatively fixed unless subjected to stresses and strains from the outside; and forms which are constantly changing, and are expected to change (means of production, transportation, communication, and the like), will continue to do so unless blocked or modified by outside forces." [7]

As the relationships of the local community to the extended community or communities are explored, the student will not lose sight of the smaller groupings within the community where face-to-face relationships are many and the degree of cohesiveness strong. These neighborhoods are the natural beginning points for community exploration and understanding at the early elementary school age. Older children will be ready to move out into the true community in their explorations, and through it to increasingly more complex relationships with the world beyond.

Conceptual Levels of the Community

The community might be thought of as having a second layer of culture over the first, and a third superimposed upon that. Since these levels lend themselves appropriately to levels of maturity in comprehending the community, they should be understood. Rugg[8] has identified them as three aspects of the culture: (1) the physical civilization (material level), (2) the social institutions (institutional level), and (3) the determining psychology and philosophy (psychological level).

• **Material level.** This is the external civilization, the *things* people use or have made, as well as the people themselves. It includes a community's natural resources; the means by which it produces and distributes goods and services; the physical setting of the community—its housing, streets, and transportation system; its parks and playgrounds; its water supply and sanitation service, communication facilities, protective services; its coal mines, bee hives, lakes, fire engines, housing projects, and the like. Children in the elementary school may appropriately undertake community study on this primary level, beginning with its simpler and more tangible aspects.

[7] Wayland J. Hayes, *The Small Community Looks Ahead.* New York: Harcourt, Brace and Co., 1947.

[8] See Harold Rugg, *American Life and the School Curriculum,* pp. 20-24. Boston: Ginn, 1936.

• **Institutional level.** Here are the organized or institutionalized ways of living, the *mass habits* of the people. This second level is less tangible, but extremely significant in determining community behavior; it is the "cradle of custom" into which each child is born. Marriage customs, family form, governmental practices, religious rituals, the language used, the number system followed, the common arrangements for economic exchange and monetary usage, all illustrate the institutional level of the culture. Intensive community study at this level should be delayed until high school years bring greater maturity of intelligence.

• **Psychological level.** Determining the customs and the material creations of the community are the *motivations* of the people. These are the desires that produce activity; the fears which inhibit behavior; the attitudes which pattern acceptable conduct; the values, goals, ideals, loyalties, and taboos which influence and direct human behavior. For example, the persistence of the one-teacher school district in many rural communities where other aspects of community living are organized on a broader basis is undoubtedly traceable to deeply rooted attitudes or values held by the people. Obviously this psychological level of community study is suited only to mature minds.

The Community's Setting in Time

Emphasis in this chapter has been primarily on understanding the *now* of the community's structure and functioning. It has been evident, however, that what now is has grown out of what was; and a future of the community has been always in the background of our thinking. The ongoingness of the community, the relationship of the *contemporary* to both the *historic* and the *future* community, should now be brought into sharper focus. This may have special significance, for, as Thaden has pointed out, "American communities are extremely youthful. It is less than 100 years ago that the initial settlements were started in three-fourths of the localities that constitute communities today. There is still a process of adjustment of population to the local resources taking place. . . . The countryside is dotted with clusters of deserted businesses and residences that bear mute testimony that they happen not to have been strategically located. . . . They cannot be restored to their former selves, except in violation of ecological forces, which can rarely be violated without too great a cost. . . ." [9] In contrast to this is the story of Tin Top, Texas, which did rebuild when the people of the community got together to do something about it.[10]

Community Evolvement through Response to Challenge

"A crisis arises—flood, fire, depression, interracial conflict, or 'boom' development, brought on by internal or external forces, gradual or catastrophic in nature—and the community must act in order to preserve itself. If the crisis is met successfully, group cohesion will be stronger than before; if it is not met, or not well met, community spirit will be weakened. Successive failures are a sign of community disintegration and, perhaps, of eventual eclipse." [11] The healthy community advances by this process of being challenged and responding effectively to that challenge. To fully comprehend the community, therefore, a review of the challenges it has faced and is facing, and the success with which they are being met, should be made.

Perspective

Any community is really a set of human relationships based upon shared experiences between people. In this chapter we have been analyzing the community's essential structure, basic patterns operating processes, resultant problems, social organization. But there is another fundamental dimension of community life: that which the experts call "status behavior." Be-

[9] J. F. Thaden, Department of Sociology and Anthropology, Michigan State College, in an address to the Great Lakes Conference on Rural Life and Education at Ann Arbor, Michigan, November 28, 1949.

[10] The story is told in the film, *Tin Top—A Community Builds*. Baylor University Drama Department, 1951, 28 minutes.

[11] *A Sociological Approach to Education*, by permission from Lloyd Allen Cook and Elaine Forsyth Cook. New York: McGraw-Hill Book Company, Inc., 1950.

cause this is a concept of major significance, it is
developed at some length in the chapter to follow.

Learning Activities

Discussion Topics

1. Can we correctly speak of a "school community," a "regional
   community," and a "world community"? On what assumptions
   are your answers based?
2. What are some of the obstacles encountered in the rural and
   smaller communities, as compared with those in metropolitan
   areas, when you seek to relate school to community? Are there
   any advantages in the smaller communities?
3. How do you see the real purpose of community study? Is it to
   improve the community, the curriculum, or the child? Why?
4. Suggest two or three other social problems for each of the social
   processes, and judge their significance for your own communities.

Group Projects

1. Make a social-base map to indicate types of land use which you
   can study firsthand.
2. Using census returns as explained in Chapter 6, study the
   population composition of this community. Report your findings
   visually, with explanations.
3. Taking your own community as an example, show how the social
   processes operate on the material, institutional, and psychological levels.
4. Preview several motion pictures in this field, and then lead class
   discussion of them after a class film forum

Individual Activities

1. Using the headings of this chapter, prepare a paper describing
   your own home-town community.
2. Do group project 1 for your home community.
3. Do the same for group project 2.
4. Write a short history of your own or another community in terms
   of the "challenge and response" thesis suggested in this chapter.

Learning Materials

Further clarification of the community concept may be desired. As a start, read two magazine articles: Clarence Pickett's "What Is a Community?" in *Progressive Education*, February 1938, and Dan Dodson's "What is Community?" in *American Unity*, May-June 1952. Pickett asserts that any defensible society must maximize personal values, that the old rural community did so but the modern city does not, and that the schools of today must therefore stress group cohesion as well as individual development. Dodson stresses the important fact that human relations *are* the community in its most real sense. Then go on to "The Community Frame of Reference" by Lloyd Allen Cook and Elaine Cook in their *Sociological Approach to Education* (McGraw-Hill, 1950). Part II outlines the nature of the community and describes community living in situations ranging from hamlet and village to the great metropolis. A more technical analysis of the community concept with statements of trends in community study is found in the section called "Human Ecology" in Georges Gurvitz and Wilbur Moore's *Twentieth Century Sociology*, pp. 466-499 (Philosophical Library, 1945). Kimball Young's *Introductory Sociology* (American Book, 1942) has two chapters of special value in this connection: Chapter 7 on "The Primary Community" and Chapter 8 on "The Secondary Community." American Communities"—Chapter 2 of *The Community School* by the National Society for the Study of Education (University of Chicago Press, 1953)—traces trends in recent community development, including leads for understanding any community's structure, organization, activities, and value systems.

Descriptions of community living offer much insight. Wayland J. Hayes' *The Small Community Looks Ahead* (Harcourt, Brace, 1947) is a study of the nature of communities—how they came to be as they are, and how they change. Jessie Bernard's *American Community Behavior: An Analysis of Problems Confronting American Communities Today* (Dryden, 1949) is a stimulating sociology of the community. Richard Posten's *Small Town Renaissance* (Harper, 1950) reviews various community self-study projects, showing vividly how people live and what they want in their towns.

The significance of the small community in human affairs is the strong concern of Arthur E. Morgan in his *Small Community* (Harper, 1942), of Baker Brownell's *The Human Community* (Harper, 1950), and of Joseph K. Hart's *Education in the Humane Community* (Harper, 1951). All, in various ways, express the reasoned conviction that only in the smaller community with its possible primary social relationships can the finer values of human living be preserved.

The physical setting of the community in relation to school studies of it is well characterized in the periodical literature, especially in various issues of the *Journal of Geography*. Perhaps J. G. Jensen's "Community Vision through Geography" (April 1945) offers a good beginning point with his suggestions regarding the gathering and use of facts. R. B. Hall's "Local Inventory and Regional Planning in the School Curriculum" (January 1934) makes specific suggestions for local community mapping. Edith Parker's "Geography and the Community" (March 1941) discusses how to analyze a community and make a community map; then considers how to use the information gained. M. J. Riggs' "Geography Field Work in a Small City" (January 1938) gives helpful suggestions for studying the spatial pattern of any city. Writing in *Education* (September 1948), Ruth E. Baugh gives help for understanding geographic factors in any state in her "California: A Type Study of a State."

Community evolvement has been the concern of several recent publications worth noting here. Wayland J. Hayes' *The Small Community Looks Ahead* (Harcourt, Brace, 1947) offers helpful discussion of community maturity and the process of community evolvement, especially in Chapters 1 and 3. Jessie Bernard's *American Community Behavior* (Dryden, 1949) analyzes the conflict situations of the changing community, and suggests essential ways by which people in communities can bring community practice into harmony with the American creed. James Dahir's *Communities for Better Living* (Harper, 1950) summarizes many current efforts at community organization in different parts of the United States. The July 1951 issue of the *American Journal of Sociology*, edited by Robert Cooley Angell, is devoted to "The Moral Integration of American Cities." The inescapable interdependency of our local communities with their regional, national, and world relationships is vividly portrayed in A. C. Krey's reminiscence, "The World at Home," in the Ninth Yearbook of the National Council for the Social Studies, *The Utilization of Community Resources in the Social Studies*, pp. 173-181. (The Council, 1938.)

Simple yet sound suggestions for analyzing any community including its structure, social processes, and problems are offered in several publications, all of value to the teacher considering a community study. Johanna Colcord's *Your Community: Its Provision for Health, Education, Safety and Welfare* (Russell Sage Foundation, 1941) is a compendium of ideas for making non-technical studies of any community in terms of such factors as its setting, founding, and development; local government; workers and wages; housing and zoning; religious agencies; foreign-born and racial groups, and the like. The National League of Women Voters' pamphlets *Know Your Town Government* (1949) and *Know Your County* present questions which may be asked to get significant data about a community's history, population, industry, public welfare, local government, education and recreation, and so on. The U. S. Office of Education leaflet *Know Your Community* (1941) offers similar suggestions for investigation and discussion.

Motion Pictures

Pennsylvania Local Government in Action. Presents many governmental service activities in such areas as recreation, welfare, housing, and council meetings. Pennsylvania State University, 1945, 22 minutes.

The Town. Shows how many of the customs of the people in a typical mid-western town are based on those of European cultures. United World Films, 1945, 10 minutes.

U. S. Community and its Citizens. Portrays the actual functioning of community life and services, as seen by a group of school children who make a community survey. United World Films, 1945, 20 minutes.

Boundary Lines shows how the "boundary lines" of color, origin, wealth, and religion result in accumulations of fear and suspicion, thus helps point up some of the problems involved in adjusting to people. International Film Foundation, 1947, color, 10 minutes.

Cities: Why They Grow portrays what the workers of the city do, thereby indicating why the city grows, as well as providing an overview of many occupations. Coronet Films, 1949, 10 minutes.

CHAPTER 4

Social Status

When people first meet, they often ask questions of subtle intent. "What do you do? Where do you work? Where do you live? Who do you know? Where did you go to school? What is your church?" No matter how the queries are phrased, the asker is seeking to place the other in a ranking system. Each one is trying to find out how the other probably will act by tentatively assigning him to a "place" in a community.

All of us live by our illusions of social status. The illusion of place in a system of rank persists because a large proportion of families maintain the same relative social position through several generations. A few are "higher," some are "lower," and others are "in the middle." Often certain individuals and families are pointed out as typical of each kind of position. Those one associates with outside of working hours constitute "reference groups" by which relative position or "place" in a community is judged. The illusion, then, becomes very real in the lives of people.

The series of ranked groups are called statuses or "social classes." The latter term is used in the sociological sense to refer a person to observed differences in reputation and participation. Status does not depend upon "class conflict" in the Marxian meaning of a "bourgeoisie-proletariat" kind of distinction.

This chapter is by CARSON McGUIRE.

Status Behavior Is Learned

Status behavior among people is learned like any other behavior. Many of the relationships are learned in childhood and adolescent years, the years through which young people attend school. Boys and girls entering school usually are viewed according to their family's status-position in the community. Very soon, though, peers begin to judge them more as individuals in the children's world. The wide-awake teacher very soon becomes aware of the ones who are approved and those who are disapproved among boys and girls of about the same age. The children themselves have a system of peer status.

The process of sorting out by acceptance and avoidance continues when the transition to adolescence is made. Girls and boys who experience disapproval by their fellows form their own gangs or friendship pairs. Some are left alone, isolated from contacts through which they could learn. A large proportion of such non-accepted and isolated young people leave school. They form a nucleus for families of lower status in the next generation.

The boys and girls who win approval usually pattern their behavior after chosen models, the children from homes of middle and higher status. Models for learning are generally the persons one knows from day to day. When accepted, a young person often learns a new life pattern. The process of *social mobility*—moving from one relative position in a ranked order to another—begins with an opportunity to learn new kinds of social behavior.

People acquire class-typed behavior patterns, or a *life-style,* through what they experience. They learn what they perceive and what they come to value as a result of their experience. Hence the formative years in a family, among age-mates, and in the school are crucial ones. These years have much to do with determining career patterns and, consequently, where the new adults are to live and with whom they are to associate. The ones who do not learn another way of life are termed *static* or non-mobile. A majority of Americans, perhaps 60 per cent, continue in the living pattern of their parents, having similar kinds of status relationships with others in their community.

Possibly as many as 20 to 25 per cent of the individuals in an age-group shift their pattern of living upward. They can be called the *climbers*. By far the larger number are from so-called lower class homes. Upward mobility is characteristic of American people for a number of reasons. Differences in birth rate, with families of middle status having relatively fewer children, makes continuous recruiting necessary. Meanwhile, some "upper crust" and middle status persons are downward mobile. "From shirtsleeves to shirtsleeves in three generations" is an old saying in America.

There are other reasons for more upward than downward mobility in America. Except in times of depression, new "white collar" career patterns and highly skilled occupations constantly open up. In the professions, recruiting of persons with talent always goes on. Moreover, individuals and families can move freely from one community to another in search of "a better way of life." And education provides a ladder for those who seek and use it.

The remaining 15 to 20 per cent, varying from community to community, seem to have difficulties. A number of those who set out to learn a new life-style, and who begin the move upward in adolescent and early adult years, fail in their attempt. They can be termed the *strainers* who either lack ability or do not perceive what others expect of them. Very often such persons are avoided by age-mates from whom they seek acceptance, or they lack the approval of older people.

Some members of each generation shift downward in their associations and way of life. Although the terms "delinquent" and "maladjusted" often are employed to describe their behavior, they can be looked upon as *decliners* in terms of status. Others, who "hang on" to the way of life of their parents in the community, can be termed *clingers*. By and large, such persons come from middle status homes and are having difficulties in achieving what is expected of them, not only with their fellows but also at school and later in an occupation. What is expected of them is governed by the position of their father and mother in the community.

Education to fit people into community living, then, has two major facets. Young people can learn skills, insights, and outlooks necessary to their "acceptance" as persons as well as their competence to be workers, citizens, homemakers, and the like. A school curriculum is a device to provide a frame of reference for the necessary experiences and the models, real and vicarious, from which boys and girls learn. Much of the science and art of teaching is concerned with finding content and procedures appropriate to the age, sex, and family backgrounds of young people.

Another facet of education is guidance and counseling, both in the formal and informal senses. Here, school people are concerned about guiding the young person and his expectations. Status relationships and what might be called mobility orientations have to be considered. There is some evidence for believing that the static person and the climber require less help than the strainer, the clinger, or the decliner. To identify young people with the different outlooks, and to work with them more effectively, we have to understand young people as persons and not just as pupils. A very important part of this understanding comes about when one is aware of the community's social climate and how it is stratified and interrelated.

The Make-up of Modern Communities

All communities tend to be more alike than different in terms of the status relationships among people living in them. Very often only a part of the pattern is to be found in a village or residential suburb. Any metropolis, of course, is a number of communities fitted together. The total structure is perceived much more clearly in an established town or city. Many people in cities carry in their heads what might be called a "status map" of the preferred and non-preferred dwelling areas. Different kinds of people live in various parts of a community.

One only has to think a bit about the parts of one's own town or city to realize the truth of the statement. A school official who has worked out attendance boundaries, for example, often is aware of the differences in life-style characteristic of families in various districts.

A diagram serves to picture the parts of a modern community. The accompanying diagram is such a schematic picture. The diagram has three dimensions to show how the parts of any community fit together. Looking at the right-hand dimension, one can recognize the several kinds of institutions beginning with the family. Along with the family, educational, religious, economic, and political institutions, there are the informal associations and the formal organizations. The seven social situations form the setting for different kinds of expected patterns of behavior, or roles, in the community.

The dimension to the left represents the basic kinds of cultural distinctions most often made in a community. Usually both the ethnic or foreign-born and the colored groups are set apart in one way or another. Much of the work in intergroup relations is directed toward establishing more lines of communication among people in the several groups. Sometimes a religious sect is regarded as if it were an ethnic group, especially if the families in it are said to hold a somewhat different set of cultural beliefs and values than do the majority of "Old American" or "Anglo" families. Barriers to communication and discrimination in a community arise out of tradition associated with beliefs and values as well as out of the "ethnic visibility" of people in communities.

Finally, the vertical dimension denotes the social class levels which may be present. Within each level one can find reference groups of persons and families who tend to associate with one another, the levels being ranked by social reputation. In established towns and cities, there often is an "upper crust" or "society" made up of "old line" families. Usually there is an upper-middle group of "community leaders" living in preferred areas and representing business and the professions, industry

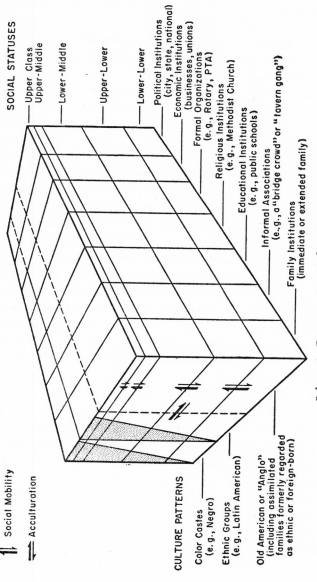

SOCIAL STATUSES

Upper Class
Upper-Middle

Lower-Middle

Upper-Lower

Lower-Lower

Political Institutions
(city, state, national)
Economic Institutions
(businesses, unions)
Formal Organizations
(e.g., Rotary, PTA)
Religious Institutions
(e.g., Methodist Church)
Educational Institutions
(e.g., public schools)
Informal Associations
(e.g., a "bridge crowd" or "tavern gang")
Family Institutions
(immediate or extended family)

Social Mobility
Acculturation

CULTURE PATTERNS

Color Castes
(e.g., Negro)
Ethnic Groups
(e.g., Latin American)
Old American or "Anglo"
(including assimilated
families formerly regarded
as ethnic or foreign-born)

Schematic Diagram of a Modern Community

and agriculture, as well as government. A much larger number in lower-middle status, both white-collar workers and skilled blue-collar tradesmen, take part in organizations and support the schools which "give their children a chance in life." Another large proportion of "hard-working, respectable people" who do not take part in community affairs often are placed in an upper-lower status. At the bottom, living a deviant way of life in lowly regarded areas of the community, are lower-lower families.

The three dimensions in the diagram thus depict the status relationships in any community. Shading of portions of the "community block" indicate that there are fewer colored families or ethnic people placed by their fellows in the higher statuses. Relatively more people in minority groups are in upper-lower or lower-lower positions. Moves upward or downward in status are shown by the lines denoting social mobility. The process of acculturation—learning the behavior and standards of another way of life—is represented by a horizontal pair of lines between the minority ethnic and the majority pattern. The remainder of the chapter discusses and illustrates with material from interviews the several aspects of community and the pattern of relationships among people pictured in the schematic diagram.

The Seven Social Situations

Situations in which particular kinds of behavior are expected can be grouped together and called the *institutions* of a community. Along with the well-recognized family, school, church, economic, and government institutions, there are informal groupings and formal organizations which tie together life in the community and its institutions. Within a set of limits, everyone knows what to anticipate from others in each institutional setting and the linking groups and organizations. The statement is true since every such social situation is made up of a particular set of status relationships which require appropriate patterns of behavior. The ways of acting are called *role-behaviors,* and they have to be learned. Although much of the learning takes place in the home and the school, many role-behaviors are learned by copying or matching one's actions to models, older or of the same age.

Certain kinds of relationships are characteristic of each institutional situation and are known as *role-expectations.* Marriage, of course, is linked with the establishment and maintenance of a family as well as the procreation and bringing-up of children. Children live with their mother and father in a family of orientation. When the children grow up and marry, a son and a daughter of another family become husband and wife in a new family of procreation. When they reach later maturity, and their children have left home, grandmother and grandfather form a family of gerontation. Thus, in a complete life cycle, every person has to learn at least three sets of expected role behaviors within the family setting.

The other situations represented in the schematic diagram also have their expected relationships. Friendship is an important part of any informal association, such as that which occurs when persons accept and interact with others in a clique or a gang. Education, in this modern world, is associated with schools and colleges. Worship, in the formal sense, is set apart and undertaken at particular times in churches. Participation in situations where people of different life-styles meet is made possible by memberships in formal organization. One can nearly always predict, for instance, how people will act toward one another in a P.T.A. meeting, a lodge session, or a service club.

Even economic and political situations have their particular relations and attitudes. Business—the creation, buying, and selling of goods and services—is the special province of economic institutions. Customers, clients, and patients, for example, are expected to act in certain ways appropriate to their status in the community and with reference to business and professional people. The members of a union, through their officials, are expected to bargain with management as representatives of employers for wages and working relationships. The ideas of democracy, as well as "politics" and the much maligned bureaucracy of officials, are a part of government (local, state, national) as it is represented in the community.

Status Relationships and Role-Behavior

Most situations are structured in the sense that certain kinds of behavior are expected according to the age and sex of the persons in them. An adult male, for example, has to learn to act as a husband and a father, an uncle, or a visitor in a home. The role-behaviors of an adult female, on the other hand, are those of a wife and mother, an aunt, or a mother-in-law in a family setting. The role-behaviors for a man or woman as a visitor are much the same. But some visitors are treated differently from others according to their status relationships to the family. The vertical dimension of status or "place" in the community, then, affects the ways in which people act toward one another as well as do their age and sex.

Young people very often carry over the role-behaviors of children to parents when they become pupils in relation to teachers. But they soon learn to act in other ways along with their "same-age" fellows. Schools are settings for children and youth to come together and respond to one another. Status among one's peers is an element in determining the social roles which are taken over by a young person. For instance, an eighteen-year-old girl is talking to a field worker about her experiences with age-mates.

Maybe I ought not to tell you—but, when I was a freshman, and a sophomore, I didn't dress very nice or pay attention to my figure. The kids didn't talk to me. I wasn't in any cliques. Cliques are natural—you like some people better than others. Then I turned to the skating rink. Because I didn't belong to any clique here in school, I tried hard to make friends at the skating rink. Then I began to pay more attention to my clothes. I worked into that crowd. Then—at school, when I looked better—the kids began to be more friendly to me. But you never get in the top crowd after your first year.

Another kind of situation is found among the churches of a community. Individuals are expected to take the role of a worshipper in a religious setting. But the actual experiences in church-affiliated groups often vary according to the person, the denomination, and the values placed upon expected role-behaviors. Acceptance seems to be a function of the extent to which a person is willing to conform to one set of moral standards as contrasted to another. The conflict is evident in an interview with another girl.

At my church there are cliques. If you come to Fellowship alone, you stay alone. If you are with a bunch, you stay with them. They don't mingle. I feel like I'm not wanted there. It's a choir gang, and I'm not in the choir—because I don't feel capable. My mother is a very good church member, but she understands why I don't want to go.

It's a bunch of kids that don't dance; they don't play cards; they don't sing popular music—don't go to shows. I feel like an outcast and I'm treated like one. In Sunday School, there is nobody in the neighborhood to go with. I'd like to go to the Federated Young Peoples; I would like them very much.

Youth become aware of the roles that older persons assume in the economic and political life of a community. They perceive the parts that different people play. In the excerpt to follow, an older boy is assessing the behavior of well-to-do individuals to whom deference is paid.

I worked on one of Mr. Bell's farms. He's a nice guy. But he's like all the other big shots that make the laws but don't live up to them. You come to a stop street. When I was riding with him, he rode right across Main and didn't look either way. He did that every time he gave me a ride out to his farm. He's the kind that give you heck if you don't obey but turns around and does the same thing himself.

Other men, who seemed to be models for learning through imitation, have an appeal to the same boy. One of them is a highly respected, skilled craftsman. Among the man's roles are those of "a pillar of the church" and "a solid citizen" at the common man level in the community.

Mr. Monelli—he's awful nice. He's always got a smile on his face. It doesn't make any difference who it is. He's a good Christian. He goes to church all the time. He works at the factory where there's a lot of swearing and he helps men to know themselves better. He talks to 'em. When you talk to a person like that you don't say things you shouldn't. When you're with guys that swear, then you do too. But I think there's a little good in even the worst ones.

School-Community Relations

Two kinds of social situations set themselves somewhat apart from the five institutional settings (family, educational, religious, economic, and political); they are the informal associations and the formal organizations. A knowledge of both can be crucial for the understanding and management of school-community relations. None of us can afford to be unaware of them and of the ways people operate through them.

Traditionally, administrators and their co-workers have made their links with their communities through memberships in dominant formal organizations. Representatives of the school, both students and teachers, appear before P.T.A.'s, service clubs, and women's organizations for entertainment and informational purposes. A superintendent often is a Rotarian. One of the principals is a member of Kiwanis. A female member of the staff is a Soroptomist. An outcome of taking such roles is the expectation of "good public relations." Educators can delude themselves, however, if they stop at establishing memberships in and "presenting the schools' case" to the dominant organizations in which "the influential people" take part.

Informal associations among people are the settings in which the basic decisions affecting community life are reached. The situation is one in which persons can move, talk, argue, and reach agreements in the relaxed, intimate association which depends upon a common understanding of an unwritten code of behavior. In the excerpt to follow, a successful school administrator reveals how his awareness of informal relationships has helped him to carry out his responsibilities as an educator.

You know we got the by-law for the new school passed. We had to work behind the scenes to get it across. First, I went to Stan Beach and talked it over. He owns the newspaper and his family's connected with a lot of things here in town. We got a sort of fireside group together. They're the fellows that really decide things in the different organizations. We met at homes—mostly—and even out at Lester Arthur's ranch. The fellows talked to others down at the Imperial over coffee, mornings and afternoons. They put across the idea that we need a new school and the service clubs and other groups backed it.

We had to get to the women too. Miss Beach and Mrs. Arthur helped a lot there. You know there's a lot that can be said across a cup of tea. . . . We couldn't have made it, though, if we hadn't reached some of the little fellows. Dick Mony—he's got a small place across the river and people really listen to him—got behind what we were doing. And Al Jenkins—he's the feedman at Darby's —did a lot of work. You have to sell your ideas to different kinds of people if you want a community to accept them.

Then you've got to consider the foreign element. They'll vote against you just like the little fellows if they think you're trying to put one over on them. Abe Chikpok, over on the east side, helped a lot. Some of us dropped in and he spread the word around. Out south of town, Dave Lange had a lot of influence. They'll go against you if you overlook them.

Principles of Inclusion and Exclusion

People are included in or excluded from a relationship on a number of bases. The most evident ones are age and sex. That is why the social scientist speaks of age and sex roles. In everyday life, we remind one another to "act your age," "be a man," or "remember you're a woman." Our schools are age-graded institutions where expectations are that a six-year-old will be beginning school and an eighteen-year-old should be graduating from high school. A young girl can date a number of men but, as she grows older, she is expected to be married. A young man begins to work with only a modest income but, as the years go on, he is expected to have a home and family which he can support as well as or better than his father did in the previous generation.

Friendships and cliques are formed partly on the basis of age and sex. The children's world of age-mates, in the middle childhood years, is largely a boy's world and a girl's peer culture intermingling in the neighborhood and at school. But boys also live apart and exchange a great deal of information, even in the mysterious area of sex which seems to concern their elders, before the pubertal change. Girls, too, have their in-groups where boys are excluded. The teen-age society involves both sexes. Only in dating do some of the girls break away to "go with" older males. Gradually, in the adult years, the age-spread of informal associations increases.

Visibility factors, especially skin color, have a strong influence upon acceptance and avoidance in human relationships. Visibility characteristics seem to operate primarily as symbols. Somehow there is an association between whiteness and purity which reinforces beliefs handed down from the past. Dark-skinned people like the Negro, and sometimes the Oriental and the *Mexicano*, find themselves set apart in a community. As the diagram indicates by the dotted lines at the top, however, there is interaction with other parts of the community in the economic and political life.

Elsewhere color barriers are encountered. Relatively explicit distinctions in the South and more implicit ones in the North mark off aspects of community life where interaction and communication are blocked. Discrimination, though, is not the only process involved. When people are set apart in a color caste, the significance of common biological descent reinforces the operation of the visibility factor. Only the possibility of "passing over," that is, changing visibility symbols, permits an escape.

Ethnicity is another factor which makes for inclusion or exclusion. Being regarded as foreign born, or of foreign descent, can set families and groups apart in a community. An older adolescent boy, for example, explains the distance between him and an ethnic girl as follows:

It seems as though there's an invisible barrier between us. If I dated her, it would be an exception to the rule because of the opinion of others. I haven't paid any attention to her so I wouldn't know if she were attractive. A lot of kids wouldn't think she was attractive. That's silly. If I knew she wasn't Polish, I don't know but what I'd think she's pretty. She just hasn't entered into my thoughts and *I wouldn't know how to enter her in,* if you know what I mean. There's too much attention paid to what others in your group have to say about that sort of thing. I wish I could be above such things. But if you try to, it appears as though you were peculiar. You have to go along with the group or you're too far apart. And *if you're too far apart, it's not so good.*

Closer examination shows that it is not just being "foreign" which is the determining factor. Successive generations often are regarded as ethnic people. In general, ethnic groups are made up of families who hold to a different tradition, especially a religious one. They tend to keep their family life, their worship, many of their associations, and sometimes the education of their children, apart from the more common pattern. People of a Jewish or a Mennonite faith, for example, understandably want to have successive generations follow their way of life. Consequently, the elders set up barriers of one kind or another to prevent the breaking away of young people.

The person, young or old, who moves out of an ethnic group or a religious sect has to become acculturated. He or she has to learn a new set of orientations. For instance, the boy quoted above has a great deal of respect for another girl from an ethnic family. He has often spoken of her as being "one of the crowd." Acceptance stems from the fact that the girl, both in the children's world and in the teen-age years, has learned a new way of life. She has taken over the social skills, the rules of behavior, and many of the beliefs of the dominant peer culture.

Some individuals who are in the process of breaking away from a traditional pattern, religious or otherwise, are marginal people. They have an allegiance to conflicting patterns. Their relationships with other people and their roles in the community are in a state of flux. Such persons can be as lonely in a community as the newcomer who has no ties and no memberships to help him meet people.

When a person or a family is actually accepted in another status relationship, assimilation has occurred. The process of acculturation and the acceptance in new roles which marks assimilation is going on in all communities. By their very nature, schools have a great deal to do with moves out of ethnic groups into the "Old American" or "Anglo" culture pattern denoted by an arrow on the schematic diagram. They permit the acquisition of knowledge and skills as well as orientations to the dominant, middle-class American way of life. They provide a meeting place for youth from many backgrounds.

Students of human relations traditionally have been concerned about minority groups. One usually thinks of those who are excluded on the basis of skin color or ethnicity. In a sense, though, there are minority groups according to age and sex. Traditionally, children and youth are subordinated to adults; and, depending upon the role-setting, one sex often is subordinated to another. Perhaps the largest minority group, though, are persons and families who form "the lower third"—a name for lower status people in many communities.

Social Statuses and Life-Styles

The vertical dimension in the schematic diagram represents the several social class statuses which may be found in most communities. As mentioned earlier, some residential suburbs have a high concentration of middle status people with only a few of "the lower third." Some smaller communities have only a few families who could move into larger centers and fit into the upper-middle groups there. Accurate representation of the proportion in each status in any particular community would require a shifting of the horizontal lines and, perhaps, an omission of a category or two. In addition, there always is a movement from one position to another denoted by vertical arrows indicating social mobility upward and downward.

One of the most effective ways of demonstrating the variations in life-style associated with the different social statuses in a community is to employ excerpts from interviews. Young people who have learned the way of life of their parents reflect the ideals, beliefs, and values which are characteristic of the family status. For instance, Lane Carter tells how his parents have gone about teaching him their way of life.

I have my own bank account. If I make a big expenditure, I consult my parents and they give me good advice. They trust me pretty much now because they think they've taught me a lot about saving. They've taught me not to be wasteful and the value of money. They gave me some and let me see how fast it goes. Then they briefed me. They weren't inclined to be a reserve bank once it was gone. They did not give me an established allowance but preferred that I work and earn my own money, rather than be an inexhaustible source of funds.

Traditional middle class value orientations are reflected in these remarks to a field worker. Ideas and sentiments characteristic of upper-middle class persons are becoming a part of the boy's value-attitude system. His parents are people well-known and active in community affairs. Both are college graduates and Lane is going on to university to prepare for a profession. A further excerpt shows the point of view he has learned.

One of our teachers is a little radical—just slightly. I differ with him on a lot of things. For instance, labor unions—he loves them. He thinks they're it—anything they want to do is right. I don't care for them at all. Last summer, either I joined the union or I lost my job. They had a closed shop. Because America had freedom, unions got started. That wouldn't be possible in a dictatorship. But once unions were established, they began to be a dictator and didn't want anybody to talk against them.

Marilu Nettant is a girl who has absorbed the standards of her family and those of her age-mates. Sometimes the restrictions put upon her by her upper-middle status parents irk her but she can see a reason for maintaining a reputation. Again one can see indications of learning a way of life which governs much of behavior and relations with other people.

I think people should be a little snobbish. I'm sure my family wouldn't want me to be with roustabouts—kids that walk the streets, people that don't have good families or reputation. You really shouldn't be that way. But you don't want you or your family's reputation to suffer. My folks don't want me to go with Joan Tipton—you know there's talk about her family. She's boisterous, she's lazy, she's for herself—but she can be very nice.

Many of the same values which are characteristic of the dominant upper-middle life-style are shared by persons from lower-middle families. The breadwinner of the family usually is a white collar employee, an owner of a small enterprise, an operator of a modest farm or ranch, or a skilled tradesman. Many youths from such backgrounds have a desire "to get ahead" which their parents had before them. Art Moran, raised in a hard-working, respectable family of this kind, phrases his aspirations and his fears that he could not attend college in a revealing excerpt.

I say a prayer to myself every night. I don't believe I've missed a night since my mother taught me when I was six years old. Most of the time I think of the future, whether I'll ever amount to anything. If I ever have a chance I want to go west. I want to be an engineer. But that's far-fetched. I can't go to college. I can't afford it nor can my family. If I had to work my way; well, I wouldn't learn as much.

The point of view also could be one commonly held by a boy or girl in a lower class home where one parent, usually the mother, holds a middle status set of beliefs and values. More commonly, though, the tendency is toward an alternate way of life and an expectation of working in a blue-collar situation. Jerry Foote reflects the difference in outlook.

My dad goes to union meetings once in a while, nothing much else. Mom—she does the prayers and the masses. My dad wanted me to get in the "T" club and I did. I won letters in two sports. I like sports and as long as I've gone to school I wanted to be in them, like the rest of the fellows. . . . I like to bowl, ping pong, play tennis, dances Thursday night. I don't go to movies much now. I find other things to do with the fellows. Smoking, pool, drinking—I just quit that. It's just one of those things you pick up as a kid. Anyone who keeps away from drinking is smart. . . . I started work when I was eleven. I make my own living. I've got quite a lot saved—enough to get married.

Jerry Foote seems to be following in the footsteps of his father—work and union membership, male friends and early marriage. He and his fellows form the solid core of people who make the modern community possible. By and large, he no more approves of the deviate life style of the "lower third" than do the youth from middle class homes who have played football with him and who will chat with him at the gas station or at a ball game in later years.

Most of the boys have avoided Tom Ding, a boy from a lower-lower status home, who finally dropped out of school. Upon leaving the tenth grade, Tom has revealed his feelings to a field worker.

I'd like to live uptown. And I'd like to have money, and I'd like to have more clothes. I'd like to go out for basketball and football. And I'd like to be in things and do things. . . . Oh, they treated me all right. But I was just different from them. They were just different from me. But when I get a job, I'll have some money and I can have dates.

By and large, however, lower-lower class people consider themselves "just as good as anybody." In the case of Tom Ding, the record shows a subtle transformation for, when interviewed the next day, he talks of doing "a man's work." He is no longer a part of his teen-age society for, as one of the middle-status youths phrases it, he has been "weeded out." An absence of recognition from his age-mates and an inability to respond to school people both have their part in keeping him in the kind of position his parents occupy. Youth like Tom Ding, who leave school early, perpetuate a core of people with a deviant life-style in a community.

At the other end of the rank order system are the relatively few families who form an "upper crust" in well-established communities. Like many upper-middle status people, the family members can visit any part of the country and find those who appreciate and value the same things. Old-line ranch as well as highly-respected merchant and professional families in smaller communities have connections and exclusive club memberships in large metropolitan centers. Although wealth at some time would seem to be necessary, the crucial symbols appear to be family lineage and high respect. An individual with money can buy goods and services at the same stores and hotels, favored by upper class families, but wealth does not necessarily purchase acceptance in American communities. The prevailing "social climate" generally demands more than that.

Undeniable Realities

The historic concepts of "social class" are repugnant to most Americans, since we tend to idealize equality as an ingredient of democracy. Yet, in the sociological sense, social class, social status, status behavior, life-styles, and role-behavior are undeniable realities. They exist, they condition the lives of us all, and as community factors they must be understood and worked with by every teacher who wishes to merit that name in a true sense.

Learning Activities

Socio-drama

Assume that your group is The Club of Ritzville High School. You are discussing the need for more members whose abilities can contribute to your club winning the annual talent show competition. Patricia Carter, president, proposes as new members Josh White, whose clothes are crude but who plays the accordion, Joe

Smith, a ventriloquist of another race; and Maria Lopez, a solo dancer. Their admission would break club traditions. There is immediate objection from some members, strong support from a few, with a majority undecided. Dramatize this meeting and then discuss its implications, both for the immediate situation and for the larger world.

Discussion Topics

1. "Human beings live by their illusions of status." How true do you believe this to be?
2. Make a blackboard summary of the most characteristic values of the upper-, middle-, and lower-class modes of life in your community.
3. Precisely how does the color-caste system operate in your community?
4. Where does your school stand in the local caste system? What range of caste and class statuses are influential in it? Why do these operate as they do? What is their history, and probable future?

Group Activities

1. The status areas of a community can be established by consulting real estate men, tax assessors, school officials, and other persons. Take a map and have each person draw the boundaries of the different residential areas as he thinks of them. Then have him rate the areas on a seven-point scale with "1" the most desirable and "7" the least desirable. The several maps should be compared to estimate agreement among informants.
2. Status relationships in a teen-age society may be investigated by interviewing boys and girls of about the same age. Trusted interviewers can lead young people into talking about the "ones who run around together" and how the different groups rank relative to one another. Compare the data for agreements and disagreements. Draw a diagram with names of youth most often grouped together and showing how the groups are ranked.
3. Choose a community and analyze the nature, history, and operation of its basic "power system."
4. Get a committee to read Hollingshead's *Elmtown's Youth* and present its major conclusions before your class, then lead group discussion of these findings in contrast to the high schools best known to the group.

Individual Projects

1. Warner's ISC, or index of status characteristics (see bibliography), is a useful means of estimating the social status of a person or a family. Employ the ISC to find the approximate social position in the community of the adults and parents of youth who have been interviewed.
2. Draw a schematic diagram to represent your community, varying the spacing of the lines to represent proportions of people at each level in terms of an estimate. Identify some of the organizations or the churches in the community and, through discussion, arrive at an approximation of the status relationships of people who are members.
3. Show the section on *Status Behavior Is Learned* to a counselor, a principal, a teacher, and a youth worker. After obtaining their reactions, write an evaluation of the statement, "There is some evidence for believing that the static person and the climber require less help than the strainer, the clinger, or the decliner."
4. Observe a person in a number of situations and write down an account of what he does and says. Compare the anecdotal records of the same person in different situations to identify shifts in role-behavior from one situation to another and personality elements which persist. Compare the records for different persons in the same kind of situation to identify common role-behaviors according to age, sex, and position in the community.
5. Describe the social behavior of some person whom you know well, and indicate where you think he stands in the class system of his group.

Learning Materials

More thorough analyses of status relationships among people may be found in *Democracy in Jonesville* by W. L. Warner and his associates (Harper, 1949). The fourth chapter (on social mobility), the eighth and ninth (on associations), the eleventh (on ethnic groups), and the twelfth (on status in the high school) should be of concern to school people. Another book by Warner and his co-workers, *Social Class in America* (Science Research Associates, 1949), explains a procedure for estimating the social status of persons and families. After reading the first two chapters, move on to the eighth and ninth to find the instructions for using the index. A series of articles by Carson McGuire in *Marriage and Family Living* should be read also. "Family Backgrounds and Community Patterns" (November 1951) tells more about the "community block" diagram. "Family Life in Lower and Middle Class Homes"

(February 1952) illustrates the way an interview is recorded. "Conforming, Mobile, and Divergent Families" (May 1952) describes the IVO technique of predicting life-styles. *What You Should Know About Social Class* by W. Lloyd Warner and Mildred H. Warner (Science Research Associates, Inc.), is a very readable pamphlet summary of basic ideas and postulates.

The impact of status relationships on youth of high-school age is the subject of *Elmtown's Youth* by A. B. Hollingshead (Wiley, 1949). Anyone who wants to study a community should read his account of field procedures in Chapter 2, and also Chapter 5 in *Intergroup Education in Public Schools* by Hilda Taba and others (American Council, 1953). "The Community and Social Class," Part 4 of Gitler's *Social Dynamics* (McGraw-Hill, 1952), presents several case-studies illustrating the meaning and types of communities and how social class and stratification actually operate in them.

Persons concerned about country communities should refer to *Rural Social Systems* by C. P. Loomis and J. A. Beegle (Prentice-Hall, 1950). Scan the first chapter on frames of reference; then, for information on social strata and the school, read Chapters 10, 11, and 15. Status relationships in a Southern community of some five thousand people, of whom 30 percent are Negro, have been studied by Hill and McCall. One of their reports which describes the use of the ISC, "Social Stratification in 'Georgia Town'," may be found in the *American Sociological Review* for December 1950.

How status behavior is learned is reported in a readable little book, *Social-Class Influences Upon Learning*, by Allison Davis (Harvard, 1948). The last half of the volume shows how experience in different family backgrounds affects mental problem-solving and performance upon intelligence tests. The fascinating topic of role-behaviors of people can be studied from different points of view, according to T. M. Newcomb, author of *Social Psychology* (Dryden, 1950). His article on "Role Behaviors in the Study of Individual Personality and of Groups" appears in the *Journal of Personality* for March 1950.

Different techniques of studying status relationships are reported in the second volume of *Research Methods in Social Relations* by Marie Jahoda and others (Dryden, 1951). A criticism of status studies may be found in Walter R. Goldschmidt's article, "The Study of Man—America's Social Classes," in the August 1950 issue of *Commentary*.

Further worth-while material can be found in these magazine articles:

"Social Status and Education in a Southern Community," Burleigh Gardner, Mary Gardner, and Martin Loeb. Shows how the school is a selective device which helps some individuals rise in the social system while perpetuating in most children the class status of their parents. *School Review* 50:179-191; March 1942.

"The School and Social Structure in a Mid-Western Community," Buford H. Junker and Martin B. Loeb. A non-technical study of one community in terms of population, class stratification, influence of social differentiation in high school, differing attitudes toward education, and the like. *School Review* 50:686-695; December 1942.

"Middletown's Split Personality," Frederick Mayer. Analyzes a town's dominant culture-patterns in simple fashion and concludes that its confusions symbolize the social lag of this era. *Social Studies* 38:195-198; May 1947.

"Social Class and the Curriculum," Celia B. Stendler. Discusses the American class structure situation and its implications for democratic education. *Educational Leadership* 7:371-375; March 1950.

"America Needs a New Social Class Theory of Education," W. B. Brookover. Since the social organization of the school reflects that of the community, educators must recognize three possible policies: (1) accept stratification as inevitable and educate accordingly; (2) reorganize schooling to promote equality and upward mobility; (3) verbalize equality and mobility values but in practice ignore them as goals. *Educational Theory* 1:97-105; August 1951; *Education Digest* 17:1-4; November 1951.

"Social Class and Teacher-Training." The entire issue of the *Journal of Educational Sociology* for April 1952 is devoted to this area.

"Social Class Structure and American Education" is the title of a special issue of the *Harvard Educational Review,* issue of the Summer of 1953 (Volume 23, No. 3).

Motion Pictures

The Greenie. A little Polish refugee boy comes to America. At first ridiculed by the boys on his street, he is finally accepted by them. Teaching Film Custodians, 1942, 10 minutes.

Color of a Man. A documentary story of discrimination and segregation. International Film Foundation, 1946, 18 minutes.

The Barrier. A morally good suburban home-owner fights against the new housing project in his neighborhood because of his social class-status prejudices, not shared by either of his children. Family Films, 1951, 30 minutes.

The High Wall. A dramatic case study of an adolescent bigot, showing how class prejudice in parents may produce delinquency in the children. McGraw-Hill, 1952, 32 minutes.

Part III

ORGANIZING
YOUR
PROGRAM

We shall doubtless all agree that the primary function of education is to transmit, create, interpret, and evaluate experience. We know that in the very process of rational learning, specific personal experiences are organized by the learner into abstract generalizations, and that these generalizations themselves become more meaningful as the context of previous experience is widened. Our instructional problem is therefore always that of choosing, using, and organizing those particular types of experience in the community as well as within the classroom which, in each specific situation, will most effectively help the individual learn to live most successfully. We must never forget that people learn best as they participate actively and thoughtfully in living—and that life is fully lived in that real world outside the schoolhouse walls.

Chapters in This Section

GUIDE TO GROUP ANALYSIS OF COMMUNITY SCHOOL PROGRAM-PLANNING

WHERE ARE YOU NOW?
(present situation)

- In Educational Thinking?
  - Book-Centered
  - Child-Centered
  - Life-Centered
- In Community Relations?
  - Hostile
  - Indifferent
  - Cooperative

WHERE DO YOU WANT TO GO?
(direction and goals)

- Immediately?
  - This Term
  - This Year
  - Next Year
- Ultimately?
  - 2-5 Years
  - 5-10 Years
  - 10-30 Years

WHAT STANDS IN YOUR WAY?
(obstacles to progress)

- In School?
  - Traditions
  - Policies
  - Personel
- In Community?
  - Climate of Opinion
  - Vested Interests
  - Pressure Groups

WHERE LIES YOUR STRENGTH?
(resources available)

- In School?
  - Administration
  - Faculty
  - Students
- In Community?
  - Climate of Opinion
  - Organizations
  - Leaders

WHAT ARE THE NEXT STEPS?
(strategy and tactics)

- In School?
  - ?
  - ?
  - ?
- In Community?
  - ?
  - ?
  - ?

HOW APPRAISE RESULTS?
(evaluation of progress)

- Opinions?
  - ?
  - ?
  - ?
- Holding Power of School?
  - ?
  - ?
- Community Improvement?
  - ?
  - ?

CHAPTER 5

Planning Community Experiences

We learn as best we can. The American Constitution cannot be understood except by manipulating words and by trying to give real meaning to those words. Swimming and tennis can be learned only by direct, firsthand experience, but proficiency in these activities can be much improved by reading about the experiences of others. In our school programs, the use of community resources cannot take the place of reading and telling any more than books, alone, can give an adequate picture of how a community lives. As we have seen in Chapter 2, learning becomes effective as the student utilizes all four of the chief learning channels: words, audio-visual materials, expressive activities, and community experiences.

What Aspects of the Community Shall We Investigate? [1]

The community cannot be understood aside from its geographic base. The Indian "old fields" explained the location of New England towns, and the exhaustion of the soil accounted for their decline. The water table in the Mississippi Valley is taken for granted there, but not so in the Salt River Valley of Arizona. Even continued economic existence of such

---

This chapter is by JULIAN C. ALDRICH.

[1] It is well at this point to review suggestions already made in Chapters 3 and 4, which deal with community processes and problems, and with status relationships of the people in the community.

regions depends upon an understanding of the geographic bases of their communities.

While location is important to some communities, it is really vital to others. Neither New York City nor San Francisco, for example, can be understood except in terms of soil, water, and hinterland. Harbors and lines of communication bring population and wealth to these communities. The difference between New York and Baltimore can be understood, in large part, by seeing the significance of the Mohawk trough.

The distribution of population in a region or community will reflect both the geographic base and the history of the area. People usually live where they can make a living, and where their families have lived before them. Some have even remained on poor land, cut off from modern lines of communication, simply because that land was home.

The kinds of people are important to study also. The nationalities of early or recent immigrants often indicate the types of work which have been needed. The shallow soil of the upper Midwest was little developed until the Scandinavians brought to it their intelligence, energy, and agrarian "know-how." Farmers and townspeople of New England and the South took with them to western communities their types of farming, their religious and cultural institutions, and their cookbooks. Irish and Chinese were brought into the United States to build the railroads; Japanese became efficient truck gardeners on the west coast. The present community can be understood, too, as one examines current census reports of occupations, and compares these with earlier times. Farm centers become financial and industrial centers. In some communities, agriculture and industry have equal importance.

Also, we must seek to understand the community in terms of its history. It can safely be said that most national movements and problems can be understood better by an examination of their impact on various regions and on local communities in those regions. To illustrate, almost any community in the Mississippi Valley can find, in its own history, the story of the

Westward Movement, and of other population trends in our nation. With allowance for acceleration by means of transportation or deceleration by lack of such, the history of any community will reflect many aspects of the history of a region and of the nation.

Local history has the color, the vigor, and the drama which is found only in the very detailed histories of our country or in historical fiction. Every community has in its own historical records the stories of people and resources woven into the pattern of our national development. The drama of railroad building can be found in almost every county and state. The struggle for soil against the forest and climate can be seen in one's own community. Constitution making, pioneering, the ages of the turnpike, the canal, and air transport can be read in the lives and times of people known in the community.

Even more important is the fact that basic social processes and problems operate in every community and can there be observed in action, as well as worked with, for, or against. Through community study of economic processes can be built the concept of an operating economy. Government can be understood in local, state, and regional terms, and through people who are familiar to the students. Social problems become concrete as we investigate them in our own communities. Possibilities and techniques of community improvement can be made vital and meaningful.

How May We Use the Community? [2]

In five fundamental ways the community may serve as an educational resource. It may provide concrete data, be seen as people striving, serve as a case study base, illustrate problems and trends in larger areas, and be the scene of civic action. Let's examine each in turn.

[2] This section is taken by permission from Julian C. Aldrich's "The Community as a Resource," in Loretta Klee (Editor), *Social Studies for Older Children*. Washington: National Council for the Social Studies, Curriculum Series, No. 5, 1952.

• **The community provides concrete data** on cultural, industrial, political, and geographic facts and relationships. These
data are tangible, see-able, and describable. "A business" may
be made real as children see "goods," "selling," and "transportation." They may see "bookkeeping," "stock," and "deposits"
made by the business representative. A talk with the business
man will give some understanding of "management." With this
conceptual background, the children may count business enterprises of a given type, compare the work done by each, consider the number of employees, and estimate the purchasing
power of those employees, thus securing a valid understanding
of these matters.

Political units may be seen on the map of the school district.
A class will find that the homes of its members, when spotted
on a map of the community, outlines their school district. The
city and the county may be placed on the same map, and their
spatial relationships made apparent. The newspapers on the
table in the classroom have illustrations of community pressures relating to local problems.

From the school building, the land-use pattern of the community may be seen: business centers, residential areas, manufacturing regions, agricultural sections.

From a higher building, the pattern of transportation and
communication may be traced. Then the children may descend
to visit each aspect seen, and perhaps to explore some in detail.

Historical depth may be seen in the community as well.
Canals, old railroads, "ghost" towns, abandoned mines and
works, even oxbows which show old channels of a river are
current data telling of the past. Old newspapers, early histories, and the recollections of older people may offer real data
on early days in the community.

• **The community may be seen as people** of varied races,
nationality origins, religions, and status relationships, all seeking opportunity for better living. The impersonality of the
printed page may be overcome by talking with people. The
local government becomes part of their own experience as

young people interview the mayor, the county supervisor, the school board member, the director of the hospital, the labor leader, the county agricultural agent. As such people tell about their work, their agencies become meaningful as groups of people working together for socially useful ends.

People run railroads, people manage businesses, people assess and collect taxes. Knowable, likable persons form the dynamic elements of American life and culture. Some are the parents of the pupils, some are their relatives, their friends. The planning of social, economic, and political life is done by these people, many of whom students may meet and know.

To the community come people from other cities, states, and countries. Yankees, Texans, New Yorkers, Oregonians may be in your midst. So also may people from other nations: Mexico, Canada, Scotland, Italy, Poland, Spain, India, Japan, the Philippines. "The World in Our Town" may indeed be a rich resource for world understanding.

• **The community may serve as a case study base** for generalizing the limitations of individual and civic action. Children and adults alike tend to romanticize their own and other communities. The selection of a few aspects (the parks, the school, the highways) for generalization about the whole ("the best little community in the world") may bolster local pride, but it does not lead to true understanding. The community may be understood better as children study and compare their own with other communities.

The city community is not better than a small town; it is different, yet it is the same. Greenwich Village, in New York City, may seem strange to the visitor from Springfield. Yet both have their residential centers, their business blocks, the "town square," their church organizations, their friendship groupings, their blighted areas, and their historical sites. The same social classes, the same social conflicts, are found in both.

Baltimore's study of its traffic problem serves to describe the political forces at work in Baltimore and in all urban areas. A study of New York City's food supply funneled by water transportation and distributed by a few centralized markets serves to highlight the economic processes at work in every town, even in rural villages. To a considerable extent, the analysis of a problem in your own community is an analysis of the problem in other communities, too.

• **The community may illustrate problems and trends** in the larger region, nation, and world. There is hardly a social problem which does not appear in some one of its aspects in the local community. Shifts in population, search for sources of tax income, community betterment, racial and religious tensions, social and economic class problems—all appear in the local scene as well as on the regional and national levels. The federal budget and the town budget are cousins. Soil erosion in Washington State is paralleled by the run-off in your own county.

But while communities have the same basic social, economic, and political problems and processes, children must also see how the particular expressions of these problems and processes differ. Feeding a small town is much simpler than feeding Chicago. The relation of a metropolis to its hinterland is more complex than that of a small city to its county. Natural resources and customs of the United States may cause our communities to behave in very different ways from what is usual and "right" in European or Asian communities.

Methods of dealing with problems also show parallels. The story of "then and now" in the community can illustrate conflicts and adjustments between social and economic groups as they have tried to solve their problems in the past. Nodaway County, for example, has tried for generations to find a suitable balance between its old agricultural way of life and a perennial attempt to "industrialize." This is essentially the conflict now apparent in Mexico and Israel. So may conflicts and adjustments be found in all communities, in the various regions, in our nation, and throughout the world.

Some international problems may be found in the community. Local products enter into international trade. At holiday times one finds many illustrations of "imports" and "comparative advantage." Local groups may be associated with others dealing with world affairs, such as a foreign policy association or a UNESCO group. Many problems of any local community —housing, political representation, taxes, law and order, economic stability—are problems of localities in other countries as well.

These parallels between local and larger communities must not encourage us to oversimplify the problems, for they are most complex. Although the problems may be similar, the approaches made to them at different levels and in different countries are always affected by the history and institutions of the area.

• **The community may be the scene of civic action.** It is in the local community that children may contribute and participate, as well as observe. In recent years, exclusive "reading about" has been replaced by "seeing for yourself" and by "improving community living." Intermediate-grade children have attended council sessions dealing with community betterment, have shared in the town's "clean-up" campaign, and have made class surveys on health and safety conditions. Older youth have served as school representatives on coordinating councils, have given volunteer services to community agencies, and have participated in town forums and in "get out the vote" campaigns.

What Kinds of Community Experiences Are Useful?

Adult study groups as well as school and college classes often ask what specific kinds of community activities may help them develop community insights, interests, and skills. Certainly no blueprinted answer can be offered because different groups will have different purposes and locales. The following few suggestions may[3] indicate the nature of such activities, how-

---

[3] This list was prepared by Edward G. Olsen to suggest activities appropriate for students engaged in community study and service as part of their professional program in teacher education. See his "Community Foundations in Teacher Education," *Journal of Teacher Education* 2:126-32; June, 1951.

ever, particularly if, with them, you review the project ideas which follow each chapter in this book. You will notice that these twenty kinds of community activities include all three levels of community involvement: *observation* (use and preparation of community materials such as documents and maps, resource people, field trips, surveys); *participation* (work experiences with community organizations, discussions with social agency representatives, social activities in homes and in the community); and *contribution* (community service projects, Parent-Teacher Association activities, civic betterment campaigns, coordinating council experiences).

Map the community area showing agricultural, industrial, commercial, recreational, and suburban areas; natural resources, water system, transportation facilities; cultural, educational and civic centers; racial and nationality residence areas and types of housing.

Study the sources of community income in terms of payrolls, investments, developments, trends, and probable future.

Study the community's financial structure in terms of the public budget, taxation policies, bonds, interest rates, personal finance companies, and so on.

Study the recreational facilities, needs, problems, and possibilities of the community, and work with interested service organizations to publicize the findings.

Survey the community's public opinion structure and processes to discover underlying local ambitions and hopes, fears and superstitions, values and taboos, and the actual social-economic-political-religious power structure.

Discover the community's tension areas and types, such as boundary disputes, residential restrictions, political and religious feuds, and from economic, nationality, and racial prejudices and discriminations.

Become acquainted with minority groups and leaders, and study their group histories, customs, contributions, and adjustment problems.

Examine state laws and local ordinances regarding protection, welfare, and education of children and youth. Discover to what extent such legislation is actually in effect, and discuss what additional laws are needed.

Study community agencies to learn their organizational patterns, philosophies, programs, and procedures.

Understand current public relations programs, philosophies, and procedures including those of community agencies other than the schools.

Make a comprehensive community survey to discover local needs, problems, and resources in such fields as health, recreation, local government, occupational opportunities, art and music, home and family life, public safety, and minority groups.

Work in a variety of community welfare agencies in such fields as these: children's welfare, public health, social case work, community councils, police department, organized recreation, youth activities.

Cooperate with lay groups and organizations interested in promoting better schools. This means sustained active participation in the P.T.A., civic service clubs, women's welfare organizations, UNESCO units, coordinating councils, and the like.

Plan, conduct, and evaluate organized field trips of various kinds, purposes, and durations with children of different ages.

Plan curricular use of community resources by developing several teaching source units utilizing a rich variety of resource people, field trips, student interviews, and related documentary and audio-visual materials.

Plan a "community resources day" whereby educational, business, industrial, farm and labor leaders may come to know each other's organizations better through field visits, discussions, dramatizations, and other methods.

Plan a "community night" program to depict the history and development of the community through song and pageant, displays and exhibits, and with child, youth, and adult participation.

Plan and organize a school-community museum in cooperation with interested local organizations and individuals.

Campaign with civic groups for improved schools, health facilities, recreation centers, employment practices, and so on.

Plot the community's probable future development, using normal expectancy figures in population growth or decline, suburban developments, technological prospects, changing tastes and the like.

By What Criteria Should Community Experiences Be Selected?

Any community experience is worthwhile only if it contributes *in greater degree than would otherwise be likely* to the educational growth of youth and to improvement of the community. Four general admonitions are in order whenever it is proposed to utilize the community as a field laboratory:[4]

• Use the community only when there are good *a priori* reasons to believe that it provides a better sort of learning experience than could be moulded within the four walls of a school.

• Use the community only when the time available is adequate to permit advance planning and later follow-up of the experience.

• Use the community only if the group is small enough to permit effective learning by all pupils at all times.

• Use the community for field studies only when it would be less effective to bring the community to the school through the medium of documentary materials, audio-visual aids, and resource visitors.

Assuming that these suggestions are observed, the next need is to appraise the proposed project in terms of specific evaluative criteria, to assure maximum educational growth and civic improvement. By such evaluation, it will be found that some proposed activities will be decidedly worthwhile, that a great many others must be considerably revised in order to promise full value, that a few would be worthless or even harmful. In this way, valid standards should save the time and energy of both teachers and students.

No set of standards can be entirely valid. Each item in the following list may have to be reworded to be fully meaningful in your particular situation. Most important, no single community project will be likely to measure up in full degree to all the criteria offered. Nevertheless, some general directives are in order, and are presented here to suggest the kind of evaluative thinking that needs to be done about every proposed community project. The criteria below are grouped under two heads: Educational Values and Curriculum Content.

[4] These suggestions are slightly adapted from Stephen M. Corey, "Utilization of Community Resources in Pupil Guidance." In William C. Reavis (ed.), *The School and the Urban Community*, pp. 76-78. Chicago: University of Chicago Press, 1942.

Criteria in Terms of Educational Values

1. Can the project be related to the present living experiences of boys and girls?
2. Does the activity contribute to the development of needed skills, habits, ideals, outlooks, and abilities?
3. Does the activity promote critical thinking?
4. Is the experience consistent with the maturity level of the children?
5. Does it provide for differences in abilities and interests?
6. May students share in planning and evaluating the program?
7. Does the activity lead to a desire to participate actively in community life, rather than to withdraw from it?
8. Does the project stimulate awareness of our need to improve human relations?
9. Does the activity cultivate a disposition to act for the general welfare?
10. Does it permit the student to assume realistic citizenship responsibilities?

Criteria in Terms of Curriculum Development

11. Does the experience acquaint the pupils with the resources of their community?
12. Does the study show the relationships between the several aspects, processes, and problems of community life?
13. Does it provide contact with persons who are seen as human beings with needs, desires, ideals?
14. Does it offer opportunity to analyze conflicts as well as cooperation between individuals and groups in the community?
15. Does the project relate to a basic process, problem, or trend rather than to superficial aspects?
16. Does the activity make vivid and real the basic trends and tensions of life today?
17. Does the experience involve firsthand participation in community living?
18. Does the experience include constructive personal contribution to human welfare?
19. Can the project actually improve the quality of living?
20. Is the activity within the power of the students to complete with a minimum of adult dominance?

What Is a Community Unit Like?

A noticeable curriculum trend is that of planning pupil-learning in terms of units of work, or units of learning-experience. Excerpts are now presented to illustrate such units in the field of community study and service. The first is from Detroit, and suggests how a group can stay in its classroom and still study about its community. The second unit, from Longview, Washington, stresses field trips by committees and by the class. The third is a resource unit definitely designed to provide firsthand experience in surveying a Philadelphia neighborhood, as a means toward planning and building a better community.

Citizenship in Detroit[5]

What the Unit Is About

"What makes the wheels go round?" is a question asked by many of us. Not only young people but adults have often wondered about such questions as: How are jurors selected? Does the Detroit Street Railway pay city taxes? Where is the intake system for the Detroit water supply? What is the effect of street lighting on automobile accidents? How are city taxes estimated? Is Detroit a healthy city?

Some of us have taken for granted many of the opportunities offered in this city of ours. When we realize that it takes a great deal of planning and organization to have things in a big city run in an orderly fashion, we will value those opportunities more and make better use of them.

If a friend came to visit us, would we be able to give him an idea of the variety of agencies which help to make Detroit one of the leading cities in the United States? If we were called

[5] From "The Detroit, Michigan, Social Studies Program for Grades Seven to Nine" by Stanley E. Dimond, in *Social Studies for Young Adolescents*, Julian C. Aldrich (Ed.). Curriculum Series No. 6, National Council for the Social Studies, 1951. Used with permission of the National Council.

upon to give information regarding family service and relief, such as are given through the Old Age Bureau, the Boys' Bureau, or the Court-Work Bureau, could we?

Did you know that in one normal year the Bureau of Markets was able to contribute more than $50,000 to the City Treasury; and that this money was used to reduce the total budget of the Department of Public Welfare? Do you know that the cost of conducting an election is almost as much for a small vote as it is for a large vote; and that much of the preparation must be made regardless of the number of registered voters who go to the polls?

To be up-and-coming citizens, and to be happy amid the conditions in which we live, we need to know something about these conditions. The American people are proud of the fact that they have local self-government. The way to get and keep good government is to be interested, not only on election day, but every day of the year. The very closeness of the local government gives its citizens an opportunity to share its services more fully. The local government gives citizens an opportunity to make known their views concerning the kind of service it is giving and the kind of service it should give. Young citizens have an opportunity to help make the local government more of a benefit to the community. Boys and girls can help to build public opinion which demands honest, efficient government.

In the study of this unit we shall attempt to reach the following goals:

1. To develop a better understanding of the city in which we live.
2. To become acquainted with the actual machinery of government in the City of Detroit.
3. To know how Detroit's finances are managed—what Detroit pays taxes for, and why.
4. To become acquainted with the variety of governmental agencies which make up the community life of Detroit.
5. To realize and appreciate the importance and value of the educational, cultural, and recreational facilities in Detroit.
6. To investigate the possibilities of earning a living in Detroit.

The Unit Outline

1. Detroit—her story and her people
   a. Detroit under three flags
   b. A new Detroit after the fire
   c. Pioneer leaders of Detroit
   d. Population growth of Detroit
   e. Industrial growth of Detroit

2. Machinery of government
   a. Types of government
   b. How cities are organized by the state
   c. Organization of Detroit's government—the City Charter
   d. Powers and duties of city officials
   e. Courts of law in Detroit
   f. Detroit's election system

3. How the Detroit taxpayer's dollar is used
   a. Why have taxes
   b. Who pays taxes
   c. Methods of raising money
   d. How Detroit uses her income
   e. Detroit's budget

4. Services provided by our city departments
   a. Protection of life and property
   b. Public health in Detroit
   c. Water supply of Detroit
   d. Public lighting in Detroit
   e. Public works of Detroit
   f. Municipal markets in Detroit
   g. Building and safety engineering in Detroit
   h. Transportation
   i. Public welfare
   j. City planning, zoning, and housing

5. Educational, cultural, and recreational advantages in Detroit
   a. Schools in Detroit
   b. Other ways of becoming educated (movie, newspaper)
   c. Cultural advantages in Detroit
   d. Kinds of recreation offered in Detroit
   e. The Detroit Department of Parks and Recreation
   f. The Detroit Historical Museum

6. Earning a living in Detroit

    a. Necessity for a knowledge of job opportunities
    b. Opportunities for jobs in industry
    c. Opportunities for jobs in business
    d. Professional opportunities in Detroit
    e. Opportunities for government jobs

Readings on the Unit

(Selected materials are listed, such as books, pamphlets, and publications of community agencies.)

Things to Do (Selections)

1. Make a diorama of the founding of Detroit by Cadillac in 1701. Show the fort and neighboring Indian villages.
3. Make a graph showing the growth of Detroit's population from 1810 to the present time.
5. Make a chart showing the relationship of the mayor, councilmen, and other city officials to the voters.
6. Collect clippings from the newspapers which tell of activities of our city government.
9. Hold a mock council meeting. Let one member of your class act as mayor, let some members act as council members, and others as heads of various departments of the city. This might be a budget hearing, at which time heads of departments explain why certain funds are necessary in terms of activities of their departments.
14. Find out from a Detroit tax notice how the tax dollar is used.
15. Make a list of city revenues other than taxes.
16. Study the proposed Land Use Plan—City of Detroit—Master Plan. Report your findings on the following elements of the plan:
    a. Community structure
    b. Neighborhood unit
    c. Housing densities
    d. Industrial, commercial, and residential plans
    e. Public and semi-public uses
24. Make a booklet containing pictures of jobs connected with the automobile industry.
26. On a map of Detroit, locate the housing projects which have

been built up in recent years. Explain why public housing is necessary in these areas.

28. A class committee could make arrangements with the school nurse for a talk on public health in Detroit.

29. Collect pictures for a bulletin board which will represent the different businesses in Detroit.

30. Look in the "Want Ad" section of the Sunday paper and find out: (a) what kind of jobs are most available in Detroit, (b) what kind of workers are most in need of jobs.

Suggestions for a Summary Discussion (Selected)

1. Show how Detroit has been under the rule of three nations. What brought about each change of rule?

4. Explain why certain fields of industry developed in Detroit.

9. Why is it more difficult for a large city like Detroit to make changes in its government than it is for a small city?

19. Do you think a city is justified in borrowing money to put in some big public improvements, such as building the Belle Isle bridge or a new sewage plant?

21. In what ways is the work of health protection in the City of Detroit different from what it was in the past?

HOW FOREST PRODUCTS AFFECT LIVING IN LONGVIEW [6]
(Eight Grade Unit)

PROBLEMS— LEARNINGS— UNDERSTANDINGS	LEARNING EXPERIENCES— SUGGESTED ACTIVITIES
I. How dependent are the people of Longview on the manufacturing of forest products? A. Number employed in various industries. B. Kinds of forest products industries.	I. A. Discussion of occupations in which parents are engaged. B. Committee contact Chamber of Commerce to secure figures about persons employed in each industry. C. Secure information from the *Longview Daily News* to learn percentage of population directly connected with forest products industry.

[6] From *At Your Service: Community Resources for Learning*. Mimeographed bulletin of the Longview, Washington, Public Schools, 1947.

PROBLEMS—
LEARNINGS—
UNDERSTANDINGS

LEARNING EXPERIENCES—
SUGGESTED ACTIVITIES

II. What forest products are made in Longview and how are they manufactured and marketed in this community?

II.

A. Sawmill
  1. Number of sawmills in Longview
  2. Source of timber
  3. Kinds of timber cut in mill
  4. Manufacturing processes
  5. Utilization of lumber
  6. Markets for lumber
  7. Transportation of lumber
B. Similar coverage will be made for each of the following:
  1. Pulp mill
  2. Paper mill
  3. Fiber plant
  4. Paperboard plant
  5. Plywood mill
  6. Shingle mill
  7. Utilization of waste products
    a. Sawdust
    b. Bark
    c. Acid recovery
    d. Binding materials

III. What occupational opportunities in the forest products industries are available in Longview?

IV. How may we plan so that forest products manufacturing may continue in the future?

A. Sawmill
  1. Discussion of forest products made in Longview.
  2. Visit exhibit display from lumber mills at Longview Chamber of Commerce.
  3. Collect pictures which show activities in the sawmills of our city.
  4. Take a field trip around the industrial area of Longview to note the location of manufacturing plants and to actually visit a sawmill to observe manufacturing processes.
  5. Make a map of Longview showing the location of forest products industries.
  6. Write letters to obtain permission to visit and to secure resource speakers and to express thanks for courtesies.
  7. See motion picture related to forest products industries.
  8. Invite guest speakers to discuss processes in the manufacturing and the utilization of forest products.
  9. Determine reasons why Longview is a manufacturing center for lumber.

  10. Observe the utilization of forest products in community.

  11. Make a map of the Pacific Northwest and locate sources of timber, indicate kinds of trees grown, modes of transportation to the mill.

PROBLEMS—
LEARNINGS—
UNDERSTANDINGS

LEARNING EXPERIENCES—
SUGGESTED ACTIVITIES

12. Decide why the Douglas Fir is a good source of lumber.
13. Gain an understanding and appreciation of specific jobs of mill workers.
14. Compare lumber production in Longview with that of the entire Pacific Northwest.
15. Write a story showing the importance of lumber in our daily life.
16. Take trip to port dock to see transportation and markets of forest products.
17. Utilize lumber in industrial arts.
18. Arrange artistically wood and lumber exhibits.
19. Produce murals showing phases of the lumber industry.
20. Make picture maps.
21. Draw illustrations for use in individual or group projects.
22. Read stories pertaining to the lumber industry in this region.
23. Do creative work in music and writing.
24. Note ways in which importance of preservation of trees are publicized in this community.

THE NEIGHBORHOOD SURVEY [7]

A MEANS TOWARD PLANNING AND BUILDING A BETTER COMMUNITY

In this unit, as in all other units, there rests with the teacher the responsibility for the selection and adaptation of this material to fit the interests and ability of a particular group. It is important that the job be limited to a practical size so that a feeling of satisfaction and success will result. To do this it may be advisable to select a single area of improvement such as housing or recreation and use techniques as informal

[7] Resource unit produced by the Curriculum Office, Philadelphia Public Schools, 1948.

as necessary. On the other hand, in the consideration of this material the children may want to expand into other areas. This should not be discouraged.

YOUTH SERVES THE COMMUNITY. The boys and girls in our schools are junior partners in building a greater Philadelphia. There is a tremendous reservoir of unused manpower in the youth of school age. One of the most promising ways of harnessing this energy is to channel it into city planning and in fact-gathering for city planning. There are definite and real directions in which pupils may function.

1. They can share in deciding what are the fundamental elements in an ideal community, such as recreational facilities, libraries, good housing, transportation, and the like.
2. They can gather data on these factors as they exist in the community today.
3. They can assist in the construction of a workable program. While this is essentially a job for the expert, school children can work out plans that can be applied to the block or the neighborhood. The function of the school is to further execution of the planning through public education and participation.
4. They can help the community absorb the plans and get the people to see the possibilities of improvement. They can do this at home, on school-radio programs, or at P.T.A. and community council meetings.
5. They can help in the execution of the plans for a better community. This is the most difficult part of the program. Older boys and girls can engage in the actual execution of community improvement projects by serving a kind of apprenticeship in the actual construction and physical improvement of the community.

I. *Title:* THE NEIGHBORHOOD SURVEY
      (A Means Toward Planning and Building a Better Community)
II. *Grades:* 4-5-6
III. *Orientation:*

    The approach necessary to arouse interest in neighborhood planning and building must be based upon the kind of community in which a particular group of boys and girls live. The youth in a blighted neighborhood face life with a different set of values and goals from those boys and girls living in a good residential area. It, therefore, follows as part of the preplanning for a unit of this type, that each teacher must personally make a study of the kind of neighborhood in which her pupils live. Intelligent teacher guidance requires a knowledge and understanding of the assets, liabilities, and needs of a given community.

    To get boys and girls thinking about their needs for better living the teacher may invite them to list the things they like about their home and neighborhood and the things they do not like. A discussion of their findings coupled with a similar statement by parents as revealed to their boys and girls will make a good beginning point for a unit on neighborhood improvement.

IV. *Suggested Method of Procedure*

    A. We Set Up Criteria for the Requirements of Our Needs for Good Living:

       1. A decent home in a good neighborhood for every person
       2. A neighborhood that is safe
       3. A neighborhood that is attractive
       4. Good clean stores and service shops within walking distance
       5. A safe place to earn a living
       6. Industries separated from home to avoid smoke, soot, noise, dirt, and odors
       7. Open space, green space, trees, flowers, and sunshine
       8. Transportation that is adequate but not dangerous; adequate parking space and wide streets
       9. Clean water and an adequate sewage and rubbish disposal system
      10. Wholesome recreation places nearby for all age levels
      11. Community center, schools, libraries, nursery schools, museums, art centers, and similar social needs

    B. We Plan a Survey of Our Neighborhood to Get More Accurate Information:

Suggestions For Problems	Suggestions For Action
1. What are boundaries of our neighborhood?	1. Teacher draws map of school neighborhood on board or on large piece of paper and class identifies streets by names.
2. How can we find where most of the boys and girls in the class live?	2. Boys and girls work on a map of the neighborhood and spot the place they live.
3. What are the good things we are going to look for?	3. Class discussion, enumeration, and evaluation.
4. What are the bad things we might see?	4. Class discussion, enumeration, and evaluation.
5. How can we record our findings accurately on the spot?	5. Discussion followed by demonstration of a block study on the board; a free hand sketch with vital comments about what they see.

Suggestions For Problems

6. How can we be sure we are going to be able to make block study?

7. How can we share the job of getting information about our neighborhood?

Suggestions For Action

6. Class goes out with teacher for a visit in neighborhood. They all map the same block together and compare their findings when they return.

7. Volunteer committees of two or more to assume the responsibility of studying a given block. (The one they live in if possible.)

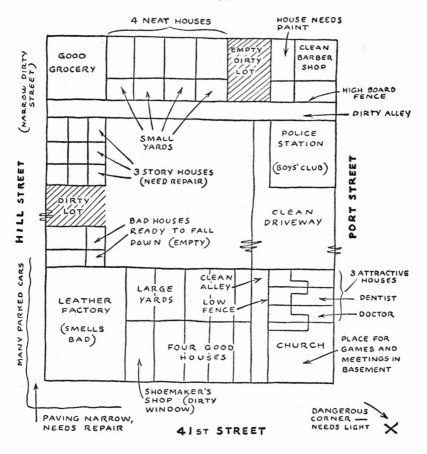

C. We Make a Survey of Our Neighborhood:

Suggestions For Problems	Suggestions For Action
1. How can we know whether we have more good houses or bad?	1. Count number of good and bad dwellings.
2. What kind of services and facilities for good living did we find?	2. Make a listing of number and kinds of service stores in block. List recreation facilities commercial and non-commercial.
3. How can we use color to help show what we found in our block?	3. Uniform color code developed and used by each boy and girl to color in each type of information on block map.
4. How can we be sure our information is accurate?	4. Boys and girls check each other's block study and evaluate the information on the block map. Compare with land-use map from City Planning Commission.
5. How can we organize the information we have discovered about our neighhood?	5. Committee compiles lists indicating number and frequency of each fact discovered.
6. How can we get a complete picture of the neighborhood?	6. Boys and girls arrange block studies side by side to give complete picture of neighborhood. Committee transfers findings to large single map.
7. What things do we need to improve in our community?	7. Class analyzes amounts and distribution of color code. Discuss notations and summary lists. Boys and girls state definite conclusions in written form.
8. What facilities do we need for better living?	8. Check findings against criteria for a good neighborhood.

D. We Evaluate Our Neighborhood in Terms of Our Living Requirements.

E. We Compare Our Neighborhood with Other Parts of the City:

1. Boys and girls contact Philadelphia Housing Association and Citizens Council on City Planning. These agencies arrange an itinerary and guide the tour made by school bus.
2. Boys and girls observe, ask questions, and take notes, which they use for a later discussion.
3. Boys and girls evaluate their own neighborhood in relation to other parts of city just visited.

F. We Select the Community Need Which is Most Urgent and that We Feel We Can Do Something About.

G. We Interest Others in This Problem by the Means of Language, Charts, Graphs, Maps, Diagrams, Pictures, and Models:

1. We plan a solution for this problem and illustrate it graphically.
2. We discuss it with our classmates, teachers, and parents through the school assembly, parent teachers association, school newspaper, and student council.
3. We visit the City Planning Commission, present our ideas, and get the advice of the experts.

H. We Modify and Readjust Our Plan to Suit Our Latest Findings.

I. We interest our neighbors through our community council. The community council studies the problem and with the help of experts, a course of action decided upon.

J. The local councilman and ward leaders are invited to a community meeting where the problem and suggested solution are offered. Governmental aid and action are requested.

K. Action is taken by the city authorities or a plan for continued and combined action is proposed.

V. *Possible Pupil Learning Experiences*

A. We Can Read

1. *Ten Communities* by Paul Hanna
2. *Community Interests*—Part II, by Berman, Fryer, and Bernard
3. *Youth Shares in Planning a Better Philadelphia*
4. Current articles in school, local, and city newspapers and periodicals

B. We Can Listen

1. To ideas of our classmates, parents, and neighbors
2. To ideas of experts from
   a. The Citizen's Council on City Planning
   b. The Philadelphia Housing Association
   c. The Redevelopment Authority
   d. The Philadelphia City Planning Commission
3. To the transcriptions
   a. Penn's Greene Country Town by Philadelphia Public School Radio Assistants
   b. The Soldier Hunts a Home by Philadelphia Public School Radio Assistants
4. To current radio programs

C. We Can Observe

1. How really to see our neighborhood
2. How to make a block study
3. The story told by pictures, graphs, and charts in the book called *Housing in the United States* by Archie W. Troelstrup
4. A demonstration of Citizens' Council Model for redeveloping the area around the Furness Junior High School
5. How to use a color code for maps
6. How boys and girls in other schools showed their ideas about their neighborhood
7. Moving pictures such as:
   a. The City
   b. A Place to Live
   c. Building America's Homes
   d. Expressways
   e. Lifestream of the City
8. Kodachromes on the Better Philadelphia Exhibition

D. We Can Take Trips to Other Parts of the City to See:

1. Good residential areas or blighted neighborhoods and take photographs
2. Well planned Public Housing
3. Recommended sites of planned improvements by the City Planning Commission
4. Early Philadelphia as revealed by pictures and maps at Logan Square Library
5. The Port of Philadelphia
6. Evidence of past lack of planning and haphazard building and evidence of the same mistakes being repeated today
7. Historical places of importance in the community
8. Well planned recreation facilities such as the Salvation Army Recreation Center at 11th and Huntingdon
9. The Philadelphia City Planning Commission

E. We Can Make and Do Things to Show Our Ideas About Our Neighborhood such as:

1. Drawing maps of our neighborhood
2. Charts, graphs, and diagrams of what we have or what we wish to have in our community
3. Constructing paper, wood, or clay models showing the present and future neighborhood
4. Paintings, pictures, and signs to tell our story
5. Collecting scrap books on our progress as revealed by newspaper clippings and other material
6. Arranging bulletin board displays
7. Planting grass, flowers, shrubbery, and trees to improve our yards and neighborhood squares
8. Organizing a clean up, paint up, fix up, campaign
9. Helping transform an empty lot into a play site

F. We Can Talk and Write About Things such as:

1. Writing letters of invitation for the experts to visit us
2. Writing letters seeking illustrative and printed material from various city planning commissions in this country
3. Writing newspaper articles for the school or local community newspaper to inform people about our plans
4. Writing plays and dramatic sketches to illustrate what we want for our community
5. Planning for graduation exercises which use neighborhood planning as a theme
6. Talking to the school assembly and parent teacher organization about our ideas
7. Talking to our neighborhood community council asking their advice and help
8. Keeping log books as a record of our daily activities
9. Speaking on radio programs and on television programs

VI. *Evaluation*

Throughout this entire unit there should be a growth of the boys and girls in many areas. There should be definite evidences of knowledge in action; a translation of thinking into doing. These may be measured by anecdotal records based on observation of pupil behavior or by check lists and other survey techniques. However in a unit of this kind there should be certain specific outcomes such as:

A. Growth in sharing ideas with others and working cooperatively

B. Growth in the ability to see a neighborhood problem and in gathering, selecting, and organizing facts to help in its solution

C. Increased awareness of change in the environment and increased courage to experiment with new ideas about neighborhood improvement

D. Growth in the ability to assume the responsibility for doing one's share of work

E. Growth in the establishment of the physical and mental health habits of cleanliness, neatness, and orderliness necessary for health and safe living

F. Growth in the ability to express findings in language and in graphic or three-dimensional form

G. Growth in the ability to make use of governmental and community agencies for improving the neighborhood

H. Such action as:
   1. Empty lots cleaned
   2. Rubbish removed from homes, yards, and neighborhood
   3. Increase of recreational facilities available to all age levels
   4. Homes repaired, painted, and cleaned
   5. Streets, paving repaired
   6. Traffic lights and street lighting installed
   7. Improved transportation and removal of safety hazards
   8. Improved school cleanliness and increased educational facilities
   9. Community organizations formed for improving the neighborhood
   10. Flowers, grass, trees, and shrubs, planted as well as other neighborhood beautification
   11. Removal of blight forming factors such as industrial nuisances, dumps, junk yards, and dangerous structures
   12. Increased cleanliness of streets particularly on rubbish collection days
   13. Improved shopping and service facilities

VII. *Teacher Aids and Resources*

A. Speakers, discussion leaders, literature, and consultant service from
   1. The Philadelphia Housing Association
      1717 Sansom Street
      Ri 6-2485
   2. Citizens' Council on City Planning
      1717 Sansom Street
      Lo 4-3288

    3. Philadelphia City Planning Commission
       Market Street National Bank Building
       Lo 4-0744
    4. Redevelopment Authority of the City of Philadelphia
       21st and Parkway
       Lo 7-0966

B. Audio-Visual Aids

    1. Sound moving pictures (see listing under Part V.) may be procured with operator and machine from Citizens' Council
    2. Model Demonstration by Citizens' Council of redevelopment of an old neighborhood
    3. Kodachromes of Better Philadelphia Exhibition from Department of Visual Education
    4. Maps—Land Use, Zoning, Census, Airport, Distribution, Recreational Facilities, Highways and Expressways. These may be secured from City Planning Commission.
    5. Models, charts, and diagrams prepared by other schools

C. Excursions—Trips planned and guided jointly by Citizens' Council and Housing Association. Itinerary may include visit to any type of neighborhood or proposed site of city improvement

D. Consultant service, equipment, and supplies furnished by Agricultural Department of Board of Education for purpose of planting neighborhood gardens and improving community parks

E. Books and pamphlets (a number were listed)

Such units of work are usually prepared by committees of teachers in the form of "resource units"—that is, a kind of file of ideas and materials from which functional learning activities may quickly be developed with the class as the need arises. Those of you who plan to assemble such units as part of your own preparation for directing community activities by students would do well to organize your unit outlines around these three essentials:

•   **Objectives**—you must know what you hope your students will achieve, and how to evaluate their success. These aims will be expressed as skills to be attained, attitudes to be developed, and knowledge to be gained.

•   **Activities**—you must tentatively plan a variety of pupil experiences to achieve the objectives sought. These experiences should be both interesting and educationally profitable, and should consist of three types: (a) *initiating activities* to give students a broad overview of the problem and its relation to the pupil and to his community; (b) *research activities* to provide opportunity for digging rather deeply into the data related to the problem, organizing the data, interpreting their meaning, and then acting upon findings for community improvement; and (c) *culminating activities* which tie together the work done and make the whole experience intellectually as well as otherwise fruitful.

• Materials—you must be familiar with numerous materials of instruction which contribute to the activities and thereby help to produce the desired modifications of pupil behavior. You will need to know how to gather various types of data, to see how particular data must be interpreted in terms of the sampling done, to draw valid conclusions from the information available, and to know what specific sources of information are likely to yield what types of needed help.

All this planning by the teacher is not in any sense a substitute for pupil planning, but is done in order to make pupil planning more effective when that occurs. The teacher's previous development of resource units will serve to facilitate pupil planning, and also to anticipate or guard against many difficulties which might discourage the students if they approached a problem for which careful preparation had not been made by the responsible director of learning, their teacher.

To What Extent Should Students Share in Planning?

Young people are actually educated in the direction of their own real purposes, rather than according to a teacher's specific aims. Particularly in the field of community study it is important to remember that the child learns what he sets himself to learn, whether that be an understanding of an industrial technique, the procedure for earning an "A," or the enjoyment of temporary escape from school. If students are to gain most from their community experiences, they must have personal interest in undertaking them, a clear knowledge of what they wish to gain, and some standards by which to evaluate the true worth of those experiences.

Pupil-teacher planning means *cooperative planning;* it is not a process by which pupils are "motivated" to do what the teacher already wants to do, or are fooled into accepting the teacher's total plan as being really all their own. It should be a real give-and-take situation. All the teacher preplanning described above is merely wise preparation by the most mature member of the democratic group to anticipate possible procedures, difficulties, and alternatives. The less mature the student group, the more essential such preliminary teacher planning becomes.

As the cooperative planning progresses, the teacher and the class members should be alert for suggestions of possible community experiences, techniques of approach, and likely problems to be encountered. If students evince no ideas for community projects, the teacher should suggest several suitable alternatives as a basis for class analysis and possible choice. However the arrangements are made, the students should feel that the community project is really their own, and that they are responsible for planning and carrying it out. Much of its value will be lost if the group feels that it is developing a project merely to please a teacher who happens to be interested in the community.

The thoroughness of group planning will depend on the maturity level of the class with which the teacher is working. With younger pupils the teacher's leadership must be more evident and definite; with older students, the teacher should continue to guide, but do so increasingly from the background. At any level, however—even in the lower elementary school grades—the students will at some time share in planning each major phase of the community project. Its purposes will be stated by them in words meaningful to them. They will examine the different possible ways of carrying out the project and will choose the ways they prefer. The teacher will act always as a resource person, aiding when necessary but never dominating the group procedure.

Students Execute as Well as Plan

Students should actively execute the community project as well as merely plan it. They can run down sources of material in the school and community libraries, call on agencies for published information, cull newspapers and magazines, search for audio-visual aids, and look for new sources of information. If resource visitors are to be invited to the classroom or assembly, the students should act as hosts and chairmen. All interviews, questionnaires, and field observations ought to be carefully planned by the student group. On field trips, surveys, and study tours and in community service projects, work experiences, and camping, the students should assume the responsibilities wherever possible. In doing all these things, however, the students should be led to recognize their need for technical instruction in methods of approach to the community and in public relations generally. Finally, students should have personal responsibility for publicly presenting the story and results of their community experience or project. A report to some local organization, an exhibit placed in the school or community library, an assembly program, a written statement for the newspaper—all of these are typical culminating activities which will conclude the community project with a fine challenge to the best abilities of the students concerned.

Learning Activities

Discussion Topics

1. To what extent and in what ways should the everyday living experiences of the pupil in the community be made a part of the school curriculum?
2. How can community resources best be used in teaching academic subjects? In citizenship education? In guidance? In vocational training? In home economics?

3. Which of the three units of work reproduced in this chapter seems to be the best? In what respects? What basic philosophy of education is most involved in each one?

Group Projects

1. Appoint a class committee to interview educational leaders such as public and parochial school administrators, curriculum coordinators, school board members, P.T.A. officers, and so on. Ask each how the schools in their community now relate to the community. Compare findings and evaluate them in the light of the community school characteristics listed in Chapter 1.
2. Outline a resource unit on community study, describing your assumptions and the educational principles involved.
3. With the help of several friends, outline some of the important content that would appear in a community study curriculum for either the elementary or the high school.
4. Suggest ways of correlating the program so as to avoid undesirable duplication if community resources are to be utilized in both the elementary and the high school in the same neighborhood.

Individual Activities

1. Using the guide on page 112, write an analysis of your own community-school program planning. Compare this with similar reports by other members of your class, identifying common and dissimilar factors under each heading.
2. Make a chart showing typical learnings suggested by your state and local courses of study and curriculum guides. Opposite each such item list varied community learning activities which can vitalize the teaching.
3. Write your home state department of education and your state education association for bulletins of possible help to you in planning a community resources study and service program.

Learning Materials

The importance of democratic group planning cannot be over-emphasized. Sound guidance and practical suggestions for such planning with children, adolescents, and adults are found in several excellent volumes of recent years. *Group Planning in Education* (1945) and *Toward Better Teaching* (1949), both yearbooks of the NEA's Association for Supervision and Curriculum Development, are good starting points. The former offers convincing evidence that democratic group behavior is inherently a matter of developing social outlooks and skills through direct experience with group planning in classroom and in community. In the latter you will find that democratic, dynamic group planning is implicit in each of its chapters, especially 3, 4, 5, 6, and 7. In their *Cooperative Procedures in Learning* Alice Miel and associates (Teachers College, Columbia, 1952) present scores of concrete, often quote-complete, descriptions of just how our generally accepted principles of group planning can actually be put into classroom practice. Loretta Klee's *How to Do Cooperative Planning* (National Council for Social Studies, 1952) presents fundamental principles in concise form. *Group Experience* by Bernice Baxter and Rosalind Cassidy (Harper, 1943) offers working answers to the query: How shall youth be taught in order to render more effective service in and for democracy?

Guides in building units of study centering about community life are scarce. Among the best is the *Santa Barbara County Teacher's Guide for Use of Community Resources* (Schauer Printing Studio, 1941) which provides excellent correlation of problems and pupil activities. The University of Minnesota's College of Education has produced *Using Community Resources: Illustrative Experience Units for Grades One to Six* (1948). This pamphlet tells how community resources enrich learnings, discusses the nature of experience units, and outlines nine units in various interest areas. *Bridges Between the School and the Community* is the title of another pamphlet; issued by the New York City Board of Education in 1949, it presents many brief cases of junior high school practice.

General directions for preparing resource units are given in most good textbooks on teaching methods. Two smaller treatments are Julian C. Aldrich's "How to Construct and Use a Resource Unit" (New York: Joint Council on Economic Education, 1951) and a *Clearing House* article (January 1952) of the same title by Edgar Draper and Gordon Gardner. Resource units in community life understanding have been published by the National Council for the Social Studies in its Community Study Series, including *The Structure of Local Government*, by Bishop and Starratt; *Parties and Politics in the Local Community*, by Fisher and Starratt; and *Community Planning in a Democracy*, by Bishop, Lamb, Smith, and Starratt. In the periodical literature you will find teaching unit outlines and descriptions such as the following:

"Workers Who Help Us Live; a Second Grade Activity," Bertha S. Shockley. Describes a two-months' second-grade unit on workers in the local community. Lists general unit objectives, progress data, trips taken and their outcomes and the script of the play written by the children as their culminating activity. *American Childhood* 23:11-16; January 1938.

"Our Community; a Correlated Social Studies Unit of Activity," M. F. Moznett. A primary and intermediate grade unit outline on the study of the local community life. Beginning with the home, the children

considered the school, the church, occupations of town and country people, protectors in the community, transportation, and so forth, and then made a social map. *Grade Teacher* 56:38-39; September 1938.
"Community Life," B. F. Carr. An illustrated unit of work, including overview, objectives, suggested procedures, sample content for primary grades, middle grades and upper grades, and possible activities based on the unit. *Instructor* 49:37-46; June 1940.
"Community Helpers; A Unit with Activities and Tests," B. G. Flath. A primary grade unit on the activities of policemen and firemen. *Grade Teacher* 58:24; February 1941.
"When We Went to the Museum; a Unit for Primary Grades," Elizabeth C. Miller. Unit outline, including introduction, preparation for the trip, the trip itself, correlations, and culminating activity. *Instructor* 51:17, 74; February 1942.
"Unit on Community Helpers," Emma Golden. Outlines a unit for primary grades, including approaches, objectives, development, materials of instruction, integration and desired generalizations. *Instructor* 54:25, 81, 83; September 1945.
"A 'Slow English Class' Investigates Community Living," Joy E. Greene. An account of a teaching unit employing firsthand experiences and inductively developing concepts with a first-term high school class. *English Journal* 40:339-341; June 1951.

Motion Pictures

Learning Through Cooperative Planning. An elementary school decides to participate in the community's annual spring clean-up and beautification campaign. Through democratic guidance, the children gain real experience in cooperative planning toward that goal. Teachers College, Columbia University, 1948, 20 minutes.
We Plan Together. A companion film for the high school level. Here an eleventh-grade group plans cooperatively for learning in its core class over a period of several months. Teachers College, Columbia University, 1948, 20 minutes.

Film Strips

The Department of Instruction and Guidance of the Chicago Public Schools is producing a *Curriculum Filmstrip Series,* first of which is "Improving Teen-Age Relationships in the Community," a 37-minute sound-filmstrip. This is an excellent portrayal of unit-development procedures in a typical city setting—40 pupils, fixed desks, and so on—showing committee activities, a community survey, field trips, resource people. Ways of integrating such activities with the three R's are stressed, as is evaluation in terms of better human relations.

CHAPTER 6

Community Materials

Teaching materials drawn from the community are of two chief types: printed or written, and audio-visual. Let's indicate specific kinds of each type:

Documentary Materials	Audio-Visual Materials
Books, magazines, newspapers, pamphlets, bulletins, diaries, church and school records, public documents, deeds, abstracts, bank statements, bills of lading —all learning materials designed to be *read.*	Charts, graphs, maps, pictures, photographs, objects, specimens, models, stereographs, slides, filmstrips, motion pictures, recordings, radio and television programs—all learning materials to be *viewed* and/or *heard.*

We may usefully consider both types of community materials in terms of their scope; that is, whether they were produced for a national or even wider market, or were designed specifically for local community, state, or perhaps regional needs. Here again a contrast may help to clarify the difference:

National Coverage Materials	Specifically Local Materials
Encyclopedias, biographical dictionaries, cumulative indexes, almanacs, textbooks; most other books, magazines, and motion pictures; network radio and television shows—all such materials intended to appeal to a geographically wide market.	State sourcebooks, city directories; photographs, slides, motion pictures, radio and television programs of local origin; tape or wire-recorded interviews—all such materials produced for essentially local community use.

This chapter is by EDWARD G. OLSEN and ALVIN B. ROBERTS.

How Are Community Materials Useful?

All community teaching materials—whether documentary or audio-visual in type, national or local in scope—help bring the world into the classroom. In books and other documentary materials is stored the whole intellectual heritage of the human race, as well as a wealth of contemporary data necessary for intelligent solution of current community problems. Audio-visual materials furnish particularly vivid experiences while also freeing the learner from sensory limitations of time and space. Special values of each basic type are well worth noting:

Documentary Materials	Audio-Visual Materials
Promote development of the scientific attitude in the analysis of community traditions, interests, values, and so forth, since of all informational sources, the printed page may be the most impersonal and the least emotional.	Make real the past as they re-create for the student dramatic and authentic episodes of history.
Stimulate needed perspective by providing comparable data from communities distant in space or time.	Provide a simplified view of complex data, and thereby render complicated physical, social, and aesthetic situations more easily discernible.
Permit intelligent solution of community problems by basing both analysis and policy-making upon accurate data.	Furnish vivid, vicarious experiences as a basis for intellectual analysis, comparison, and generalization about community processes and problems.
	Economize time by presenting a wealth of impressions in a well-organized, concise, and intrinsically interesting manner.

Many learning materials of national scope are of great significance but will not be mentioned here, even though they may be used to excellent advantage in local community study and service projects. This chapter deals only with teaching materials which are directly related to local community situations, or are specifically produced by local community interests for their own vicinity. We shall look first at documentary materials, then at some audio-visual approaches.

What Community Information Can Documentary Materials Provide?

Every ten years Uncle Sam collects a vast deal of information about all of us, ranging from the month of the year in which we were born to the income we receive—and whether or not we own a television set. Rural and urban sociologists have made thousands of surveys of such matters as standards of living, status of youth, housing conditions, social disorganization, and consumer interests. Many agencies and organizations, both public and private, are constantly gathering and frequently publishing social data of many kinds. Much of all this information about community living is readily available to the student of the community if he knows where to look for it. So let's see now what documentary sources are most valuable in local community study. We shall examine some sources useful in five areas of interest: population, local history, economic conditions, social welfare, and intergroup relations.

Population

Who are your neighbors? If you really want to know their characteristics as groups, your primary source of documentary information is the latest United States Census. Here you can find detailed facts about such matters as these:

Age, sex, and racial composition
Number of foreign-born by country of origin
Marital status
School enrollment
Number of years of schooling completed
Kinds of work done by employed people
Family incomes
Changes in residence

These and many other important factors are shown for the nation as a whole, for each of several large geographic regions, for every state, every county, every urban place of over 2,500 people, every rural non-farm and rural-farm part of each county, and for all unincorporated places of 1,000 or more inhabitants.

The *Characteristics of the Population* Census volume is published as 51 separately bound books, 49 of which cover the states and the District of Columbia. Each state volume duplicates the information given for that state in the general volume on the *Number of Inhabitants.* Separate data for the non-white population are given for some areas. Very detailed information is published also for extremely small areas (the "census tracts") and even for single city blocks. Census tracts, of which there are more than 10,000, are the small, largely homogeneous areas into which over 60 cities (including all cities of over 250,000 people) and their adjacent territories have been divided for census-taking purposes. Since these census tracts generally remain constant from one census period to another, we can refer to their reports for accurate comparisons over a period of decades, and thus readily determine social trends and economic development within the stated areas. The Bureau of the Census publishes a series of Census Tract bulletins presenting population and housing characteristics. For tracted areas containing 10,000 or more non-whites, separate data are shown. The cost of these bulletins is nominal if ordered from the Superintendent of Documents, Government Printing Office, Washington 25, D. C.

Not all data tabulated for census tracts are actually published. These unpublished statistics can be had upon request, the only charge being the cost of transcribing them. For complete description of such unpublished data, consult *United States Censuses of Population and Housing: 1950, Key to Published and Tabulated Data for Small Areas,* published by the Superintendent of Documents as a pamphlet.

If you happen to live in one of the cities which had a population of over 50,000 in the previous Census year, you can find in the current Census reports much information classified by city blocks. These figures are published in a series of bulletins, one for each of the "block cities." Maps included in these bulletins permit identification and location of each block within the entire city.

If you live in a rural area, you can turn to the *United States Census of Agriculture* for considerable information about the people of your county, including their age levels, types of residence, their color and race, years on the farm, and their tenure as farm operators.

Compact "ready reference" volumes summarizing the Census returns are the Census Bureau's own 1952 *County and City Data Book* and its similar publication of 1953. The former presents in compact manner 101 selected items of data on the economic and social characteristics of each county in the United States, and 92 items for each of about 400 of the larger cities. The latter includes statistics from the 1950 Censuses of Agriculture, Population, and Housing, as well as selected series from the Censuses for Business, Manufacturers, and other fields. Both are designed for those who need a compact, single source of data relating to counties, cities, and metropolitan areas.

Should you require more statistical information about a particular community than appears in the Census reports, you can ask the government to provide it for you. The Bureau of the Census, the Bureau of Foreign and Domestic Commerce, and the Bureau of Labor Statistics, among other federal agencies, will make special tabulations of unpublished information at the cost to you of transcribing or assembling the needed data. The requested information can be supplied, if desired, by census tracts; that is, by the original small enumeration districts themselves. The usefulness of these small districts is illustrated by the case in one community where opinion was sharply divided as to whether or not to build a new school, and where to locate it, if built. Examination of the census tract data on population showed that 70 per cent of the actual and 75 per cent of the potential school enrollment lived in three of the thirteen enumeration districts involved, the rest in the other ten. This simple fact explained the reason for the community conflict and provided part of the basis for its settlement.

Local History

However small your community may be, a little searching will surely disclose many kinds of documentary materials bearing upon its early settlement, later development, local crises, noted leaders, major advances and set-backs. Newspaper files, legal records in the county courthouse, documents preserved in libraries and by historical societies, old letters and diaries treasured by local families, church and synagogue records, minutes of the proceedings of local organizations, local and county histories—such are some of the primary sources of community information which can be used to make local history really live.

Much research has been done and state histories written for all of the American states. These histories usually include detailed references to many local communities within the state, and often reproduce significant local documents and other record materials. Your State Library and State Historical Association can refer you to such histories, some of which may not have been published but are available for inspection in manuscript form.

During the 1930's, the Federal Writers' Project of the Works Projects Administration compiled and had published a wealth of valuable information about our country's local history and geography. These publications may be found in most public libraries. They include the *American Guide Series*—a valuable set of guidebooks, one for each of the states—and the *American Life Series*, along with numerous booklets, pamphlets, and leaflets reporting on many aspects of local communities' history, culture, and development.

Inexpensive books and pamphlets dealing with local and regional history, geography, and biography are published by the Government Printing Office and are for sale at nominal cost. Free price lists of such materials may be secured from the Superintendent of Documents in Washington, D. C.

Historical and contemporary fiction can do much to infuse the breath of real life into otherwise musty records and dry statistics. Among the best of such regional and locale writings are the books of Hervey Allen for the Colonial frontier, Joseph Lincoln for Cape Cod, Dorothy Canfield Fisher for Vermont, Walter Edmonds for New York State, Ellen Glasgow and Erskine Caldwell for the South, Zona Gale and Willa Cather for the Midwest, Edgar Lee Masters and Harold Smilan for Illinois, Walter Havighurst for the Great Lakes region, William Faulkner for Mississippi, Marjorie Kennen Rawlings for Florida, and Zane Grey, Rex Beach, Vardis Fisher, and Eugene Manlove Rhodes for the West. There are also books like Partridge's *Country Lawyer*, Hough's *Country Editor*, and Della Lutes' *Country Schoolma'am* which offer rich insight into earlier community life and its human values.

Economic Conditions

From the Census reports you can discover the numbers, age-groupings, color, and nativity of workers employed in your community in each of the more important kinds of occupations. By contrasting these findings with similar items in previous decennial Census volumes, you can analyze major occupational trends and problems. In similar fashion you can work out a kind of general index to community economic welfare (and hence to a host of related considerations) by noting the numbers and working out the percentages of local families by their income levels.

To illustrate, the 1950 Illinois census volume shows the following classification of incomes in two adjoining towns, both suburbs of Chicago:

Family Income Level	Number of Families Receiving This Income	
	Town A (4,025 families)	Town B (4,435 families)
$3,000-4,000	350	180
4,000-5,000	380	270
5,000-6,000	595	485
6,000-7,000	395	530
7,000-9,000	480	815
over $10,000	260	1,075
median income	$4,676	$6,703

In the light of these figures, in which town would you think it best to live if other things were equal and your family income was $5,500? Why?

In rural areas the Census of Agriculture, taken every five years, is most useful. This gives detailed statistical data on these and other significant items by counties and state economic areas:

Number of farms, acreage, value, and farm operators
Farms by size, by color and tenure of operator
Facilities and equipment, farm labor, farm expenditures
Livestock and livestock products
Specified crops harvested
Farm characteristics for commercial farms
Farms classified by value of products sold, by type of farm, and by economic classification
Value of products sold at the source

This report is published in 34 parts, covering all geographic regions of the United States and with individual bulletins for each of the agricultural states. A second major volume provides these statistics classified by subjects rather than by counties, thus permitting interesting comparisons of local developments with trends in larger areas. Other Census of Agriculture volumes deal with irrigation and the drainage of agricultural lands.

By using census figures through two decades, for example,

a class in Allen County, Kansas, could quickly locate such information about its county as shown in the accompanying table.

ITEM	1935	1940	1945	1950
Number of farms	2,166	1,949	1,757	1,665
Average size (acres)	141.3	153.7	175.6	179.5
Full owners	749	687	675	809
Tenant farmers	1,041	952	658	421
Percent of tenant farmers	48.1	48.8	37.5	23.3
Number of chickens	351,992	253,259	187,043	171,513
Number of apple trees	9,783	6,355	5,043	3,055
Telephones	—	935	969	1,036
Electricity	—	426	659	1,356
Tractors	—	834	994	1,226

Some interesting trends appear here—with real significance for those considering agriculture as a career in Allen County. Apparently farms are declining in number while increasing in size, and that more and more farmers own their own land and have been able to electrify and mechanize their holdings. Perhaps former diversification of products—as represented by chickens and apples, at least—is declining, though this assumption, like all others thus made, would require careful checking against other factors before being accepted as valid.

Social Welfare

The community school needs adequate and accurate data concerning community housing, health, recreation, social agencies' activities and the like. Not otherwise can it expect to become effective in helping to improve the quality of living through education. Facts are the tools of intelligent action for community improvement. So we turn once more to the Federal Census as a primary source of information.

The 1950 United States Census of Housing offers detailed

data concerning the housing conditions of the American people, including these factors:

Number of dwelling units classified by occupancy and tenure
Type of structure
Condition of structure and plumbing facilities
Year built
Number of occupants and persons per room
Heating fuel used
Refrigeration equipment
Television
Contract monthly rent
Value of one-dwelling-unit structures

This housing information has been published also for each of the 209 "block cities" (population over 50,000). There is one bulletin for each of these cities. Maps included permit identification and location of each block within the city.

Housing conditions in cities and in counties may be studied through use of the Census of Housing volumes, one for each of the states. Page 19 of the *Indiana* volume, for example, shows that Gary, Indiana, has a total of 38,283 dwelling units, of which 4,576 have neither bathtub nor shower. Gary is an industrial city, with special problems of cleanliness because of that fact. We would surely expect community schools in Gary to take account of this problem as they develop a life-centered curriculum program, just as we expect community-minded educators anywhere to have similar concern for significant problems in their own communities.

Local health conditions and problems may well be studied with *Vital Statistics of the United States, 1949* as background materials. This volume, published by the Federal Security Agency, Public Health Service, National Office of Vital Statistics, presents detailed statistics on births, marriages, and deaths (including infant mortality), median age at first marriage, death rates by age, race, and sex, and numerous other subordinate aspects. Many of the data-categories are analyzed by states and counties. Comparisons between communities may offer interesting insights, particularly if you secure figures from the County Medical Association on numbers and types of physicians and other health personnel in the area.

General social welfare information can be secured from local welfare agencies and organizations such as community chests, family welfare bureaus, visiting nurses associations, county and city offices of public welfare, private employment agencies, and the like. Many cities have Councils of Social Agencies which publish directories, have access to member agencies' reports, and maintain active research departments. Sometimes local reports of real significance to the community school program have been publicized only in local newspapers, and exist only in typescript form. Often your public library and your local college or university department of sociology will have preserved such reports.

Information on juvenile delinquency and adult crime can be secured from court judges, police records, or from social workers such as probation officers. If a social base map (see page 160) is made to spot such factors as delinquents' residences, value or rentals of their homes, segregated housing sections, locations of recreational facilities, and the like, some significant associations are likely to be found.

Intergroup Relations

The extent, intensity, and significance of group prejudice, discrimination, and segregation should be of primary concern to every community, and certainly to the community school. Race, religion, nationality origin, and socio-economic status are the major factors here. As already indicated, much data of these kinds can be secured from the census reports. Information about the religious denominations may be found in the United States Census of Religious Bodies. Denominational beliefs and rituals may be better understood by reference to appropriate articles in such standard encyclopedias of religion as the *Catholic Encyclopedia*, the *Jewish Encyclopedia*, and the *Encyclopedia of Religion and Ethics*.

In all of the larger cities and in many of the smaller ones there are active human relations agencies, some private, such as the National Conference of Christians and Jews, the Anti-Defamation League of B'nai B'rith, and the Urban League, and others governmental, such as state and municipal commissions on human relations. Their publications and reports will be eye-openers to most people not otherwise informed about the progress and problems in intergroup relations in our local communities generally, as well as throughout the nation.

The status of civil rights in your community may be indicated by local laws and municipal ordinances, by newspaper stories and editorials, and by local reports of intergroup agencies. If yours is one of the states or cities which has Fair Employment Practices legislation you may secure information in this area from the appropriate government agency.

What Audio-Visual Materials Are Useful?

Literally hundreds of different audio-visual items are available as "open doors" to enrich and actualize the community school program. Let's examine ten major categories of such learning materials to see how this can be.

Graphic Documents Are Vital

Although charts, graphs, and maps are in one sense documentary materials, they are listed here because they all involve a greater degree of visual perception than do printed and written words alone. All are schematic representations of reality rather than verbal descriptions of it; they are, therefore, properly included among other visual aids intended to help students interpret the community more meaningfully.

Tables and organization charts; pictographs, line, bar, and area graphs; physical, population, historical, literary, health, and relief maps are all among the various kinds of graphic documents which may be used to picture such categories of community data as the following:

• **Population:** Sex, age, racial and nationality composition; changes in numbers and types; present residential areas.
• **History:** Early settlements, community growth and extension, chronology of dates, location of existing historical sites and buildings, genealogy of famous families.
• **Geography:** Land use and productivity in relation to natural factors such as mountains and plains, waterways, climatic conditions, vegetation, animal life, soil composition, scenic areas, mineral and oil deposits.
• **Political Organization:** Political areas and boundaries, seats of government, principal cities, relationships between governmental divisions, lines of administrative authority and responsibility.
• **Economic Conditions:** Land ownership and values, industrial development, agricultural regions and products, changes in price level, financial balance sheet, productive capacity, unemployment by years.
• **Public Welfare:** Occupational distributions, delinquency areas, housing conditions, racial and nationality residential groupings, health conditions, illiteracy rate, recreational facilities, life expectancy among different races, frequency of accidents, welfare agencies.
• **Transportation Facilities:** Streets and highways, railroads, bus lines, ship and aviation routes, locations of terminals, toll roads.

Specific directions for preparing most types of graphic documents need not be given here. Three newer varieties of the graphic document, however, do merit brief mention because they are so very useful in the community study procedure. Let us therefore consider the techniques of fashioning pictorial charts, land-use maps, and social base maps.

Pictorial Charts

Sometimes called a "pictograph," this chart is an arrangement of realistic or symbolic pictures in such manner as to tell a statistical story. To make a pictorial chart, standardized symbols appropriate to the subject matter are either purchased or drawn. These symbols are cut out and pasted upon a paper or cardboard background, which is then properly lettered and titled. Excellent examples of this technique may be found in the Public Affairs Pamphlets and in the University of Chicago Round Table Transcripts.

Sheets of standardized pictorial symbols have been especially prepared for schools, and may be purchased at small cost from Pictorial Statistics, Co., 144 East 24th Street, New York 10, N. Y. Interested teachers will find a comprehensive treatment of pictographic possibilities in Rudolph Modley's *How to Use Pictorial Statistics.*

Land-Use Map

This is a special type of map, constructed to show just how the land space of a given area is utilized for productive (or nonproductive) purposes. It is an original drawing, done to scale upon the basis of actual field investigations, and is best finished in the following commonly used colors:

LAND-USE AND COLOR DESIGNATIONS

TYPE OF LAND-USE	SUGGESTED COLOR
Forest	Dark green
Water areas	Light blue
Farm land	Golden yellow
Dwellings (1-2 family)	Orange
Dwellings (multiple)	Light brown
Commercial buildings	Red
Industry (light)	Violet
Industry (heavy)	Purple
Transportation	Black
Public buildings and grounds	Pink
Recreational areas	Lemon yellow
Scenic and historical places	Dark blue
Welfare institutions	Dark brown
Vacant land	White

Often it will be necessary to differentiate land-use within one or more of these major categories; that is, to distinguish superior, average, and inferior housing areas, or to indicate agricultural land devoted to corn in contrast to that sown in wheat. In such cases, subdivide the map accordingly, and then color the subdivisions with contrasting hatching—vertical lines, horizontal lines, diagonal lines, dots, and the like.

Helpful in a study of land utilization are the soil surveys of the United States Department of Agriculture. These surveys consist of a descriptive report and a large, colored map showing the kinds of soil in each area or county surveyed. For a list of surveys available, write to the Superintendent of Documents.

Land-use mapping may be facilitated by the preliminary use of a good topographic map of the area in question. The United States Geological Survey (Department of the Interior), has published large-scale topographic maps, size 16½ by 20 inches, for over half of the nation. An index map of any state, listing the local topographic maps available for that state, will be furnished by the Survey upon request and without charge.[1]

Social Base Map

This map is similar in general nature to the land-use map just described. It differs in that its chief purpose is to locate specifically the various *agencies* serving a local community or a neighborhood, rather than to visualize the general purposes to which the land surface of an area is put.

To make this useful community-study aid, a large-scale outline map of the area in question is necessary. Such a map may be drawn in the school, but it is preferable to purchase it if one can be found. For an urban area, a large-scale map can sometimes be secured from the city or county department of engineering, health, or taxation, or from the local council of social agencies. Rural area maps of sufficiently small scale are more difficult to find; lacking others, however, the Rural Delivery Maps issued by the Post Office Department may be used

---

[1] There is available from the Superintendent of Documents, Government Printing Office, Washington 25, D. C., a map entitled "Major Land Uses in the U.S." (1950). The scale is 1:5,000,000. Also available from the same source is "Graphic Summary of Land Utilization in the U.S." (1947).

even though their scale of one inch to the mile is rather small for most effective results as a social base map.

The next step is to procure or make a number of small graphic symbols to indicate the generic types and geographic locations of different governmental, educational, religious, welfare, social, recreational, commercial, and other community agencies. The Russell Sage Foundation (130 East 22nd Street, New York 10, N. Y.) has developed a series of standard symbols. Pins or thumbtacks with variously colored heads may also be used to designate major types of agencies. Their chief disadvantages are that the agencies they represent are not self-evident—as they are in the case of the printed symbols—and also that in order to affix them the map must be mounted in some rigid fashion.

The final step is to attach the chosen symbols in their proper places upon the map, and to add appropriate captions and a descriptive legend. Then the map is ready for display and use.

The construction of such a local land-use or social base map often stimulates student interest in the larger community areas, and in their relationships to the immediate locality. To illustrate: if the map is designed to show the community's important industries, the questions will arise: "Where do these industries get their raw materials? And where do the finished products go?" The answer to these and other similar questions calls for study of larger and larger areas, and of other local communities both near and far away. Thus the pupil-made maps of their own immediate locality become a nucleus for the further study of regional, national, and international resources, relationships, needs, and problems.

Exhibits Spur Interest

Literally thousands of material objects, specimens, and models can be used to enrich and amplify the community school program. Such exhibits are widely available through purchase, donation, loan, and excursion viewing. The following list suggests merely a few of the many exhibits that can fruitfully be used to deepen student understanding of the physical, biological, and social environment:

Animals: rats, mice, rabbits, kittens, squirrels, chickens
Building materials: brick, tile, wood, metal, paint, nails
Flowers: wild and domesticated; fresh, pressed, preserved in plastic
Fuels: wood, oil, coal, peat
Indian relics: arrowheads, flints, celts, hatchets, harpoons, pottery
Insects: moths, butterflies, grasshoppers, flies
Plastics: anatomical models, scale-size reproductions of buildings
Raw materials: cotton, flax, silk, latex, foodstuffs, ores
Rocks: stones, minerals, ores, fossils, petrified woods
Weeds and weed seeds: types, control methods, commercial uses

Exhibits such as these may be secured from varied sources such as pupils' homes, industrial and commercial concerns, fairs and other public exhibitions, public and private museums, school supply houses, and from other schools through exchange or loan. Some items may be obtained for permanent exhibition; others can be borrowed for temporary use. Many useful models can be made by the students themselves, either in the school classroom or shop, or in their homes, for display at school. Steel construction sets, for example, may easily be utilized to build working models of machinery and mechanical appliances. Lifelike papier-mâché models may easily be constructed from newspapers, paste, and a little paint.

Evolutionary exhibits can be effectively built. Typical demonstrations are the life cycle of the butterfly, moth, or beetle; the reduction of ores; the fabrication of alloys; the growth of plants and flowers; the manufacture of soap or the preparation of sugar. Students may even design and execute more complicated exhibits, such as a habitat or similar nature grouping.

Every school should and can have its own museum of materials illustrating community life. Many persons, adults as well as children, enjoy collecting items of various kinds, and many students already possess collections of their own. Such a group project is both intriguing and educative to students and faculty alike. Cooperative planning, obtaining, classifying, mounting, and labeling exhibits, evaluating one's own and one's neighbors' efforts, and generally working together for the common good bring pronounced educational benefits.

The school museum is not completed when the exhibits have been made and labeled; they must also be located accessibly and displayed attractively if they are to become effective educational materials. The important thing is to locate the exhibits where they can be used easily and without formality, utilized without disturbing other students and teachers, easily moved to various classrooms, suitably protected and indexed, and grouped to represent an artistic appearance. But whatever the location chosen for the school museum, care and discrimination should always be used to the end that only truly educative materials be collected or constructed. We must always keep in mind the fact that a good museum is not merely a collection of miscellaneous items gathered at random from the community; it is rather a usable collection of significant community realia.

Pictures Illuminate

Photographs, sketches, cartoons, paintings, post cards, pictures clipped from magazines and newspapers, and many other similar "flat pictures" provide a wealth of valuable information about your community. Such pictures are easily available from many sources, inexpensive and convenient to collect, make, mount, and use. Having been mounted and titled, they may then be passed about among the students or displayed upon the bulletin board.

Pictorial materials should always be properly mounted in order to enhance their attractiveness, make them more usable, and preserve them better. Being mounted, they are more easily passed around, handled, and otherwise used by students; furthermore, mounted pictures can be laid down, stood upright, hung on the wall, and conveniently filed away.

Slides and Filmstrips Appeal

Slides and filmstrips are particularly useful since many thousands of them, covering all aspects of the environment, are available from commercial and professional agencies, on a sale or loan basis, and also because they can readily be made by students and teachers. As a general rule, photographic slides, regardless of size and type, may be classified in two groups: those prepared by local amateurs for the study of the immediate locality, and those produced by technical experts to report the basic social processes of living in the larger regional, national, and world areas. We shall confine attention here to the amateur productions, merely noting in passing a few titles of the second type to indicate their value:

Food From the Land	*Community Helpers Series:*
Life On a New England Farm	*The Baker*
Democracy Is Home Made	*The Fireman*
Homes in the City	*The Grocer*
Air Transportation	*The Policeman*
Carrying Freight	*The Postman*

The photographic slide is a splendid medium for reproducing many such community-interest items as these:

• Old Documents: Maps, original manuscripts, blueprints, deeds of sale, old photographs, and so forth, which may be found in every community and photographed for projection purposes in the school.

• Slides Made From Old Negatives: Community activities of many kinds are photographed by local camera fans, who will be glad to loan their negatives for reproduction as slides. Likewise, scenes of many years past may be found in the files of long-established commercial studios and may also be borrowed.

• Current Photographs: The various scenes which may be currently photographed even by amateurs are too numerous to mention. When we consider the many natural sites, scenic points, industries, occupations, means of transportation, community festivals, special celebrations, and so on, we shall begin to grasp the possibilities of slide-making for local community study.

Most photographic slides are of the 2- by 2-inch variety,

either black and white or in full color. Yet the hand-drawn 3½- by 4-inch "standard" slide of several types may be used in presenting a wealth of ideas pertaining to the community. Since these slides are so adaptable to a wide range of materials, the most commonly used forms are mentioned here:

• Etched-Glass Slides: This type is most often used to repro-duce maps, charts, graphs, diagrams, and other materials of a simi-lar graphic nature. The etched slide is simply a plain piece of glass, roughened on one side with acid so that one can draw or write on it with pencil, colored pencils, or ink. The image or picture is traced or drawn on paper so that it will come within the 3½- by 4-inch di-mensions of the standard slide. The glass, roughened side up, is placed over the image to be reproduced, and the tracing is made. The slide is then ready for use.

• India Ink Slides: A bright and clear outline or diagram may be produced by using India ink on a plain cover glass. A thin coat of shellac on the glass makes a better surface on which to draw.

• Cellophane Slides: This type of slide is used most frequently for projecting written material. To prepare it, cut a piece of cello-phane the size of the slide. Then cut a piece of good carbon paper 6½ by 8 inches in size, and fold the carboned sides together. Place the cellophane inside the folded carbon, and write or type the de-sired copy. Remove the cellophane on which the words now appear, and mount it between cover glasses to protect it and give it rigidity.

• Silhouette and Paper Cutout Slides: The figure to be repro-duced is cut out of opaque paper and then inserted between two cover glasses. If the figure itself is used, the silhouette is obtained when the slide is projected. But if the paper from which the figure was cut out is utilized, all of the slide surface except that of the figure will be dark. Such "cutout" slides may be made more attrac-tive by using colored cellophane. Sometimes several colors may be used to advantage, either together or in slide sequence.[2]

The filmstrip is a 35 mm. continuous film carrying a number of photographs called "frames" or pictures. Filmstrips have become increasingly popular in recent years, and are espe-cially useful for easy amateur recording of community scenes,

[2] An excellent film showing how to make slides is *How to Make Handmade Lantern Slides* produced by Indiana University, Bloomington, 1947. In this film basic production techniques are outlined, with suggestions for uses of slides on various grade levels.

later to be projected in the classroom as part of the trip report. Such filmstrips can be shown with accompanying oral comment, or the spoken explanations, complete with musical and other sound effects, may be transcribed upon phonograph records or tape or wire recorder for synchronized use with the projection itself.

Motion Pictures Stimulate

Through motion pictures we can almost literally bring the world into the classroom. By using different types of photography, such as the time lapse, slow motion, animated cartoon, microphotography, miniature, and the like, practically every form of physical phenomena and life activity may be realistically reproduced.

As in the case of slides and filmstrips, motion picture films may be grouped in two broad divisions according to their general availability: (1) those useful in the study of the local or immediate environment, and (2) those which reproduce features of more remote community areas. Again we shall consider only the first type.

Many interesting motion picture films can be produced by the school, the photographic class, the teacher, or by mature students. The new "tape-on-film" as a method of sound recording and reproduction reduces considerably the cost of producing sound films. The preparation of a local film always arouses widespread interest, and at the same time provides many significant learning experiences and excellent technical training for all members of the producing group. Preparing the script, planning the scenes, placing the people or objects in each scene, preparing the titles, arranging photographic equipment and "shooting" the pictures—all these activities provide rich and vital experiences.

In making local films, emphasis generally centers about two aspects of the school-community relationship: interpreting the school program to the community residents, and depicting other time-periods or important events of the community.

All who have worked in the public schools know how difficult it is to get the parents and other people of the community to visit the school where they can actually see the children in action. Consequently, the motion picture film can be used very effectively to show the people just what schools are attempting to do for their children. One of the best films of this type is *East Aurora In Review*. This is a 1600-foot film in color showing just how the schools of East Aurora are attempting to serve the needs of the students of that community. It explains the objectives of the instructional program on the kindergarten, intermediate, junior high, and high school levels. The narration and musical background for the film were put on tape. This film has been used very effectively in Aurora, Illinois, in acquainting the people of the community with their schools.

In depicting other time periods or important events in the community, 16 mm. film also has a part—especially in the photographing of pageants or other events dealing with earlier periods in the history of the community, if they are staged. The staging of such events by the school can be a very worthwhile project of the dramatic department; the production can be filmed for future use in helping the students understand the history of their own community.

Commercially prepared films are often of real value in studying even your own community. Such titles as these are indicative:

Birth of the Soil	*State Legislature*
Home Town Paper	*County Government*
Port of New York	*Country Town*
Seed Dispersal	*Ohio Town*
School in Centerville	*Expanding World Relationships*

Radio Impresses

The radio is not only a resource to be used for purposes of school instruction, but it is also an excellent medium whereby the students can publicize in the community their own findings concerning community life, developments, and problems.

Many communities have their own broadcasting stations. Although purely local in coverage (apart from network programs), these stations generally have a large audience within the region served. Many colleges and universities either maintain their own stations or have access to local broadcasting resources. The programs of all such local stations may often include broadcasts dealing with the history, growth, industries, occupations, social needs, and other concerns of local radio listeners. Many schools, conversely, are using local radio stations to acquaint their patrons with the school activities, especially those involving or reporting upon school-community relationships and programs.

Schools often arrange series of radio programs, covering both school activities and local community affairs as they impinge upon the curricular program. Broadcasts portraying early events, describing historic buildings and sites, interviews with leading citizens and with technical specialists in varied fields, analyses of local occupations and social problems are all suggestive of the programs which are frequently presented. Such programs serve the double purpose of better acquainting the students with their community, and of better informing the community about its schools.

Larger school systems sometimes own and operate their own radio stations, beaming programs directly into the classrooms throughout the school day. Their programs are thus made a definite part of the established instructional activities, being prepared as curriculum materials and announced to all teachers well in advance. Under this arrangement, opportunities for using community resources via radio are virtually limitless. In Chicago, as a single example, the Board of Education, through its Radio and Television Division, recently broadcast a 13-week series of 15-minute programs dramatizing the work and civic contributions of locally operating human relations agencies. Each agency planned its own program, illustrative of the types of problems and needs it is prepared to serve. The accompanying Teacher's Handbook stated that "*Good neighbors in action* introduces classroom listeners to the work and the services of various Chicago-area welfare and human relations agencies. Designed to remind Americans that prejudice and discrimination have no place in our democracy, the series represents a cross-section of problems on intergroup tensions and offers suggestions for positive treatment contributory to better intergroup understanding and interfaith relations."

Recordings Enliven

Literally hundreds of excellent recordings and broadcast transcriptions are suitable for serious instructional use. Among these are many which are especially appropriate to the larger community areas, to the institutional and psychological levels, and the historic, contemporary, and future time-periods (see Chapter 3). Schools which have equipment with which to make their own recordings will find rich opportunities for more realistic community study and public reporting through this vital medium.

The tape or wire recorder can be used effectively as a means of recording student interviews with old-time residents of the community, thus preserving their firsthand stories about the community's early development and later events. Similar use can be made of recorded interviews with new arrivals to the community, and with visiting celebrities.

Dramatics Are Fun

Pageants, plays, and skits all have their important place. They serve especially well as culminating activities for large units of work; and since they require considerable physical, emotional, and mental activity, they are excellent media for developing both intellectual understandings and emotionalized attitudes. Dramatics integrate logical fact with emotional feeling; they simultaneously impart information and cultivate attitudes.

Brief skits, longer plays, extensive pageants are all suitable for the dramatic treatment of many themes which are central in the life-centered school curriculum. The history of the community, scenes of pioneer life, origins of national holidays, minority contributions to common welfare, the ideals and problems of democracy—all these suggest topics of interest and vital concern in life-centered education. Full-length plays and pageants obviously require more elaborate staging and preparation; they may therefore best be presented on important school occasions and as part of community festivals. Skits and one-act plays obviously require less preparation and may be well utilized for classroom or assembly portrayals of more limited theme situations.

Television Enthralls

The educational potentialities of television are still largely unexplored, but as increasing social use is made of our advancing technology, we may find this among the greatest of all audio-visual aids to mass instruction. Instantaneous viewing of historic events may become commonplace; visible interviews with prominent personalities in all fields of endeavor may be a regular part of the school curriculum; master lecturers upon any conceivable subject may be freely utilized; televised laboratory experiments may be clearly demonstrated to scores or hundreds of students simultaneously; television excursions into industrial plants, technical laboratories, museums, art galleries, churches, welfare centers, historic sites, community festivals, engineering projects, cooperative communities, experimental schools, and a host of other such community centers may await the flick of a switch.

Where Can We Get Community Materials?

Documentary and audio-visual materials are essential to realistic community education programs. Such materials are procurable from five chief sources: commercial publishers and supply houses, governments, business and labor organizations, civic associations, and educational agencies. Let's note some typical items in each group.

Commercial Publishers and Supply Houses

Numerous publishing and supply houses (including university presses and newspapers) issue material useful in community understanding. Much of this is valuable as general background for local situations, for making comparisons between local conditions and those elsewhere, and for basic study of larger community areas. No comprehensive list of such materials can be offered here, but the following sources are perhaps suggestive:

Encyclopedias

Americana   *Britannica*
Book of Knowledge   *World Book*
Catholic Encyclopedia *Jewish Encyclopedia*
Encyclopedia of Religion and Ethics
Encyclopedia of the Social Sciences

Biographical Dictionaries

Dictionary of American Biography
Who's Who in America
Who's Who in New England, Who's Who on the Pacific Coast, and so forth.
Who Knows—and What

Cumulative Indexes

Education Index   *Educational Film Catalog*
New York Times Index   *Public Affairs Information Service*
Readers Guide to Periodical Literature

Annuals, Handbooks, and Yearbooks

American Year Book. Excellent narrative accounts of the year's developments in such broad fields as history, economics, public resources, social conditions, government, literature, education, science, religion, etc. Lists of relevant periodical references and of related organizations are included.

Book of the States. An authoritative summary of governmental affairs in each of the forty-eight states. Tabular comparisons are made for such items as state election laws, state expenditures, state employees and payrolls, industrial relations, marriage laws, crime control legislation, motor vehicle regulation, etc. Rosters of state administrative officials are included.

Municipal Year Book. Annual résumé of activities and statistical data for most American cities. Gives comparable data on such matters as crime rates, population shifts, accident deaths, library expenditures, school enrollment, tax rates, names of chief administrative officers, etc.

Social Work Yearbook. Authoritative articles on all aspects of social work such as city planning, housing, youth problems, unemployment, and so forth.

Statesman's Year Book. Concise and readable manual of descriptive and statistical information about governments of all countries in the world. For each country, it gives data on government, education, religion, justice, social welfare, industry, etc. Valuable bibliographies are included.

World Almanac. The most comprehensive and useful handbook of miscellaneous information. Contains much data on industry, government, history, education, religion, biography, and similar subjects.

Governments

Federal, state, and local governments publish much valuable material. Many items are either free or very inexpensive, thus putting them within financial reach of most teachers and all schools. Many federal agencies issue documentary and audio-visual materials which may provide useful information concerning the national, regional, and even local community areas. Especially noteworthy are these Departments and their sub-divisions: Agriculture, Commerce, Justice, Labor; Health, Education, and Welfare. Lists of publications issued by these and other Departments may be obtained without charge upon application to the Superintendent of Documents.

A majority of the states publish annual or biennial handbooks such as the *New York Red Book* and the *Oregon Blue Book.* These provide official information concerning such matters as state legislation, school systems, law enforcement, planning and housing, names and titles of state officials, and the like. You should communicate with the relevant state agency about such a handbook of your own state. Information from such a source may enable you to discover how your own county, and often your own community, compares with others in your state.

State education departments publish lists of materials and sources specifically available or suitable to schools. So do offices of county school superintendents, and those of many local school systems.

Counties and even municipalities often publish comparable reports, the latter especially in New England. In one Massachusetts town, this report runs to three hundred pages and is sent to the citizens. It provides financial data for all departments such as fire, police, health and sanitation, education, libraries, highways, charities, recreation, unemployment, debt, and interest. It lists all appropriations, reports on assessments and tax collections. It presents, in addition to this financial data, careful discussion of the work and accomplishments of each department, as well as other significant data.

City directories are common and very useful sources of detailed information in metropolitan areas. New York City's *Little Green Book*, for example, boasts over five hundred pages, is almost an encyclopedia of data about the city's government, and is a local best-seller.

Business and Labor Organizations

Major sources of documentary materials are the business and labor organizations of your community. Despite the private character and interested nature of their activities, such agencies should not be overlooked as sources of community information. Chambers of commerce naturally seek to present an attractive picture of the community, but even so they do often collect and record valuable data, especially about economic development and related matters. The larger labor unions generally maintain educational departments which collect much local information pertaining especially to welfare and industrial conditions. Trade associations and real estate boards are among other business groupings which often gather information about local economic matters and may be willing to share findings with the school.

Civic Associations

In nearly every community there are several or many local, county, and state agencies of an essentially civic nature which collect significant community information and gladly make it available upon request. Among them are such as these:

Historical societies	Human relations agencies
Patriotic associations	Housing authorities
Social agencies	Farm and home bureaus
Fraternal and service clubs	Women's organizations
Churches	Selective Service boards
Cultural minority associations	Civic planning agencies

The larger the community, the better and more complete all these sources of information are likely to be.

Educational Agencies

Many local and state school systems, colleges and universities, and professional education associations have produced local community learning materials of real significance to their own areas, and are samples of what can and should be done in every locality. Among these are some excellent resource units and handbooks specifically designed as guides to selected aspects of local community processes and problems.

PRODUCTION SOURCE	TITLE
Burbank, California, Public Schools	*The Citizen and His Local Government*
Detroit Public Schools	*Citizenship in Detroit: A Source Book on Detroit's Civic Life*
Louisville Public Schools	*Louisville in Kentucky*

Production Source	Title
Los Angeles Public Schools	*Community Life Series: Milestones and Landmarks, Parks and Recreational Centers, The Civic Center,* etc.
Los Angeles County Public Schools	*Industrial Units Series: The Walnut Industry, The Petroleum Industry,* etc.
Philadelphia Public Schools	*Curriculum Reference Pamphlets: Speaking of Elections, They Carry the Mail,* etc.
Syracuse University (Maxwell Graduate School of Citizenship and Public Affairs) and the National Council for the Social Studies	*Community Study Series: Structure of Local Government, Parties and Politics in the Local Community, Community Planning in a Democracy,* etc.

Every school large enough to own or have access to a mimeographing or other type of duplicating machine can produce documentary materials like these. They are especially valuable in terms of local interest and probable actual use if lay people and students, as well as teachers, have helped to prepare them.

Audio-visual materials reflecting community history, people, processes and problems have likewise been produced by schools in every part of the nation. Most common are colored 2- by 2-inch slide sets picturing historic sites and monuments, and portraying basic industries in operation. Motion pictures are widely utilized to interpret to the community the school's program and policies. Instructional materials bureaus, maintained by city and county school systems and sometimes by universities, often produce audio-visual materials of local value for loan to local schools and to community groups.

How Can We Produce Local Community Materials?

Important and useful as they are, already-prepared materials will never be enough—simply because even at their best they cannot provide adequate coverage of your changing local scene, needs, and resources. The community school requires full information about its supporting area as well as data about the larger world. It needs pictures of local factories—to be studied before field trip visits to those centers, and then reviewed again afterward. It should have specific facts and figures about local population groups, health and employment situations, birthrate and migration trends, intergroup tensions and developments. Students ought to have at hand film or tape recordings of relatively inaccessible local resources, such as a meeting of the city council which occurs too late at night for students to attend. Local events of civic or historical significance should be recorded at the time for future school and community use. Every community concerned about its civic morale—which means its own future—will use such ways to build local pride as well as stimulate wider and more intelligent participation in local community life.

Every school should produce documentary and visual materials to supplement direct learning experiences. Always the field trip, the resource visitor, the interview, survey, work experience, or service project should be fully "tied in" with appropriate books, maps, audio-visual materials, and constructing activities, as we have seen on page 29. Learning is always a unified process, and is best stimulated through many coordinated approaches.

What kinds of local, specific materials do schools produce? Many kinds—field trip outlines, descriptions of historical events and industrial processes, district and regional base maps, floor charts of fire stations and bakeries, flow charts of dairies and lumber mills, enlarged photographs and color slides of scenic spots, historic sites, industries, government activities, school-community projects of all kinds.

A dairy plant, for example, is usually a rather noisy place. This makes it difficult for the plant guide to make himself heard as the group walks through. Many members of the party may not be able even to identify the various machines, let alone hear the guide's description of their functions. Their impression of the dairy plant is likely to be one of confusion, even resentment. But this difficulty can be largely overcome if a diagrammatic floor and flow chart with keyed explanations has been prepared in advance and given to each visitor before he enters the plant. Such a chart with process explanations is reproduced on the following pages. Some dairy plant managers are glad to place numbered placards or even permanent signs on or over each machine, so that by easy reference to individual floor charts all visitors may understand better what they are seeing. Such signs may be made by school students in the art room or the industrial arts shop.

Simple narrative and visual materials describing its own community should certainly be produced by every school. These materials may deal briefly with selected aspects of the community's life, portray some such aspects in considerable detail, or present a comprehensive overview of the community's structure, people, group processes, and social problems. All materials should be planned for the reading and experience levels appropriate to children, to older boys and girls, to adolescents, and to adults.

In most cases these materials are developed by committees of teachers as part of their workshop or in-service programs. Sometimes students in English or in social studies classes originate the project, and often they assist in it. Multilithing or lithiprinting is the best way to duplicate documentary materials cheaply. These processes costs only a little more than mimeographing, and permit inclusion of as many photographs as desired without additional printing charges. Sometimes local school systems produce illustrated materials describing selected aspects of their own communities. *Indianapolis at Work* is one such series; it is a group of brochures together with books, film strips and other visual aids which together tell the story of the city's business enterprises to pupils in grades four through twelve. An advisory committee composed of representatives of business, industry, labor, the press, the

MILK PROCESSING AT THE KITSAP DAIRY

1. Milk Receiving Room

As the milk is poured from each farmer's cans into the weighing vat, a conveyor system carries the can to the washer where it and the lid are washed, sterilized and then conveyed to the truck for return to the farmer.

2. Holding Vats

The milk is weighed, a sample taken from each shipment for testing, it is pumped to the cooler, and then into holding vats, each of which holds 1,000 gallons. Here it is agitated to keep the cream from rising until it is ready for separation or bottling.

3. Testing

A sample of each shipment as taken from the weighing tank, is placed in a test tube where sulphuric acid is added to it. It is rotated violently to mix the chemical, which brings the fat to the place where it can be measured on the graduated stem of the tube.

4. Separator

When the milk is ready to be separated it is pumped first to the preheater which heats it to a temperature of 95° F., then to the separator where centrifugal force sends the cream to the center of the bowl and the skim milk to the periphery. Cream then is pasteurized, cooled, and bottled, or used in making butter. The buttermilk is also pasteurized and bottled.

5. Homogenizer—Clarifier

The whole milk is pumped to the homogenizer, where pressure breaks up the fat globules so that they cannot rise to the top as cream. The clarifier is a type of filter in the line.

6. Pasteurizer

In the pasteurizer, the milk is passed between stainless steel plates with hot water in alternating plates. The temperature is raised to 163° F., then the milk is sent through the pipe which circles the pasteurizer and passed through another series of plates which reduces the temperature to 38°F. The whole process takes 3 minutes, which gives the name "short time pasteurizer" to this piece of equipment.

7. Control Panel

The control panel behind the pasteurizer shows accurately and automatically the temperature of the milk at each step in the process.

8. Bottling

Pasteurized milk is sent to the holding vat and into either one of two types of bottling apparatus. The traditional glass milk bottle is filled by the machine on the right of the holding vat, after the bottles have been thoroughly washed and sterilized through 5 solutions and rinses.

The new type of fibre bottles are made and filled in the other piece of equipment to the left of the holding vat. This is one of three bottle makers produced since the war, and is something of an innovation both in Bremerton and the whole state of Washington.

KEYED EXPLANATION OF CHARTED PROCESS
Bremerton, Washington

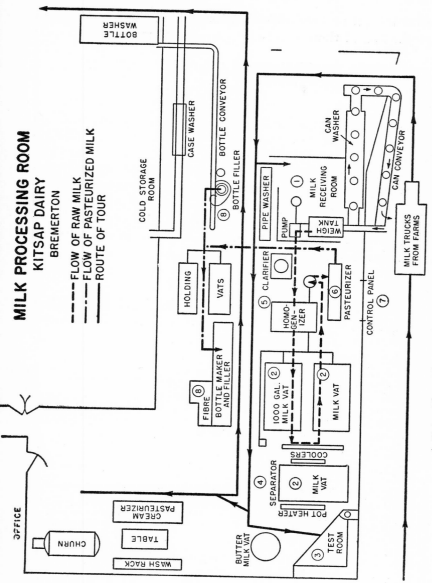

MILK PROCESSING ROOM
KITSAP DAIRY
BREMERTON

- - - - FLOW OF RAW MILK
- · - · FLOW OF PASTEURIZED MILK
——— ROUTE OF TOUR

BOTTLE WASHER

CASE WASHER

COLD STORAGE ROOM

BOTTLE CONVEYOR

BOTTLE FILLER

CAN WASHER

MILK RECEIVING ROOM

PIPE WASHER

PUMP

WEIGH TANK

CAN CONVEYOR

MILK TRUCKS FROM FARMS

HOLDING

VATS

CLARIFIER ⑤

HOMO-GEN-IZER

PASTEURIZER ⑥

CONTROL PANEL ⑦

FIBRE ⑧

BOTTLE MAKER AND FILLER

BOTTLE FILLER ⑧

1000 GAL. MILK VAT ②

MILK VAT ②

COOLERS

SEPARATOR ④

MILK VAT ②

POT HEATER

BUTTER MILK VAT

TEST ROOM ③

OFFICE

CHURN

TABLE

WASH RACK

CREAM PASTEURIZER

① MILK RECEIVING ROOM

A Dairy Plant Floor and Flow Chart—Bremerton, Washington

179

schools, and parents' organizations guided the planning and production of these excellent instructional materials.

How Should Community Materials Be Used?

Specific directions for utilizing each of the documentary and audio-visual aids just mentioned are beyond the province of this book. Detailed suggestions may be found in any textbook devoted to teaching materials as such, and in every good handbook on audio-visual methods. Yet some general suggestions are in order here, and will be offered as three fundamental principles which must obviously be applied to particular situations. These principles have been drawn out of much practical experience, and their observance generally will enable you to use both major kinds of community teaching materials with full confidence and success.

Know the Limitations of Your Materials

Despite their real value, both audio-visual and documentary materials have certain marked limitations as teaching avenues. These you will keep always in mind as a skilled teacher. Let's itemize them like this:

Documentary materials	Audio-visual materials
Impersonality is characteristic of most printed materials, and is especially evident in such statistical matters as census reports and survey summaries. Such materials definitely repel many people by their very lack of human "warmth."	The entertainment function may be predominant. The intrinsic interest of these materials, in contrast with traditional classroom procedures and equipment, may permit them to become ends in themselves, rather than means to other and superior purposes.
Gullibility concerning the written word is unfortunately very prevalent. Many people tend to accept as true anything they see in print. The "authority of the printed page" is still so great that it is genuinely hard to make immature readers critical of the assumptions and attitudes underlying the materials they use.	They are no substitute for firsthand experiences. Closely related to the first limitation is the danger that reproduced reality in the classroom may habitually be substituted for direct experience with that reality in the community. Projected pictures of birds, in lieu of an excursion to a nearby aviary, would be most inappropriate.

Documentary materials

Verbalistic learning may be mistaken for education. Words are highly abstract symbols, and frequently arouse quite different meanings in different minds. And since written words are necessarily inflexible in the sense that their author is not present to interpret, amplify, or clarify *his* meaning, it is evident that documentary materials must be used with exceeding care if their true meaning is to be commonly understood by all readers.

Audio-visual materials

Over-simplification of complex situations is likely to occur. Because audio-visual materials are largely edited representations of reality, they often present a deceptively easy picture of man's environment, activities, and problems, thus leading the learner into either naivete or cynicism concerning the deeper problems and ultimate possibilities of community improvement.

Use Materials as Teaching Tools for Chosen Purposes

Every conceivable audio-visual or documentary aid is undoubtedly valuable for certain purposes, with selected groups, under given conditions. But under different conditions, with different groups, with different purposes, any such aid may prove useless or even harmful. We must always remember that educational techniques are only relatively valid; that there is thus no "best" type of learning material for all purposes, groups, and conditions. It is highly important to understand the specific possibilities of all types of community learning materials if each is to be used with maximum advantage.

Never should materials be used as virtual ends in themselves —as often happens, for example, when the children in grades five, six, seven and eight are all herded in to see a film secured for the seventh grade general science class, and yet shown to all the others also on the ground that the school paid rental for the film, and besides it is interesting and valuable, isn't it? Every teaching "tool," from a census report to a television program, should be used because—and only because—it bids fair in that particular situation to stimulate better learning than would any other kind of "aid" available. The specific educational objectives sought must always control the choice of methods. Materials are aids to good teaching, not substitutes for it.

Remember That Materials Vary Greatly in Reliability

We must always check carefully, particularly when objective data are essential, upon the source, the author, or the producer of the material, the purpose for which it was prepared, and the methodology used. Newspapers, for example, always have a point of view which often reflects the attitudes of special interest groups, and it is important to recognize this viewpoint in order to make full allowance for it. Chamber of commerce and labor union films will similarly show a bias, although more so on some questions than on others.

Since practically all aids are edited in some fashion (by the very choice of subject matter and techniques of presentation, at least) they easily become media for deliberate or even unconscious propaganda. American nationalists, for example, may unconsciously prefer that pupils use the Mercator projection of the world map, while proponents of full international responsibility use the newer "polar view" projections, which are less likely to generate an isolationist stereotype than does the Mercator.

We must also be always aware of problems relating to the methods used. We need to know something of the conditions and assumptions under which the source materials were prepared. As one example, we must be sure that terms used are truly comparable before we attempt to make contrasts. In one city, to illustrate, birth data collected are based upon live births, while in another city such data include all births, whether live or stillborn. Again, it is well to know that churches use different bases when compiling figures on membership. Protestant churches generally count the names of individual members; Catholic parishes automatically include all children of Catholic members; Jewish synagogues commonly report all Jews in the synagogue area, whether or not they are congregation members. Uncritical comparisons of birth rates or of church membership would obviously be quite misleading.

Essential Tools

Documentary and audio-visual materials are essential tools for community understanding. In succeeding chapters we shall examine other equally necessary avenues of learning.

Learning Activities

Discussion Topics

1. What are the values and dangers of using commercially prepared community study materials?
2. How could educational television be utilized in community study and to interpret the school to the community?
3. What kinds of local community materials could your class or school produce? What would be some first steps toward such production?
4. How valuable for your teaching and learning purposes in your own situation are the U. S. Census reports? Be specific.
5. What are some possibilities for using socio-drama in community study?

Group Activities

1. Plan a script for a motion picture film which will interpret the school or some phase of its program to the community.
2. Study some local industry and prepare a script for a series of slides which can be used to interpret its operations to a class. If possible, actually take the pictures and record a commentary.
3. Check your school buildings for space, and then plan and develop a school museum.
4. Put on a radio program (either actual, over a local station, or simulated with microphone and amplifier) reporting dramatically some of your community findings.
5. Let a committee preview available motion pictures and recommend the best of them for class viewing.

Individual Projects

1. Prepare a graph, chart, or other device to interpret an important community problem to parents.

2. Collect and display old photographs of your local community, with explanatory captions.
3. Use a tape or wire recorder in interviewing interesting people in the community. Bring these interviews into class, and evaluate them as instructional materials for specific grade levels and subject fields.
4. Make a chart contrasting the advantages and limitations of audio-visual techniques in community study.
5. Write supplementary reading materials designed to help explain selected community resources to students.

Learning Materials

As you think about producing your own local documentary materials, you will do well to look over these sources of good ideas:

"Producing Curriculum Materials about the Community," Mary F. Sanders. Outlines problems each school faces in preparing its own instructional materials about the local community. *Elementary School Journal* 43:601-606; June 1943.

"Educational Action for Development of Regional Materials," John E. Ivey, Jr. Explains how such regional materials as those of the Sloan Experiment in Applied Economics, the New Dominion series and the Tennessee Valley publications were actually planned and produced. *High School Journal* 28:217-244; October 1945.

"Use of Local Historical Documents in Teaching the Social Studies," Daniel L. Van Leuvans. Suggests school uses of early church records, military lists, handbooks of academies, maps and surveys, deeds, and so on. *Social Studies* 39:26-28; January 1948.

"School-Made Teaching Materials," Maurice F. Seay. The story of the locally produced textbooks designed to improve community living through the Sloan Experiment in Kentucky, Vermont, and Florida. *Nation's Schools* 41:25-27; February 1948.

"Ghost Towns of Minnesota," Neal R. Merritt. A junior college class found local history came alive when they tracked down and secured data on many "ghost towns," and then planned to publish their findings. *Clearing House* 23:473-474; April 1949.

"Developing Instructional Materials in the Sloan Experiment," Ruth Hillis Seay. Explains how these teaching materials were planned, written, tested, and revised. *Educational Leadership* 8:417-421; April 1951.

"Civics and History at the Registry of Deeds," Edna M. McGlynn. Detailed description of how teachers college students used a county registry of deeds in research for local community history. *Social Education* 15:333-335; November 1951.

"1950 Census—Its Significance for Schools." Summarizes the latest population facts that have special significance for those who work in the field of education. *National Education Association Journal* 40:639-640; December 1951. See also "Schools and the 1950 Census," the NEA's December 1951 *Research Bulletin* for a more extensive analysis.

"Locating Resources for the Teaching of Local History," Ralph Adams Brown. Over half the states now require schools to teach local history, and in over half of these the instruction is given in both elementary and high school. This article offers many specific suggestions for using such materials as public documents, newspaper files, cemeteries, published histories, business records, and the like. *School Review* 60:292-297; May 1952.

"Fresno County's Community Life Series," Walter G. Martin and Lars Barstad. Explains twelve steps taken by joint committees of local industrialists and educators to produce curriculum materials on basic local industries for classroom use. *Social Education* 17:321-322; November 1952.

"Community Economics for the Third Grade: A New Venture in Textbook Writing," Marcillene Barnes. How a group of sixty teachers, working with children, wrote a book designed to help primary grade children understand and appreciate their city. *Social Education* 17:339-340; November 1953.

In the audio-visual field, standard textbook and similar sources are numerous. Among the best to draw upon for community study ideas and techniques are these:

Anna C. Chander and Irene F. Cypher, *Audio-Visual Techniques* (Noble & Noble, 1948).

Edgar Dale, *Audio-Visual Methods of Teaching* (Dryden, 1946).

E. C. Dent, *Audio-Visual Handbook* (Society for Visual Education, 1944).

Charles F. Hoban, C. F. Hoban, Jr., and Samuel B. Zisman, *Vitalizing the Curriculum* (Cordon, 1937).

James S. Kinder, *Audio-Visual Materials and Techniques* (American Book, 1950).

Harry C. McKown and Alvin B. Roberts, *Audio-Visual Aids to Instruction* (McGraw-Hill, 1949).

National Society for the Study of Education, *Audio-Visual Materials of Instruction* (University of Chicago, 1949).

L. Harry Strauss and J. R. Kidd, *Look, Listen and Learn* (Association Press, 1948).

G. G. Weaver and E. W. Bollinger, *Visual Aids, Their Construction and Use* (D. Van Nostrand, 1949).

W. A. Wittich and C. F. Schuller, *Audio-Visual Materials, Their Nature and Use* (Harper, 1953).

If you are interested in producing your own films, you will find several specialized sources useful. *Producing School Movies* (National Council of Teachers of English, 1941), by Eleanor D. Child and Hardy R. Finch, aims to acquaint the student and the teacher with the making of school films. *The Preparation and Use of Visual Aids* (Prentice-Hall, 1950), by Kenneth B. Haas and Harry Q. Packer, is designed as a basic or supplementary text. "Make Your Own Sound Movie," by Carlos De Zafra, in the *Clearing House* of October 1949, gives ten steps and some short cuts to making classroom movies. "Teacher Makes an Instructional Film," by Z. Ross, in *Journal of Business Education* of April 1950, includes motivation and production of films for business education classes, along with problems involved. A good film, *Basic Motion Picture Technique* (32 minutes), produced by Celluloid College, demonstrates techniques of panning, using the tripod, shot breakdown, screen direction, matching action, buildup, composition, indoor lighting, and applied technique. E. E. Brodbeck's *Handbook of Basic Motion Picture Techniques* (McGraw-Hill, 1950) is a worthwhile book for the beginning cinephotographer.

Amateur radio producers should consult J. W. Callahan's *Radio Workshop for Children* (McGraw-Hill, 1948), especially Chapter 19, which deals with "Pupil Community Programs." *

If you are planning a school museum, you can find help in several magazine articles. "Why Not Start a Museum?" by H. L. Williams, in *Parents' Magazine* of August 1938, is an enthusiastic challenge. "A Low-Cost School Museum" is described by William G. Hart in *Educational Screen* of May 1942. Priscilla A. Pearl's "An Elementary School Science Museum" offers many suggestions in the *N.E.A. Journal* of November, 1946. "School Museum," by L. L. Winslow, in *American Childhood* of March 1950 presents the function of a school museum, its arrangement, and plans for a museum showcase. "Vitalizing the Classroom: Museum Exhibits and Dioramas," by S. S. Blanc, in *School Science and Mathematics* of June, 1952, gives a general discussion of the function of a school museum and what to place in one. See also *Children's Museum: How to Start One*, by J. B. Cheny, published by the American Association of University Women, 1634 1st St., N. W., Washington 6, D. C.

Suggestions for preparing educational exhibits are found in *Educational Exhibits—How to Prepare and Use Them*, a United States Office of Education publication which includes many ideas for preparing exhibits, charts, maps, and other visual aids which can be planned easily and at minimum cost. "Better School Exhibits," by W. P. Allen, in *American School Board Journal* of October, 1947, is an article which presents the purpose of the school exhibit, along with practices found successful. "School Exhibits," by E. W. Osgood, in *Industrial Arts and Vocational Education* of November 1949 gives detail plans for a display

---

* See also *Radio and the School*, by Woelfel and Tyler (World Book, 1945), Chapter 8, which deals with student broadcasting. Helpful suggestions for the local radio program will be found in *Radio in the Classroom* by Margaret Harrison (Prentice-Hall, 1938), especially Chapters 4 and 5.

unit and suggested groupings of such units. Marjorie East, in her book *Display for Learning* (Dryden, 1952) aims at showing teachers how to produce visual materials and how to use them in and out of the class-room. Theory, materials, design, mediums, and appraising of displays are included

CHAPTER 7

People as Resources

Every community, no matter how small or isolated, has within it dozens of people of rich and varied backgrounds who can "open doors" to vivid learning experiences. The butcher, the baker, the candlestick-maker—and the homemaker, the scientist, the musician, the traveler, the hobbyist—all these and many more are the community's human resources waiting to be utilized by the enterprising teacher to enrich and vitalize the school program.

Human resources are not limited to any particular areas of interest or to any special age groups. The third grade may enjoy a puppet show given by two parents whose hobby is puppetry. A fifth grade art period may be used to watch a potter demonstrate his craft, with children's questions popping up on every side. A junior high school class may ask a chemist to speak to them about plastics, while the ninth grade home-makers see a mother bathe her baby and explain simple safety measures that are important in the process. A group of future farmers may ask a successful grower the secret of a bumper sugar beet yield; a college class committee may interview the county commissioners.

The term "resource people" is applied to persons of any age and background who can share their specialized knowledge of living with students, and who are able and willing to do so

This chapter is by Margaret Koopman Joy and Eldon W. Mason.

by coming into the classroom or by being interviewed elsewhere. Resource people are utilized for serious educational purposes, not merely for entertainment.

The general function of any resource person is to contribute
to the solution of problems, to help enrich and broaden meanings, to awaken and help build worthwhile interests, to acquaint students with varied aspects of their social and physical
environment, and to develop deepened sensitivity to people,
their ways of living, accomplishments, and problems.

It is a safe rule to bring resource people into the classroom,
or to interview them in the community, only when they can
make some contribution which has direct bearing upon the
activity, problem, or unit which the pupils are planning or
working upon. The exceptions are in the case of an outstanding
personage or an important event in which there is general
interest, or when there is definite likelihood of broadening
children's outlooks and interests. Such general needs are most
often met through assembly programs. Below are suggested
some kinds of resource persons of real value to appropriate
learning programs of the school:

Early settler to describe pioneer days, changes in the community,
contrasts between old and new in home life, school methods, customs, beliefs.

Recreation Director to analyze community recreation, to solicit
and instruct volunteer workers, to correlate school and community
recreational programs.

Public Health Nurse to discuss health in the community, build
wholesome attitudes toward the public health program, solicit cooperation in specific health projects, advise on school health problems.

City Manager to explain functions of government, local civic
problems.

Community Council members to interpret the function of the
Council and explain its plans for improving community living.

Conservation officer to show movies and discuss reforestation, soil
erosion control, plant diseases, conserving wild life, how schools
can cooperate in the conservation program.

Red Cross worker to explain the services rendered by the organization, to organize a Junior Red Cross program, to teach classes in first aid, home nursing, child care, nutrition.

Clergymen to describe social services of the churches and synagogues, to analyze community problems, to solicit volunteer workers for community projects in social welfare.

Theater manager to talk about film selection, how to appreciate motion pictures, how movie equipment works, new developments in motion picture making, outstanding movies.

Librarian to discuss services of the county or city library, new books of interest to the group, how to use the library; to tell stories and interest children in the library story hour; to discuss the work of a librarian.

Newspaper editor to describe how news is gathered and how a newspaper is printed; to discuss what makes a good newspaper, advertising, vocations in the field of journalism, how to read a newspaper.

Farmers, dairymen, fruitgrowers, agricultural workers to analyze problems related to farming and country life.

Industrialists to discuss technical processes, relation of industries to the community, labor policies.

Labor organizers to explain problems of the worker, reasons for organizing, social security, government and labor; to describe the work they do; to explain training required for unskilled, semiskilled, skilled, and technical workers.

Business people to talk about prices, distribution problems, wise buying, cooperatives, merchandising.

Scientific workers to talk about scientific processes, the scientific and social significance of their labor.

Social workers to discuss actual cases, types of aid available, the Social Security Act, social service as a career.

Director of an employment office to describe the activities of the office, shortages and surpluses of labor, movement of workers between areas and industries.

Safety Council Director or Fire Chief to discuss and demonstrate safety measures.

Hobbyists to show collections, dances, animal-training, and the like, and to discuss recreational and avocational hobby interests.

Special-event speakers for Brotherhood Week, United Nations Day, Book Week, I-am-an-American Day, and the like.

Friendly, direct-contact experiences like these can do much to make a school program really meaningful, even gripping, to many children and young people of all ages. For this technique:

• **Helps students realize** that people as well as books are desirable sources of information and inspiration.
• **Creates better understanding** of many different types of people, and helps students identify themselves with other people and their problems.
• **Promotes social experiences** shared by youth and adults to their mutual interest and satisfaction, thereby increasing the respect of each age group for the other.
• **Provides opportunity for developing social skills** in real life situations—letter writing, telephoning, making introductions, receiving guests, carrying on a conversation, interviewing, listening attentively, leading discussions.
• **Allows adults to learn, through their own experience,** what modern teachers are trying to do for, and with, students.

How Can Classroom Visitors Best Be Utilized?

When the class feels the need for some outside assistance it is time for the class group and the teacher together to do some exploratory planning. What kind of resource visitor is needed to meet the situation? Who is available? Who is most suitable in terms of his background and the maturity levels of the group? Should he be invited to come to the school, or would an interview in his own locale be better? What are the problems of advance arrangements, transportation, and the like? Answers to these and similar queries should of course be readily available in the school's directory of community resources as described in Chapter 13.

Preparing for the Visitor

In the planning stage the class and teacher working together might well follow such steps as these:

• **Specify the Need.** Discuss such questions as why an outside person is needed at this point in the class work, how his general area of competence fits into the class program, what he would be likely to contribute to the group's understanding,

interests, and skills. Decide just what should be found out from
the expected visitor. Decide whom to invite by first consulting
the community resources' directory and then by canvassing the
group for further suggestions. Formulate some questions for
the desired visitor, and perhaps choose different members of
the class to ask them and note the answers when the time
comes.

• **Plan the Form of Presentation.** This might be an exhibit
and informal talk, a demonstration with explanations, a panel
discussion, a luncheon meeting with planned conversation, a
formal talk followed by questions, an interview before the
class, an illustrated talk, or the like.

• **Extend the Invitation.** This should be done well in advance. If an invitation is accepted orally, it should be con-
firmed in writing as soon as possible. Be sure to tell the invited
person about the group and about the arrangements made and
desired: age level; subject field; number of students; date,
time, and place of meeting; any needed traveling instructions;
length of time for the meeting; name of person in charge, and
names and positions of any other participants in the program;
a statement of the group's major purpose or need for the occas-
sion; and, in some circumstances, a list of the questions which
will be asked by the class.

• **Make School Arrangements.** Special rooms, projectors
and screens, maps, tables, and so on, may be needed; if so,
be sure they will be ready at the proper time and place. Plan
where, when, and how to receive the guest at the school, and
also for any necessary entertainment after the class session if
the visitor does not plan to leave the school or the town immediately. Choose a chairman and a recorder if desired by the
group. The recorder's function is to write a factual account of
the meeting as it progresses, noting the most important events
or ideas. It is generally better to have one person or a small
committee act as recorder since a better summary is likely to
result and the group as a whole can give undivided attention
to the speaker. Decide also how to thank the guest afterward.

Appreciation may be expressed by applause, orally by the chairman for the group, in later conversation, by letter, or by a combination of these ways.

• **Check All Arrangements the Day Before the Visit.** Remind the speaker by letter or telephone call, and be sure that all needed equipment and services will be ready on time. Agree upon standards of behavior to be observed such as paying careful attention, participating as opportunity develops, being responsible if one has been asked to arrange the room, to telephone, greet the guest, serve as chairman, or perform any other needed function in the program. All such group planning provides both motivation and meaning for the experience itself.

The Visit

At appropriate times, the activities already planned by the group should be carried out by them. This will involve meeting and welcoming the visitor, and being thoughtful of his wraps, his desire for last-minute grooming, and his wish to see the room before he talks in it. Before introducing him to the group, be sure you know enough about his background and accomplishments to make a personalized introduction. Be very sure to pronounce his name clearly and correctly. After the talk or other presentation, escort the visitor to the exit from the building, or to whatever further entertainment has been planned for him.

• **Be Ever Conscious of Public Relations.** Students should be fully aware that such a visit is more than an educational experience for themselves; it is also a venture in public relations on the part of the school. The care with which they plan, their cordiality and receptiveness, their participation, the use they make of the experience in the school and in the community—all such factors will surely impress the lay visitor for good or ill, and will mould his opinion of both the character and effectiveness of the entire school.

Interpreting the Experience

As soon as possible after the visit, the teacher and students together should analyze the value of the experience, decide upon next steps, and record their impressions in some tangible form. The group's planning should be appraised, as well as the guest's contribution and the participation of the students.

• **Plan Appropriate Follow-up.** Opportunities for constructive follow-up activities in classroom, school, and community should be explored, and plans made while enthusiasm is still strong. Some record of the speaker with a general evaluation should be placed in the community resource file, and a description of the whole experience might well be written for class use and for publicity purposes.

Through such a process, the resource visitor's contribution is better understood and appreciated by the class, and is more likely to lead into further educational activities. Frequently the outside person stimulates the group to creative participation in community processes, or perhaps provides some entrée into local activities. The alert teacher will capitalize to the full upon all such opportunities.

How Should the Outside Interview Be Managed?

In every community there are many people whose experiences, interests, knowledge, hobbies, viewpoints, or accomplishments would add much to school learning, yet who for one reason or another cannot be brought into the classroom as resource visitors. They may, however, be interviewed in their own homes, places of work, or other community locales. The interview technique is especially good in giving students a personalized view of community living and of some of the values and ends to which selected residents would direct youthful attention. Through their eyes, and in man-to-man informality, young people may come to see community processes in operation; with these adults they may explore and assess local human relations. The interview also provides for fine experi-

RESOURCE PERSON EVALUATION FORMS

PITTSBURGH PUBLIC SCHOOLS

Division of Guidance and Child Accounting

PROGRAM EVALUATION

School_____ Date of Program_____

Speaker_____ Representing_____

Subject_____

Number in Group_____ Check (Boys _____
                                         (Girls _____
                                         (Both _____

Evaluation: Superior_____ Good_____ Fair_____

Suggestions for Improvement:_____

_____

Other Comments_____

_____

_____

                                   _____
                                        Signed

In Pittsburgh, the teacher's report goes to Guidance and Child Accounting

STRICTLY
CONFIDENTIAL

Name ....

Collection or Information ....

....

Grade.. Size of Group.............................

Quality of Presentation ....

Adequacy of Collection or Information ....

....

Other Remarks ....

....

_____   _____
        School   Teacher

Please send this card to Director of Instruction and Guidance
RESOURCE FILE EVALUATION—THE PUBLIC SCHOOLS—MONTCLAIR, N. J.

*In Montclair, New Jersey, the report goes to Instruction and
Guidance*

ence in meeting people, itself an important social skill. The child or adolescent who has talked successfully with a mature person about matters of common concern has himself advanced toward maturity in that experience.

"Interviews" are informal personal conferences wherein one or more students question an adult to get authoritative opinion or information of some sort. As a method of community study, the interview technique is similar to that of using resource people. It nevertheless differs from it in two notable respects: (a) the interview is held in the expert's usual place of work or residence, rather than in the school classroom, and (b) the interview is primarily a question-and-answer procedure; it does not require of the interviewee a prepared talk, demonstration, or other type of organized program. The interview, in short, uses resource people for educational purposes, but does so under somewhat different conditions from those involved in bringing resource visitors into the classroom.

The values of an interview are matched by its dangers, none the less real because they are complex, elusive, hard to observe. Illustrative of what may happen is the case of one interview in which a thoughtless and prejudiced adult belabored a pupil with his personal animosity toward the school administration. That pupil's adjustment to society was definitely retarded by that act. Of equal misfortune is the case of another interview in which one student's bumptious aggressiveness was considerably increased by the indulgent pampering of an easy-going adult sentimentalist.

If interviews are to be really profitable so far as the pupils' growth toward maturity and sensitivity to the community are concerned, they must be carefully developed on an individual basis by a teacher who is alert to the personality characteristics of both interviewers and interviewee, and who can therefore sensibly match the personalities involved.

It is taken for granted that no student should be sent out for very many interviews of a formal character, and that no adult will have his time and energy exhausted by the arrival of too many interviewers. As with all educational techniques, the program of interviews must be administered guardedly.

Preparing for the Interview

When definite need for expert outside aid is felt and the resolve taken to seek it through interview, the class should cooperatively determine the purpose and decide whom it wishes to interview. If the problem in question is a controversial one, be sure that all viewpoints are represented in the interview program as a whole. Do not allow a situation to develop in which a minority opinion goes unheard. When these decisions have been made, the next steps follow.

• **Learn All You Can About the Interviewee.** If pertinent, worth-while questions are to be framed for him, the interviewing committee must be aware in advance of his general experience and specific responsibilities. Such information is essential for a second reason also: it provides a basis for knowing what is "common ground" and hence enables the interview itself to get off to a good start.

• **Analyze the Qualities of a Good Interview.** The student goes not merely to listen, but to converse; he must therefore have in mind the questions he wants answered—including questions or comments which are intended to bridge awkward gaps and halts in the interview—and should, if possible, have something definite to contribute to the conversation from the school itself. There should be tentative decision as to how many students shall participate in the interview; the form in which it is to be recorded; whether notes are to be taken during the interview or subsequent to it; how the interview is to be terminated.

• **Decide What Questions to Ask.** All questions should reflect sober thought. They should relate to significant aspects of the work or experience of the person to be interviewed, and must never be superficial or malicious. When decided upon in final form, the questions should be typed in triplicate, the original copy for the interviewee, and carbon copies for the committee chairman and the class librarian.

•   **Designate an Interview Committee.** This committee should be composed of three or four class members, and should include a chairman and a reporter. The latter's function is to write up the interview after it has been held; he should do this as an objective reporter of questions asked and answers returned. No part of his responsibility in writing will have to do with interpretation; his job is that of recording what happened.

•   **Make Initial Contact with the Interviewee.** Unless the students are quite mature, it is wise for the teacher to make first contact with the citizen to be interviewed. This contact will preferably be through personal interview by appointment, although a telephone call or letter may be sufficient in some cases. The purpose of this teacher's initial contact is to acquaint the interviewee with the objectives of the project, and to be sure that he is willing to cooperate with it. After that the chairman and one other member of the committee should call upon the interviewee in person. They should outline the general purpose of the interview, and then explain what the full committee would like to talk about when they come. A copy of the questions listed by the class should be given to him, and a time for the full committee interview arranged.

•   **Make Travel Arrangements.** A public conveyance is preferable for travel because of the safety hazard involved in the use of private machines (see Chapter 14). Determine the time needed for the committee to get to the interview location, and then add fifteen minutes to allow for those unforeseen delays which are always probable.

•   **Emphasize Good Behavior.** The group should anticipate that people will ask what school they represent—either because the committee members are crude, loud, and boisterous, or because they appear to be well-mannered and quiet. Of such impressions is a school's public reputation made, and of this fact the class as a whole should be fully aware.

These steps should all be taken well in advance of the day set for the interview proper. Although casual and unplanned interviews may occasionally be highly successful, continuously good results require conscious and careful planning of every predictable detail.

Conducting the Interview

When the committee arrives at the interview point, the chairman should be the spokesman stating the business of the group. Good social sense on the part of the other committee members is also important. The group should stay together, and not monopolize an outer office while waiting for the interviewee. Boys' hats should be removed. Voices should be softened. Members should be seated, if possible.

When the committee is invited in to begin the interview, the chairman should first introduce each member of the committee individually, then state briefly the purpose of the visit. Here is where understanding of the interviewee's background, responsibilities, and interests bear fruit. Tactful mention and brief discussion of interests held in common help to clear the psychological atmosphere and stimulate good will.

• **Give Full Attention.** Busy persons have no wish to talk with students who exhibit slight interest in their conversation. This is not to suggest that committee members should react in starry-eyed amazement to everything that is said, but only that outward signs of interest, sympathy, and understanding should always be shown.

• **Make No Attempt to Dominate the Situation.** Let the interviewee talk as he wishes without interruption and without disagreement. Seek to understand *his* view, whatever it may be, and to draw him out in exposition of it. Listen as much for what he does not say as for what he does.

• **Take Notes Only as Needed.** The mechanics of note-taking during an interview should be of such nature as not to

hamper the psychological freedom of the person being interviewed. Two or three words jotted down for each major point
may be enough at the moment; these reminders can be expanded in detail as soon as the interview is over.

• **Ask Questions Intelligently.** The person being interviewed may or may not use the set of questions previously
given him. The committee will have to adjust its interview to his
decision in this matter. In any case, the chairman should have
his list of questions before him in order to be sure that the
ground covered by those questions is not ignored. All committee members should be certain they do not ask questions that
have already been answered; for to do so wastes time and
clearly indicates a discourteous lack of attention. If questions
come to mind which do not appear on the prepared list, they
should be interjected at transition points in the interview, not
simply thrown out in a hit-or-miss fashion.

• **Conclude the Interview.** The committee should be very
careful not to outstay its welcome. When the chairman feels
that the ground has been covered, or when the interviewee
indicates by some sign or mannerism that he has finished, the
chairman should express appreciation in behalf of the committee and the whole class, and then lead the group out of the
room.

• **Expand the Notes Taken.** As quickly as possible after
the interview, each committee member should expand his
brief notes into full form. The sooner this documentary record
is made the better, for notes rapidly become "cold" and even
unintelligible as the vivid memory of the immediate experience
begins to fade.

Interpreting the Interview Experience

Although the interview has been concluded, the committee
now has the further responsibility of organizing its findings
and reporting them to the class as a whole. It should therefore,
as soon as possible, engage in several significant follow-up
activities, as follows:

• **Reconstruct the Interview.** The committee should meet as a group to decide just what was said in the interview. The official reporter might well summarize aloud the substance of the interview, thus permitting other members to check him and each other upon such items as figures and dates, as well as upon less specific factors noted.

Having reached a measure of agreement as to what the interviewee actually said, the committee is now ready for analysis and interpretation. What is the real significance of the remarks made? Were the ideas of the interviewee guarded in their expression? Was he holding anything back? Was he on the defensive? Was he seeking converts to his point of view? Was there anything peculiar about his situation which may minimize the worth of his opinion? Such are the types of queries to be asked within the group. Before beginning analysis of this nature, however, students should be warned that usually there are several sides to any question, with consequent possibility that even varied interpretations of it may be equally correct. Dogmatism and pat definitions are both unscientific and dangerous.

• **Record the Data.** After the committee has thus summarized and interpreted the interview, it should proceed to make a written record of its findings. The reporter may be expected to write out a summary statement; when completed this should be submitted to the committee as a whole for checking of questions asked, answers given, and figures included. Committee members should not hesitate to suggest needed improvements in grammar, sequence, or construction. After the report has thus been corrected and approved, it should be put in permanent form and deposited in the class or school library, museum, or social studies laboratory. Such reports, if properly annotated and permanently filed, may add richly to a school collection suitable for laboratory study and comparison in subsequent years.

• **Report to the Class.** At the appointed time, a formal, oral report should be given by the committee to the class it represents. All committee members should share in making this report. Attention should be focused upon specific purpose of the interview, questions asked, answers given, general findings, conclusions, and interpretations. If the committee's opinion upon any of these areas is not unanimous, both majority and minority reports should be presented for further analysis by the entire class. In any event, full class discussion of the committee report should be encouraged.

Significant Avenue

Through such procedures, the essential contributions of the resource person will best be defined, clarified, and perpetuated for the class and the school. This technique thus takes its place as another significant avenue of realistic, life-centered education.

Learning Activities

Discussion Topics

1. What measures might the school take to avoid the over-use of willing resource people?
2. Is it desirable to assign certain resource people to definite subject fields and grade levels?
3. If not, how can you avoid duplication of resource persons in a given student's experience?
4. Should resource people be expected to donate their services?

Group Activities

1. Send a committee to interview the local superintendent of schools concerning the field trip and resource visitor program operating in that system. Report to the class, with recommendations.
2. Divide the class into small committees for field interviews with leaders of labor organizations, better business bureaus, child placement agencies, historical associations, religious organizations, and the like. Plan interview purposes and techniques beforehand, and analyze their effectiveness afterward.
3. Develop some criteria by which your school might decide which

of the many possible resource people should and should not be used by the school.

4. Have a committee bring before the class a resource person in the field of community resources, using and evaluating the steps suggested in this chapter.

5. How can a teacher help students understand their role in building good public relations in interview situations?

Individual Projects

1. Chapter 13 reproduces record cards used to catalog resource people. After examining these, choose one, or devise your own, for future use.

2. Compile an extensive list of possible resource people appropriate to your teaching grade level or subject field. Annotate the list briefly.

3. Take any unit of work useful to you and show specifically how certain resource people might advantageously be included in it.

4. Write an article telling how a particular school might feasibly go about developing an organized resource person program.

Learning Materials

Ways of utilizing resource persons in the classroom have been vividly portrayed in *Fifty Teachers to a Classroom* (Macmillan, 1951), a pamphlet prepared by the Metropolitan School Study Council which describes plans used in various schools for finding and bringing into the classroom many resource people. Olsen's *School and Community Programs* (Prentice-Hall, 1949) gives Chapter 4 to fifteen dramatic case studies of "Resource Visitors and Interviews." A browse through the following magazine articles will also prove richly rewarding:

"Use of Community Resources in Rural Schools," Inga E. Brown. Vivid account of how early settlers, immigrants, state officials, and so on, may be utilized as stimulating resource visitors. *Social Education* 5:520-524; November 1941.

"Forgotten Men and Women," Paul J. Misner. Resource people of great value live in every community and work in every school. Suggests who they may be and how they can enrich children's education. *Progressive Education* 19:18-20; January 1942.

"City Council Comes to Wilbur Wright Junior High School," Clarence Killmer. Six council members came as resource people, told of their civic activities, and answered questions. *Social Education* 12:305-306; November 1948.

"Retailers Make Good Professors," Glen Rice. Explains how a college "raids Main Street" to secure teachers for many business-education courses. *Business Education World* 24:272-273; January 1949.

"Everybody's School," Andre Fontaine. Vividly describes one high school's program for using resource visitors frequently and well. *National Parent-Teacher* 44:10-13; September 1949.

"Community's Career Night," John Caffrey. Describes a vocational guidance plan using lay people. The ten steps taken to organize the program are listed. *California Journal of Secondary Education* 24:399-401; November 1949.

"Play Fair with the Resource Citizen," Ben Sweeney. Warns against abusing the willingness of resource people to help in the school, and suggests safeguards for them. *Nation's Schools* 44:43-44; December 1949.

"Parents Utilized in the Curriculum," Lowell W. Beach. Tells how a junior high school uses special talents of its pupils' parents on an extensive scale in many courses. *Clearing House* 24:342-343; February 1950.

"Careers Day: Community-Planned at Hamilton High," John C. Fry. Explains how the school faculty and the business and professional leaders of the community cooperatively organize the annual Careers Day. *Clearing House* 25:153-156; November 1950.

"Guest Speakers within the Classroom," Sarah L. Miller. Tells how a ninth-grade social studies class uses resource visitors from many fields to vitalize their study of current problems. *Ohio Schools* 28:413; December 1950, also in *Education Digest* 16:32-33; April 1951.

"Will You Walk into My Classroom?", Bess B. Lane. Describes the activities of one school in encouraging parent visitation. *Childhood Education* 28:249-252; February 1952.

"Using the Community's Human Resources," Vernon Hicks. Reproduces resource persons' survey blank, covering letters to parents, and card form used in one community. *National Elementary Principal* 32:122-125; September 1952.

Values and techniques of field interviews by students are likewise suggested in a number of excellent articles. Be sure to see also Spencer Brown's *They See for Themselves* (Harper, 1945), a stirring account in small-book form of how high school students interviewed community lay people to get needed intercultural information.

"Interviewing for English Classes," Ward S. Miller. Step-by-step procedures in arranging, conducting, and writing up an interview are described. *English Journal* 26:18-22; January 1937.

"Interviewing in Social Research: Basic Problems of the First Field Trip," J. E. Hulett, Jr. Practical suggestions, especially designed for the social interviewer going into a new community to interview local residents. *Social Forces* 16:358-366; March 1938.

"Real Interviews for High-School Seniors," C. W. Willis and R. C. Henley. Explains a program whereby all interested students may interview local business executives concerning employment-interview techniques. *Clearing House* 14:464-466; April 1940.

"Interviews with Celebrated Persons Motivate English," Alta McAffee. A technique through which fully prepared, eighth-grade student teams successfully interview celebrities who appear on local music-lecture programs. *English Journal* 31:323-325; March 1942.

"Personal Interview as a Method of Utilizing Community Resources," Leonard Gernant. Reports a five-year experiment in the use of the interview in vocational guidance. *Educational Administration and Supervision* 30:415-423; October 1944.

"Using the Interview to Understand Judaism," Albert R. Brinkman. World history students interviewed a rabbi to understand better such topics as the differences between Judaism and Christianity, the principles of Zionism, and so forth. *Social Studies* 38:102-104; March 1947.

"Five Steps to Minneapolis' Senior Job Conference," Margaret E. Andrews. Explains in detail how vocational guidance conferences are arranged for students with successful, interested adults in their own places of work. *Clearing House* 22:334-338; February 1948.

"Interview Helps the Student," Louise R. Grover. Outlines plans for interviews as an English assignment with government officials, editors, judges, union officials, zoo manager, and the like, each to be followed by oral and written reports of findings. *English Journal* 37:85-88; February 1948; also in *Education Digest* 13:40-42; April 1948.

"Intensive Interviewing in Community Research," Floyd Dotson. Describes motivations of people in the community who will or will not consent to be interviewed; suggests how the interviewer can best secure cooperation. *Journal of Educational Sociology* 27:225-30; January 1954.

"Planning the Career Day Program," Charles R. Foster and Robert O. Stripling. Specific planning and programs are described. *School Executive* 73:74-77; March 1954.

Motion Pictures

Community Resources in Teaching. Although chiefly concerned with the technique of the field trip, the film shows also the values of using resource visitors in the classroom. Iowa State University, 1950, 20 minutes.

CHAPTER **8**

Field Trips

Every American community, however small or isolated, is a microcosm of western civilization, since within its own borders go on the essential processes of living. That is why every school can richly extend its curriculum by utilizing local resources through experiences—and perhaps by going further afield to explore selected aspects of its region, the nation, and even countries abroad. Although field trips have many non-academic values, their major purpose is instructional, and as such, they are not to be identified with school trips taken to participate in athletic, musical, or forensic contests, with hikes or picnics organized for pleasure purposes, or with sightseeing journeys taken by graduating classes. None of these activities can properly be called a field trip.

The term "field trip" is commonly used to designate any organized visit to points outside the classroom, taken by school people as an integral part of their academic work, and primarily for educational purposes. It may consist of anything from a walk around the school building to a trip around the world.

Field trips or study tours may relate directly to the study of social processes such as sharing in citizenship, making a living, maintaining health, enjoying beauty, and the like. They are also major approaches to the study of social problems such

This chapter is by CHARLES UGER and JOHN ROTHSCHILD.

as housing, intergroup relations, old-age security, and waste of natural resources. Trips and tours may prove just as useful in conventional academic fields such as art, geography, history, nature study, science, and vocational guidance. The better traditional schools as well as all community schools make wide and constant use of the field trip. And such schools are making more and more use of extended study tours.

The motivating reasons behind a given field trip may be varied, but it is probable that among them one or more of the following are predominant: securing information, changing attitudes, awakening interests, developing appreciations, promoting ideals, enjoying new experiences. All, of course, may be significant goals or by-products of the field experience.

Some excellent field trips may require only a few minutes of time, as when a class goes into the school yard after a heavy rain to observe the effects of small-scale erosion. Other trips will require a full class period, several hours, or perhaps an entire day. Longer trips, involving one or more overnight stops, are usually called field studies, study tours, or educational field study. Such longer tours combine the essential elements of an extended trip and a survey; that is, they take the group out of its home environment and into a new one for purposes of serious field analysis over a period of time. Such a study may last from several days to several months; its geographic area may be local, regional, national, or international; it may work in one community, or it may travel thousands of miles. The members of the group work, learn, and generally live together.

Although a field trip may properly include opportunity to "see the sights," it should never be mere sight-seeing. Whereas genuine field study measures up to academic standards in definition of subject matter and rigor of methods, the sight-seeing excursion rushes from place to place, its members absorbing sensory impressions largely devoid of intellectual or emotional substance. Too often, sight-seeing trips masquerade as "education," and too often teachers are accessory to that deception.

How Does the Field Trip Prove Its Worth?

Firsthand acquaintance with varied natural and social phenomena is an essential aspect of realistic education in any field. Field trips:

• **Stimulate imagination and learning** by providing sensory perceptions which cannot otherwise be experienced—the taste of fresh milk, the odor of wild flowers, the roar of machinery, the heat of a steel mill, the sight of real things in the real world of adults.

• **Deepen insight into even familiar phenomena** in the environment, for as these matters are freshly interpreted, they take on new meaning. No one really knows his own environment and his own neighbors until he has compared them with something different.

• **Integrate classroom instruction** by exposing the artificiality of conventional subject matter divisions, and by enabling pupils to view facts and forces as they exist in their everyday relationships in living communities.

• **Arouse student interest** in new areas of thought and activity, thereby often leading to further reading and field explorations outside of school. Such personal exploration and discovery utilizes natural curiosity, and thus develops the best motivation for school work.

• **Treat students and teacher as complete personalities.** The limited and somewhat hierarchical relations of the classroom are discarded. The teacher is no longer merely an instructor; he is now also parent, companion, arbiter. Students are no longer detached from their backgrounds; it is now as though they have moved into the classroom, bag and baggage.

• **Teach the art of living with others.** The day-in-and-day-out association—traveling in the same conveyances, sharing rooms, sitting at the same table, participating in the same experiences, getting deadly tired together—is not without strains and stresses. Idiosyncrasies and character defects come to the surface; so also do traits of nobility. The purpose of field study is to focus attention upon the outside world, but in the business of living and working intensively with others, the student also gets under his own microscope. Insight is developed and character built.

• **Expand emotional and intellectual horizons** by making us acquainted with people whose manners, customs, living standards, outlooks, and interests may be quite different from our own.

Planning the Field Trip

"Going places and seeing things" is an educational technique of prime significance—providing always that it is used with care, discrimination, and intelligent foresight. Always there should be the closest interrelation between technical travel arrangements and curricular and social programs. One does not first do the travel planning and then the program, or vice versa. The planning must be one indivisible process: travel arrangements are naturally shaped to the purposes of the trip and the curricular and social programs by which those purposes are to be achieved; on the other hand, curricular and social arrangements may be modified by exigencies of a technical nature, and often plans of either a technical or non-technical nature have to be revised more than once before the preparations for the trip are completed. Following are the principal things to be considered in preparing for either a limited field trip or an extended study tour.

Plan Democratically

Student participation in planning is the first step in making the trip democratic. It may be simpler for the teacher by himself to define the objectives, formulate the program, and make the travel arrangements. But a trip which in its inception is authoritarian will not be democratic in execution. If students share responsibility for decisions, they can also be expected to share responsibility for carrying them out.

Democratic planning does not imply an unrealistic division of labor between teacher and students. There are some things which the teacher can do best, and these he should do. Example: It is desirable that someone visit in advance the various locations of the field course in order to learn essential facts and make necessary arrangements. Obviously, the teacher is the one to do this. In such cases, the democratic principle will be served if the problem has been thoroughly discussed in class and the teacher goes as the representative of the group.

Everything depends upon the teacher or group leader. The better he gets along with others and the more he knows about the subject to be investigated, the greater is the likelihood of the trip's success. Yet character and temperament are more important than specific knowledge or experience. The teacher best qualified to conduct a field trip is student-centered in his thinking, has administrative ability, and is truly democratic in his human relationships both with students and with adults, regardless of their race, color, creed, nationality background, or social-economic status.

Determine Purpose and Locale

The next need is to decide the type of trip to be made. Shall it seek to secure information, arouse new interests, awaken deeper appreciations, develop sensitivities, combine some or all of these elements? Should it concentrate on some specific social process or problem, or seek a more generalized base? Is it to be carried on in the local community, elsewhere in the region or in the nation, or outside in foreign lands? Each of these fundamental queries must be answered in terms of many factors inherent in the needs, interests, and purposes of the particular group.

It is important that every pupil, as well as the teacher, become fully aware of just *why* this particular trip is being planned, and of *how* it relates to his own classroom experiences and activities. General group discussion is excellent in this connection.

The determination of locale can be made with relative ease if the field trip is to be in the local community, or even elsewhere in the United States where advance data is readily obtainable. But deciding where to go abroad is much more difficult. A group planning a public housing study in Europe, for instance, will probably be unable to gather the requisite preliminary information from American sources. The best plan would be to establish connections with some competent

European organization. But doing that is not easy, and consultation at such long range takes considerable time. In such cases, the services of an educational travel agency may become essential.

The most fruitful field trips in the United States are those which concentrate on a specific topic or focus on a local community. But since the concentration of interest which is possible at home can hardly be expected abroad, it is obvious that the general cultural tour and the general overview curriculum are both more popular and usually more desirable for the foreign locale—especially for those taking their first trip outside the United States. Such generalized field studies offer valuable learning experiences, providing they do not cover too much ground, are built on contacts with people, and penetrate below the sight-seeing level on which most tourists pursue their way smoothly, comfortably, and in almost perfect isolation from the life around them.

The specific study, on the other hand, offers superior advantages to those who already possess a general background derived from previous travel, and to those whose special interests are already sharply defined, whether or not they have already been abroad.

Study the Field in Advance

Intellectual preparation is essential before any field trip is actually undertaken. Teacher and students alike need to study the problem at hand in order that they may possess sufficient background to make the excursion itself really meaningful. Relevant documentary materials should be utilized by the teacher, by individual pupils, by committees, or by the class as a whole, and all worthwhile information found may be shared with the group through reports, panel analyses, or in general discussion. Appropriate audio-visual aids may also be used, both for initial motivation and for general orientation to what will be seen on the trip itself. In these and other similar ways central issues should be identified, basic problems recognized, and major purposes further clarified and made specific.

Best results will be obtained if the teacher goes over the entire itinerary in advance. This is essential so that he may be thoroughly familiar with the best route, bus stops, parking facilities, provisions for guide service, things to be seen and done by the group, aspects or phases of the resource center to be stressed or ignored, eating and toilet arrangements, time needed at each stage of the trip, special safety hazards, and similar factors. Through such preliminary observations, the teacher can also determine the best sequence in which various centers may be visited on a single trip.

Even if an extended tour is planned it is desirable that the tour leader visit the locations of the course and make arrangements on the spot. This does not mean that the teacher has to interview everyone who is to participate in the program. The purpose of such a reconnaissance is achieved if it enables the teacher to survey the resources and to find competent local people, to work out the general plan with them, and to convey to them his point of view and its requirements. The detailed planning can be carried forward from that point by correspondence between the teacher and those whom he has chosen to work with in the local communities to be visited.

Plan the Curricular Program

A good field study has coherence, deals with live material, and is arranged with an eye to dramatic development. Planning the program involves knowing the needs, resources, and capacities of the group. And the more the students know about the study subject in advance, the greater will be their zeal and achievement in the field. Students should therefore be given background and overview by means of orientation talks and through assigned reading. It may be worthwhile to get them to do preparatory individual or group research, and to share their findings with the rest of the group. In any event, maps showing political, economic, cultural, and demographic factors should be fully utilized.

Individual and committee assignments may be desirable—such as questioning, taking notes, photographing, collecting specimens, keeping a "log," and the like. While careful advance preparation is always essential, it should not be made in too great detail; room should always be left for some surprises and for the thrill of personal exploration and discovery in the field.

Make Necessary Arrangements

[The following sections, pages 213-229, deal with arrangements required for field trips of less than one day's duration. For help in planning longer tours, see pages 229-243.]

Cooperative planning of the trip itself is now in order. Class committees or the whole group should work with the teacher to arrange as many of the following details as are relevant in the particular situation:

• **Secure administrative consent for the trip.** Your building principal must give his consent well in advance. If your school has a well-organized community resources program, you will probably use such a request form as those shown on pages 214-216, and may receive a confirmation form like those on page 217.

• **Invite a few helpful parents.** Be sure they understand what is planned and how they can best assist the project. Let them be present at the preparatory class sessions.

• **Secure permission to visit the chosen centers of interest.** How approach their officials? A telephoned request is easy to make, and equally easy to refuse. A letter is somewhat better, but it, too, may easily be refused or neglected. A personal visit will accomplish more, yet it is costly in time and effort. Best of all approaches is a personal introduction by an interested third party—an influential parent, business executive, civic organization secretary, or the like.

• **Complete all necessary business arrangements** with the proper officials involved—with executives, speakers, auditorium managers, transportation companies, and so forth.

• **Arrange with hosts and speakers for a definite schedule** and sequence of events, and for specific time limits on their talks and

FIELD TRIP REQUEST FORMS

School—————————————— Date——————————

To Field Trip Office:

Please arrange a field trip to:

Grades———————————— Number of Pupils——————————

Date———————————— Day—M T W Th F   Time——————

Method of transportation: (check ✓)

    Chartered bus   ☐   Chartered Streetcar   ☐

    Regular streetcar or bus ☐   Within walking distance ☐

Names of teachers who will accompany group:——————————————

I have indicated on the back of this card the pupil's educational interests which this trip may further.

Teacher ———————————————— Principal ————————————

FIELD TRIP REQUEST

878 (ZM 9-49) Vocational School Print Shop

MINNEAPOLIS PUBLIC SCHOOLS
VISUAL EDUCATION

Minneapolis

BOARD OF EDUCATION
of the
CITY OF ST. LOUIS
Department of Instruction

APPLICATION FOR EDUCATIONAL FIELD TRIP
(To be submitted in duplicate — separate applications must be submitted for each room)

School..Date ....

Approval for the following educational field trip by pupils and teacher is requested:

Room .... Grade ...... No. of Pupils ...... Destination ....

Date .... Time: Departure from School........................ Return to School ....

The primary purpose of this trip is to help achieve the objectives of the Course of Study for the

....Area by—

....

....

(over)

Type of transportation to be used: ....

Approved:

....
Teacher

....
Principal

....   To be signed by the principal or by the teacher
Assistant Superintendent   and principal.

Form IN-15 July '50 5040

St. Louis

FIELD TRIP REQUEST FORM

EDUCATIONAL EXCURSIONS DENVER PUBLIC SCHOOLS · Department of Special Services

STUDY PLAN

School.. Grade............ No. of pupils.............. Date.....................

Place to be visited...

Date of visit.. Length of visit...

Purpose of excursion...

List what you have done to prepare pupils for the excursion:

1. ....

2. ....

3. ....

List plans you have prepared for evaluation:

1. ....

2. ....

3. ....

BUS REQUEST

School.. Grade............ No. of pupils.............. Date.....................

Place to be visited...

Address...

Name of official granting permission for visit...

Date bus needed..

Time bus to call at school for pupils...A.M ....P.M

Time bus to call at place visited to return pupils to school....................A.M. .............P.M.

Bus requested by.., Teacher

Request approved by.., Principal

Denver

FIELD TRIP REQUEST FORM

Form 78.30—1521 Sets—1-48
To be made out in Quintuplicate.
Original, Duplicate, Triplicate, and Quadruplicate
to Pupil Transportation Office,
Business Division.
Remove carbons before forwarding.

Original

LOS ANGELES CITY BOARD OF EDUCATION

APPLICATION FOR SCHOOL JOURNEY AND/OR USE OF SCHOOL BUS

Date...........................

SCHOOL...........................

TEACHER IN CHARGE OF GROUP...........................

DESTINATION OF GROUP...........................

ADDRESS...........................

NUMBER OF PUPILS...........GRADES...............NUMBER OF TEACHERS...........

NUMBER OF BUSES DESIRED...........................

DATE OF TRIP ....
DAY   DATE

SCHEDULE:

LEAVE SCHOOL	ARRIVE AT DESTINATION	LEAVE DESTINATION	RETURN TO SCHOOL
A.M.	A.M.	A.M.	A.M.
P.M.	P.M.	P.M.	P.M.

UNIT OF INSTRUCTION...........................

I HAVE THE SIGNED FORM 34 EH 17 "PARENT'S REQUEST" FOR ALL PUPILS IN THE ABOVE GROUP...........

METHOD OF TRANSPORTATION: SCHOOL BUS...........................WALKING...........

COMMENTS...........................

SIGNED...........................
PRINCIPAL

Do Not Fill Out Below This Line

APPLICATION FOR APPROVAL AS A SPECIAL TRIP

Estimated Cost...........................

☐ Approved   ☐ Denied

ASSISTANT SUPERINTENDENT

Date Bus Scheduled...........................

Date confirmation sent to school...........................

Date confirmation sent to firm...........................

Application No...........................

Four copies of this are made and sent by the clearing house to the place to be visited, the school involved, the Pupil Transportation Office and the Business Division.

TRIP CONFIRMATION FORMS

COMMUNITY RESOURCE

Arrangements have been completed for your trip to

_____

_____. The bus will be at your building

at_____ to pick up your group and will return by

_____.

The person you will contact is_____.

I hope you have a profitable trip.

Bernadine Batters

Vancouver (Washington)

To_____
        Teacher   School   Date

We have scheduled the field trip you have requested as follows:

_____
Place   Time of Starting

M T W Th F _____
              Date   Time of Returning

Number of students_____ The cost of this trip will be_____.

The school will be billed for extra charges at the rate of $1.50 for each half hour or fraction thereof if the time is extended beyond the hours indicated, or if detours involving additional mileage are requested.

Make checks payable to the Board of Education and mail to the Field Trip Office within two weeks after the date of the trip.

Will you please fill out the evaluation report on this trip. Include suggestions for improving this field trip service. Your comments furnish the data by which to determine the educational value of this trip.

FIELD TRIP CONFIRMATION
883 (2M sets 7-50) Vocational School Print Shop

MINNEAPOLIS PUBLIC SCHOOLS

Minneapolis

instructions. And be sure that they include within these time limits adequate opportunity for questions from the group.

• **Send written reminders** to all these persons a day or two in advance of the trip itself. In case of any doubt, also telephone them.

• **Make adequate provision for meeting the necessary expenses** involved in the trip (see Chapter 14 in this connection).

• **Decide what wearing apparel is appropriate,** what materials such as pencils, note pads, maps, cameras, baskets, measuring tapes, knives, hammers, magnifying glasses, flashlights, and similar items, should be taken along, and by whom, what kind of lunch to bring if one is required, and so on.

• **Develop a guide sheet** to be given to each excursion member. This sheet should list at least the itinerary, traveling directions, and names of speakers with their topics. It may well also include some significant problems for thought, questions to be answered, and reading references for further investigation.

Secure Consent Slips from Parents

No elementary school pupil or high-school student should be taken on a field trip unless an official consent slip, signed by the pupil's parents and properly dated, has been filed in the principal's office. The legal importance of the consent slip is a topic to be treated in Chapter 14; it is sufficient at this point to say that teachers cannot generally be held liable in the event of accident to a pupil providing the teacher can demonstrate that reasonable care had been exercised. One evidence of such reasonable care is the procurement of parental consent slips before children are taken on scheduled trips. See samples on pages 393-394.

Agree Upon a Code of Behavior

The success of any field trip depends in part on the code of behavior which governs its participants. There has to be agreement regarding the function, responsibility, and authority of the teacher, the relations of students to each other, and the relation of the group to those it meets along the way (hosts, informants, guides, servants). It will not be difficult to define the position of the teacher or to develop rules of conduct within the group. But the formulation of attitudes toward outsiders requires imagination.

There are a few fundamentals: People in all walks of life are glad to talk about their jobs, their interests, and their problems—*provided the inquiry is genuine, intelligent, and not condescending.* The secret is to establish a degree of identification with all whom one meets. Once this has been done, it is possible to be searching in one's queries without giving offense. There are situations of conflict and tension in which great tact is required, but it is generally possible to meet all factions and get all points of view, provided partisanship is avoided. The right of students to learn facts for their own enlightenment is conceded, so long as there is no feeling that the students are "slumming," or that they are going to take sides or "expose" anyone. The watchwords of any field study must be humility, friendliness, and sincerity.

Punctuality is a group obligation which must be impressed on everyone. Nothing is more destructive of group morale and good public relations than the thoughtlessness of laggards.

Conducting the Trip

The day of the excursion has arrived. Before the class actually departs upon it, there are several important details which the teacher should check upon. These may seem like trivialities, but we all know how an apparent triviality, if overlooked, may destroy the best-laid plans. After these smaller matters have been cared for, the trip may proceed.

Make Last-Minute Check

Before the trip begins the teacher in charge of small children should do as many of these things as seem desirable:

• **Check on physical condition of the pupils.** Those with symptoms of illness should be left behind in care of the school nurse.

- Note the appearance and dress of the students; see that each is appropriately attired.
- Determine whether each pupil has brought his correct car-fare, lunch, equipment, and so forth.
- Be certain that consent slips for each child have been received.
- Summarize and clarify the purpose of the excursion.
- Ascertain whether those pupils with special assignments understand their responsibilities.
- Emphasize again the importance of safety first, and indicate the nature of special hazards, if any, to be avoided on the trip.
- Review the essentials of good behavior, stressing the fact that all will be guests at the centers of interest and will wish to act as such.
- Permit the class to get drinks and go to the toilet.

Provide for Those Left Behind

When it is necessary to leave someone behind, the teacher should send the pupil in question to another teacher's room. So far as feasible, he should go there with some special assignment directly related to the class trip underway; thus he can maintain some feeling of sharing in the enterprise and contribute his bit to it in succeeding group discussions. The names of all pupils left behind, together with their temporary room numbers, should be sent to the administrator's office.

Organize the Group for Travel

Public relations, as well as physical safety, require that the teacher have some definite procedure for insuring discipline during the trip, and also for making routine checkup upon pupil attendance at various points along the way. These needs are especially important on the elementary school level, but are by no means to be neglected with even college students.

What can be done? One suggestion, particularly appropriate for children, is to organize them into squads of four, with every odd-numbered child on the curb side of the route acting as captain of the child on his right as well as of the two children immediately behind him, thus:

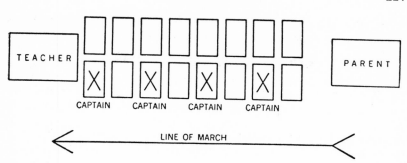

With such younger groups, it is well to give the squad captain some special badge of distinction, have him realize the nature of his responsibilities, and see that he lives up to them throughout the trip.

Older pupils, of course, need not be organized so thoroughly, but they too must be carefully checked at intervals, and to that end, the use of small groups with chosen captains is recommended even though no formal order of march need be maintained.

Proceed En Route

As the group leaves the building, the teacher takes his position at the head of the line, while a parent or other adult brings up the rear (see diagram). The teacher, knowing the way, leads the group while the assistant follows to prevent straggling and falling behind. Certain general considerations for the happy and orderly conduct of the trip itself should now be observed:

• **Encourage the group to sing,** if traveling in its own bus for an extended time. Such vocal expression of student enthusiasm is desirable, since it develops a desired esprit de corps and also drains off a certain amount of youthful exuberance before the more serious part of the trip begins.

• **Halt approaching traffic,** if necessary, before the group attempts to cross a street. If no traffic officer is on duty where a crossing must be made, the teacher should stand in the middle of the street and stop the traffic by raising his hand. The assistant, meanwhile, should hurry to the head of the line and lead the group across the street, the teacher then bringing up the rear onto the opposite sidewalk.

•   **Point out and interpret interesting items** to be seen along the way. Ability to do this will require careful advance preparation by the teacher. If a private bus is being used, the telling of relevant anecdotes en route may heighten general interest in the trip itself while also relieving the tedium of a lengthy ride.

•   **Keep the group together.** In wooded sections and in cities some audible signal such as a whistle or horn is essential for the teacher's use. In noisy situations such as a busy station, a raised handkerchief or similar visual signal is necessary unless the group is very small.

•   **Avoid side-interests** or stops not directly related to the major purposes of the excursion. Too many sensations will diminish interest, confuse comprehension, and induce emotional as well as physical fatigue.

•   **Watch constantly for signs of fatigue** and lagging behind. Keep stragglers up with the party through friendly encouragement; hold back the more impetuous.

•   **Stay on schedule.** Always endeavor to be just a little ahead of time at the next point, so as to allow for unforeseen delays. Allot each place its time and be sure not to overstay your allotted time in any one place.

•   **Approach your destination (if in a city), from the opposite side of the street.** This approach enables the group to see their goal to best advantage before they reach it, thereby heightening their sense of expectancy.

•   **Hold the group outside the resource center** while the teacher goes inside. When the guide or other host has been located, the students may enter. Introductions should now be made. These may be personal if the group is small and composed of relatively mature people; otherwise a general presentation as a class will be sufficient for the occasion.

•   **Arrange for the speaker, guide, or host to talk with the students most of the time,** rather than with the teacher or his assistant. While en route or during a meal together, have him walk or sit in the midst of the group in order that they may benefit to the full from his presence. If a meal is to be served, see that he starts eating first so he can be finished before his hearers. This can be arranged by having the waiter serve him first, or by putting him at the head of your line in a cafeteria.

Stimulate Learning at the Center

Although the resource center has assumedly now been reached, your vigilance must not be relaxed. Even if professional guides have taken charge of the student group, you have a number of new responsibilities which should not be overlooked. To illustrate, you should now:

• **Arrange opportunity for the pupils to carry on their previously chosen learning activities** such as questioning, taking notes, sketching, photographing, collecting specimens, making maps, conversing with workers, and so on.

• **Keep authorized groups together;** do not allow aimless wandering about or undue attention to irrelevant exhibits, however interesting they may be.

• **Be sure that insofar as possible every pupil is able to see and hear** what is occurring for his benefit.

• **Remain constantly sensitive to background factors** such as weather conditions, traffic movements, seating arrangements, ventilation, emotional atmospheres, amorous interests, and similar influences of present or potential significance.

• **Watch the time carefully.** If guides, speakers, or hosts take more time than was previously arranged, the teacher should be tactfully insistent upon moving on at the appointed time. Failure to do so at one center will invalidate schedules planned with others, or will end the trip at a later hour than announced.

Promptly at the designated time, therefore, the group should leave the resource center. The teacher will then thank the guide or host at an appropriate moment; the pupils should be encouraged to express their appreciation also as they go out. Everyone who has served the group should personally be thanked for his efforts if that can be done without disrupting the excursion schedule.

Dismiss Pupils from the School

If the class departed from the school then the class must be returned to the school upon completion of the trip. Under no circumstances should a teacher take it upon himself to dismiss an elementary school class from any other place, such as a bus or railroad station. Such action in the case of immature pupils would be evidence of failure to exercise reasonable care. (See page 390).

At the school, and before final dismissal, the teacher should check quickly to see that everyone is present and everything is all right. Not until then should the pupils be released from the jurisdiction of the school.

Interpreting the Field Experience

Completion of the excursion proper does not end it as a project. On the contrary, much still needs to be done before the trip's full educational value can be realized. Definite follow-up activities form an integral part of any well-managed excursion. Such activities, if properly planned and carried out, will result in more vitalized education—not only from the curricular point of view, but also in improved pupil-teacher relationships. Since the trip has enabled teacher and students to share interesting common experiences, it provides excellent intrinsic motivation for further study. The wise teacher will be well aware of this fact, and will take immediate steps to capitalize upon it.

Follow-up activities are of two chief kinds: (1) those which analyze and appraise the trip itself, and (2) those which grow out of information, appreciation, or interests developed on or as a result of the trip. Suppose we notice each type in turn.

Appraise the Trip

As soon as possible—else interest and enthusiasm will cool— the field experience should be analyzed by the group in general free discussion. Information gathered and incidents remembered should be discussed and evaluated. Often, the emotional experiences of a trip are of more permanent value than is the factual information received. Yet such experiences must be analyzed in retrospect if they are to be of most value. More specifically, therefore, the group should:

- **Evaluate the trip** in terms of the **purposes** originally established for it.
- **Diagnose mistakes, difficulties,** and other lost opportunities from the standpoint of how to improve future excursions.
- **Discuss the conduct of the group and appraise it,** in specific but impersonal terms.
- **Write letters of thanks** to officials, speakers, guides, bus drivers, parents, and all others who helped to make the excursion possible.
- **Record the highlights of the trip** in some permanent form for future use.

Honest evaluation of this nature will do much to mature the thinking of pupils, for it will force them to appraise their own educative process in concrete terms. A further excellent outcome will be that of improved pupil-teacher and pupil-pupil relationships for the future. Now the teacher is ready to fill out a trip evaluation form like those pictured on pages 227-228.

Express Emergent Interests

Every really successful trip will arouse new interests which, properly stimulated, may be of great educational significance. Every opportunity should be provided for appropriate mental, physical, and emotional activities as personalized outgrowths of the excursion experience. Individual projects, committee work, class activities of many sorts should now develop as a definite part of the total project. Such activities as these are eminently suitable as follow-up procedures of this second type:

- **Discuss the significance of things learned** as they relate to the subject, unit, or problem which originally inspired the excursion itself.
- **Express ideas and feelings** through oral reports, written compositions, scrapbooks, photographic exhibits, graphs, maps, sketches, drawings, murals, scaled models, public addresses, role-playing, socio-drama, and the like.
- **Relate important findings to other subject fields** or areas of experience. By so doing, the student becomes more aware of the essential unity of all knowledge.

TEACHER'S EVALUATION REPORT—FIELD TRIPS

School_____ Person Reporting_____ Date_____

Place Visited _____

Grade_____No. of Pupils_____No. of Teachers_____

Method of Transportation_____Hours of Starting_____Returning_____

How much time was spent in traveling to and from place visited?_____

Arrangements: Were transportation plans satisfactory?_____If not, how could they be improved?

_____

_____

Were arrangements made in the Field Trip Office dates, guides, etc. satisfactory?_____

What suggestions can you give for improving this service?_____

_____

Value of Trip: State the specific values of the excursion. (If an Art Institute Trip, also state lecture topics.)_____

_____

_____

_____

Would you recommend it for other pupils of this grade?_____

What suggestion can you give for improving the experience?_____

_____

TEACHERS' EVALUATION REPORT—FIELD TRIPS
884 (2M 9-49) Vocational School Print Shop

MINNEAPOLIS PUBLIC SCHOOLS
VISUAL EDUCATION

Minneapolis uses a 4 x 6" file card

School............................. Teacher or Sponsor. .... Date...........

Class or Committee... Number of Pupils............ .... Hour...............

Place Visited...

Official of Firm Who Granted Permission: Name... Position..................

Remarks: (Special features, difficulties, etc.)..

....

....

....

....

....

DENVER PUBLIC SCHOOLS
UTILIZATION OF COMMUNITY RESOURCES
EVALUATION SUMMARY

FORM 1240-X/S D&P 12-48-100 PADS M-473-58M1

Denver prefers a 5 x 8" card

TEACHER'S EVALUATION OF FIELD TRIP
NOTE: Please complete this form and give it to the
building principal. All returns will be carefully
studied to improve our field trip opportunities in
the future.

DATA

Teacher's Name _____ Date _____

Place Visited _____

Basic Purpose _____

Grade Class _____ No. of Pupils____ No. of Adults____

Method of Transportation _____

Time Left School _____ Arrived destination____

Time Left Destination _____ Time returned school____

ARRANGEMENTS

Were transportation plans, guides, food and toilet arrangements etc. satisfactory?_____ What suggestions can you offer to improve these and other
factors next time?

VALUES

Summarize the instructional and social results of this experience as specifically and objectively as you can:

Instructional Values	:	Social Values
(information, appreciation,	:	(attitudes, habits, behavior,
motivation, etc.)	:	etc.)
	:	
	:	
	:	
	:	
	:	

PLANS

What plans have been made to follow up this experience through further
group and individual activity in school and community?

SUGGESTIONS

Do you recommend this trip to other classes of this grade or field? _____
Comment:

What other suggestions can you give for improving this field experience in
the future?

Kent, Washington

REPORT ON SCHOOL JOURNEY

Name of School_____   Teacher_____

Date_____   Grade_____

No. of children participating_____   Unit of Study_____

No. of teachers participating_____   _____

1. Purpose of trip:
(Problem or problems to be solved;
interest to be stimulated, ideas,
processes of learnings to be
clarified, etc.)

4. Guidance provided at place visited:
(Is a guide provided? Does he guide
children to objects related to their
problems or unit of study? Is he
selective in choice? Does he know
how to talk with children?)

2. Safety Features:
(Provided or recommended)

5. Follow-up Activities:
(Indicate outcomes. Include examples
of the outcomes -- letters, reading,
construction, dramatic play,
language, etc.)

3. Values received from trip;
(In relations to purpose,
appreciations, attitudes,
citizenship.)

6. Remarks:

Los Angeles

• **Test for increased information, deeper insights, changed attitudes.** This, of course, assumes that comparable pre-trip testing has been done.

• **Share the experience with others.** Committee visits, classroom displays and exhibits, dramatic skits, class newspaper, special assembly programs, and the like are all excellent means whereby other pupils may share the excursion experience.

Carefully planned, conducted, and interpreted field trips provide realistic and vital educational experiences. Out of them come enriched knowledge, increased maturity, sustained interests, and personal satisfactions of a high order. The alert teacher, knowing these results and appreciating their lasting value, will make wide use of the technique in his local community.

Planning the Extended Study Tour

Generally speaking, extended field study should come at a later stage in education than local excursions. This is an activity for the maturing mind. Graduate students and people already practicing their professions get more from extended study trips than do college undergraduates. The latter, in turn, benefit more than high school students. It is questionable whether educational returns commensurate with the effort and expense can be obtained at a lower level than senior high school.

When a group of adolescents or adults travel together, their administration presents obvious problems. First is the feasibility of combining the sexes. This will depend upon the social pattern which has governed their previous relation in school life and in the community, on the intellectual intensity of the experience being offered, and on the teacher's character and personality.

Fifteen is the maximum number that any teacher should try to supervise single-handed. Larger groups, even if the teacher in charge has adult assistance, tend to become unwieldy. The larger the group, the more formal its program and the less opportunity there will be for intimate discussion with hosts and informants, and for that casual observation which is so often the most revealing.

Brothers, sisters, and friends of the same age level should be taken only if they are otherwise qualified for the experience that is planned. The inclusion of qualified students who are native to the locality to be studied can greatly enrich the group's experience. Parents and other adult relatives should generally be excluded. To succeed in their work the students have to develop a group life; the presence of non-functional adults, especially with ties to particular students, is invariably disruptive.

Establish Standards of Travel

Uniformity of standards is more important than quality. A group which accustoms itself to simple standards will be happy as long as it does not spend a night in a first-class hotel. On the other hand, a group which alternately stays in cheap and de luxe hotels is likely to be continually discontented. However, fluctuations in standards which are due to lack of facilities, or which have educational reasons, will always be understood and accepted. Groups accustomed to staying in comfortable inns have thoroughly enjoyed being billeted in farmhouses without modern conveniences.

Decide Whether to Use a Travel Agency

An obvious first thought in planning an extended tour is to turn the business management over to some travel agency. Unfortunately, however, there are few competent agencies. Most travel agents know only how to sell transportation and to retail the standard tours which they purchase from wholesalers such as Thos. Cook & Son or the American Express Company. Furthermore, the services which they sell—excepting transportation, for which there are standard rates—are designed for middle class and wealthy tourists; these services are basically expensive and the surcharges of the wholesaler and the retailer are excessive.

STANDARDS IN THE UNITED STATES	STANDARDS ABROAD

TRANSPORTATION

The ideal arrangement is for the group to have its own automobiles. This facilitates mobility in carrying out the program, and makes possible diversification of activities. The problem is to recruit cars with safe drivers. The cost of such transportation, when prorated among the group members, is very low. Where the use of private cars is not feasible, a school bus may be used. This, however, has the great disadvantage that all must do the same things at the same time, and that the group is conspicuous wherever it goes. Train travel is generally inadequate because it leaves the problem of local transportation unsolved. Over long distances, however, railroad or air travel may prove most feasible.

There are three classes of ocean travel: first, cabin, and tourist. Students and professional people generally travel tourist class.

The use of private automobiles is not feasible abroad. Transporting cars from this country is exceedingly expensive and renting them abroad is likewise expensive. A foreign field trip therefore generally relies on common carriers for all transportation. In Europe there are from two to four classes of rail travel, depending on the country. Students and teachers generally use the cheapest, except for long journeys.

LODGINGS

Group rates can often be secured at a standard hotel which compare favorably with the rates of an inferior hotel. It is frequently feasible to use the Y.M.C.A. and tourist homes, the one disadvantage of the latter being that it is likely to necessitate scattering the group. Where a field trip spends considerable time in one place, it may be advisable to rent a house. This was done by a field course which studied a Maine textile town; the group lived in several cottages on a lake five miles from the town center and did its own cooking, with the result that the charge to each student for living and travel during six weeks was well under a hundred dollars.

There are various distinct grades of hotels in Europe, with corresponding price differences. It is a good rule to patronize small hotels and pensions (a combination boarding house and hotel, and generally a family institution); these are often very comfortable and the food excellent. Such places are overlooked by the commercial travel trade, but agencies catering to students will know them. There are also student hostels, clubs, and, in a few instances, International Houses connected with universities. These facilities should be available through the special type of travel agency recommended in these pages.

BOARD

In rapid movement, hotel dining rooms, restaurants, and cafeterias must be used. But when the group settles down for an extended period, it may be possible to utilize boarding houses or even to establish cooperative housekeeping arrangements as suggested above.

It is usually cheapest to take all meals in lodgings. This arrangement is known as "full pension." However, such an arrangement necessitates return to lodgings in the middle of the day and hampers the educational program. It is therefore best to take breakfast and dinner, or only breakfast, in lodgings.

231

The school which plans a study tour in the United States does not need a travel agency. Arranging transportation, lodgings, and meals in home country is not difficult and goes hand in hand with the elaboration of the program. To illustrate: the local people who help to arrange an educational program in their community can also be relied on to find lodgings at minimum cost. But the technical planning of a tour abroad requires organization and experience which no school is likely to possess. Transportation from the United States, the intricacies of foreign timetables, connections, standards of travel and rates, the procedure of getting reservations, payment in foreign currencies are all functions of specialists. Among such specialists who are fully dependable are these:

Council on Student Travel, 179 Broadway, New York 7, New York, should be able to assist in obtaining low-cost trans-Atlantic steamship transportation and to advise regarding travel bureaus which are equipped to serve educational needs.

U. S. National Student Association, 48 West 48th Street, New York 36, New York, in conjunction with student organizations of other countries operates low-cost tours for American students.

The Open Road, 128 East 56th Street, New York 22, New York, assists educational institutions in arranging low-cost trans-Atlantic air charters.

The Institute of International Education, 1 East 67th Street, New York 21, New York, does not itself operate any travel services but may be able to advise in case any of the aforementioned organizations is not able to do so.

The Division of Travel Service of the National Education Association conducts numerous summer tours for teachers and others. Alaska, Hawaii, Canada, Mexico, South America, and Europe are visited.

Construct a Time Schedule

The next important step in planning successfully is to build a calendar. This must show the dates planned for each place, the exact times of arrival and departure, and the details of routings and connections between points. Such a schedule outlines the technical structure of the trip. On it are based

```
                          AMSTERDAM 2½ DAYS
                  July 22 Evening through July 25 Morning

Organizer                                              Accommodations
Miss Olga van Delden                                   Hotel Polen
ISHA-in-Holland                                        Kalverstraat
105, Statenlaan                                        Amsterdam
Telegrams:  VANDELDEN STATENLAAN HAGUE
Telephone:  553115
Der Haag


July 22          On arrival the group went to the hotel where dinner was served.

Evening:         Free

July 23

9:30             The group was shown through the new open air school for healthy children
                 of Amsterdam.  This school has now been in operation for about 7 years
                 and Mr. Janssen, who has taught there during this entire period, led the
                 group.
11:00            Visited Miss Bienfait's private Montessori school, where Miss Bienfait her-
                 self gave detailed information about her methods of teaching and theories.
12:00            Visit to the Rijksmuseum.  Lunch at the Hotel Polen.

Afternoon:
14:30            Boat trip through the canals and harbor of Amsterdam.  Rest of afternoon free.
                 Dinner at the Hotel Polen.

Evening:
20:00            Lecture on Dutch nursery schools, kindergartens, etc. by a young student
                 in this branch.  Miss T. van Poelje of The Hague.

July 24

8:30             Left for The Hague by bus.
10:00            Visit to a municipal nursery and Montessori school in the Delagoastraat.
                 The group watched the children at work and at play and special demon-
                 strations were given for the benefit of the group.  The principals, Miss
                 Smit and Miss de Haan, showed the group around.
11:30            Visit to the Municipal open air school for children with noncontagious
                 cases of tuberculosis at the Doorniksche straat in Scheveningen.  The
                 gardens of this school are right in the dunes.  The group was shown around
                 by the principal, Mr. Wagner.

Afternoon:
13:00            Lunch at "Seinpost" in Scheveningen overlooking sea.  Short walk on beach.
15:00            Visit to the municipal school museum of The Hague.  Short lecture by the
                 Director of this museum, Dr. W. E. van Wijk.  Tea at the museum.
                 Free for shopping.

Evening:
18:30            Dinner at historical Witte de Witt mansion, where national Javanese food
                 "Rijsttafel" was served.  Through The Hague visit the group was also ac-
                 companied by Mr. Wimmers of the municipal school inspection.

July 25          Lv. Amsterdam. . . . . . . .10:15    MISS VAN HOYTEMA LEAVES
                 Ar. Vlissingen . . . . . . .13:37        (Dutch Guide)
                 Lv. Vlissingen by boat . . .13:50
                 Ar. Harwich. . . . . . . . .19:10    MRS. MUNRO JCINS
                 Lv. Harwich by train . . . .19:55        (English Guide)
                 Ar. London Liv. Str. St. . .21:30
```

*Typical Page from A Field Study Schedule. European Field Course in Nursery
School, Kindergarten, and First-Grade Education*

cost estimates, reservations, and the timing of the study program.

When the calendar has been provisionally drawn, many details will emerge for consideration. One knows how many nights of lodging must be reserved in each place; how many meals there will be at each center, and what meals have to be provided for en route between points; exactly how much working time the group will have in each place, and so on.

With the skeleton calendar in hand, it is possible to start organizing the study program. As engagements are made and events are scheduled, they should be entered in the calendar so that upon completion of preparations, there will be a day-by-day, hour-by-hour record of all that is planned. Such a calendar will be indispensable in operating the trip as well as in planning it.

A common defect of study tours is the overcrowded schedule. Adequate time must be allowed for each event, and there must be enough time, between events, for getting from one place to another. Furthermore, the day must not be too full. It is a good rule to leave a third of each day—morning, afternoon, or evening—free from prescribed activities. People need time to digest experiences, to do things on their own, and to attend to personal affairs and interests. This is the best insurance against jangled nerves and jaded sensibilities. Those who construct field tours, like those who arrange public meetings, often overestimate human endurance. A program which looks meager on paper often overtaxes its participants.

Estimate Costs

In establishing a cost estimate, calculation should first be made for the group as a whole; this figure may later be divided by the number of participants to determine what each individual should pay. Some items can be estimated with precision; others can only be approximated in advance. It is well to add a small sum or percentage to the total of any estimate as a safety margin. Students can be assured that any surplus will be returned to them at the conclusion of the tour. Complete cost estimation on a day-to-day basis is the only safe course to take.

COSTS WHICH CAN BE DETERMINED IN ADVANCE

EXTENDED TRANSPORTATION: Money can often be saved by buying all transportation as a single unit. Round-trip rail, bus, or airplane tickets can be purchased from any point in the United States at a saving. Steamship and air lines give free trips to group leaders. Discounts for small groups are not obtainable on American railways, but the government-controlled railroads of Europe generally give discounts to travel groups.

LODGINGS: Many standard hotels, here and abroad, give group rates which are lower than their ordinary tariffs; many of them also give free lodging to the person in charge of the group.

BOARD: Meals in lodgings can be precisely estimated. The cost of meals taken outside is more difficult to calculate and a certain amount of guesswork may be unavoidable.

GUIDES' FEES: These can generally be known in advance.

COSTS WHICH MAY BE ONLY APPROXIMATED IN ADVANCE

LOCAL TRANSPORTATION: Where common carriers are used for local transportation, one can either allocate a lump sum by guesswork or ascertain the transit rates and work out a budget accordingly.

ENTRANCE FEES: Many museums and historic places, local sight-seeing trips, theaters, movies involve entrance fees. Some information may be obtained in advance, but an arbitrary allowance will probably have to be made.

INSTRUCTOR'S ADMINISTRATIVE FUND: The teacher in charge should have at his disposal funds to defray such incidental expenses as telephone, telegraph, cable or radio charges, tips, porterage of luggage, reciprocal hospitality to hosts and informants, occasional treats for the group, and minor expenses which cannot be foreseen. These contingency funds should be sufficient so that it will not be necessary to take up collections from the group members. "Treats for the group" may mean an ice cream soda at the psychological moment on a hot day, or a snack when the next meal is too far off.

ORGANIZATION EXPENSES: It is best if the school meets the expenses of organizing the trip. Such expenses may include guide books; source materials; stenography; telephone, telegraph, and cable charges; and travel expenses incurred when arranging the program. To the extent that such items are not met by the school, they must be prorated among the group members.

Secure Registration

When plans are sufficiently definite, a prospectus should be prepared for the information of all concerned. It may be necessary to issue a preliminary prospectus along general lines, to be followed by a final prospectus when the plans are in final form and the price which each participant must pay has been established. The prospectus should include the following data:

General statement regarding the aims of the project, the way it has been conceived and is to be carried out, who is eligible, and so forth.

Summary of the program planned. This may, but need not necessarily, include a calendar in detail.

Description of standards of travel and of living accommodations.

The services provided for the stated price, with a statement of possible services or extras which are not covered by the inclusive price.

Price to the student. This figure may be merely a total, or it may include a breakdown of that price in some detail.

Good management requires that business relations between the school and the participants (or their parents if the travelers are minors) should be clearly defined and stated from the outset. This is best accomplished by means of a registration blank to be signed by the parent or guardian at the time he enrolls his child in the trip. See page 237 for a sample blank.

Plan for Payment

It is advisable to collect a deposit at the time of registration. Payment of the balance should be required before the start of the trip. It is common practice to collect in full thirty days before departure. Payment of an initial deposit is the best evidence that the student really intends to go, while collection of the balance a month in advance is the final test. This allows time to enroll another group member in the event of a cancellation.

Provide Insurance

Insurance is a form of financial protection which should be utilized to the full for all extended travel. Four types of insurance are applicable to extended field trips:

•   **Public Liability:** The school should protect itself against claims by parents in the event of accident.

TO THE RICHARD ROE SCHOOL:

Having read and accepted the terms and conditions contained herein,
I herewith enroll my son
                       daughter _____
in the _____
                    (name by which trip is known in prospectus)
I make payment herewith of $ ____ deposit, it being understood by me that
the balance of $ ____ is due ____ days before the trip begins.

Date _____ Signature _____

Terms and Conditions

The engagement of services is secured by payment of a deposit of ____
per cent of the total price of the trip. The balance is payable ____ days
before service begins.

On cancellation made ____ days before services begin, the full amount received will be refunded. In case of later cancellation but prior to the date when services begin, the school may retain up to ____ per cent of the price of the trip as compensation for losses sustained.

Students who find it necessary to absent themselves from the trip while in progress are requested to notify the teacher well in advance. Where this is done, the school will use its best efforts to effect cancellation of those travel facilities which are not to be used. Such amounts will be refunded as the cancellations enable the school to save on the total expenses of the party. The decision of the school as to the amount refundable shall be final and shall bind all parties. Should the conduct of a student oblige his elimination from the party, refund will be made in accordance with the above.

In view of the character of the trip, the school reserves the right to decline to accept or retain any person as a member at any time. It also reserves the right to withdraw the trip and to make such alterations in plans as may be found desirable for the convenience of the party and the proper carrying out of the program.

Prices are subject to marked fluctuation in rates of international exchange. (To be included of course only in a trip outside the United States.)

All expenses due to delay, deviation or alteration of plans, arising from causes, or as a result of causes, beyond the control of the school shall be borne by the student.

The school, except for the wilful negligence of itself or employees, disclaims all liability of whatsoever nature for loss or damage to property or injury to the person of a student.

The exercise of judgment granted herein to the school may be delegated by it to such agencies or persons as may have immediate local control or charge of the trip, with full power to them or any of them to act in the premises as the exigencies of the case at the time being may warrant.

Registration Blank for Field Study used by The Open Road, Inc.

- **Individual Accident Insurance**: It is recommended that students be required to buy individual accident insurance policies. Premiums should be included in the price of the trip.
- **Baggage Insurance**: This form of protection is desirable unless the effects of the student are already covered by a family floater or by provisions in family fire and theft policies.

•   **Automobile Insurance:** If private cars are recruited for group travel, the school should see to it that each car owner carries adequate public liability insurance on his car. Any automobile utilized on a field trip should carry public liability insurance in the sum of $100,000/$300,000. If the owner is insured for less, the school should request the above figure and itself pay the difference in premium, which is negligible. The insurance company should be notified of the use to which the car is being put, lest policies be invalidated.

All insurance problems should be taken up with a *first-rate* insurance agent for the following reasons: it may be impossible to obtain a standard public liability policy which protects the school, in which case the agent must be capable of securing a special policy; a number of companies write individual accident policies, few of which are adequate; and the general assistance of a good agent may be most helpful, not only in writing insurance, but also in the event of claims.

Make Reservations

After the calendar has been established, and at the earliest possible date, tentative reservations should be made for boat or plane accommodations, for lodgings, and for any other service for which there is heavy demand. It is often necessary to make deposits for such reservations, which is another reason for requiring them from participants at the time of registration. Care should be taken to assure that deposits on tentative reservations are refundable in case the contemplated number is reduced or the trip cancelled.

As the contemplated numbers in the trip increase or shrink, the tentative reservations should be increased or reduced accordingly, so that good relations are maintained with carriers, hotels, and the like. When the exact number of participants is finally known, the tentative reservations should immediately be made definite.

Develop a "Who's Who" of the Group

Those who are to receive the group must know with whom they will be dealing. Be sure to tell them about the size of the group, the age level, the balance of the sexes, and the stage of intellectual development of the group as a whole. Sometimes it is a good idea to prepare a *Who's Who* of the membership which lists each individual's name, major field of study, special interests, and so on, and to circulate this among those who will meet the group.

Arrange Passports and Visas

These credentials are required for foreign travel and must be secured before leaving the United States. Up-to-date information can be obtained by writing to the State Department, Washington, D. C.

Loss of a passport is attended with great inconvenience and it is advisable that the leader of an immature group carry the passports for the group. In any case, the leader should have a list of passport numbers.

Advise on Clothing and Other Equipment

The less one takes, the better. Neatness and suitability are the essentials. Students are advised to consider the packing qualities of clothes and to avoid things that must be freshly laundered or pressed to look well. Shun objects that make bags heavy—like weighty cold cream jars. Valuable jewelry should be left at home, also electrical appliances, unless the group is to spend a period of weeks in one spot. American appliances are useless abroad. Room should be left in suitcases for the things one will want to buy en route. It is suggested that before the tour begins the group come together to decide what type of clothing will be needed and how it can be kept at a feasible minimum.

Specify Baggage Limitations

It is desirable to keep baggage to the minimum. Group members should be furnished with a list of needed and recommended items. Limitations on baggage should be enforced.

For those traveling by sea, rail, and automobile. Several group suitcases should be taken on voyage; heavy clothing needed only on shipboard can then be packed in the suitcases when the port is reached. Arrangements can be made with the steamship line to store the cases and to deliver them on board the return vessel.

Each student should be allowed to take one suitcase measuring about 29 by 17 by 9 inches maximum size, and one handbag not exceeding 18 by 12½ by 6 inches in size. There are good reasons for these specific limitations: the larger case is the biggest that can conveniently be packed in the luggage compartments of automobiles or fitted into luggage racks of trains; the smaller case is of a size which the individual himself can carry at all times and for some distance if necessary. If the large bag exceeds the recommended limits, it will be a continuous annoyance; if the small one is larger than suggested, it may involve extra charges for porterage. If automobiles are to be used, it will be necessary to make an exact study of the luggage capacity of each before issuing baggage instructions, for it will frequently be found that the limits outlined above are too generous. Luggage can satisfactorily be shipped from point to point in the United States by common carrier. Doing so abroad is more troublesome and delivery is less certain.

For those traveling by air. Where air transport is used between continents or to any extent while abroad, weight limitations have to be considered. The usual baggage allowance on a tourist flight across the Atlantic or between points in Europe is 44 pounds per passenger. There is a charge for excess weight.

Leave Mailing Instructions

Nothing is more essential to group morale than hearing from home and friends. Arrangements for the handling of mail must be carefully worked out. A memorandum should be prepared and each student given enough copies to cover his correspondence list.

If the tour is in the United States, the memorandum should contain a list of addresses, with the dates of each. If the trip goes abroad, it is advisable to have all mail addressed in care of the central foreign office of the travel agency, for these reasons: it is almost impossible for friends at home to gauge the time a letter will take to reach its destination and mail is likely to arrive after the group has left; time tables and hotels often have to be changed in the course of the trip; only the central foreign office of the agency will know where the group is going to be at all times, and so be able to send mail to the right place at the right time; the slight delay occasioned by the re-directing of mail from a central foreign office is overbalanced by the greater certainty of delivery.

The mail instructions should contain advice to address the student as

Mr. John Doe
Member, _____ School Group,
Address

By identifying the student with the school or the name of the trip, the problem of forwarding mail is greatly simplified. Also it saves the teacher the trouble of including all names in his forwarding instructions to a hotel when the group leaves it.

Carry Funds Safely

It is recommended that individuals put their personal funds into traveler's cheques. The teacher should also carry group funds in traveler's cheques unless the sum exceeds a thousand dollars, in which case a letter of credit may be advisable.

Divide the Labor

The teacher carries the general responsibility, but he cannot attend to every detail and also perform his essential intellectual, social, and guidance functions. It is therefore advisable that as many jobs as possible be assumed by students, perhaps in rotation. Some of these student assignments might be:

• **Laundry:** Immediately upon arrival in a place where there is to be a sufficiently long stay, arrangements should be made to get laundry done.

• **Mail:** Inquiry must be made concerning mail which has already arrived; it must be distributed; and, in departing, a group forwarding address must be left.

• **Room assignments:** Accommodations must be checked and assigned.

• **Accounting:** Someone should check bills before they are paid, and also collect from individuals for items which they personally owe.

- **Recording secretary:** It may be desirable to have someone keep a record of the names and addresses of persons with whom the group has contact, and of all the important events which occur.
- **Social secretary:** Perhaps some individual should see that everyone who extends hospitality or assistance to the group receives a suitable acknowledgment.
- **Confirming technical arrangements:** Some member might arrange for meals to be taken outside of lodgings; check time of plane, train, or bus departure and reservations; time and place of meeting with guides, and similar items.
- **Confirming curricular arrangements:** There may be someone in the group sufficiently mature and adroit socially to check the engagements with institutions, speakers, etc., insofar as this may be necessary.

Plan Learning Activities

A field tour affords only limited opportunity for reading. It is well, however, to carry a small selection of books, periodicals, and reports to which students can refer. But in the main the learning activities are the gathering of impressions from life, their organization, interpretation, and evaluation.

Students must be taught how to conduct interviews, both as a member of a group and individually. This calls for thought and experimentation on the part of the teacher. But the gathering of data is a much simpler business than the reflective process by which meaning is derived from impressions. Obvious devices for this are group discussions and the preparation by individuals or committees of reports to form a basis for such discussion. It may also be desirable to have each student keep a notebook or "log" in which he summarizes those facts which he has learned and which seem to him important, and in which he records reactions to experiences. Such an intellectual diary induces reflection, thereby carrying the learning process to a higher level than is usual with young students. A further value of such notebooks is that they furnish a basis for discussion between teacher and student regarding the latter's habits of observation, sense of the significant, clarity of thought, imaginative freedom, and the like.

Other forms of recording and expression are photography, sketching, and the making of collections. While interesting and useful, these media are not as fruitful for intellectual development as is the reflective diary and are of secondary value.

Great American Custom

"Going places and seeing things" is a great American custom. Field trips and study tours represent two of the community school's avenues of effective learning. Every community is rich in learning resources which that school should know well how to use.

Learning Activities

Discussion Topics

1. Are junior high school people mature enough to profit from such field trips as those to city council meetings, or should these be restricted to older students?
2. Should a school class be administratively limited to a fixed number of field trips each year?
3. Should extended study tours be taken by elementary school children? (Scan the literature before you answer.)
4. What can be done about the high school teacher who disapproves of field trips and penalizes students who miss his class because of trips scheduled by other teachers?

Group Activities

1. Divide into interest committees, each to work out plans for a field trip upon which the whole class might go. Then vote upon the one of greatest value, and let that committee organize and conduct that trip.
2. Check through your state teachers' association journals of the past several years for descriptions of field trips and extended study tours taken by school groups in your state. Evaluate these as best you can in terms of basic learning values.
3. Select a committee on field trips to recommend class excursions which will help the group to master the major techniques involved.

4. What seems to be the general attitude of business houses and industrial concerns toward class visits to their plants? Make a sampling survey to get your local answer.

Individual Projects

1. Do a research study on the history and development of the school trip in other countries and in the United States.
2. Through a "man-in-the-street" interview technique, determine the attitudes of a significant number and range of educators and lay people toward the use of the trip as a learning activity. Summarize your findings in chart or other visual form as a basis for class report.
3. Scan the recent literature for examples of field trips different in kind or purpose from those described in Olsen's *School and Community Programs*.
4. Secure samples of parent permission slips used in several schools or school systems near you. Analyze these for legal validity, and also for parent appeal—after you have looked into Chapter 14.

Learning Materials

The origins and development of the school excursion have been traced in a doctoral study by Henry C. Atyeo, *The Excursion as a Teaching Technique* (Teachers College, Columbia, 1939) and reported in his Chapters 2 and 3. Charles F. Hoban, C. F. Hoban, Jr., and Samuel B. Zisman's *Visualizing the Curriculum* (Cordon, 1937) devotes its 2nd chapter to the school journey as a means of instruction, and includes some historical background of its use. Healthy warnings about trips and tours in general are offered by Marvin Rife whose "Tours in Dynamic Education" (*Educational Method,* February 1941) lists some fundamental questions to be asked about field trips before their values can be assumed. In his "Is This School Trip Necessary?" Alexander Frazier warns against using the trip merely to collect meaningless data or to take excursions simply because opportunity offers (*Educational Administration and Supervision,* March 1946). A tremendous challenge to extend the field tour program nationwide was issued by Beardsley Ruml in his "Learn as You Go" proposal that every year two million high school students travel 10,000 miles each on national study tours as a regular part of their school experience (*Coronet,* March 1945; also in *Secondary Education,* February-March 1945).

Vital case studies of field trips on all grade levels are presented in Olsen's *School and Community Programs* (Prentice-Hall, 1949), Chapter 5, which describes seventeen successful trips of many kinds. His pamphlet *Social Travel: A Technique in Intercultural Education* (Hinds, Hayden, Eldridge, 1947) describes and analyzes field trip programs whereby intergroup attitudes may be improved. Chapters 6 and 7 of Elizabeth V. Hubbard's *Your Children at School* (John Day, 1942) recount in detail the enthusiastic activities and reactions of primary school children as they enjoy excursions. George E. Pitluga's *Science Excursions into the Community* (Teachers College, Columbia, 1943) is a handbook for teachers of grades four through eight, filled with ideas and suggestions for fourteen science trips and related activities. Other useful accounts will be found in the literature now suggested under five headings.

Elementary school cases may be sampled in a number of excellent reports including these:

"Young Explorers Make Discoveries," C. Skiles. Vital account of how a group of children became interested in making a visit to the airport, arranged to spend the entire day there, and developed weeks of follow-up classroom activities. *Childhood Education* 12:358-363; May 1936.

"The Excursion Method in Primary Reading," Hattie Ewald and W. W. Ludeman. An interesting account of how a teacher used a farm excursion as a means of motivating reading and providing content for it in the first and second grades. *Educational Administration and Supervision* 24:172-176; March 1938.

"Some Experiences in Using Community Resources," Anna B. Jones. Describes a host of activities through which children study their local community. They learned about the railroad, planned a model home, visited dairy and turkey farms, various stores, offices, libraries, and took trips to the zoo, Chinatown, old ranch house, and so forth. *National Elementary Principal* 18:458-464; July 1939.

"Fourth-Grade Excursion to Another City," Dale Robertson. Detailed account of how 71 children accompanied by five teachers, four parents, a trained nurse and the principal make a trip from Indiana to Chicago. *National Elementary Principal* 18:481-488; July 1939.

"We Visit Our Cold Storage Plant," Norman R. Kelley. Outline of a fact-finding trip in terms of its initial preparation, objectives, preliminaries, arrival at the office, order of the tour, activities, correlations with other subjects and values. *Instructor* 50:61; November 1940.

"Learning Through Seeing," Helen M. Waltermire. Urges the importance of using the summer vacation to explore the community and tells how children in one community did just this. These experiences, organized by one teacher, provided invaluable socialization as well as much background for the following school year's classroom work. *Instructor* 50:14; June 1941.

"Developing Language Skills Through the Use of Community Resources," Ruth I. Thomas. How a sixth-grade class utilized local resources through excursions to have experiences as a basis for writing, speaking and reading. *National Elementary Principal* 20:543-548; July 1941.

"Being Six in the City," Dorothy Stall. How the six-year-olds in a modern school learned about their city environment through a series of field trips, each growing out of the previous experience, and each followed up in song, dramatics, map-making and the like. *Childhood Education* 22:190-194; December 1945.

"Grocery Store: A Problem Unit," Helen M. Sylvia. A second-grade class visited a chain store and then established a grocery store in their classroom as a means of learning arithmetic. *Education* 69:337-339; February 1949.

"Developmental Education," Leone D. Cummings. Extensive account of how a first-grade class built meaningful concepts through actual experiences using field trips and resource people in relationship to reading and socializing activities. *Nations Schools* 46:37-41; October 1950.

For the high school level, see these articles for further ideas:

"Let's Interview the Government," Herbert J. Abraham. A high school trip to Washington need not be superficial sight-seeing. This class went "behind the scenes" for three days, with great educational benefit to all. *Educational Method* 17:16-19; October 1937.

"Geography Field Work in the Small City," M. J. Riggs. Describes how a class used excursions through different areas of their own city (business, manufacturing, poor residential, low middle class residential) as a basis for understanding the typical spatial pattern of any city. *Journal of Geography* 37:28-31; January 1938.

"Youth Visits Industrial Detroit," William A. Van Till. Step-by-step account of how an Ohio high school class planned and carried out a four-day field study in Detroit. Letters to parents, student diaries, question lists and final student comments are reproduced. *Educational Method* 18:266-271. March 1939.

"The Local Community as a Resource for Teaching High School Geography," Walter Crewson. Warns against superficial looking in excursions and illustrates concretely just how deeper understanding of industrial processes may result from adequate geographic knowledge about them. *Journal of Geography* 39:105-109; March 1940.

"The Nation, Our Campus," Alvin B. Roberts. Detailed account of the extended field study program carried on by a small high school in Illinois. Each student in the school may make twenty or more tours covering the state, as well as four regional trips averaging 3,000 miles each. *Educational Screen* 20:5-8; January 1941.

"Seeing the United States From a School Bus," L. Maude Hall. Describes a 4,500 mile, 22-day bus trip taken by a senior class. They carried cots and sleeping bags and stayed in school gymnasiums at a total cost of about $2.00 per day each, half of which was paid from class funds and the rest by the individual student travelers. *School Activities* 18:205-206; March 1947.

"Our School Trip to Kentucky," Don Chapman and others. High school students vividly describe their six-day, 1,100-mile trip. The trip was made during the academic year with academic preparation and follow-up. *School Activities* 18:246-247; April 1947.

"Two-Week Tour: 2,400 Miles by Bus," F. C. Thomas and Annette Sheel. Forty-five high school seniors from Illinois had a 13-day tour to Eastern cities. Preparation for the trip and its educational values are stressed. *Clearing House* 22:554-556; May 1948.

"City Hall and Court House," Ruby Strickland. Tells how an American Problems class goes into the community to delve into local governmental agencies, watch them in operation, and get firsthand information from the officials in charge. *Clearing House* 24:344-345; February 1950.

"Learning by Hosteling," Elizabeth Wadsworth. Describes the bicycle hosteling program of one high school. *National Education Association* 39:364-365; May 1950.

"30 Visits to Study Community Problems," Francis Tiernan. Shows how economics and sociology high school students learned about community problems at firsthand, through visits and interviews in a wide variety of agencies and organizations. *Clearing House* 26:149-151; November 1951.

Trips and tours on the college level, including those in teacher education, are described in Olsen's *School and Community Programs.* See also Jean Carol Trepp's *Uses of Field Work in Teaching Economics* (Sarah Lawrence College, 1939), a detailed account of the Sarah Lawrence College's field trip program, and Helen M. Lynd's *Field Work in College Education* (Sarah Lawrence College, 1945), a more comprehensive description of the same institution's program with emphasis on the implications for liberal education of the field work approach. A brief statement of this program by its field work director is Soloman's "Beyond the Classroom" in *Educational Leadership,* November 1946. Stimulating articles on field work in other colleges are these:

"Teachers in the Community," James A. Michener. Describes and evaluates a Harvard Graduate School of Education community study course. The group spent the first week on campus orienting itself to its problems; then a week in each of three different New England communities, studying them and their social processes through extensive interviews; after which a final week at Harvard summarized their findings. *Social Studies* 32:219-221; May 1941.

"Education Takes to the Tall Timber," Ralph B. Price. Firsthand studies of five Colorado communities were made in a 2,000-mile journey during summer session; cattle raising region, sugar beet region, coal fields, gold mines, dust bowl. Stirring accounts of educational values in each are the heart of this article. *Clearing House* 15:531-532; May 1941.

"Studying the South Firsthand," Gordon W. Blackwell. Describes a field course in southern conditions by Columbia University's Teachers College. Each year fifteen students from the North and West join Southerners in a scientific study of a typical southern community. *Educational Record* 23:271-282, April 1942.

"Field Work in Politics," Paul S. Jacobsen. Describes Colgate University's Washington Study Project in which ten honor students spend a full semester studying federal government firsthand. *Educational Record* 28:162-171; April 1948.

"Geographic Study Tours for Undergraduates," V. Calvon McKin. Analyzes preparation, equipment, materials and safety measures needed; then suggests procedures for the field study of relief and topography, soil, climate, minerals, vegetation, erosion, opulation, and land use. *Education* 69:9-15; September 1948.

"TVA Journey 1948," Ryland W. Crary. Describes a field study course on the Tennessee Valley Authority taken by graduate students at Teachers College, Columbia. *Teachers College Record* 50:179-185; December 1948.

"Travel Courses Can Be More Than Sightseeing Trips," E. C. Beck and W. C. Smith. Describes an American Literature travel course involving two weeks in the field. Students prepare before starting the tour, hear lectures en route and at literary shrines, and take examinations. *Nation's Schools* 47:44-45; April 1951.

"The Field Trip—A Technique in Natural Science Teaching," Richard Beidleman. Tells about the spring field tour taken annually by students and faculty from the Forestry School at Colorado A & M College. *School Science and Mathematics* 52:105-118; February 1952.

"Conservation Across the United States" and "Some Techniques of a Conservation Tour," by Raymond Kienholz. Describe an extended study tour taken by 32 adults who covered 12,000 miles through 26 states in a two-month summer period. The group traveled by bus, accompanied by a mess truck which furnished the meals. *School Science and Mathematics* 53:178-186; March and May 1953.

Student exchange programs are a more recent development of the study tour technique. An annual program whereby Canadian and American high school students visit each other is described by Kenneth Gell and Alfred Hobbs in "The Trans-Lake Study Groups," in *Clearing House*, September 1948; also in the *Education Digest*, February 1949. The story of an exchange between schools in Concord, Massachusetts and Hyattsville, Maryland, is told by O'Connor in "Our Next Class Meets in Dixie" in *Nation's Schools*, August 1951. Reports of how the Macon, Georgia and Manitowac, Wisconsin exchange originated and developed have been written by Ann Holmes as "Magnolias and Bratwurst" for *Clearing House*, May 1952, and by Angus Rathwell in his "Wisconsin and Georgia Enthusiastic About Student Exchange" in *Nation's Schools*, August 1952. An ambitious yet intriguing plan for exchanging a million high school students a year with families in other nations is outlined by Kneller in his "One Million Ambassadors" in *Progressive Education*, March 1946.

Business-Education days involve visits of students or teachers to industrial and commercial centers, with possible return visits by business men to the schools. In the *School Executive,* May 1950, A. F. Olney describes a program through which 60 high school students spent a full day visiting business establishments. Interesting accounts of teacher visits have been published by Alvin T. Stolen as "Teachers Learn Brewing, Baking and Money-Making" in the *School Executive,* April 1953.

Motion Pictures

Near Home. A junior high school class gets interested in local history and present community processes, and takes planned excursions to get needed data. International Film Bureau, 1946, 25 minutes.

Field Trip. Depicts the ways in which a junior high school biology class plans, conducts, and follows up an excursion. Many suggestions for all types of trips are given. Virginia Department of Education and Norfolk County Schools, 1949, color, 10 minutes.

Outside School Walls. Shows teachers the technique of conducting a trip by portraying a junior high school class's visit to the headquarters of the United Nations. New Tools for Learning, 1950, 15 minutes.

Community Resources in Teaching. Shows in detail the class and committee planning, executing, and follow-up of a field trip. Iowa State University, 1950, 20 minutes.

CHAPTER 9

Surveys

From earliest childhood pupils go about exploring the world around them. Much of this activity is both unconscious and unsystematic in character, but it is clearly purposive for all of that. Through such activity, the growing child is developing personal understanding and control over his own physical and social environment.

The community survey, practically speaking, is only an organized and systematic procedure whereby the random explorations of childhood may be transmuted into conscious adult capacity for intelligent local, regional, national, and international planning. The survey may deal with a single aspect of the community, as the provision for recreation in a given neighborhood, or it may involve a general overview or cross section of the entire locality, as in a professional analysis of a community. Yet in either case, the survey may be defined as an accurate determination, through organized study, of social or physical data, particularly with reference to its spatial patterning and causal relationships.

If the survey is properly adjusted to the maturity of the pupils, the making of it may be an excellent educational experience—not alone for the data it reveals, but also for the cooperative planning and activity it entails. A survey is likely

This chapter is by ELDON W. MASON.

to involve field trips and interviews, and to combine them with
library research and all the activities of a classroom laboratory.
Under good conditions, the making of a survey is a project
with all the merits which were attached to project teaching
in its original sense. The survey technique:

• **Fosters comprehensive understanding of community structure and processes** in their everyday operation, interaction, and
complexity.

• **Stimulates depth of insight into vital community problems
and trends** as these have been influenced by past conditions, present developments, and future prospects.

• **Discloses problems which should be met**—not because
teacher or textbook loftily says so, but because the evidence itself
inescapably reveals the need.

• **Suggests possibilities for student participation** in the ongoing
processes of the community. Such constructive participation, cooperatively carried on, provides fine personal satisfactions as well
as essential training in democratic citizenship.

• **Develops awareness of human interdependence** and of the
practical necessity for general civic cooperation in carrying on successful individual and group living.

• **Promotes superior citizenship** by providing extended experience in the making of critical judgments concerning existing conditions. Students learn, through personal actions, to base conclusions
and recommendations upon factual data carefully assembled, objectively interpreted, and meticulously verified.

Every community carries on the fundamental social processes
and experiences some of their related social problems. Every
school can vitalize its students' education by encouraging them
to make selected local surveys part of their academic experience.

What Are the Types of Surveys?

Surveys may well be classified according to the types of community factors they examine. It will be remembered that Part
II presented a pattern for analyzing any community in terms
of several major factors, and that these factors were further
divided and even subdivided as follows:

Community Structure

Physical Setting   People   Social Organization

Processes and Problems

Improving Material Conditions	Protecting Life and Health
Appreciating the Past	Improving Family Living
Adjusting to People	Securing Education
Exchanging Ideas	Meeting Religious Needs
Making a Living	Enjoying Beauty
Sharing in Citizenship	Engaging in Recreation

Levels

Material   Institutional   Psychological

Time Period

Historic   Contemporary   Future

Status Relationships

Class   Caste

Now it becomes evident that a community survey might be undertaken to discover how (one, some, all) of the *social processes* operate through *social organizations* (institutions, agencies, groups) on the (material, institutional, psychological) *level,* as influenced by the (class and caste) *status relationships* of the *people* in their *physical setting* during the *time period* under consideration. Mathematically and practically, there are hundreds of possible combinations among these important variables. Actually, however, most useful community surveys emphasize some variation of two fundamental patterns:

• Extensive, general overview of a community structure or of many social processes as they operate contemporaneously in the local or regional community upon one or more of the three levels.

• Intensive, detailed analysis of one social process and related problems as it operates in all time periods and upon all three levels in the local community, and as it is influenced by the status relationships of the people.

It is evident that any aspect of the community which has meaning for young people may properly be considered an appropriate field for school surveys. The scope and depth of each survey will depend upon the time available for the study as well as upon the maturity of the pupils involved.

How Can the Survey Best Be Used?

In many instances, a survey is a mere mechanical piece of busywork, an arid accumulation of knowledge for its own sake. One school proudly reports a survey, participated in by almost three hundred pupils and covering an area of many city blocks, in which the outcome was apparently the preparation of thirty statistical tables summarizing such varied items as number of houses in each block, number of persons in each family, number of college graduates, number of illiterates, number of homes with gardens, amount of home ownership, amount of sickness, the number regularly attending church, and the number of books in each house. While these are potentially valuable data in some respects, they are unrelated in their own parts or to any general purpose. Such rudimentary counting might well be the beginning of a survey, but hardly its outcome. It needs to be followed by an analysis of relationships or of problems or of social changes. Any survey of educational significance is not merely an experience in tabulation; it is tabulation for the definite purpose of interpretation and social action. The means ought not to be confused with the ends, yet many surveys made by pupils or by adults do not go beyond the accumulation of undigested data. At its best, the survey is a creative rather than a routine procedure. Anything less than enlightening interpretation of accumulated data is to be avoided by the school. Let us therefore examine the characteristics of a truly constructive survey, noting these according to our threefold pattern of (1) preparing for the survey, (2) making the survey, and (3) interpreting the survey experience.

Preparing for the Survey

A number of significant procedures are in order in this initial planning stage. These procedures may well be outlined as follows:

The Teacher Must Prepare in Advance

If you are to be effective in stimulating pupil interest, you must orient yourself to survey possibilities well in advance. Inadequate preparation will quickly be sensed by the pupils; they do not readily follow a leader in whom they detect signs of uncertainty, indecision, or lack of confidence. While the teacher should always work with students in a spirit of mutual adventuring and should not appear to know all the answers in advance, it is equally important that he possess some definite awareness of directions and possibilities before such explorations are undertaken by the group.

A number of brief pamphlets[1] will help you get the basic survey idea well in mind. Among these are *Know Your Town* and *Know Your County*, both published by the National League of Women Voters; *Know Your Community* by Bess Goodykoontz; *Let's Look at Ourselves*, issued by the National Citizens' Council on Civil Rights; and *Your Community Looks at Itself*, available from the Southern Regional Council or from the Anti-Defamation League. Several books should also be examined at this stage, including Colcord's *Your Community* and Sumption's *How to Conduct a Citizens School Survey*.

In addition to your reading, you will need to spend as much time as possible in personal observations of the community in order to get the "feel" of it. The printed page springs into life as you supplement it by immersing yourself in related community activities.

Arouse Student Interest

Little of lasting value will result from a survey if pupils look upon it as just another assignment. Assuming that the area, process, or problem to be examined has genuine social significance, the teacher's task is to translate that significance into terms which will motivate his students to personal interest and

---

[1] Consult the chapter bibliography.

group action. If the teacher cannot relate the proposal for a survey with factors that already touch the lives of his pupils, it would be better not to proceed any further.

In this world "aching with vividness," there are innumerable areas of activity which carry deep and personal significance for youth. The resourceful teacher will seek, wherever possible and within reasonable limits, to let the survey have its basis in the achievements, good and bad, of people. A survey of juvenile delinquency, for instance, will be much more eagerly approached by pupils if they are not initially frightened by too many statistics. Let them come to know something of the human factors first, and then go on to statistical summaries and generalizations. *Start with people* and the survey will come alive.

Is it to be a survey of public health agencies? There is romance, heroism, defeat, victory in the lives of people engaged in this field. Lift the cold statistics from the printed page and blow life into them through some revelation of what men and women have done to throw safeguards around human life. What has happened to American life expectancy in the past hundred years makes only indifferent statistical reading. But dramatized in personal, human terms, it becomes a thrilling story.

Genuine student interest will depend, to a marked degree, upon what answers can honestly be given to these two basic questions, both of which are useful criteria for appraising the choice of survey:

• **What difference does it make?** If there is to be an adequate development of pupil interest in the survey, the teacher must be sure that a positive answer is returned to this query. Unless students can see a functional value in the making of a survey, they will properly remain uninterested in it.

• **What can we do about it?** Besides recognizing the real value of a survey, students need to feel that they themselves can actually help to improve conditions disclosed. If they cannot actively contribute, either now or in the future, they will often develop feelings of frustration and eventual indifference or cynicism.

It is of crucial importance that the teacher does not assume the position of taskmaster, but rather that of a colleague engaged in mutual research. Beware of that I've-been-through-all-this-before attitude, and be sure never to reflect boredom. Teacher and students can work cooperatively together in a spirit of shared research, seeking information which is of genuine significance. To the extent that this is done, the survey will not be just another assignment; it will possess the breath of life itself.

Identify the Purpose

The basic necessity in planning a survey is the thoughtful, precise formulation of the major purpose or end toward which it is directed. The first step in reflective thinking upon any problem is always a clear definition of the question involved. One of the paramount values for pupils making a survey is the exercise it may afford in clear thinking—and that thinking must be initiated in the question: *just what are we trying to accomplish?* It is relatively easy to accumulate data, but there is little value in collecting them in random fashion or in the vague hope that they will turn out to be interesting or illuminating. Only when the purposes for which data are wanted are precisely known, can they be assembled efficiently. There can be no efficiency in any survey until its purpose has been stated and all its aspects related to the achievement of that purpose. The more thorough the planning, the less lost motion there will be.

Michener suggests that the survey problem be formulated as a question, and that this question be checked against five criteria as a means of appraising its educational validity. The central survey question should thus: (a) Contain one idea, (b) Be comprehensive, but not involved, (c) Not be answerable by a simple "yes" or "no" reply, (d) Be unambiguous and pertinent, (e) Possess social significance.[2] "Can We Believe

[2] James A. Michener, "Participation in Community Surveys as Social Education." In Ruth West (ed.), *Utilization of Community Resources in the Social Studies*, 144-63. (153). Ninth Yearbook, National Council for the Social Studies, 1938,

HOW GOOD IS YOUR TOWN?

What is your honest opinion of your town as a place to live, work, and bring up a family?

What will you find if you measure your town against recognized standards for a good American community?

Below are ten standards you can use in rating your town. Keep in mind that *the community is the people.* Check (X) your town as either *good, fair,* or *poor* on each standard.

COMMUNITY STANDARD	YOUR TOWN IS		
	GOOD	FAIR	POOR
Standard No. 1. EDUCATION Modern education available for every child, youth, and adult. Uncrowded, properly equipped schools in good physical condition. Highly qualified, well paid teachers.			
Standard No. 2. HOUSING AND PLANNING Every family decently housed. Continuous planning for improvement of residential areas, parks, highways, and other community essentials. Parking, traffic, and transportation problems under control.			
Standard No. 3. RELIGION Full opportunity for religious expression accorded to every individual. Churches strong and well supported.			
Standard No. 4. EQUALITY OF OPPORTUNITY People of different races, religions, and nationalities have full chance for employment and for taking part in community life. Dangerous tensions kept at minimum by avoidance of discrimination and injustices.			
Standard No. 5. ECONOMIC DEVELOPMENT Good jobs available. Labor, industry, agriculture, and government work together to insure sound economic growth.			
Standard No. 6. CULTURAL OPPORTUNITIES Citizens' lives strengthened by ample occasion to enjoy music, art, and dramatics. A professionally administered library service benefits people of all ages. Newspapers and radio carefully review community affairs.			
Standard No. 7. RECREATION Enough supervised playgrounds and facilities for outdoor activities. Full opportunity to take part in arts and crafts, photography, and other hobbies.			
Standard No. 8. HEALTH AND WELFARE Positive approach to improving health of entire community. Medical care and hospitalization readily available. Provision made for underprivileged children, the aged, and the handicapped. Families in trouble can secure needed assistance.			
Standard No. 9. GOVERNMENT Capable citizens seek public office. Officials concerned above all with community betterment. Controversy stems from honest differences of opinion, not from squabbles over privilege.			
Standard No. 10. COMMUNITY ORGANIZATION An organization — community forum, citizens' council, or community federation — representative of entire town, is working for advancement of the whole community. Citizens have opportunity to learn about and take part in local affairs. There is an organized, community-wide discussion program. Specialized organizations give vigorous attention to each important civic need.			

TOTAL SCORE FOR YOUR TOWN: GOOD (10 points for each item) _____
FAIR (5 points for each item) _____
POOR (0 points for each item) _____

Source: New York State Citizens' Council, *Scoreboard for Your Town,* Adapted by Harold Bottrell, University of Houston.

What We Read in the Newspapers?" and "What Human Relations Tensions Exist in Our Community?" are examples of survey problems which satisfactorily meet these five criteria.

Persons active in the field to be surveyed should be consulted as the survey problem is being defined. Some of these people, together with the teacher and a committee of students, should meet once or twice at the outset to define the limits of the field, and should also meet as often as necessary during the whole period of the survey in order to check both direction and progress.

Gain Perspective upon the Problem

Students should now be immersed in a reading program as the springboard for direct contact with the field. It would be a grave mistake to start field contacts if the students have no background of general understanding in the area chosen for survey. Only as they come to know a given field in terms of its literature, as well as its immediate phenomena, will they secure an intelligent understanding of it.

Documentary sources must be chosen with care, and must always be appropriate to the mental level of the students using them. These materials should first deal with general aspects of the problem, and thus provide an initial overview for all of the students concerned. With that background in common, the reading program may then be diversified for detailed treatment of specific sub-problems by various committees or individuals.

Such general and specialized reading, accompanied by adequate classroom discussions and interpretations, should enable the students to sense the "topography" of the problem and thus be in position to break it down into its component elements.

Analyze the Problem

The chosen problem should next be divided into several constituent sub-problems. This should be done by the students and teacher in free discussion. *What are the essential and detailed features of this problem?* To stimulate thinking it is well to develop an outline on the blackboard; each student making his own notebook copy after it is completed. A sample breakdown of one fundamental question might thus be outlined somewhat as follows:

"Can We Believe What We Read in the Newspapers?"

1. What is a newspaper?
2. How is news gathered?
3. How is news edited?
4. How is a newspaper financed?
5. What connections may exist between editorial policy and advertising revenues?
6. How do publishers decide what political issues or candidates to support?
7. Is the news censored in any way?
8. What ethical standards are expected and maintained in journalism?

In developing such a breakdown, the subtle skill of the teacher will be of paramount importance. Much time can be saved if students are prevented from getting too far afield in pursuit of relatively unimportant features. The incidental and inconsequential must not be allowed to obscure the fundamental issues; neither must any really significant aspects of the problem be ignored. A good analysis always simplifies the general problem, stimulates insight into its interrelated elements, and facilitates division of labor among several committee groups.

Discover the Practical Limits of the Survey

Having identified and analyzed the problem, the teacher and pupils are next confronted with three basic questions concerning the desirable range of the survey being planned. Those three questions are these:

• **Are the pupils mature enough?** In a survey of housing, for example, it is obvious that the approach made by a class of seventh-graders would have to be different from that employed by a group of college seniors. The mental maturity of the students must always determine the *depth* of the survey they undertake; that is, the degree to which they probe beyond the material level and into the institutional and psychological levels of the housing problem. Furthermore, their mental development should always condition the *extent* of the survey: their study of regional, national, and international housing trends and policies as related to the local housing situation. Both depth and extent of student interest and ability will depend in large measure upon their general grade level.

• **Will community morés permit?** Pupils must not be sheltered from reality, but at the same time the school cannot usually go much beyond dominant community attitudes in its teaching program. In some sections, for example, a survey of minority political opinion or of religious or racial tensions may be charged with social dynamite. The teacher who knows his community will be able to avoid areas of investigation about which local feelings run high. This is not to suggest that controversial issues be avoided—quite the contrary—but only that good judgment be used to avoid areas which are "untouchable" and thus free the teacher for more active social leadership where he may be effective.

• **Is the survey over-ambitious?** It is better to do an adequate survey in a limited field than to spread efforts so thin that results are necessarily sketchy and unsatisfactory. Let's remember that pupils should learn something of the technique and spirit of the survey, as well as find genuine personal satisfaction in its results. If too pretentious a survey is attempted, both these values will be lost. Time is a real factor here. Such matters as distance between the school and the survey-field, post-school availability of pupils, and means of transportation must also all be taken into careful account.

Determine What Data Are Needed

The obvious next step is to decide what types of information may be secured to throw most light upon the problem chosen. To illustrate, the class may conceive its purpose as that of finding out how public opinion in the local community is formed. With this objective in mind, the pupils may then consider the availability and relative usefulness of data on citizens' reading habits, on the use of commercial advertising, on the extent to which people use the radio and the types of programs they select, on the influence of movie newsreels, television programs, or public forums. Probably it would not be feasible to tap all these sources of information, but within practical limitations the sources chosen must be selected in terms of their pertinency to the general purpose of the survey.

Decide upon Techniques to Be Used

Now comes the problem of determining what survey techniques to use—source documents, audio-visual aids, resource people, field interviews, excursions, questionnaires, public opinion polls, and the like. Detailed suggestions have already been given for using most of these approaches, so attention here will be confined to brief descriptions of questionnaires and polls.

Questionnaires should be relatively simple and brief, and should deal with materials fairly easily recorded and tabulated. Since comparable replies to the questionnaire are desired, as extensive use as possible should be made of check lists and mechanical markings on the form devised. A questionnaire, once prepared, should be tried out on a small group and then revised before final and extensive use of it is made. The persons to whom it is taken or sent should be carefully selected. An accompanying letter, perhaps signed by the school administrator, should explain the purpose the school seeks in allowing pupils to circulate their questionnaire.

In many respects the opinion poll is similar to an interview. The techniques developed by professional analysts of public opinion, such as the Gallup Poll, are useful; they involve especially critical care in two areas: the selection of subjects in the sampling used, and the careful formulation of the questions asked. The sampling need not be large but should be representative. The questions chosen should be direct, unequivocal, and simply phrased.

Some schools have found it useful to secure generalized data through reports made by the pupils of themselves, or of their families. Records of reading done, recreations enjoyed, purchasing habits, church interests, and the like may serve many educational purposes. Care must always be taken that items to be reported by pupils be very clearly understood by them in advance, or the reports may not be accurate or even be returned. And every precaution should be taken to avoid the appearance of prying into personal affairs. Data must be generalized and impersonalized if their educative use is to be possible.

Obviously the variety of techniques to be used is as great as the variety of possible purposes or the number of areas to be surveyed. The choice of each is dependent upon the local situation and upon the alertness and ingenuity with which the teacher approaches the project.

Organize Class Committees

Having general plans well in mind, the students and teacher now turn to the matter of committee organization. The committee approach is recommended because it makes for economy of effort, and it provides a situation where students may work intimately together, where group responsibility may be readily shared, and where observation of individual efforts is expedited. Committees should be established on the basis of student interests.

The number of committees will depend upon the number of significant areas or sub-problems requiring attention. Each committee should number between three and seven. Fewer than three members fails to provide sufficient opportunities for intra-committee discussions, and bears the further hazard of not providing sufficient numbers to cover the field adequately. More than seven may result in no-participation by some members, with consequent loss of interest by all of them.

Each committee should now select a recorder, a chairman, and a librarian. The librarian's function is to keep a list of sources in the field to be surveyed, adding to it references brought to his attention by committee members. He keeps a file of newspaper clippings, and acts also as custodian of all audio-visual aids utilized by the group. The recorder keeps an account of the planning and progress of the group, and also assists the chairman in checking over the reading program of individual committee members.

Before the committees go into their reading programs, the teacher should give the class some practical suggestions about efficient taking of notes. This is important, for if students are allowed to make a laborious task of recording notes on reading and observations, they will lose interest in the project itself.

Nothing so dulls the ardor of committee members as fumbling conduct of meetings. To forestall this possibility, the teacher should explain and demonstrate *simple* rules of parliamentary procedure before the committees hold their first sessions.

Define the Committee's Function

We have already stressed the importance of breaking down the problem into its constituent elements. Within each committee, the same process should now be repeated; each subquestion should in turn be analyzed into *its* logical aspects. Continuing the newspaper illustration offered on page 259, let us suppose that Committee 6 is composed of pupils who are especially interested in subquestion 6. This committee might therefore break down its problem somewhat as follows:

"How Do Publishers Decide What Political Issues or Candidates to Support?"

(1) How does the editorial page differ from the rest of the newspaper?
(2) What general training do editorial writers have?
(3) How much do editorials influence readers' opinions?
(4) What is the relationship between the news and the editorials?
(5) What is the relationship between editorial opinion and the news presented?
(6) What is the relationship between the publisher and the editor?
(7) How does the business office influence both publisher and editor?

Each committee member chooses one or more questions on which he will report. Then he makes his investigation in the literature and also in the field, and reports findings to the whole committee or to the entire class. All members should watch for items and sources of information useful to fellow members.

Hold Teacher-Chairmen Conferences

A schedule of conferences between the teacher and all the committee chairmen should be worked out. These meetings will permit the teacher to check upon progress, to inject a sense of direction as needed, and to stimulate rapport between the various chairmen. The student chairmen are the key people of the class, and the success or failure of the whole survey will usually hinge upon their attitude and sense of responsibility toward it.

Seek Lay Advisors

"Lay advisors" are persons active in the problem-field who may be induced to help with the survey of that field. Even busy people will cooperate in this manner if they can be convinced that the students are serious in their purpose and intelligent in their planning. It should be remembered that nearly everyone is trying to *sell something*—an idea, a service, or a commodity. This being true, nearly everyone will respond to a request for counsel in the area of his interest. Since these lay advisors are actually "resource people," they should be utilized according to the techniques outlined in Chapter 7.

At suitable times, the committees most concerned, the teacher, and the lay advisors should meet together. The latters' function is chiefly that of interpretation, direction-pointing, and stimulation of student interest. Being human, they have their own prejudices and predispositions, all of which must tactfully be taken into account as the survey progresses.

Assuming now that these steps of survey-planning have been successfully completed, the class is ready to start the actual field survey.

Making the Survey

All preparations have now been completed, and the stage of active investigations in the field has been reached. Five major steps now become necessary: gather the data, report findings within the committees, present committee reports to the entire class, synthesize committee findings, and verify conclusions.

Gather the Data

Keeping foremost in mind the central and subsidiary purposes of the survey, the committees now proceed to gather the data needed. This they will do by utilizing those varied techniques of investigation already chosen. Before any of these techniques are actually attempted by the students, however, all the suggestions already offered for their effective use should be carefully reviewed. As a final safeguard, the teacher should once more stress the vital importance of cultivating public goodwill in all the field investigations about to be made.

Report Findings Within the Committees

Some definite plan for reporting individual and sub-committee findings is essential to sustained interest and group efficiency. Such a plan must include at least seven significant aspects, as follows:

• **Schedule report meetings.** Each recorder should prepare a report schedule after teacher-committee discussion of progress and needs. A copy of this schedule should be given to the teacher, who thus knows where responsibility lies in each committee all of the time. Committee members likewise know definitely on what days they are to make their reports. If the chairman constantly checks upon the reading and field research programs of all committee members, much "cramming" for report days will be avoided.

• **Maintain a balanced program.** No fixed rule for the frequency of reports can be suggested. That will depend upon the age of the students, the volume of material available, the abilities of individual pupils, the number of class periods devoted to the survey, the amount of time that committee members can work upon their assignments, and similar factors. At all times, the teacher must seek to maintain a nice balance between the requirements of a thorough investigation and the limitations of committee members.

• **Require adequate notes.** If the teacher has helped students with the mechanics of note-taking, the presentation of reports will be much more meaningful than is likely if pupils have little idea of what is important or trivial, significant or irrelevant. Adequate notes will do much to foster such discrimination. Notes should be carefully taken and organized, and preserved together in a notebook of reasonable size.

• **Present oral reports.** According to the committee schedule, individual members make oral reports of findings to the committee as a whole. It is important that the notes from which these talks are made be prepared upon cards in basic outline form. The student's original notes, whether of reading done or of conditions observed in the field, should not be used directly. The reason for this is that the student will have taken notes about many items which will not be very important in a summary talk. If he speaks directly from his original notes, the fumbling which ensues injures effective presentation. The talk should be made in such a manner that the other members readily discern its outline, and should be concluded with a brief summary which says in effect, "Now, out of all I have told you, here are the highpoints."

• **Make progress reports to the class.** During the course of the survey, reports from each committee should be made before the entire class. This procedure provides excellent general motivation since it introduces an element of desirable group competition, and it also enables the teacher and students to comment profitably upon good and bad techniques of presentation.

• **Summarize committee findings.** The final step within this purely committee procedure is to bring all the individuals' findings together for organization, summary, and interpretation. This can best be done in a discussion group composed of the entire committee, the lay advisors, and the teacher. The blackboard should be freely used as an aid in visualizing ideas, relationships, and relative significance of findings. When the group has agreed upon its completed summary, the recorder should write out that summary in full and have it typewritten in triplicate—one copy for the class or school library, one for the committee chairman, and one for the teacher.

Present Committee Reports to the Entire Class

When a survey is thus undertaken on a committee basis, it is as though a structure, let us say a house, is to be built in sections and later assembled. Each committee is given responsibility for a part of the whole; each "crew" must contribute its share to the total project. Not to do so adequately would produce something less than a finished structure. The reading and the field research programs are the materials out of which each committee constructs its allotted portion of the common dwelling.

• **Schedule each report.** The committee chairmen and the teacher should schedule the various committee reports. The amount of time allowed each committee will depend upon the significance of the total problem, the importance and proportionate value of each committee's findings, and the time which the teacher feels can be devoted to presentation. In a survey of newspapers, for example, the time allotted to the committee on censorship might be greater than that assigned to a committee on newspaper finance.

• **Decide what to present.** In preparing its class presentation, each committee should bear constantly in mind this essential query: "What should the intelligent member of this community know about this problem-field?" Every committee will have uncovered numerous details which it would be pointless to present to the entire class group. What should be known and remembered? What is genuinely significant? What information does our committee have which will help our classmates?

• **Determine the form of presentation.** Each committee must next decide how and by whom its report is to be presented. The nature of the material will naturally determine whether panel discussions, motion pictures, dramatizations, tape recordings, charts, drawings and sketches, or direct talks are most appropriate. A committee may utilize one, several, or possibly all of these devices. In any event, presentation should not be restricted to the "star" members of the committee. In the interests of general pupil growth, it is always desirable that every committee member participate in some way.

• **Hold a "dress rehearsal."** Whatever the form chosen, the committee should practice its report. It is helpful to use a tape or wire recorder so students may evaluate and improve their techniques. Committee members should know their material well enough so they will not be too dependent upon notes or other props. This is not merely "making a report"; it is telling a story of vital import.

•   **Stimulate audience questions.** When the committee has completed its report, all students should have a clear understanding of the facts uncovered by that committee, and of the significance of those findings for the entire survey problem. Such understanding is not likely to be complete upon the basis of the committee's presentation alone; it requires questions by the audience and replies from committee members. If students are not thus stimulated to ask questions, it may be taken for granted that the committee presentation was either perfect or most inadequate.

In such manner, the entire class is made aware of the major findings, conclusions, and generalizations reached by its respective committees. The obvious next need is for the class as a whole to organize these separate findings into a coherent general picture.

Synthesize Committee Findings

After all committees have reported, general class discussion of their findings is in order. The teacher should serve as chairman of this class discussion, since he alone has been constantly in touch with all committees throughout the survey, and since he is presumably more skilled in organizing data and in detecting relationships. Yet he must avoid dominating the group since students need real experience in analyzing, relating, and interpreting discrete data. If the teacher acts in a residual capacity, the students will enjoy that experience and yet will be safeguarded against serious error in their interpretations of data.

Conscious effort should thus be made to crystallize all reported data into three or four major generalizations, each concisely stated and subject to verification in the future. Meanwhile, however, one further step should be taken; this is to refine these several generalizations into one inclusive statement.

In other words, an hypothesis is formed as the intellectual basis for appropriate social action in the future.

Verify Conclusions

Every effort must now be made to verify the data, the generalizations based upon the data, and the hypothesis crystallized from the generalizations. Verification may be sought by submitting findings to the best available experts for review and criticism. Lay advisors and other resource persons should be invited to evaluate the validity of the data and the logic of interpretations made from it. In the light of their criticisms, objectively considered, necessary changes should be made in the generalizations and hypothesis itself. Only after both facts and logic have been verified, is the class justified in assuming the truth of its findings.

Thus it is apparent that the whole process of planning and conducting a survey is properly a directed exercise in reflective thinking: identifying and analyzing the problem, gathering and synthesizing data, formulating and verifying hypotheses. But thinking unrelated to action is sterile, and so is a survey which fails to eventuate in some form of social activity. Now we pass into the third basic stage of the survey project: acting upon the findings.

Interpreting the Survey Experience

Community study should not "evaporate into thin air." Data are to be accumulated and recorded, not merely to fill up files, but to be *used*. One test of the value of a survey is the extent to which it is the basis for further study and for wider activity in the community itself.

The data of a survey, however reported and recorded, are finally to be closely related to the basic purpose for which the survey was undertaken. Until the data are used to answer the question for which they were collected, the project has not been consummated. All that has been said about follow-up teaching of an excursion is equally pertinent to the final phase of teaching through the making of surveys. "What do these data mean for us and for our community?" ought to concern pupils and teacher jointly. In addition to the careful interpretation they demand, the survey data should be made the basis for social action on the part of the students. Such action should consist in the application of data to problems within the framework of the basic community processes (see Chapter 3).

Prepare Visual Aids

Having tabulated and interpreted its data, the class ought now to plan how to present its findings to wider audiences.

The language of graphs, diagrams, charts, and pictograms is becoming a language of the common man in an age where quantitative analyses were never so important as now. It is therefore imperative that students be trained in the making, use, and interpretation of such aids to learning. Visual expressions of data should not, of course, displace written and oral reports, but they ought to be extensively used.

The class should construct whatever "visual aids" are appropriate and feasible as media for presentation of survey data. Among such aids frequently utilized are these:

photographs	land use maps	charts
relief maps	social base maps	graphs
scale models	pictorial charts	diagrams

Suggestions for construction of these and other visual aids were given in Chapter 6.

In developing these visual summaries, it is economical for the students to work as small committees. These committees may be either those which originally gathered the data, or new committees formed on the basis of individual interest in the construction of different visual media. The latter is generally preferable since it provides better for personal creative interests, and serves also to promote wider cooperation between class members. Thus the survey, beginning as a class project, proceeding through committee endeavors, again becomes a class interest as it moves along in this third major stage.

Publicize the Findings

Teacher and students should constantly be alert to ways in which the survey findings may be related to life concerns within the school and the local community. What, then, might be done to bring findings to the attention of a larger audience? Among many vital possibilities such projects as these are suggested:

• **Prepare an exhibit of material** for school, library, or museum display.

• **Write news and feature stories** for school and community newspapers or magazines.

• **Speak before school classes,** one member representing each interest committee.

• **Conduct a colorful school assembly program,** using visual aids, panel discussions, or dramatic productions.

• **Mimeograph a summary report** for distribution to parents, lay advisors, other resource persons, local newspapers, etc.

• **Address business, professional, and service clubs,** utilizing all avenues of publicity before and after the event.

• **Hold a public meeting to present findings,** and send special invitations to all people who were interviewed, all lay advisors, all teachers and parents intimately concerned, and all local newspaper editors.

• **Broadcast by radio and television,** and offer to send mimeographed summaries to all listeners who request them.

Through scores of such approaches, the school and community publics may be reached. And in reaching these publics, students gain invaluable personal experience in speaking, writing, organizing, interpreting, as well as in the more fundamental processes of scientific thinking.

Take Community Action

At its best, the survey will achieve the triple aim of community study generally; that is, it will (a) deepen participants' *understanding* of community structure, processes, and problems, (b) develop positive *attitudes* leading to group attack upon disclosed problems, and (c) provide extensive practice in applying social *skills*. Any survey which ends in cold understanding, untouched by enthusiasms and skills directed toward the making of needed community improvements, is hardly justifiable in the community school.

The ultimate value of the survey project thus appears as it leads into constructive, cooperative, and civic activity within the community itself. Specific suggestions for planning, executing, and evaluating such community *service projects* are offered in Chapter 12 and need not be previewed here. At this point, let us simply emphasize again that the purpose of the survey is not to *be* an activity complete in itself; rather it is to *result in* further social action.

Learning Activities

Discussion Topics

1. Should a community survey be limited to the kinds of information of use in the present curriculum, or should it include other types of data? Be specific.
2. Have a panel discussion on the values and the limitations of the survey as a learning activity for different age levels and in varied teaching fields.
3. Are there areas of community life such as politics, intergroup relations, or religion that should not be surveyed by school students?
4. How can you provide for individual differences in ability and interest when planning a class survey of the community?

Group Activities

1. Organize a number of committees, each to survey one "social process" and its related social problems in your community. Be sure not to neglect the three community levels or the status relationships explained in Chapters 3 and 4.

2. Plan how you might report these findings verbally, visually, and dramatically to interested adult groups in the community, as well as to the local press and broadcasting stations.
3. Get a committee to seek arrangements for the presentation of these findings as planned above.
4. Have a panel discuss effective ways of involving parents, teachers, church workers, and social agency officials in a community survey initiated by the school.

Individual Projects

1. Make a written analysis of some ways in which you could utilize the survey approach to strengthen your own teaching.
2. Tell how a school might organize its instructional program to make good use of community survey findings in the school itself.
3. After scanning a number of magazine articles and books reporting practice, explain how these surveys apparently affected the schools' public relations.

Learning Materials

Community surveys by school students are sampled in *School and Community Programs,* edited by Olsen (Prentice-Hall, 1949), where a dozen such projects are reported in Chapter 6. Other challenging accounts are listed now.

"Participation in Community Surveys as Social Education," James A. Michener. Includes values, criteria, analysis of typical surveys, techniques used, and answers to common objections. In National Council for the Social Studies Ninth Yearbook, *Utilization of Community Resources in the Social Studies,* pp. 144-163.

"Studying the Local Standard of Living," Mildred P. Ellis. Detailed account of procedure and findings in a community survey by high school students. *Harvard Educational Review* 9:175-183; March 1939.

"Study of Battle Creek Community," O. I. Frederick and E. C. Geyer. Outlines a plan for surveying a community cooperatively. The study group, numbering more than 100, was divided into seven committees, each to study one major aspect of the local community. *Curriculum Journal* 10:325-327; November 1939.

"Society Is Our Laboratory," Arthur Repke. Reports student-teacher experiences in making local surveys. Describes the student committee planning, the individual investigation procedure, the correlative reading program, the class procedures and the student forum to which findings were reported. *Social Education* 3:620-622; December 1939.

"A Housing Study—Correlating a National Problem with a Community Project," Joseph C. Baumgarter. A housing unit in which field study of local housing conditions led into a larger study of housing as a national problem. The topic outline for the unit is presented, together with correlated class activities in the field study of local housing. *Social Education* 4:470-473; November 1940.

"School Serves the Community," Neal F. Myers. Explains the step-by-step procedures followed by a high-school class in making and reporting a local housing survey. *National Association of Secondary School Principals Bulletin* 26:97-101; February 1942.

"A High School Class Surveys Its Town," Margaret Stowell. An economics-geography class made a land-use map of their city as a two-weeks' project. Steps taken are detailed and final map is illustrated. *Journal of Geography* 41:179-185; May 1942.

"Schools Learn From Industry," Elizabeth K. Wilson. Ten school districts cooperated with employers in making an occupational survey of the city. As a result, the school curricula were modified in many fields and much good feeling between schools and industry developed. *School Executive* 63:40-41; November 1943.

"Social Science Surveys Diet," John E. Hoar. A high school class surveyed its community to discover dietary habits and problems. Procedures and findings are reported, the latter in both tabular and summary form. *American School Board Journal* 108:23-25; March 1944.

"A Student Survey of Local Occupations," J. Fred Murphy. How three civics classes in the senior high school made an occupational survey of the city of 18,000 population. Describes the purposes of the survey, the method of procedure, the limitations of the survey, the facts obtained and the uses made of the data. *Social Studies* 27:474-476; November 1946.

"Word Concepts: Economics Class Polls Community," Joseph L. McKinney and Avery F. Olney. Students made semantic investigation of public opinion concerning the words "union," "strike," and "closed shop." Findings and conclusions are reported. *Clearing House* 23:156-159; November 1948.

"High-School Seniors Survey Job Opportunities," Katherine W. Dresden. An account of a youth survey which provided occupational guidance, increased rapport between school and community, and led many of the seniors to desire to stay in their own community as workers. *Occupations* 29:32-35; October 1950; also in *Education Digest* 16:4-6; January 1951.

"The Bellevue Community Study," Bernard Haake. Anecdotal description of a four-day community survey made by 23 students from a state teachers college. *Education* 73:121-125; October 1952.

Social process aspects of the community which may suggest survey possibilities have been listed in several excellent publications. The best is Johanna C. Colcord's *Your Community* (Russell Sage Foundation, 1941), which provides a detailed analysis of any community's structure and functioning. Similar helps in pamphlet form include *Know Your Town Government* (1949) and *Know Your County* (1937) by the National League of Women Voters, and *Know Your Community,* issued by the United States Office of Education (1941).

Suggestions for methods and techniques for school-made community surveys are apparent in many of the case-accounts listed above. In addition, you would do well to look into Margaret Koopman's pamphlet, *Utilizing the Local Environment* (Hinds, Hayden & Eldredge, 1946) which briefs the philosophy and objectives of community study and gives some directions for making social-process surveys. M. M. Chambers and Howard M. Bell's *How to Make a Community Youth Survey* (American Council, 1938) outlines the essential steps in making a youth survey, and points out the limitations as well as the significant features of such a survey for school and community action in solving youth's problems. If you are interested in occupational surveys, see the United States Office of Education's bulletin *Community Occupational Surveys* (1942) which reports on 96 surveys and suggests specific steps to be followed in making a good survey. The New York State Department of Education has a bulletin, *Community Surveys in Determining Needs for Vocational Industrial Education* (1945), telling how to conduct a community survey and suggesting needed statistics and forms. In his "School Socio-Economic Survey," Sigmund Folger offers directions for making an effective survey of a school's community to provide background for understanding child behavior (*Journal of Educational Sociology,* October 1945). Douglas S. Ward raises the question of "Community Surveys for Junior High Schools?" and warns against them unless they are well-organized and executed (*Social Education,* December 1940).

Teachers and lay people interested in conducting local surveys can find much material of real help. *Schools Look Around* by Elizabeth N. Layton and Justin B. White (Longmans, 1948) is a book about local surveys for teachers. In recent years, citizens' school surveys and community self-audits have become valuable allies of the modern school; in this field Merle Sumption's *How to Conduct a Citizens' School Survey* (Prentice-Hall, 1952) tells how to organize a committee, take a child census, analyze the financial ability of a school district, conduct a study of the educational program, and the like. Such state education department publications as Michigan's *Guide for Area Studies* and Vermont's *Guide for School Area Survey* will also be valuable to teachers working with lay groups.

Your Community Looks at Itself (Southern Regional Council, undated) is a detailed manual for the home town local survey, giving basic suggestions and check lists for getting data in such fields as population, health facilities, law enforcement, and housing. A brief guide for conducting a community self-survey of civil rights is *Let's Look at Ourselves,* published by the National Citizens Council on Civil Rights (undated). A comprehensive handbook in this important area is Margot H. Wormset and Claire Selltiz's *How to Conduct a Community Self-survey of Civil Rights* (American Jewish Congress, undated) which documents a scientific method of investigating the prevalance of discriminatory practices in community life. The Philadelphia Public Schools have issued *The Neighborhood Survey: A Means Toward Planning and Building a Better Community* (1948). This teaching unit, reproduced in Chapter 5, is an outline for the lower elementary grades, and includes suggested procedures, possible pupil learning experiences, evaluation ideas, and lists of teacher aids and resources.

Motion Pictures

U. S. Community and its Citizens. Begins with a newspaper story that the class is to survey the community. History is traced and maps made; then small committees study particular aspects of local living and the class as a whole makes a film of its findings. United World Films, 1945, 20 minutes.

Near Home. A class and teacher study many aspects of the community in which they live, then report to the town through a public exhibit of findings. International Film Bureau, 1946, 25 minutes.

CHAPTER **10**

School Camping

Woods, hills, plains, valleys, lakes, and streams are becoming part of the community school plant. In such an outdoor setting, an ever-increasing number of schools provide educational experiences for students and teachers, using the natural environment for real and direct learnings. These adventures in learning in a nature setting are made richer when boys and girls and their teachers go to camp for several days as a regular part of the school program.

School camping is part of a great surge of interest in the out-of-doors arising in this mid-century. Today's adults are already two generations from the land, but camping and outdoor experiences can become the heritage of every child as community schools thus extend their operations. Current interest in camping and outdoor education by schools may be explained as follows:

• There has been organized camping in America for more than 75 years, and people generally regard camping as a good and wholesome experience for children.
• School administrators and curriculum makers have been seeking for more direct-experience learning opportunities for which school camping is a "natural."
• The drift to cities and the rapid tempo of modern living is creating a felt-need for people to find more opportunities for roots in the soil, thus developing a closer relationship between human beings and natural resources.

This chapter is by JULIAN W. SMITH.

One of the most hopeful aspects of school camping is the fact that it is being considered a part of general education and an experience that is good for all children and teachers. Efforts in camping involve the use of many resources and necessitate teamwork with a variety of local, state, and federal agencies, particularly those that have responsibility for custody and management of public lands. Mobilization of these resources for the education of youth and for the improvement and development of the community itself is a unique operation of the community school. It results in the improvement of community living through the efforts of the school as a service agency and, at the same time, provides additional opportunities for a more complete education of all. School camping, like other community school activities, is planned by the participants—students, teachers, and parents—and the learning activities are tailored to meet the needs of children, youth, and adults.

What Is the Nature of School Camping?

Fortunately, Nature imposes no required curriculum or sacred sets of activities for those who seek education and recreation in her environment. In school camping, the program may be planned to meet both the general and special needs and interests of those who participate. However, it is only logical to make the maximum use of the natural environment and the living situations available in the camp setting. The greatest case can be made for the out-of-classroom activities when the program centers on those experiences that can take place most effectively outside of the central school plant. There are many applications and real situations relating to classroom learnings that occur in the camping program.

School camping encourages direct learning experiences and has potential life situations that are conducive to the most effective teaching methods—that is, through learning by doing, seeing, hearing, tasting, smelling, feeling, with a minimum of answer-giving by teachers and by resource leaders. The school camp is essentially a miniature community with the campers and teachers as citizens. Many of the problems faced by the home community are inherent in the camp, such as the handling, preparation, and eating of food, sanitation, sewage disposal, housing, health habits, social and cultural differences, and the process of representative government. The camper finds real opportunities with the group for self-realization, recognition, and security.

The most significant aspect of school camping is that it is a phase of general education and does not belong exclusively to any interest area, such as science, physical education, recreation, guidance, or health. School camping is unique also because it is an integral part of the total educational experience for a group of children and their teachers. Being a part of the community school program, the camp activities are related directly to the curriculum. In a school camp, there is ample room for special interests, such as conservation, spiritual and aesthetic appreciations, outdoor sports, hobbies, and countless others. School camping periods are shorter than usually found in other kinds of camping. Camping experiences in school create a continuing interest in the out-of-doors and many students will desire to attend other camps for more extended periods of time in the summer. School camping conflicts or competes in no way with private and agency camping.

We must understand that school camping is only one way to secure learning experiences in the out-of-doors. Field trips, school farms, gardens, and day camps are other patterns for outdoor education. The resident camping experience, with its democratic group living, adds many more values and learning opportunities than are available in other types of outdoor activities.

How Has the School Camping Movement Developed?

The interest and growth of school camping during the past few years has been phenomenal. While there were reports before 1940 of occasional camp activities sponsored by schools, they were usually spasmodic and occurred for short periods of time. In several instances, such as the Los Angeles Camp in California (in the early twenties), camping for school children was provided during summer months and vacation periods as a recreational opportunity. In other cases, such as the Tappan Junior High School, Ann Arbor, Michigan, junior high school students spent short periods at a distant camp as a part of an excursion trip. Some school districts in the United States have owned camp properties for a number of years, but usually operated them during the summer months as a community recreational activity. School-sponsored camping occurred in Cadillac, Michigan, and Atlanta, Georgia, in the thirties. The literature in the past frequently mentioned school camps as being desirable. With the establishment of Life Camps in the thirties, L. B. Sharp, Director, began to encourage and promote public school camping. It was not until 1940, however, that the first year-round school camp went into operation on the assumption that school camping should be an integral part of the curriculum. This first year-round camp was made possible by the W. K. Kellogg Foundation of Battle Creek, Michigan. This Foundation made its Clear Lake Camp and staff available to three Michigan schools—Battle Creek–Lakeview, Decatur, and Otsego—for a year. Students from grades four to twelve participated for two-week periods, and the new venture was so successful that the Battle Creek Public Schools and other schools of Calhoun County initiated a similar program in the years that followed.

In 1945, the Michigan Department of Public Instruction gave state leadership to this promising educational venture, and soon thereafter initiated a demonstration research program of school camping and outdoor education in cooperation with the Department of Conservation and the W. K. Kellogg Foundation. In a period of six years, upwards of 100 school districts in Michigan developed school camping programs. School camping in Michigan has had public endorsement in the form of an act passed by the Legislature in 1945 which enables the school districts to acquire camps and operate them as a part of the regular educational and recreational program of the schools. Later, the Legislature set aside funds in a State School Aid Bill to encourage secondary schools to initiate camping programs.

Following the lead of the Clear Lake Camp program in Michigan, San Diego, California, organized the city-county camp commission which, for a period of years, has provided extensive camping opportunities for children in the city and county schools. A number of other California schools, such as Long Beach and Los Angeles, now have programs. School camping is also under way in Washington, New York, Texas, Florida, Illinois, Massachusetts, North Carolina, Ohio, Pennsylvania, Alabama, South Carolina, Utah, New Hampshire, Indiana, Georgia, Iowa, New Jersey, Maryland, Missouri, Tennessee, Minnesota, Arizona and others are in the planning stages.

The school camping idea has had considerable attention on the part of national leaders in education. In the early 1940's, the W. K. Kellogg Foundation sponsored a conference at the Clear Lake Camp in Michigan which delineated many of the educational values of camping experiences for school children. In 1949, a National Conference on Community School Camping was held in Michigan, during which more than 100 leaders from various parts of the nation observed the Michigan program and carefully studied this rapidly unfolding adventure in education.[1] Notable among the pronouncements of the group was that community school camping is a partial answer to the problems of youth, a vitalization of the educational content and method of the school curriculum, a utilization of human and natural resources, and involves the cooperation of the many agencies concerned with youth and natural resources.

In recent years many books and periodicals have devoted attention to school camping, and the topic has been considered

---

[1] See *A Report of the National Conference on Community School Camping*, by Lee M. Thurston, Department of Public Instruction, Lansing, Michigan, 1950.

at numerous state and national conventions and conferences. The Educational Policies Commission in its 1944 *Education for All American Youth* suggested that camping and outdoor education be made a part of youth education generally. The acceptance of school camping as a part of general education and the rapid growth in the number of programs indicate that the community school has found another successful avenue of learning.

What Is the Camp Program Like?

The general plan of school camping is very simple. Teachers and their students go to camp together, usually on school time. Most schools today are using the one-week period; but a good case can be made for two weeks or longer, and no one would say that less than a week would not have some value. The week period is easier to administer; obviously more children can be involved if the school has a series of shorter periods. In selecting leadership, the school administrator usually asks a teacher to direct or coordinate the camping efforts, and the regular classroom teacher along with other teachers in the system compose the staff. In most instances, the staff is made up of classroom teachers and others who have special skills and interests that are important in the camping program. Some of these include teachers interested in science, conservation, health, physical education, nursing, social science, agriculture, homemaking, vocational subjects, and recreation.

It is neither possible nor appropriate to suggest a program for a school camp that would be applicable to all schools. All we can do is indicate some of the general principles for program planning, and to enumerate some of the learning possibilities. It has been pointed out before that the school camping program should include those experiences that cannot be achieved as well, or at all, in the classroom. In addition, the camp experiences should supplement and enrich many of the in-school learning opportunities. There is no question but that school camping makes unique and significant contributions to general education, as follows:

- Learning to live happily and healthfully in the out-of-doors.
- Experiencing democratic living.
- Understanding the physical environment and how to use natural resources wisely.
- Providing additional real situations, including work experience, where many of the skills and attitudes developed in the classroom may be applied.

The camping experience has great value to all groups. For children in the upper elementary grades to go to camp as a part of the educational experience for that age group is a logical and natural development. Obviously the problems of organization and administration are simpler in the elementary school. On the other hand, a strong case can be made for the junior high school with its exploratory functions, and there is little doubt that the traditional secondary program needs the vitalizing and freshening influence of the camping program. Experience in Michigan, California, and Washington has demonstrated that the interest and enthusiasm of secondary school students is equal to that of any other age group, and the values appear to be just as significant. The development, naturally, will be slower in secondary schools because of the departmentalized system, but there is little doubt that an ever-increasing number of high schools will develop a flexible curriculum and schedule to include camping and outdoor education experiences.

In the elementary school camp, much stress is placed on the exploratory trips throughout the camp area, along with cookouts, shelter building, trail blazing, the use of the compass, and a great variety of other skills that have meaning and interest to children. For those of secondary school age, specific projects to improve the camp community have great interest, such as building of shelters, improving the park, timber management, studies and activities in game and fish management, correction of soil erosion. Interspersed with all of these are the trips and explorations to points of interest such as marshes, quaking bogs, glacial lakes, sand dunes, high cliffs, desert areas, tropical swamps, sawmills, and gravel pits. Appropriate activities depicting the folklore and history of the area are also unique in camping: Indian life, lumbering, mining, transportation, and land management are illustrations.

There will be in each instance the arts and crafts associated with the native materials. Among these will be making and using archery equipment, basket weaving, excavation of Indian relics, painting, music, poetry, and dramatics, all of which develop from the natural and uninhibited interests of children.

It is interesting and significant that the types and patterns of school camping vary greatly particularly in the beginning stages. In the elementary school, the problem is relatively simple because an entire classroom goes to camp together; but in the junior or senior high school, some special group has to be chosen. Some of the units selected in the various Michigan schools include homerooms, science classes, core courses, unified studies, and all or part of a chosen grade group or other special interest area. In general, it is desirable to choose a group of students and teachers who are associated together throughout the school year. Ideally, a group, associated with a teacher or teachers having wide interests in guidance may get more of the real values of a living experience, while special interest groups, such as a science class may devote more attention to the exploration and study of the natural environment. However, it should be re-emphasized that the school should begin where the best interests of the school and community can be served by the camping program. The determining factor in many instances might be the interest and readiness of the teachers, because experience has indicated already that students and their parents are very enthusiastic about the development of the school camping program.

The contribution made to the camping program by specialists, technicians, and all those having special interests in the out-of-doors, professionally or through hobbies, is extremely significant. These people render maximum service when there has been careful planning for the learning experience. The teacher should never abdicate or forsake his role as teacher-counselor in the camp activities. The resource leader, with his understanding of the problem involved, aids the teacher in making the experience real and meaningful. At the same time that the teacher is learning about the out-of-doors, the resource leader gets a better understanding of the learning process and methods of teaching.

As teachers participate more in camping programs, there is less dependence on resource leaders, but there will always be a need for the practitioneer, whether state conservationist, health specialist, or hobbyist, to help bridge the gap between academic concepts and life as it goes on within the camp. It would be difficult, for example, to conceive of a good community school camping program that took place in the vicinity of forest areas, if campers, during their stay at camp, did not see the forester, the game specialist, or the park ranger in action, and perhaps have a part in helping him.

While most school camping is devoted to general education purposes, special groups should utilize the out-of-doors for more intensive study, such as science, history, music, painting, conservation, and the like. Let's illustrate with a possible day's activity in a Michigan school camp. There might be an exploratory trip over the area with a cook-out or overnight stay; a work project, such as planting trees, building shelters for game, repairing boats, or otherwise improving the camp; responsibility for the common activities of daily living, such as the preparation of food, cleaning the camp, and cutting wood for the fire; participation in interest activities, such as crafts, dramatics, music, fishing, archery, or games around the fireplace; helping to plan the evening's activities, which might include square dancing, story-telling, or Indian ceremonies; helping evaluate the day's program; meeting with the camp council; and trips to points of special interest, such as a stone quarry or an unnamed lake. Included in all of these would be the friendly and genuine associations with teachers and resources leaders. Among the usual course of events might be the items of business, such as writing letters home, getting food out of the commissary for cook-outs, running the camp store or bank, and planning for parents' visits. These are only a few of the many fine activities that can take place. The sample

AN ELEMENTARY SCHOOL CAMPING PROGRAM

DAY	GROUP I	GROUP II	GROUP III
Monday	Planning and hiking around lake Cook-out Paul Bunyan stories	Planning and hike to abandoned farm Weather study Building shelter	Planning and camp cruise Tapping trees Square dance
Tuesday	Blacksmith's shop Scavenger hunt	Logging Make ice cream	Treasure hunt Plant trees
	Sock Hop		
Wednesday	Boiling sap Cutting wood Weather station	Cook-out Hike around the lake Tree planting	Fire building Compass hike Crafts
	Square dance		
Thursday	Breakfast cook-out Compass hike Visit grist mill	Compass hike Plan for council fire	Cook-out Bird census
	Council fire		
Friday	Clean up and pack Evaluation session Go home		

Other daily activities include housekeeping, meals, banking, camp store, crafts shop activities, camp library, and bedtime stories.

A HIGH SCHOOL CAMPING PROGRAM

DAY	PROGRAM GROUP I	PROGRAM GROUP II	PROGRAM GROUP III	PROGRAM GROUP IV	PROGRAM GROUP V
Monday	Weather Station — Historical hike	Hike to old homestead	Felling trees and cutting wood; Archery	Building a dam	Bird hunt; Blazing a trail and woodcutting
			Sunset Vespers		
Tuesday	Fish conservation; Evening cook-out	Trip to Old Indian Village; Noon cook-out and hike	Planning session; Building game shelters	Building animal shelters; Fish conservation	Trip to Devil's Soup Bowl; Cook-out
Wednesday	Build brush shelters for game	Find depth of lake; Fish conservation	Tree planting	Tree planting; Archery	Fish conservation (scaling); Bird trip
			Deer Census		
Thursday	Axe Demonstration — Gun demonstration; Scaling and lumber mill trip	Fire arms safety; Clearing underbrush; Build brush piles; animal shelter; Felling trees	Gun demonstration; Trip around lake; Noon cook-out; Historical hike	Trip to gravel pit; Noon cook-out; Study of lake	Axe demonstration; Gun demonstration; Sawmill visit and cruising
Friday	Camp improvement	Camp clean-up	Camp project; Evaluation	Camp improvement	Camp clean-up

EVENING ACTIVITIES

Day	Camp council	Singing	Games	Snacks
Sunday	Planning by group			
Monday	Planning session and daily evaluation by groups	Singing	Square dancing	Snacks
Tuesday	Guest speakers	"	Storytelling	"
Wednesday	"	"	Square dancing	"
Thursday	Storytelling	"	Social dancing	Snacks in cabin

Note: Each group was responsible for planning only one evening's activities.

programs illustrate how the various groups schedule a week's activities.

Many of the great values of school camping will be the concomitant learning resulting from situations that often cannot be foreseen, as well as the guidance that takes place around burning embers at bedtime, or when an understanding teacher helps a camper meet a difficult personal or social problem. Not the least of these is the effect upon children of the beauty of sunrises and sunsets; birds, animals, and plants in their natural habitats; and perhaps the real fury of a storm.

How Is a School Camp Organized and Administered?

Like other aspects of the community school program, camping is tailored to meet students' needs. The administrative patterns and program activities of the many schools now having camping programs are different, and it would be unwise to attempt to standardize them. The camp and land areas, whether the property of the school district or owned publicly or privately, are considered a part of the school's educational plant, and the only functional difference from the other community school facilities is the distance to the woods and the uniqueness of the natural environment.

Since school camping is an integral part of the curriculum, the same general plans for administration and instruction that would be found in a good community school should be applied in the camping program. The camp staff members are professionally trained and certified as teachers. The regular classroom teachers go to camp with the children. The director should have training and experience comparable to other supervisory positions, with special competencies in camping and outdoor education. The school also should assume full responsibility for transporting pupils to and from camp inasmuch as the camp is part of the program. Instructional materials go from the school to camp, as does the necessary equipment. Food and supplies are purchased through the regular school channels.

School policies with respect to health and other special services should be followed in camp, with appropriate variations to meet special needs, since the camp becomes both the students' home and school during the camping period.

More than other factors, the types and availability of facilities have tended to shape operational patterns and organizations of school camping. To date, schools have used good judgment in making the best use of facilities already available, and in starting modestly and experimentally to develop their programs. The general patterns in existence at the present time might be described as follows:

• The operation of a camp by a school district on a year-round basis, usually having a central staff and a continuous program.

• The use of existing camps and facilities by schools for shorter periods of time, with classroom teachers making up the camp staff. This program is much more prevalent and provides a high degree of program flexibility, depending upon the staff and the groups that have the camp experience.

• A school camping program provided by a college or university which has acquired camp facilities for teacher education, and at the same time makes it possible for schools of the area to participate.

The school camping program should be financed the same as any other aspect of the school program, namely, from the regular school budget. This applies particularly to instruction and facilities, inasmuch as the home should provide for the food and clothing of the children while at camp. The following principles have been generally accepted as a guide to the administration of the camping program:

• The family should assume the cost of food and clothing for the students while at camp. The home should retain its responsibility for the maintenance of its members.

• In camping, as in other aspects of the school program, the board of education should provide instruction and necessary equipment and materials for school-age children and youth.

• For those families that cannot pay for their children in camp, the regularly constituted social agencies which normally care for them at home should assume the responsibility here also. Local service clubs and organizations that believe in the camping program

frequently provide additional funds so that no child will be denied his camping experience because of family finances.
• Camp sites and other facilities should be provided by the school district or other appropriate governmental unit, such as state or county.

As the number of schools that provide camping programs increases, the matter of administrative procedures and facilities will become a more important problem. Experience to date indicates that adequate camp facilities can be shared by a number of school districts. This might be accomplished by having a larger school own or rent a camp and then contract it to other schools. Matters of policy, with respect to staff and program, can be formulated by an advisory group from the participating schools. If not too cumbersome a procedure, the property may be held jointly by a number of school districts. In any event, the use of a camp and land area can be arranged cooperatively by schools without duplicating facilities and services, as has been done so often in the past. A large school system needs one or more camps of its own, and can operate them efficiently through continuous use—day and night, winter and summer.

A good example of cooperative action is the case of the city of Battle Creek, Michigan. The school leases the Clear Lake Camp from the W. K. Kellogg Foundation and then makes it available for nine other school districts, each paying its own proportionate share of the instruction and maintenance costs. In many places, schools already own land on which simple facilities can be built, and the development of a camp itself might be a significant educational development. In Michigan, Wisconsin, and some other states, schools have been deeded land by the state. It would be appropriate in many instances for the school to develop a camp or shelter to encourage elementary and secondary school students to use it as an educational laboratory.

It appears that much of the publicly owned land in the United States could and should be made available for educational purposes. In Michigan, for example, the state owns more than 4,000,000 acres, much of which is usable for educational purposes. The state has some camps already built in these areas and has made them available to schools. In some instances, as in the case of state and national parks and forests, it might be necessary to change the laws with respect to the use, leasing, and sale of lands to school districts. When schools purchase land for camping purposes, it is advisable to buy relatively small parcels of land, adjacent to large publicly owned areas, which can and should be used in the venture.

The home pays the cost of food at camp, which averages approximately $7.00 per week in Michigan, and the school furnishes the instruction, transportation, rental of the camp, and instructional materials. The usual ratio of teacher to children found in classrooms is not adequate in camp because of the increased responsibilities in a 24-hour-day situation. A common practice is for the administrator to select additional teachers, often hiring assistants to take their places while spending the week at camp. While there is no fixed ratio, many schools have found it possible to conduct successful programs with one staff member to twelve to fifteen campers (with this leadership supplemented, however, by resource personnel). In the matter of cost of food and maintenance, where it is difficult for the family to assume these costs, agencies and interested groups in the community have made funds available so that all of the children of a selected group may go to camp if they desire to do so.

The cost and difficulty in initiating a school camping program are oftentimes used as reasons for not attempting it. For the comfort of those who feel that it is too expensive, the costs reported by the 33 secondary schools in Michigan that provided camping programs in 1951-52 will be encouraging. While some of the costs may be hidden, since most of the leadership and many of the materials are already in the existing budget, the following figures indicate the expenses above those in the regu-

lar school budget. The items listed are the amounts per camper
per week:

Food	$6.08
Rental of camp	2.00
Additional instructional costs	3.73
Transportation	1.37
Miscellaneous	.84

TOTAL COST PER CAMPER PER WEEK.... $14.02

The superintendents of the 33 secondary schools reporting
commented in each case that the program was very successful,
and the recommendation for improvement was that the opportunities be expanded to include more students.

The question of liability of the school and teachers while
children are in camp is often raised. In this case, the same
policies apply that would in the school or on the playground.
In most states, the only situation where liability would be a
problem is in gross negligence on the part of the teacher. Accidents in a well-run school camp are actually rare and are
fewer in number than occur in the regular course of playground and gymnasium activities. Many schools make the services of the school nurse available all or part of the time, while
in other instances the county health nurses and local community health staff members assist. Medical care generally can be
arranged with the physicians in the nearest town.

What Facilities Are Needed?

Schools are often able to use many facilities already available,
such as state-owned camps, social agency camps, and those
operated by private organizations or individuals. The fact that
most of the camping is done on school time has made it possible
to use camps that otherwise stand idle after the expiration of
the summer period. In the northern climates, it is necessary
to remodel and winterize many of the existing facilities. The
time is near in some states when new camps will have to be

constructed, either by the school district or by other appropriate agencies—state or, perhaps, federal.

In considering facilities, it is highly important that we think
first of the program of school camping. Camp buildings should
be designed so as to be conducive to group living conditions,
with maximum opportunities for the best of guidance. Camp
buildings for sleeping could be constructed in units accommo-
dating 15 to 20 campers each, with counselor quarters and a
living room between two sleeping units. In the northern climates, particularly, toilets should be adjacent to the sleeping
units. Central dining rooms can be supplemented with eating
facilities for small groups. Other buildings, such as recreation
halls, first-aid center, and shops, should be provided as needed.
Much attention should be given to locating the camp on or
near large land areas that are available for exploration, study,
recreation, and conservation.

There are those who feel that the camp should be extremely
rough and primitive, but if it is to have year-round use it must
be constructed for all kinds of weather and in such manner as
will serve the needs of all in the community—children, youth,
and adults. Those who desire rough camping in small groups
will find plenty of room in the out-of-doors for occasional activities of that nature.

All community agencies concerned with camping should plan
cooperatively so that the various youth-serving organizations
can use the camp in the summer months, making it available to
schools for the rest of the year. It would be a mistake for every
group to plan its own camp independently of the others. In
some sections of the country we can already find examples of
poor planning in that respect.

Long-range planning will be necessary to provide adequate
camping facilities near large cities. Federal and state governments may have to acquire marginal land, in some instances
higher-priced parcels, in order to make the necessary facilities
available to the more densely populated areas. An example of
this farsighted planning was given when the Michigan State

Legislature appropriated money and authorized the Department of Conservation to purchase approximately 50,000 acres of land in a semicircle around the metropolitan area of Detroit, and within an hour's drive from nearly any point in the city. On these lands, many of which are unsuited to agriculture, there are found activities such as picnicking, camping, hiking, and fishing, with the possibility of a variety of others. Also in these same areas are several camps that have been used continuously since the beginning of the Michigan school camping program.

How May a School Camping Program Be Developed?

School camping can be made available to all children only by complete cooperation between those concerned with the education and welfare of children, and those who have responsibility for the management and protection of natural resources. In several states the Departments of Public Instruction and Conservation operate as a team, at the state level, in helping communities make the best use of available facilities and leadership. Such cooperation and utilization of existing resources has resulted in the wide use of skilled personnel and technicians as resource people to assist schools in the use and improvement of parks and camps, in the preparation of materials, and in the expansion of in-service education activities. The same is true at the local level in many communities where schools, agencies, and various organizations join together in providing opportunities and facilities for the development of school camping.

Camping leadership and facilities are often already available to provide the beginning of an excellent school camping program. Departments of education, conservation, and health; soil districts, county agents, colleges, parks, and national forests are powerful resources because many of them have personnel, materials, equipment, and facilities that can supplement the efforts of schools in initiating and conducting camping programs. Teamwork will be reflected in joint meetings of staff members on planning committees, participation in conferences, coordination of field activities, and cooperative endeavors in the development of documentary materials and films.

Organizations such as civic groups, camping associations, Audubon societies, garden clubs, sportsmen's clubs, and a host of others have leadership that is often enthusiastic about the extension of camping experiences. Many schools have found dozens of local resource people who are more than willing to assist in the process.

There is little excuse for departments and organizations that have mutual interests, such as camping, conservation, and outdoor education, to be at cross-purposes or to be selfish with their facilities and leadership when they are receiving financial assistance from the communities themselves. The time is near at hand when the citizen is going to require cooperation and the wider utilization of funds and resources before he will support many of the interests seeking financial aid for themselves.

There is no secret formula for the development of any good program except that of careful planning. School camping programs can be initiated much the same as one would approach the problem of improving the health program, or more effective industrial development, or better streets, or a library, or whatever the people desire. In school camping, it has been found that individuals, organizations, and departments concerned with natural resources, parks, and outdoor interests should be a part of the planning at the local and state levels. A logical procedure for a school just starting to work on a camping program might include these steps:

• Form a planning committee, made up of teachers, parents, students, and community lay leaders, to study the possibilities, collect ideas, survey other school camping programs, and then suggest the best planning procedures for local needs. The final step would consist in a recommendation to the board of education that an experimental or pilot program be undertaken.

• Organize an action group if the community, through the board of education, approves of a camping program as a part of the offering of the school.

• Survey available camp facilities and resource leadership.

- Visit camps already operating to see programs in action.
- Provide in-service camping experiences for school staffs.
- Interpret proposed plans to all citizens of the community.
- Collect helpful materials, including books, periodicals, and films, which document school camping experiences.
- Organize student and teacher planning groups to visit the camp to be used or developed, work out class projects, and make preparations for the new experience.
- Plan with resource people who might include teachers, conservationists, Audubon society members, sportsmen's club members, garden club members, health department technicians, and the like.
- Arrange with colleges and universities for the participation of student teachers in the new camping program.
- Continuously evaluate the developing program in terms of both educational and public-relations values.

The initiation of a school camping program is relatively a simple and easy process, and one which is within reach of most school districts, whatever the size. This is true because the beginning should be reasonably small and experimental in character. The planning steps suggested above are particularly appropriate for the smaller school where, in many instances, it is easier to get community support, and the out-of-doors itself seems closer at hand and therefore more important. Some of the best programs have started when one or two interested teachers and a roomful of excited youngsters have planned and developed their own program on a day-camping basis, and later moved into camp with the approval of the board of education and the administrators. It is not unusual for interested parents to assist in the camp itself.

In most parts of the country there is an actual or potential camp site within range of the school district, either publicly or privately owned, which could be used at least during the warm weather. It would be unusual if a school administrator in any school in the country could not find some help in the planning of such a program from the college serving the area, from state departments, or from some of the other agencies mentioned previously.

The entire school staff should share in developing the camping program. While all staff members might not be equally interested in participating, careful planning will usually insure the cooperation of all, at least for the initial pilot effort.

In summary, it should be repeated again that the same planning should be done for school camping as for any other aspect of the community school's operation. Most educational leaders and curriculum makers now believe that the planning of a curriculum is the right and the responsibility of the local community and that, outside of necessary minimums for protection, the regional, state, and national agencies and departments should assume a leadership role in helping the community help itself. If school camping develops this way, it will be a part of the general education of the community, and its goodness will be reflected in the interest and enthusiasm of citizens in maintaining the best kinds of educational opportunities for all children, youth, and adults.

What Teacher Preparation Is Required?

Since school camping is an integral part of the curriculum and the experiences involved are of general educational nature, the most important factor in the success of the program is good teaching. A teacher who likes children well enough to want to live with them for a period of time, and who understands the learning and growing process, will find himself quite at home in the school camp. He is most successful when he enters into the new learning experiences as one of the group, calling on resource people when needing the assistance of specialists. Good elementary school teachers are already working with children in informal situations, and are involved in a variety of activities ordinarily found in the self-contained classroom. Not minimizing the need for teachers to understand the physical environment, it is far more important that he know and understand children and be able to use the teachable moments that occur in the camping experience. As we view the implications of community school camping for teacher education, some of the most important concerns appear as these:

- Experience and training in informal situations, such as are characteristic of good camping.
- Training in outdoor situations where there is opportunity to understand the physical environment and natural resources.
- Opportunities to learn about children as they live together in camp and participate in informal learning activities.
- Relating camping and outdoor education to the school curriculum.

It would be wrong to assume that all teachers should have a highly specialized type of training peculiar to the out-of-doors, conservation, crafts, and the like. This might encourage a separate kind of education, even a dual system, that would take place in the woods and might be otherwise quite unrelated to the total educational program. Ideally, the good teacher should feel as much at home with the children in camp as in the classroom, the playground, or the music hall. The school camp director or coordinator needs to have broad training and experience in outdoor skills, camp administration, and the interpretation of the outdoors.

Many schools and colleges have already initiated teacher education activities in connection with school camping. Hundreds of teachers have attended in-service training institutes, workshops, credit courses, extension courses, and conferences where field training experiences have been available in camping, conservation, and outdoor education. These activities have been made possible through the efforts of colleges and universities, state departments of public instruction and of conservation, and by other agencies and groups. A large number of these training activities have occurred in outdoor environments, such as school camps and conservation laboratories. Resource leaders, specialists, and technicians in conservation, health, the physical sciences, social living, and other fields have participated in such activities. Some school systems have developed their own continuous in-service training programs and give many of their teachers camp experiences prior to the beginning of the school camp periods.

Much consideration is also being given to pre-service teacher education. An increasing number of colleges and universities are developing their own camps, while others participate in the ongoing school camping programs in their areas. Notable among these are Cortland Teachers College, New York; Sargent College, Boston University; Florence Teachers College, Alabama; Southern Illinois University, Carbondale; Antioch College, Ohio; and Northern Illinois Teachers College, DeKalb. Similar programs have been reported in California, Tennessee, and Washington State. It is interesting to note that five out of the eleven teachers' colleges in New York already have their own camps and are preparing to give prospective teachers more camping experience. In Michigan, all the public educational institutions for teachers are responding to the growing needs for training in school camping and outdoor education. Michigan State Normal College, Western Michigan College of Education, Wayne University, and Michigan State College provide experiences in school camps for student teachers; Central and Northern Michigan Colleges of Education and the University of Michigan offer credit courses for teachers in summer camps; and Michigan State College has added Outdoor Education to the School of Education.

When a college or university has a camp and a training program for outdoor education, it is possible to offer the following advantages:

• Laboratory and field opportunities for training in biology, geology, conservation, physical education, camping skills, recreation, wood crafts, and other special areas.
• Child growth and development classes which participate in a school camp with children.
• Opportunity for all prospective teachers, elementary and secondary, to spend some time in a school camp situation. Schools of the area and the campus laboratory school can share in such a program, thus combining school camping with teacher education.
• Student teaching experiences or internships in school camps for a large number of prospective teachers.

Institutions can participate actively in the camping and outdoor education program by using existing school camps as resource laboratories to improve and evaluate school camping, and by giving continuing consultant services to schools in a variety of such fields as child growth and development, science, and conservation.

Training programs such as described have had successful beginnings in some states where college students have already had student teaching experiences in existing school camps. As schools include more groups for camp experiences in the curriculum, school administrators will employ increasing numbers of new teachers who have had some personal experiences helping to make them more competent in school camping developments. There is no doubt but what such teachers will participate with greater interest, understanding, and competency as a result. The basic principle of learning by thoughtful doing applies as much to teachers and to adults generally as it does to children.

Classroom in the Woods

School camping is a natural and logical aspect of the community school. The concept that the whole community should be the students' learning environment is generally accepted today, and the actual extension of school operations into the pulsing community is becoming a reality in many places. The camp, a classroom in the woods, then becomes a part of the larger community. The outdoor environment in and around the camp represents added resources for the better education of children, youth, and adults. The opportunities to learn, work, and play amid the natural resources of the area contribute greatly to the growing-up process, and also stimulate interest and concern for the protection and wise use of the many natural resources of the community.

Learning Activities

Discussion Topics

1. By what kinds of instruments and procedures could you best evaluate a school camping program?
2. Select a given community and then outline how an effective school camping program might be developed for it, specifically.
3. Should camping be an integral and required part of every child's regular school experience?
4. Would this chapter's recommendations for school camp financing be acceptable in your community? Who might object, and why?
5. What responsibility should your state department of education assume for the promotion of school camping programs?

Group Projects

1. Make a study of public lands and facilities in your area which might be available for a school camping program. For information, write to the National Park Service and to your state departments of education and conservation; also to state camping associations and to the American Camping Association.
2. Find out the locations of school camps near you and, if possible, arrange for a field trip to one or more of them.
3. Suggest needed changes in public policies that would tend to encourage school camping. This would include policies with respect to the sale, leasing, and rental of public lands and facilities, state and federal aid, and various kinds of assistance that could be given by state and national organizations and departments.
4. Outline a model school camp weekly and daily program in terms of your own community's situation and needs.

Individual Activities

1. Study legal provisions and regulations at the state level that would make possible or tend to encourage school camping. Suggest needed changes in your state's legislation.
2. Summarize the findings of research that would have bearing on school camping.
3. Appraise the old Civilian Conservation Corps program in terms of what was learned about group camping.
4. Design the physical setting for a model school camp.

5. Check the *Education Digest* and other sources to see what colleges and universities are offering school camp leadership training, then write to them for further information.

Learning Materials

The philosophy of school camping is stressed in *School Camping* by George W. Donaldson (Association Press, 1952), a little volume which uses the camping program of the Tyler, Texas, school system to illustrate values and approaches. Frank L. Irwin's *The Theory of Camping* (Barnes, 1950) relates camping with educational thinking. A positive answer to the query of whether children's learning is affected by their going to camp on school time is evident in *Extending Education Through Camping*, a pamphlet report of an experiment published by the New York City Board of Education (Life Camps, Inc., 1948).

Other accounts of school camps in action should be noted also. A brief description of school efforts in camping throughout the United States is found in Helen K. Mackintosh's *Camping and Outdoor Education Experiences in the School Program*. (Gov't Printing Office, 1947). James M. Clarke's *Public School Camping* (Stanford University Press, 1951) is a rather complete description of the San Diego, California, city and county program which is different in many respects from other ventures, especially in administrative structure. *Camping and Outdoor Education in California,* published by the California State Department of Education, discusses different school programs in that state, with attention to the objectives and legal aspects involved. School camping programs in Michigan are described in text and pictures in *Community School Camping.* (Michigan State Department Public Instruction, undated.) This State Superintendent of Public Instruction has also produced *A Community School Work-Learn Camp* which reports the educational experiences of youth from three high schools who spent a semester in a camp where the outdoor curriculum was tailored to the needs of these young people who were school drop-outs or potential drop-outs.

Procedures in planning, organizing, and initiating school camping programs are explored in Helen Manley and M. F. Drury's *Education Through School Camping* (C. V. Mosby, St. Louis, 1952), a resource book which also gives a good description of the school camping program at University City, Missouri. A monograph of value to schools starting their camping activities is the Los Angeles County Office of Public Instruction's *Outdoor Education*. Those interested in designing and constructing camp facilities for school use will find many suggestions in *Community School Camps,* published by the Michigan State Office of Public Instruction.

School camping has been the theme of several issues of professional journals. See especially the May 1947 *Bulletin of the National Association of Secondary School Principals* which presents over twenty camping articles, the May 1950 issue of the *Journal of Educational Psychology,* the

School Executive of January 1947, the *Phi Delta Kappan* of December 1938, the *National Elementary Principal* of February 1949, and *Education* for September 1952.

Valuable magazine articles on school camping are constantly appearing. You will find the following among the best to date:

"Role of Camping in Education," W. H. Kilpatrick. The nature and psychology of effective learning as it develops in group camp living. *Education Digest* 7:46-48; March 1942.

"Education's New Look: Camping," Harry B. Gilbert and J. Wayne Wrightstone. Reports research findings on a fifth- and a seventh-grade school camping experience. The evaluation proceedings, results, and interpretation are indicated. *School Executive* 67:31-34; June 1948.

"Children's Work and Play Experiences in a School Camp," Elizabeth Hosking. Describes the what, where, who, and why of the Battle Creek, Michigan, school camp. *Childhood Education* 25:166-169; December 1948.

"Year-'Round Public-School Camping," Lotene Willare. Describes the Long Beach, California, school camp as used a week at a time by successive sixth-grade classes with their teachers. *National Education Association Journal* 38:576-577; November 1949.

"Classes That Camp Out," Esther Bristol. Outlines the philosophy and implications of school camps. *National Parent-Teacher* 44:94:22-24; May 1950.

"Classroom in the Cascades," Milton J. Gold and Harley L. Robertson. Describes a work-study camp experiment in which 65 high school boys and girls spent a week on conservation activities. *Clearing House* 25:80-84; October 1950.

"My Two Weeks at School Camp," Elena Harap. This is a day-by-day diary of a seventh-grade girl who, with her classmates, spent a fortnight in camp in April as an integral part of their school work. *Educational Leadership* 8:276-282; February 1951.

"Educational Leadership in School Camping," George W. Donaldson. Lists and explains four kinds of leadership responsibility of school camp directors. *Camping Magazine* 23:20-21; May 1951.

"What Is Outdoor Education?" L. B. Sharp. A summarizing statement which includes field trips in its concept, but stresses the superior values of learning in school camp. *School Executive* 71:19-22; August 1952.

"The School Camp in Winter," Leslie Clark. Describes the winter phase of year-round school camping. *Journal of the American Association for Health, Physical Education, and Recreation* 23:10-11; January 1952.

"Legal Authority, Restraints, and Liabilities," Madaline K. Remmlein. Reports the general legal situation with respect to school camping. *Education* 73:44ff.; September 1952.

"School Camping—A Potent Factor in Guidance," Marion J. Sack. How an elementary school uses its fifth- and sixth-grade school camping experiences to help children understand themselves and others. *Education* 73:501-503; April 1953.

"Camping—Introduction to School," Sarah E. Goodhue. A camping program for sixth graders, planned cooperatively by a school committee, is enthusiastically described by an elementary school principal. *Journal of the American Association for Health, Physical Education, and Recreation* 25: 37-38; January 1954.

"Let's Go Outdoors," Julian W. Smith. An appeal to all classroom teachers to include school camping and other types of outdoor experiences in the school program. *Michigan Education Journal;* April 1954.

Motion Pictures

School Time in Camp. Two groups of children are taken to camp for a three-week period during the regular school term. The film shows boys and girls retaining each vivid experience of a new life in effortless absorption. Life Camps, 1947, color, 18 minutes.

To Live Together. A sensitive documentary treatment of an interracial camp sponsored by two leading Chicago community centers. The interaction of the children at the camp revealed many of the problems involved in intergroup relationships. The film attempts to show that only by living what is to be learned can children overcome their prejudices toward other groups. Association Films, 1951, 30 minutes.

Wisdom Grows Outdoors. Several Michigan state group camps are shown in use by schools and youth-serving agencies. Michigan Department of Conservation, 1951, color, 24 minutes.

Classroom in the Cascades. An account of the pilot camping program conducted by the Highline High School and the Washington State Department of Public Instruction. Conservation projects are a part of the camping program for these high school youth. Washington State Department of Public Instruction, 1952, color, 20 minutes.

CHAPTER 11

Work Experiences

Our world's human need is for a new generation of youth inspired by the clear vision of a democratic, efficient, harmonious world society, yet ever sobered by an intimate acquaintance with the workaday world and with the patient, painstaking kind of effort that lasting social progress requires. To the development of such youth, planned work experiences can contribute enormously in both inspiration and realism. A youth is never fully mature until he is self-supporting in his own job. Society must now stand ready to provide jobs for all who wish to work, and must initially offer adequate opportunity for personal, sustained, and carefully supervised working experiences as a part of general education for all young people, not only for those enrolled in courses in distributive education, in diversified occupations, and in office practice. It is true, of course, that many students are forced to work within the home, on the farm, or in the family business enterprise. Such "work experience" is important, but is not likely to develop fullest educative value for the adolescent unless it is carried on with personal interest and insight. In such situations, the school's responsibility is to stimulate that insight and interest by continuous official recognition of the student's work and of its genuine significance to him, his home, and to society in general.

This chapter is by MORRIS R. MITCHELL.

Enterprising young people always go outside the home to find remunerative minor jobs for themselves—selling newspapers, shining shoes, delivering groceries, picking fruit, caring for children, Saturday clerking in stores, and the like. Paid work experience of all these varieties is tremendously valuable to youth, providing always that they labor in jobs which permit growth in initiative, reponsibility, and skills, and also that they are not physically, financially, or morally exploited in the process.

Sometimes systematic occupational training is given by community industries and offices working in close cooperation with the school's vocational education program. In such programs, students study part time, work part time, and are supervised throughout by officials representing industry and labor as well as the school. On the college level, cooperative work-and-study plans are well exemplified by the "Antioch Plan," whereby students alternate periods of work off campus with periods of study on campus. Yet regardless of the specific administrative plan, this type of work experience stresses the integration of vocational and social thinking with vocational skills as a fundamental, shared responsibility of school and community.

Work experience is sustained and interrelated activity of body and mind, carried on for purposes which are primarily prevocational in nature. More specifically defined, it means "practical activity in the production or distribution of goods or services exercised in a normal way in business, industrial, professional, and institutional fields." [1] Student clerking in a store at Christmas time is thus a form of work experience; so is after-school service in a social settlement, and a summer assignment as a farmer's helper. Such experiences may or may not include financial remuneration for work done. To be sure, they may often eventuate in a genuine civic contribution, and should always be infused with the spirit of cooperative service for social welfare, rather than that of grasping exploitation for

[1] Warren C. Seyfert and Paul A. Rehmus (eds.), *Work Experience in Education.* p. 6.

personal gain. Yet, fundamentally, the aim of work experience is to help young people to acquire the vocational orientation, the specific skills and interests, and the sustained self-discipline essential to their individual success in some vocational career. In this process, the community becomes partner with the school. Thus understood, work experiences:

• **Offer occupational orientation and exploratory experience.** In this realistic laboratory setting, the student can more clearly define his career aspirations, evaluate his previous expectations, discover the specific nature of further training needed, and decide in which particular occupational area his life will prove most useful to society and most satisfying to himself.

• **Stimulate a healthy attitude toward work,** including the desire to secure needed occupational information, skills, habits and discipline—not the least of which is a growing ability to "take it" in doing responsibly the necessary work of the world.

• **Deepen civic insight as it brings firsthand contact with varying social-industrial conditions** in their relation to problems of employment, wages, conditions of work, unions and employers' associations, government regulation, consumer income, and the economic meaning of wealth production.

• **Identify the adolescent with the adult group** through their cooperative attempts to meet a real need in a real situation. This psychological identification can be highly satisfying to both adults and adolescents, for as it develops adult status for the adolescent, it promotes genuine cooperation between the two generations in the accomplishment of socially useful work.

• **Relate doing with thinking.** Purely verbalistic education is not adequate. The mind and the body are one, and must be educated as a unit. Broad work experience, based on sound values and devoted to the development of marketable vocational skills, employs mind and body in one functional interrelationship.

• **Help bridge the gap between students** of different social status, since an organized work experience program is an integral and required part of the modern curriculum.

Thus does work experience, of a cultural as well as prevocational nature, vastly enrich our educational program. This it does by fostering greater realism, by building personal character, generating wholesome attitudes toward self and society, developing useful career skills, and by actually contributing to the general welfare. Suitable work experience thus becomes significant as one vital aspect of *general education*, as well as a means of vocational placement. Providing as it does for continuing firsthand experience with the vocational world, work experience should be made a primary avenue for the development of sound social, economic, and civic insight and responsibility.

The school obviously can have little or no control over the home or part-time job type of work experience, although it should surely be fully informed concerning the nature and extent of such work or jobs being carried by its students. Group service-work projects and individual vocational training, however, are both officially sponsored and primarily controlled by the schools. Suppose that we therefore notice certain broad principles of operation which should be observed in administering such programs of work experience.

Planning the Program

Careful planning is particularly important in the area of community-centered work experience. Although resource visitors, interviews, field trips, surveys, and school camping all involve considerable public cooperation, all of those "doors" are open briefly in terms of time; that is, each individual project is planned and completed in relatively short order. But an ongoing program of sustained work experience requires the development and maintenance of cooperative and cordial relations with the same community groups, for identical purposes, over an indefinite period of years. The best assurance of maintaining such cooperation is to use every care in planning for it, both initially and continuously.

Develop a Sound Philosophy

Work experience should not be advocated through any ascetic concern for the inherent value of severe or prolonged physical activity. There are sounder reasons than that for introducing curricular work experience of a socially useful nature.

Physical toil has been so arduous, yet so necessary during the three thousand centuries of mankind's existence, that even our religious writings have referred to the "sweat of his brow" as man's inescapable fate. Yet his efforts to escape that toil have been constant and profound. The more intellectual sought means of substituting mental for physical labor; one result of these efforts was the progressive emergence of technological short cuts, such as machines. Another common form of escape was through exploitation of the weak and less gifted by the strong and the ruthless. A third escape was through the rendering of professional services such as preaching and teaching. Formal education thus often became an instrument whereby people might further refine their techniques for escaping the exigencies of physical toil.

Out of all this arose an exaggerated distinction between physical and intellectual activity, with a greatly emphasized prestige and hence formal stress upon the latter. Our traditional schools, with their tendency to divorce curricular programs from vital life-needs, are merely the educational reflection of this artificial, yet deep-seated dualism. Many such schools, especially on the secondary level, have maintained curricula which were fundamentally unsuited to most of the children "educated" within them. Adolescents of limited mental ability cannot cope successfully with the traditional book-learning, and in consequence are usually directed into narrowly vocationalized trades; there they attain limited personal skills, but without adequate insight into their social and civic responsibilities. An equally dangerous consequence of the traditional school program, however, is that to the mentally gifted children. Many of these children, commonly considered too "superior" or too "promising" to work with their hands, go through school on a basis of planned inexperience with various kinds of physical labor. Emerging from school as "intellectuals" or "artists," their concepts and attitudes toward society are founded almost entirely upon vicarious rather than direct experience with the hard realities of the working world. Yet these children also, like those of lesser mentality, will each have his vote in helping to shape the political, economic, and social policies of the community. Neither group is apt to be *adequately* prepared for democratic citizenship in this critical era; the first because its members often work without thought about the social implications of their labor; the second because it becomes easy to think grandly yet often impractically through lack of direct appreciation of what human toil means and must mean to the world. Nowhere is the virtual immorality of disassociating *social thinking* from *vocational doing* more apparent than in many schools and factories of this twentieth century. That separation has left many intellectuals out of sympathetic touch with the people, while business managers, technicians, and laborers often show little concern for the promotion of general human welfare.

Any educational program designed to bridge this gap must therefore include as an essential aspect an integrated program of thought-in-work experience for all students, regardless of their mental abilities and future prospects. It is apparent also that such an integrated program, to be effective, must be built upon a new conception of the significance which socially useful work must have in our developing civilization.

We must increasingly judge the social value of production and work in terms of their ultimate human consequences. We shall do well, therefore, to begin by insisting that any work experience to which we give school approval shall be carried on in productive areas that are of *true value to human society,* as well as of manifest educational worth to the participating students. The school must help the employer understand that he is participating in a community endeavor to prepare young people for occupational life and adult citizenship. He must be willing to cooperate with the school by allowing a school representative freedom to work with the student's immediate supervisor on the job when necessary, in order to correlate study in school with the work experience, and to assure adjustment by the student to the job and progress through the total training program.

Arrange Work Opportunities

It is advisable to proceed slowly in developing the commercial, industrial, agricultural, and institutional contacts which may provide suitable work experiences. No wholesale solicitation of such opportunities should be made, for to do so is likely to cause administrative complications, difficulties in personality adjustment between the center's personnel and the working students, and even some likelihood of requests for student help under conditions which would endanger or exploit them. It is much better to add one or at most a few placement centers at a time, and to do so only after quiet but thorough investigation. Such centers should be chosen with an eye to affording a wide range of learning experiences suitable to the different aptitudes and interests of the students. There is danger that work experience selections may be limited by the special vocational interests of the teachers involved; this should be clearly recognized and provided against. And every opportunity should be sought whereby urban youth may secure rural working experience, and vice versa. All programs must obviously be planned in accordance with labor laws and other regulations.

Develop Job Analysis Sheets

A job analysis sheet should be worked out for each training situation. This may best be done in active consultation with the employer and the student involved. Such a sheet should state the general agreement made and should include the specific objectives and activities planned. If more than one employer in a given occupational grouping is participating, it is good procedure to get them all together to decide upon the training program for that occupational area. In many communities, the program as a whole, as well as the job analysis sheets, should be developed in close cooperation with organized business and labor.

Adapt the School Schedule

Extra-class activities, service projects, work experiences, and other less formal aspects of education are constantly—*and properly*—impinging upon the traditional school program of arbitrarily scheduled learning periods. Specific suggestions for meeting this problem are given in Chapter 14 of this volume. Here we shall simply note that teachers who desire to develop such vital learnings must be patient with those other teachers who are still satisfied with the formal disciplines, and that every care must be taken to arrange a reasonable balance between educational values sought through field projects and those obtained within the academic classroom. Actual details must obviously be settled in terms of each school's particular situation. It is well to note, however, that under stress of a broadening curriculum, both the school day and the school year tend to be considerably lengthened.

There are few who still doubt the value of work experiences. But many object to such experiences being made an integral part of the school program. There are those who oppose "credit" for work experiences on the ground that they are not measurably or comparably educative; others who feel that the "credit system" has been stretched to the breaking point, believe that we must move to a more intrinsic basis of motivation and evaluation. In some schools, credit is given where work experience is substituted for a "course." But most high schools that offer work experience opportunity grant some credit, one credit per semester being the most common practice.

Supervising the Work Experience Program

Adequate supervision by qualified adults is an essential aspect of any successful work experience program. Without going into minor details, let us therefore examine several significant considerations which must be observed as the program moves from the planning into the active phase.

Provide Competent Supervisors

Supervision of work experiences can provide admirable opportunities for guidance at its best. So often guidance has been a periodic affair, designed to meet crises rather than to prevent them. Work experience requires constant adjustment. Sound adjustment means personal growth. The teacher should therefore meet regularly with the students working under his direction, should maintain close contact with the employers involved, and should be regularly in touch with the students' parents.

Sometimes an outsider can best be called in to supervise work experience. In such cases, however, the wise teacher will not dismiss his own responsibility for the safety and educational growth of his students. He will make sure, for instance, that the learners enjoy a flow of changing purposeful activities; that they demonstrate capacity to carry through their purposes despite wearying repetition; that they do not become content with mere perseverance after growth has ceased; that they are relatively free from periods of rush or overstrain, and of slack times and even idleness.

Associate Study with Action, Thinking with Doing

Various work programs divide the school day into a formal, closely scheduled morning (to insure "mastery of fundamentals"), and a free afternoon of diverse practical activities. This is like separating flavor from food. Flavor has a function in digestion. Thought without action is futile. Action without thought is unethical. Functional education does not consist in mornings devoted to thought and afternoons dedicated to action. Thinking and doing are inseparable aspects of sound human growth. This basic principle is the foundation of educational advance during recent decades; it has already given us both the activity school and the community school. The functional program of work experience will therefore relate thinking and doing—planning, organizing, executing, and judging—in organic unity, rather than in artificial sequence.

Adjust the Work to the Student's Needs

Young people enjoy hard work if they feel that the job is their own. Work that is too easy offends. Yet work that is too hard may cause serious overexertion, particularly if the worker is stimulated by a new environment, by the presence of spectators, or by the prospect of high material reward. A nice balance must be maintained between the physical condition of the student and the physical demands of the job-situation. We must remember how completely most city children are accustomed to a life involving little sustained physical effort. In most instances, their muscles are flabby and their body tissues are soft. When such a child spends several hours or a whole day in driving a tractor, in haying, in helping build a house, a dam, or the like, a severe strain is thrown upon him as a physical organism. Every possible effort must therefore be made to prevent work experiences from causing undue fatigue or excitement at the outset.

Beware of Excessive Monotony or Stimulation

Guard against both excessive monotony from repetitious work (most such work can be done better mechanically in any case), and against undue stimulation from a new environment. Children new to the city will not concentrate upon planting, along streets, the trees they have brought from the country; neither will city children mend a pig fence until they have made friends with the pigs. If work experience is to be successful, the learner-worker must be challenged by the situation, and at the same time find himself purposefully identified with it.

Be Cautious but Not Over-Protective

Avoid extremes of over-concern for the students' safety and of unwise disregard of danger. There should be a nice sense of challenge and courage, but never of recklessness. Furthermore, we must be careful neither to under-estimate nor to over-estimate the learner's technical knowledge. The former is resented. The latter leads to frustration. Every supervisor of work experience should know first-aid, and should have adequate first-aid equipment constantly on hand in the work center itself. Comfortable work shoes, loose clothing, and gloves for soft hands are important. Sunburn should be avoided, and so should overheating. In the case of a prolonged job, involving strenuous exercise, it is well to begin with a work period of an hour or so the first day, and then lengthen each day's work by an hour or two until a proper balance between work, study, play, and rest has been achieved.

Remain Alert against Exploitation

Public desire to safeguard children against exploitation has led to regulations which often make difficult the provision of needed, vital, hand-work experience. What is desirable is not a complete exclusion of children from work until they reach some given age such as fourteen, but rather a gradual introduction of children into work situations on a guidance basis. Such a program would be practically impossible to administer on any other than an educational basis, and even here it is difficult to organize, particularly in urban situations where work opportunities for the immature are far fewer than they are in rural areas.

A more immediate consideration is that of making sure that students are not exploited through school approved or directed work experiences which are inexpertly managed, that are not socially useful, that demand exertion beyond the capacity of the young people involved, or that endanger them physically, emotionally, or morally.

Keep Adequate Records

Think through the problem of records in terms of the educational purposes of the work experience itself. Avoid

becoming enslaved to the time-consuming task of filling in unnecessarily detailed forms. In planning the needed records, ask
such questions as these: Will this item assist the student, the
employer, the parent, or the school in better guiding student
growth? Will this item help us to appraise the real value of
this particular work experience? Will this information be useful
to the administration in deciding whether to continue this work
experience opportunity? Under such practical scrutiny as this,
every recorded item of information is assuredly functional in
considerable degree.

Interpreting the Work Experience

Concern for the student's educational growth through work
experience requires that he, as well as the school and the cooperating community organizations, be led to evaluate that
experience constructively. Such appraisal, to be adequate, must
be continuous, and it must make provision for such evaluative
procedures as presented in the following five paragraphs.

Encourage Constructive Criticism

Encourage the student to evaluate his own work; encourage
the group to appraise each individual's work; and encourage the
group to judge its own work. The best evaluative approach emphasizes favorable points first, and then goes on to discuss the
unfavorable factors. A truly objective viewpoint will not offend
learners accustomed to such evaluation; on the contrary, they
may even want to wave aside compliments in their desire to
learn how best to improve their efforts in the future.

Analyze the Procedure

There is real need to analyze the procedure in work experience in order to make clear to the learner, and often to his
parents, that genuine educational growth has occurred. Extra-
neous rewards and punishments have so long and so often been
used to exaggerate the value of formal learning, that the highly
significant values of a *doing* program may be obscured by the

less important items upon which pencil-and-paper examinations are based. That is why we must analyze the learning process with our students, and thereby help them to understand that in an activity program, many valuable learnings are achieved even though these learnings are often not of the traditional type. Socialized attitudes, new personal interests, deepened appreciation of labor, ability to "take it" in completing a contractual task—all these are learnings of tremendous significance to the individual as well as to society at large.

Summarize the Values

Measure the learner against his former self and against the problems still ahead. There should thus emerge a rising sense of confidence and of reasonable hope. In case there has been partial or complete failure, by individual or group, determine the cause; carefully select a new course; then move forward toward the original purpose. But if that purpose was itself unworthy or too difficult, judge it accordingly and develop new purposes for the future. In such ways, even failure may hasten and strengthen educational growth.

Seek Improvements

One of the more important aspects of guided work experiences is a needed sensitivity to suggestions from the students and from those with whom he works. By all means invite everyone concerned with the work experience program to criticize it constructively and in detail. Such desire for criticism is but one aspect of that cooperative (and hence democratic) relationship that should increasingly characterize all group effort. Honest criticism, pointing forward to future improvements, is the surest guarantee of genuine progress.

Publicize the Plan

The public is so aware of the need to make education more functional that it will welcome the inclusion in the school program of properly organized and directed work experiences.

The community status of the school will therefore be strengthened as sound publicity is given to those broader opportunities for learning which confront our youth through fruitful work experience in industry, agriculture, commerce, social welfare agencies, and the like. The school has both duty and opportunity to keep its community informed concerning work experience programs, developments, and needs. In preparing such publicity, stress should be laid upon the civic contributions made through student work experience, as well as upon the extended learning values thus available to the individual students.

An Integral Aspect

Work experience, at its best, is not a fitful, infrequent interruption of an otherwise "normal" curriculum. On the contrary, such experience will be an integral and habitual aspect of the regular educational program in the life-centered community school. Yet there must always be careful preparation, competent supervision, and constructive evaluation of each individual's work activity and program.

Learning Activities

Discussion Topics

1. List the major arguments for and against work experience as a part of general education, and evaluate the validity of each one.
2. Should a student receive both school credit and wages for work experience? How can the amount of credit be decided?
3. Should a student attend school a part of each day and work a part of each day, or should he attend school for a few weeks and then work for a few weeks?
4. Is there a place for youth work camps in American education? If so, what?

Group Activities

1. Visit one or more school systems which have operating programs of work experience. Compare their arrangements with those suggested in this chapter, and evaluate the contrast.

2. Invite several work experience coordinators or directors to present a panel discussion before your class.
3. Have a committee systematically review the literature as a basis for a symposium on the problem of how the school can prevent exploitation of child labor in connection with work-experience programs.
4. Organize a speakers' team to discuss "Work Experience for All Youth" before a local service club or other community organization.

Individual Projects

1. Write your state department of education for information about school systems which have developed work-experience programs of the kind described in this chapter.
2. Secure from the superintendents of the indicated schools further data and evaluations.
3. Prepare a radio or television script reporting the values and progress of the work-experience movement in American education, with special reference to your own local and state developments.
4. Call to class attention some current magazine reports on work-experience programs.

Learning Materials

The work experience movement is examined in several volumes well worth your attention. Wilson H. Ivins and W. B. Runge's *Work Experience in High School* (Ronald, 1950) defines the nature and objectives of a work experience program, shows step-by-step procedures for putting it into operation, and suggests how to correlate it with the existing curriculum. *Work Experience in Secondary Education* by Harold J. Dillon (National Child Labor Committee, 1947) is another excellent presentation of the whole subject. Milton J. Gold's *Working to Learn* (Teachers College, Columbia, 1951) reports and evaluates many work experience programs in America and abroad, and proposes a high-school curriculum centered about man's occupational activities. Paul B. Jacobson's "Educating Through Work" in the NEA Department of Supervision and Curriculum Development's *Toward a New Curriculum* (1944) outlines the philosophy, types, values, programs, criteria and problems of work experience on both the elementary and the secondary. school levels. A concise statement is A. E. Joyal and W. G. Carr's "Work Experience Programs in American High Schools" in the *Annals of the American Academy of Political and Social Science* of November 1944. A United States Office of Education bulletin by Coraline Legg, Carl Jessen, and M. M. Proffitt called *School and Work Programs* (1944) reports a study of experience in 136 school systems. *Work Experience* by Walter D. Cocking (Hinds, Hayden & Eldredge, 1945) and *Work Experience in Education* by Warren E. Seyfert and Paul A. Rehmus (Harvard University Press, 1941) are pamphlet reviews including program characteristics, planning, values, and development.

Work camps are a more intensive type of experience, usually involving community service emphases. For brief descriptions, see Kenneth Holland and George L. Bickel's *Work Camps for High School Youth* and Holland's *Work Camps for College Students* (both by American Council, 1941). In *School and Society* (77:83-86; February 1953) Oscar E. Janson describes an established cooperative group experience program of secondary-school people in his "Week-Long Work-Camp Project." Seth Phelps' "Community Looks at a High School Work Camp" in the *School Review* of April 1948 analyzes the social benefits brought to an Ozark Mountain region by an American Friends Service Committee work camp. "Work Camps and Education," by Raymond Dennett, in the *Harvard Educational Review* of March 1942, characterizes the divergent work camp philosophies reportedly held by the Service Committee and the Work Camps of America organization.

Some other magazine articles present the philosophy of work experience incisively. See, for example, several of the following:

'Philosophy of Work Experience," Howard Y. McClusky. Psychological analysis of man's biological capacity and need for work. *Progressive Education* 19:72-75; February 1942.

"What the Schools Can Do to Provide Work Experience," G. D. Humphrey. Schools must develop an adequate philosophy of education through experience and then proceed to make work experience a part of the general curriculum for all American youth. *Southern Association Quarterly* 6:274-281; May 1942.

"Work Experiences: Basic Issues," F. P. Haskyn. A semantic analysis of the values commonly claimed for work experience, with relevant suggestions for making "work" a real "experience." *Curriculum Journal* 14:22-25; January 1943.

"Values of Work Experience," Bertram L. Lutton. Work experience increases the individual's importance and value both to himself and to society. He receives vocational training and guidance, democratic conditioning, and can establish broad standards of social value in the area of intergroup relationships. *School Executive* 64:55-56; August 1945.

"Working With Children as Workers." Entire issue devoted to varied accounts and analyses of work experience for modern children. *Childhood Education* 23:255-275; February 1947.

'Working to Learn," Milton J. Gold. Outlines a secondary school program which brings work experience into the general education of all school youth. *Educational Leadership* 7:375-379; March 1950.

"How Much Work Experience in Our Programs for Youth," Wilson H. Ivins. Suggests the range of work experiences on a scale between extremes of narrow vocational training and broad social participation; suggests values relative to such types of work experience. *National Association of Secondary School Principals* 36:179-183; March 1952.

Secondary school programs of work experience are described along with elementary school programs in Chapter 10 of Olsen's *School and Community Programs* (Prentice-Hall, 1949), as well as in some of the books just mentioned. For the periodical literature, see these fine accounts:

"As off to Work They Go," C. P. Young. A program in which boys and girls over sixteen spend one half their time in school and the rest as apprentices in stores, offices, shops, and factories. *School Executive* 59:11-14; October 1939.

"Implications of Co-operative Work for Secondary Education," Leo F. Smith. Emphasizes several ways in which work experience for high school youth is now provided, discusses some of the difficulties connected with these approaches, and describes the program at the Rochester Athenaeum and Mechanics Institute. *School Review* 50:17-23; January 1942.

"Rotary Gives Youth Vocational Experience," C. A. Weber. Describes a Chicago Rotary Club project through which youth receive practical vocational guidance and well-organized work experience. Reports from students, employers, teachers, and parents are reproduced. *Occupations* 21:464-468; February 1943.

"Work Experience in Secondary Education," Paul J. Leonard. Urges the importance of work experience for "understanding and experience in democratic living; development of competence to do productive work; development of individual interests." *National Association of Secondary School Principals' Bulletin* 28:29-35; May 1944.

"Can Job and School Mix?" A. O. Michener. Popularly written account of how work experience programs operate in better high schools. *Parents Magazine* 21:24-25; November 1946.

College-level work experience programs are less frequent, except in a few institutions which have made work experience an integral part of their entire curriculum, sometimes the "core" of the college experience. The well-known Antioch College plan for work experience is described in Algo D. Henderson's *Vitalizing Liberal Education* (Harper, 1944) and in *Antioch College* by Henderson and Dorothy Hall (Harper, 1946). In the periodicals, see these accounts:

"Behind the Counter They Go to College," Edward G. Mason. How junior colleges across the nation are cooperating with business enterprises to provide valuable practical training for young people. *Nation's Business* 29:66; May 1941.

"Cooperative Work Programs," Leo F. Smith. Reports a descriptive study of the school-community work programs in colleges and universities. Present status, trends, and implications are stressed. *Journal of Higher Education* 15:207-212; April 1944.

"Practical Education Through Internship," Grace B. Carleton. Values and activities of a department store selling experience program for junior college girls. *Junior College Journal* 15:308-309; March 1945.

"Terminal Program Dovetailed with Industry," A. J. Cloud and W. C. Marsh. Hotel and restaurant, insurance, merchandising, floriculture, commercial art and laboratory technique are the six fields in which a San Francisco junior college integrates field experience with classroom instruction. *Junior College Journal* 16:10-15; September 1945: *Education Digest* 11:41-44; November 1945.

"Experiment in Educational Techniques," Chase Going Woodhouse. Connecticut College in cooperation with a large department store gives ten selected students each year extensive experience in all aspects of store management, personnel relations, and so forth. *Annals of the American Academy of Political and Social Science* 251:153-156; May 1947.

Operating principles, techniques, and problems in work experience development may be examined more closely by reference to the several publications here listed:

Work Experience in Education, Warren C. Seyfert and Paul A. Rehmus (eds.). A workshop report upon work experiences, stressing the administration, supervision, evaluation, and coordination of such experiences. Harvard Workshop Series No. 2. Cambridge: Harvard University, 1941.

Youth and the Future, Chapter IV, American Youth Commission, American Council on Education. The Commission's statement of principles that should govern relations between youth work programs and the schools. Washington: The Council, 1942.

"Work Experience in Secondary Schools," Henry A. Cross. General principles to follow in developing work experience programs. *National Association of Secondary School Principals' Bulletin* 26:36-43; March. 1942.

"Six Errors About Work Experience," Robert G. Andree. Errors cited are too much red tape, failure to work with unions, preoccupation with work for pay, failure to recognize that many youth already work, failure to see that neither problem nor solution is new, and the school's presumption in trying to do the job alone. *Clearing House* 16:518-520; May 1942.

"Providing Work Incentive for Co-operative Students," Donald K. Beckley. Suggested incentives for improving course work of part-time working students are: send marks to employers; refuse to allow deficient students to continue cooperative work; give school credit for job performance. Values and limitations of each device are analyzed. *School Review* 52:346-349; June 1944.

"Planning a Work Experience Program," Ormsbee W. Robinson. School and community together must plan the work experience program if it is to be truly successful. Pertinent aspects of such planning are analyzed. *School Executive* 64:52-54; August 1945.

"Guides for a Work Experience Program," Joseph Leese. Presents basic principles around which to organize an effective work experience program for youth. *Nations Schools* 36:43-44; December 1945.

Education through Work Experience. A handbook of suggestions, proposals, and references dealing with work experience. New York State Education Department, Division of Secondary Education, 1948.

"Work Experience Within Our Schools," Edward K. Hankin. Summarizes current practice and thinking in many areas of the work experience field: activities, pay, needs of pupils, philosophy and objectives, staff, scheduling, limitations, and unsolved problems. *Educational Record* 32:217-230; April 1951.

"High School Work Experience Programs in Action," Stuart Anderson. Reports factually a study of work experience programs in thirty-eight cities; deals with nature of supervision, selection of students, credit given, grade placement in the program, pay of students, and similar items. *American School Board Journal,* August 1951.

"How Much Work Experience in Our Programs for Youth," Warren C. Seyfert. Advises resistance to further stretching the credit system so as to include work experiences, strongly approves this "novel curriculum element"; feels work experience should never be required for graduation. *Bulletin of National Association of Secondary School Principals* 36:184-189; March 1952.

Motion Picture

Campus Frontiers. Portrays the work-study program of Antioch College, showing how job experience invigorates classroom study and promotes good citizenship on campus and in community. Association Films, 1942, color, 28 minutes.

CHAPTER **12**

Community Service Projects

Education will never be realistic and practical and important in our time if it is merely book knowledge filed away and soon forgotten. True education must be grounded in extensive, guided, firsthand experience with significant community affairs. When children and young people actively share in community improvement programs, both they and the community benefit accordingly. But without a sense of belonging, of being wanted for their ability to contribute to the family or to larger common welfare, children as well as adolescents become problems to themselves and others. Much of our juvenile delinquency and young adult crime is rooted in the failure of these persons to achieve satisfying, responsible participation in the normal activities of adulthood. Their consequent feelings of frustration and inferiority lead easily into compensatory aggression. With Lloyd Allen Cook, we may well guess that "no past generation has been so detached from its culture, so blocked in what was once the normal pathway of social integration, so wavering between conflicting viewpoints and behaviors. Community schools have a practical mission. They are relating their life and work to breakdowns in the socialization process. Their function is to make such contributions as are possible toward the induction of youth into adulthood, to discover ways of doing what our society can no longer do well outside the school." [1]

This chapter is by MORRIS R. MITCHELL.

[1] Unpublished manuscript. Used by permission.

Service projects are cooperative group activities organized and carried out by students as specific contributions to civic welfare. Being primarily *civic* in both purpose and motivation, such projects never include financial remuneration although they always provide for deep personal satisfactions of other kinds. Involving individual activity of an integrated mental-physical-emotional-spiritual nature, service projects eventuate in genuine educational value to the student as well as in significant social value to society.

If our children and young people are ever to fulfill their proper role in a democratic society, they must have every chance to study, to criticize, and to contribute to better living in their own communities. They must learn to work with each other and with interested adults in developing intelligent programs of community improvement. The youngster who serves his fellows as a safety patrolman or as an assistant in the library, office, or laboratory gains a feeling of personal significance, a sense of belonging, a new maturity and a finer loyalty to his school community. In similar fashion, those who leave their classrooms to plant seedling trees on denuded hillsides are doing more than setting out trees or even increasing our nation's wealth—they are also developing deep roots of personal responsibility, of social concern. By actively identifying themselves with group welfare they are also increasing their civic devotion and strengthening their own moral character.

Service projects lift education from the dull routine of leading each generation in the footsteps of its predecessor, to earnest yet joyous adventures in cooperative social welfare. Service project values are most clearly perceptible among youth who sense the transition crisis of our times, and devote themselves to local community betterment through work camps, improving intergroup relations, building cooperatives, fostering international organization, and other progressive movements. Thus, service projects:

• **Give hope and courage** to youth who are in danger of demoralizing frustration. They promote change from despair at the thought of a "world like a hog trough too full of feet," to an eager desire to help build, for all men, that kind of truly civilized community which this earth could become.

• **Effect definite social improvements** and thereby enable youth to contribute in significant fashion to the social progress of his group.

• **Promote status for youth** by enabling adults of the community to understand and approve the contributions being made by youth to the common welfare. Such recognition is most critically needed during the adolescent period.

• **Stimulate all-around growth and development** of the students, since the projects undertaken are of such nature as to require sustained and integrated effort of mind, emotion, and physique.

• **Create more functional patterns of education.** Each century, each generation, we have outgrown our previously prevailing notions about education. As researches into the psychology of learning moved many teachers, during the 1920's, away from support of the traditional school, so our new insights into the nature of human relationships are now drawing us forward to uphold the community, life-centered school.

• **Help to make world citizens out of provincial youngsters** because they lift the imagination from personal matters of the moment to the enduring life concerns of all peoples everywhere.

"Culture" has long been considered an ethereal value acquired through certain historical disciplines and is often centered in fields of study relatively remote from current experience. Consequently, it is difficult to persuade parents, or even students, that true culture involves the intelligent meeting of human problems, both personal and social. We accordingly find our schools still placing great emphasis upon curricular subjects of traditional prestige, and upon intellectual tasks carried on in the classroom and within regular school hours. Community service projects, on the other hand, do not lend themselves to the regimentation of standardized assignments, grading, state-adopted textbooks, paper-and-pencil examinations, and other ritualistic aspects of traditional school education. There is an element of daring, an adventuresome challenge in learning through service projects that calls for a different set of educational values and procedures.

Community improvement projects are most apt to become a vital part of the school program if the teachers and administrators of the school are themselves identified with the constructive forces of the community. Even by joining civic luncheon clubs and engaging in other conventional social activities, teachers are sure to bring more freshness of purpose and perspective to the classroom. Today there are newer moving forces: groups interested in promoting better intergroup relations, the cooperative movement, international understanding, decentralism. Teachers should be leaders in such groups, and should help to stimulate local thinking to the end that a "current of true and fresh ideas" may hasten right transition in these troubled times.

The first essential, then, is that the teacher himself live constantly in an atmosphere of responsible social participation. Most teachers are the products of generations of academic inbreeding. Many are teachers, despite the low salaries, because teaching offers institutional protection against the hazards of other careers. Too many of us teach for immediate and selfish reasons solely, rather than from long-range professional and social considerations. Under such circumstances, our social leadership role is not likely to be very influential.

Of course there are limitations upon student participation in social processes and problems. There are handicaps of physical, mental, social, and emotional maturity. It is important not to thrust children prematurely into areas of activity they do not understand. But we often exaggerate these limitations, and make them excuses for retaining children in community "observer" roles even when they are ready to participate and to contribute. Studying *about* the community is important, but it is never enough. Because children cannot participate completely, cannot wholly solve a problem, is no reason for their not taking such part as they rightly can. Psychologists know that the vivid imagination of the normal child easily carries his emotional participation far beyond the real. A child placed a few bricks in a wall and thereafter sincerely believed that he had, with some help, built the entire structure. Such children are not dishonest; they are merely victims of alert imaginations. We must treasure and feed by experience this hunger for participation. The child who is never introduced to social-civic problems until he is relatively mature is not likely to develop desirable vision and sensitivity then. There is no magic formula that makes 8- or 21-year-olds civic-minded.

Guided social participation is the essence of true educational method. Schoolroom walls will largely disappear; home and school will work together; student-community enterprises will function much more fruitfully when we view education as broadly as it must be conceived if it is to meet the challenge of our crisis culture.

Planning the Community Project

It is essential that the community service projects undertaken by the school be planned, executed, and evaluated with extreme care. There is no surer way to discredit the life-centered educational philosophy among colleagues, students, and lay people generally than to undertake and fail in some ill-planned community improvement project. As with all other vital educational techniques, the service project must be administered with care and discretion. Let's note some useful guidelines.

Discover Community Needs

Exhortation to social action is the wrong approach. To be sure, the teacher may invite his students to join in civic projects in which he is already active—in planning for street improvement, smoke-nuisance abatement, malarial control, inter-religious fellowship, slum clearance, and the like. But, for the most part, the students should discover their own service projects through a growing personal awareness of social needs identified through community surveys and other informational learning activities. In some communities, real courage is required to plumb the open or secret economic greed and political chicanery. Much can be done, however, if a constructive enthusiasm is maintained, and if emphasis is constantly placed upon the importance of positive and democratic civic responsibility by all good citizens, including the school students. This psychological atmosphere, surrounding the students' discovery of social needs, should enable them to sense right directions, kindle group purpose, and act with responsible vigor.

Select Projects with Care

If the community experience is to be of most educational and civic value it must be chosen with considerable care. Certainly all proposed service projects should be appraised in terms of specific standards by which their educational and civic validity may be determined. Six such criteria are now suggested.

• *Is education the primary goal?* Community improvement projects are justifiable only if they operate as superior educational experiences for those who participate in them. It is indeed true that the major function of the community school is to improve the quality of living, but this must not be pushed to the possible extreme of exploiting children in the performance of needed community services, however beneficial such a project might be to the community as a whole. Recently it has become almost fashionable in community school circles to assert that "the major task of the school is to help improve its own community" and that schools should "accept the function of aiding in community improvement as their principal, if not their only, task.[2] Persuasive as this view may appear, there are clearly dangers in it. Perhaps our standard of judgment might better be this: Does the community project in question seem likely to improve the quality of living of the students personally involved, as well as that of the community at large? Schools are only incidentally social welfare agencies; their first and foremost task is that of educating people. Social participation, civic contribution, community improvement are all valid avenues of educative experience, but they should never become sole goals in themselves.

• *Is the project really constructive?* Community service projects, however laudable they may appear, must not be of such nature as to further entrench social practices which are actually lament-

[2] See "The Editors' Perspective," *School Executive* 72:38-39; January 1953.

able. A project of providing Thanksgiving baskets for the poor, for example, will lessen suffering of the moment but does not even approach the real community problem involved: that of inadequate family incomes. And it may even help to perpetuate an existing situation by giving more fortunate members of society a smug satisfaction in their "sharing," blinding them to the need for more fundamental efforts.

• *Is it suitable for young people?* Many civic problems are the direct concern of children and youth because they vitally affect their well-being. But there are many aspects of community life needing improvement which must be solely or largely the responsibility of adults. Youth should not be made responsible for righting these wrongs nor for the unpleasant task of cleaning up social festers which adults would like to leave to more eager hands. This criterion must not be interpreted too narrowly, however. Throughout this volume we are urging projects in which all members of the community—children, as well as youth and adults—together tackle problems of cooperative community improvement. In such a conception of a project, the adults perform those duties that are clearly their responsibility, and the young find their field of contribution in tasks appropriate to their maturity and ability.

• *Can the project develop a spirit of joint effort?* Our world needs cooperative effort far more than charity. Service projects must not nurture "an attitude," of condescension or servility. Arrogance destroys rather than fosters responsible comradeship in facing mutual problems. Hence the social necessity for being sure that the chosen community project is of such nature as to permit development of mutual effort, of genuine feelings of doing *with*, not for.

• *Is there real chance for success?* Of course there are projects beyond the physical strength and endurance of children—problems too complex, too remote, too costly, too dangerous, problems requiring advanced knowledge, skills, techniques, problems socially too involved or too delicate. But such real difficulties must not blind teacher or students to the rich array of community improvement possibilities that are everywhere available. Nor must success be too narrowly judged. Failure, after determined effort and against calculated risk, may be an important tempering element in growth. Remember also that you will risk censure from some defenders of things as they are if you lead school people in seeking to improve any aspect of community living. That is why in some places the first community improvement project might well be that of educating public opinion about the educational soundness of the service project as part of the life-centered community school.

• *Does the project interpret broad areas of social concern?* Soil erosion is such an area. Civilizations have fattened on harvests of the soil itself; gully and sheet erosion and soil mining are universal principles of destruction. Housing is such an area. In a sense, the slums of any city in America are part of the slums of Hong Kong, Bangkok, or Algiers, since related causes are at work. Health is such an area. So is recreation. And education. So is each of the other basic social processes already identified in Chapter 3. Your community service project should thus exemplify a basic social process or problem, and thereby help students gain perspective upon numerous other instances which cannot now be sampled. In that process you may stimulate genuine critical thinking and constructive social action.

Gain Background and Insight

Most of the specific suggestions already advanced in Chapters 5 through 9 are fully applicable as the group first examines its chosen community project. Without amplification here, let us simply summarize the essential steps which may be taken to secure needed insights and understanding necessary to the development of a successful service project.

• **Utilize documentary materials** as a primary source of data concerning the problem-area chosen.
• **Employ audio-visual aids** to dramatize the need and to illustrate significant approaches to it already made in this or other communities.
• **Invite resource visitors** to explain the need and the problem, and to suggest possible courses of action toward solution.
• **Arrange interviews** to gather data and suggestions, advice and aid, and to enlist cooperation and support of key adults.
• **Conduct field trips** to develop common insight and to stimulate purpose.
• **Make surveys** to assemble data, define and refine the problem, and then to evaluate results after the service project is completed.

In using any of these approaches, remember to do so with the special needs of your service project foremost in mind. For the goal now sought is the successful completion of the chosen project, and all the other "doors" into the community are, in this instance, merely means to that end. They are now warranted only to the extent to which they do actually develop intellectual, emotional, and ethical background for the selected service project itself.

Clear with Administration

The teacher who senses a social cause in some community problems—such as mosquito control or the need to demolish an adjoining "lung-block" to gain space for a playground—should always approach his school administrator before engaging in any general discussion of the project. This precaution is professionally courteous, and also avoids the possibility of jealousy at headquarters, of conflict or overlapping of plans among various teachers, and of the embarrassing necessity of retraction, should the proposed plan prove administratively unfeasible. Besides avoiding these negative possibilities, initial consultation with the administration will often result in the project receiving its full support from the very outset.

Organize the Class

Effective group organization now becomes essential. In stimulating such organization, the astute teacher will take steps as follows:

- **Sense student interests.** Assuming that the project which the teacher has in mind is appropriate for school sponsorship, he should be able to find, in the diverse interests of the boys and girls, some adequate opportunity to lead them in the desired direction. But in so leading, the teacher should not pretend merely to follow the students' interests when he is actually guiding the group thinking toward some preconceived plan or program. To do that is to be fundamentally dishonest. The desirable alternative is for the teacher and students together to recognize the importance of having proposals presented for group analysis, and then to work together for the improvement of these proposals. Good rapport between instructor and class is the heart of this problem; where that exists it avoids both domination from above and sentimental over-emphasis upon the validity of students' suggestions.

• **Condition the psychological atmosphere.** Pupil attitudes are highly responsive to environmental changes. The teacher can there-fore do much to direct students' feelings and expressions of interests by a judicious choice and use of pictures, charts, posters, books, slides, recordings, radio programs, motion pictures, scientific ex-hibits, and the like.

• **Observe conditions of effective organization.** Whatever spe-cific plans are made, the procedure followed should always be:

• *Democratic.* Because our schools were so long organized after an authoritarian, often autocratic pattern, they have too fre-quently not themselves been democratic. It is now crucially important that we deliberately bring America's finest politi-cal tradition into our everyday classroom planning.

• *Efficient.* Technology is efficient precisely because it recognizes and utilizes special talents and training. These qualities are not identified by a system of selection based upon popularity won through emotional oratory, appeal to prejudice, joviality, or pre-election generosity. In the scientific world, it is results that count, and superior results are not expected from inferior ability or education. We should lead our students to recognize this principle, to apply it in the world of human relationships, and therefore to choose democratic leaders in terms of such factors as natural aptitude, special training, demonstrated efficiency, motives of social service, ability to stimulate co-operation, loyalty to the highest ideals of human brotherhood, and the like.

• *Creative.* Designated leaders and committees should be allowed as much initiative and responsibility as discretion will permit. The teacher who is changing from more traditional forms of instruction to the use of service projects must remember that he can no longer expect to dominate in every assignment and to check up on every achievement. His older responsibility for these items must now be gradually and increasingly shared with the students. In the best community improvement pro-grams, pupils are often working on projects located blocks or miles away from the school. The sharing of responsibility—which is so strong a characteristic of the service project type of teaching—actually releases the teacher from much burden-some detail in working with large numbers, and makes possible far more individual attention where guidance is especially needed. Service projects may thus be carried on with as great a number of students as is customary in more formal methods.

Approach Community Leaders

Real service projects deal with community problems and thereby involve community sensibilities. For this reason, let it be said frankly that service projects may sometimes involve controversial issues. But this fact must be faced and not escaped, or else we shall accumulate unsolved social problems that may bring increasing suffering and civil strife.

Some community leaders may prove far from receptive to proffered aid from schools. They may be contemptuous of teachers for their academic-mindedness, and of students for their immaturity. Occasionally they may fear scrutiny of their own inefficiency or dishonesty. Yet thousands of American teachers are shouldering civic responsibilities, and doing so with public gratitude. In hundreds of school systems, children are winning the increased respect of adults by the initiative they show, by the hard work they are eager to do, and above all, by their demonstrated capacity to understand civic problems and to act upon them constructively. In the light of extended experience, however, we can say that unless community leaders are first approached and their confidence gained, most ambitious service projects will probably be doomed to failure. Jealous officials can find many quiet ways to discredit and thwart the best-planned service project program. Conversely, however, community leaders whose cooperation is sincerely sought, will often do much to smooth the way and promote the success of projects in which they are interested.

Work Through Community Groups

To the parents through the children, and directly by personal contacts, the teacher should enlist the support of such organizations as parent-teacher associations, civic clubs, churches, newspapers, and the like. The service project should always be the community's project, never the teacher's nor even the school's. Let the teacher be not too greatly concerned about personal praise for achievements made; far more will be accomplished if major credit is attributed to community leaders and organizations who have given their aid. But be sure that the students know their successes have been appreciated, and that even their mistakes were considered to be fruitful aspects of worthwhile learning.

Secure Needed Supplies

Service projects often require some technical equipment and supplies. The group must therefore think ahead and arrange for the procurement of such materials. Example: red oxide of iron mixed with burnt motor oil was found to be a possible material for painting homes and barns in a rural area where many of the buildings had had no protective covering whatever. Again: to change the quality of native nut trees to the most superior varieties calls for a few simple tools and such other items as strips of linen, beeswax, rosin, and linseed oil. Unless such materials are made available at the needed time, student interest may lag or die. In a sense, then, the service project must be planned to operate somewhat on an assembly line basis; all necessary tools and supplies should be available at the exact time they become necessary to the progress of the project.

Plan Essential Safeguards

Necessary physical safeguards depend largely on the type and location of the service project undertaken. When fighting forest fires in the Rockies, for example, adequate precautions must be taken against injury from the fire, against the fever tick, and against poisonous snakes. By contrast, the safeguards necessary to the construction of toys for the community's lending library would be simple. In any case, it is usually desirable for the teacher or administrator to contact the parents of elementary and high school students to discover in advance the existence of any possible parental objections. Sometimes parents ignored at such times have later injected emotionalized barriers into a project even after it has been well advanced.

The group should also be sure to ascertain the existence of any legal barriers to any aspect of the proposed project. If this is not done, the group may unwittingly violate the law—as one class did when it trucked an apiary across a state line and thereby incurred the possibility of a fine and the imprisonment of the group's leader. Legal barriers are not usually obscure, but it is better to be informed in advance rather than in retrospect.

Executing the Community Project

No definite line should divide the preparatory from the executing aspect of the service project, for these two aspects are merely progressive phases of one ongoing process. Yet it is important to move out of the planning and into the practicing stage, else the project itself will never mature. In this second stage also there are certain fundamental procedures which may well be followed.

Give Definite Initial Direction

Many service projects have failed because of the seeming lack of responsiveness among the pupils. A class may show great interest in planning a project, but when the actual work in the field begins, may lapse into a disappointing indifference. Sample: a group has decided to repair a pig house and then to raise pigs to get funds to give to the Red Cross. The pigs have been purchased with money borrowed from the school's credit union. The necessary carpenter tools and the whitewash ingredients are all on hand. Students are aglow with anticipation, but when they get to the scene of supposed activity there is only indifference; the children fool around chasing one another, while conversation is devoted to quite irrelevant affairs. Teacher urging does no good.

What is the trouble? Many factors may be in the picture, but among them all, there is probably one of dominant influence: the pupils have planned their general policies well enough, but they have not adequately planned their *precise techniques*.

Perhaps none of them have ever mixed lime with water to make whitewash, to say nothing of the more complicated formula involving also soap and alum. They may never have seen a fence built, nor helped to build one themselves. Under such circumstances, preliminary planning should have provided for very specific initial directions, both for the exact sub-jobs to be done and for the particular pupils who were to do them. With such definite initial direction, otherwise reluctant groups have been known to grow greatly in both self-direction and technical competence.

Let Emotional Satisfactions Attend Each Step

The first law of learning is that activities which bring personal satisfaction tend to be both repeated and fixated thereby. Nowhere is this psychological principle more apparent than in the development of successful service projects. Specimen: In one rural school, long given to formal instruction, a propagating house for ornamental shrubbery was developed upon the basis of textbook teaching of botany. Now, many years later, that school is enjoying the use of its third propagating house. Its nursery covers three acres. Fifteen hundred shrubs beautify the school grounds, and a half million ornamentals add to the charm of nearly every home within a six-mile radius. The example of this project has spread to fifteen or more schools within that state, and even to schools in other states.

The real success of this initial botanical service project was due to the fact that from its very inception, care was taken to see that each step in its progressive development brought emotional satisfaction to the pupils and the patrons of that school. This fundamental satisfaction led to widespread community approval, and as a consequence dozens of other service projects followed—a cooperative hatchery, cooperative curb market, student-built gymnasium and baseball park, school apiary, pupil-operated public library, and the like. School and community approval of such projects was further stimulated by the judicious use of public meetings wherein such activities were discussed, and the point was always made that from service projects like these the students were constantly achieving highly worthwhile learning values. Through such precautions, community support was assured, and no serious criticism has ever been encountered in that area because of the now-phenomenal extension of community improvement enterprises in the school.

Be Considerate of Other Teachers

It is important that the principal and all affected teachers know of any disruption to the regular program which the projected service project will occasion. In many schools, some of the faculty have joined in coalition against others who favored service projects, largely because their classroom teaching of the students involved had been interrupted with little apparent concern. We must never forget that the difference between the routine procedures of formal schooling and the vigorous challenge of learning through social action is so basic that the utmost tact, patience, and unfailing goodwill must ever be observed by those engaged in service project work.

Keep Permanent Records

Sufficient records should be kept to enable teacher, students, and parents to review their course of effort and to evaluate it at its conclusion. Such records should be as complete as necessary to enable one group to profit from a previous group's experience. Somehow, a nice balance must be maintained between the extremes of keeping no written records and keeping too many. The former course fails to make adequate provisions for the later sharing of experience with other groups; the latter becomes burdensome and frequently degenerates into an end in itself. An illustration of the latter extreme: a college seminar class spent a year making an exhaustive and exhausting survey of a community; when it finished the task, its members had no strength or enthusiasm left for directing an attack upon the community needs thus revealed. The written report of its findings was filed away in a bookcase, whereupon the discovery was made of the report from an exactly similar survey made twenty-five years before, and which revealed almost identically the same problems about which neither group had done anything. Records, like service projects themselves, should be guides to action, not ends in themselves.

Secure Appropriate Publicity

Publicity is important and necessary, but it should be sought and used for constructive educational purposes, never as an agency of personality projection or of student exploitation. It is unworthy of the great purposes of community-centered education for ambitious teachers or administrators to seek advancement of their own status by advertising their small part in this democratic movement for social betterment. Publicity can and should be used only as an educational means of acquainting the general public with the purposes, plans, procedures, findings, and activities of the projects undertaken, and to interpret fairly the whole philosophy of the community school.

Interpreting the Community Service Experience

If greatest educational growth is to occur—and thereby validate the primary purpose of the service project—it is essential that the whole experience be critically evaluated. This evaluation will be continuous throughout the project, but it should also serve as final interpretation of it. In planning this critical summary, there are three areas which should be examined with care. The first two relate to the fundamental objectives of the service project technique itself; the last is concerned with using the present procedural experience as a basis for planned improvement in the future.

Identify the Learning Results Achieved

There is real danger that many of the non-intellectual learnings inherent in the service project may go unrecognized, even by the teacher. The notions of external discipline and of learning as a dull chore are so deeply ingrained in our consciousness that it is hard for many to comprehend how enjoyable the most wholesome growth experiences can and should be. Teachers and students alike need to realize that it is educationally as important that they learn to work together, to integrate their thinking, to compromise their differences, to develop social sensitivity, as it is that they acquire an increasing fund of factual information. A helpful way of clarifying the reality of such varied growth is by recounting the problems met and solved, or met and still unsolved. True development is the by-product of a succession of problems constructively met with all the intellectual, emotional, and physical resources at one's command.

Summarize the Social Contribution

The second major purpose of service projects, it will be recalled, is to advance community welfare. Just how is the community now a better place in which to live because this particular project has been completed? To what extent and in what manner has this project actually penetrated into a real civic defect, rather than merely ameliorated a surface symptom? Thoughtful group consideration of such queries as these is another essential aspect of the final evaluative process.

Analyze the Group's Procedure

Evaluation should now go one step further to include analysis of the part played by each participant in the group enterprise. While this process is sometimes carried to such an extreme that the students become too self-conscious about their own development, it is well that they do not ignore such factors (and their opposites) as a cooperative spirit, the willingness of each to accept suggestions, the endurance of purposefulness, creativeness, promptness of action, resourcefulness in suggesting feasible means to the attainment of desired ends, and the like. These factors, after all, are likely to have been central to either success or failure. If democracy is to work, our youth must have opportunity to make considered judgments upon their own and others' growth toward competence in the basic skills of democratic action.

The Heart of Democratic Education

Today we realize as never before that practical citizenship must be the very heart of democratic education, and that this citizenship must be learned through satisfying personal experiences in community improvement projects during the period of formal schooling as well as afterward. Teachers of foresight and patience can do much to provide functional, realistic, democratic education based partly upon cooperative community service whereby students and community mutually benefit.

Learning Activities

Discussion Topics

1. Drawing on some of the suggested readings, discuss through a panel the basic philosophy of community service in relation to the democratic way of life and the ethical teachings of the great religions.
2. How should the school decide how far to go in participating in community chest drives, civic reforms, social services?
3. How can such annual events as Brotherhood Week, Education Week, Clean-up Week, and Youth Week be made more functional throughout the year?

Group Activities

1. Compile a list of community service projects which are appropriate to the age groups which will be taught by members of your class.
2. Debate the proposition that the job of the school is to educate people, not to improve community living.
3. Investigate the community service program of the American Friends Service Committee, and through a dramatic sketch report your findings to the class.
4. Making each member responsible for a different magazine, find all the examples you can of service activities programs reported in recent journals.

Individual Projects

1. Investigate the extent to which community service is now part of the school program in your home community, and also in the community where you now are.
2. Survey your community's service, civic, and social welfare organizations to discover kinds of service projects in which you and other students might participate.
3. Devise an acceptable system of permanent records which would be helpful in developing and evaluating the community service efforts of your school.
4. In a brief paper answer the question: Is there any valid reason for making young children aware of community shortcomings?

Learning Materials

The purposes, values, and kinds of service project possibilities are indicated in a number of books. *Youth Serves the Community* by Paul R. Hanna and Associates (Appleton-Century, 1936) describes several hundred projects in public safety, civic beauty, health, agricultural and industrial improvement, civic arts, local history, surveys and protection of resources. The Introduction to that volume, written by William H. Kilpatrick, is a definitive statement of "The Underlying Philosophy of Cooperative Activities for Community Improvement." The Educational Policies Commission's *Learning the Ways of Democracy* (1940), Chapter 5, gives many challenging accounts of how schools across the nation are studying and serving their own communities and in that very process providing effective education for democratic citizenship. A similar accounting is found in "Experiences in Civic Action in the Secondary School," pages 98-113 of the 1950 yearbook of the National Council for the Social Studies. Olsen's *School and Community Programs* presents fourteen stories showing how children and young people planned and carried through civic service projects as outgrowths of school programs. Scores of successful projects for improving intergroup relations are described and analyzed in Chapter 5 of *Intergroup Education in Public Schools* by Taba, Brady, and Robinson (American Council on Education, 1953). Maurice E. Troyer's "Educating Through Community Service" in the National Education Association's Department of Supervision and Curriculum Development 1944 yearbook *Toward a New Curriculum* (pp. 41-55) cites several good examples of community improvement projects. In their *Small Communities in Action* (Harper, 1946) Jean and Jess Ogden have collected numerous brief and challenging accounts of citizen programs at work in small communities, including some with school participation.

Educational reasons for community service projects are examined in a number of significant magazine articles:

"Bring Our Youngsters into the Community!" Stuart Chase. A dramatic account of what young people are doing in and for their communities, emphasizing the basic values involved. *Reader's Digest* 40:7-10; January 1942.

"Education Through Community Improvement," Verner M. Sims. Critical analysis, stressing desirable manner of approach, points of emphasis, ways of working, and evaluation principles. *Progressive Education* 19:332-335; October 1942.

"Social Cement for Group Unity," Harold R. Bottrell. Basic suggestions for developing group service projects in colleges and universities. *Educational Leadership* 4:298-303; February 1947.

"Citizenship Laboratory," Raymond Nelson. Urges that no student be allowed to graduate from high school unless he has first engaged in community service work which is an integral part of his regular study. *School Review* 56:156-162; March 1948.

"Everyone Shares in City Planning," G. Leslie Cushman and John T. Mladjen. Philadelphia has incorporated city planning into the curriculum at all levels and in many teaching areas in order to launch all youth on careers of civic-mindedness and action with adults. *Educational Leadership* 6:227-231; January 1949.

"Undergraduate Social Service and Research in the Community," Arthur Katona. Outlines four approaches to community study and work for the student: observation visit, social analysis, social research, social services. *Social Education* 13:234-236; May 1949.

"A Place for Youth on the Community Team." Community service provides opportunity for children and youth to gain status and acceptance, and thereby develop patterns of responsible citizenship. *School Executive* 72:66-72; January 1953.

Community service by elementary school children is discussed in *Community Living and the Elementary School*, 1945 yearbook of the Department of Elementary School Principals of the National Education Association. See also these special articles:

"Service Above Self," Georgia Englund and Minnie Fuller. Seventh- and eighth-graders may elect "work" as a subject. This includes care of handicapped children, cafeteria, library, office, and maintenance activities. *School Executive* 64:59-60; August 1945.

"We Declared War on Poison Ivy," Aline V. Higgins. Tells how fourth-graders undertook to solve a community program. *Childhood Education* 27:373-376; April 1951.

"Learning to Serve," Margaret Marshall. Reports interesting volunteer work projects by school children from kindergarten through the sixth grade. *Childhood Education* 28:166-169; December 1951.

High school accounts are more numerous. In addition to those reported in the books previously mentioned, you might scan these articles for ideas:

"Youth Has a Part to Play," Morris R. Mitchell. Describes 167 case-study examples of youth service to the community. *Progressive Education* 19:87-109; February 1942.

"Biology Class Led Fight Against Mosquitoes," L. W. Anderson. Students in a mosquito-infested town studied the problem and then campaigned for the fight that brought a more healthful community. *Clearing House* 17:267-270; January 1943.

"Boulder Pupils Work for the Community Chest," T. Eldon Jackson and Lindley J. Stiles. Students organized themselves as teams to raise money for the local Chest, and then sent official representatives to serve on the Chest's board of managers. *Clearing House* 17:275-276; January 1943.

"Substance of Things Hoped For; How High School Students of Montgomery County, Va., Planned and Built a Community Center," Jean Ogden and Jess Ogden. High school students needed a community recreation center, so they planned and built one. They drew plans, figured costs, issued and sold bonds, made speeches, adopted a constitution, and otherwise secured community cooperation and support. *Recreation* 39:297-299; September 1945.

"Volunteer Student Social Service Project," Emma L. Bolzau and Emily D. Stevenson. Describes the program started eight years ago in the South Philadelphia High School for Girls. *Social Education,* 13:237-238; May 1949.

"Learning and Serving," Robert C. Taber and Hettie R. Bachman. In Philadelphia, a large number of students serve as volunteers in social agencies during the summer months, and a few throughout the entire school year. *National Education Association Journal* 38:612; November 1949.

"An Experiment in School Community Cooperation," Muriel C. Kovinow. Junior girls in a New York City high school have a Community Service Corps through which each member devotes two after-school hours per week to some institution where she can be of help—schools for the blind, social settlements, and so forth. *High Points* 32:45-48; September 1950.

"Plea to Voters," H. G. Walters and Rose E. Boggs. Explains the plan whereby some 80 per cent of the students in a junior high school call on every home and business office in the district to urge adults to vote at election. *Clearing House* 25:337-340; February 1951.

"Bold New Program in Our Schools," Elizabeth Fagg. How the Citizenship Education Project initiated at Teachers College, Columbia University, in 1949 is helping young people learn community responsibility through their own civic service projects. *The Rotarian,* August 1953; condensed in *Reader's Digest,* August 1953.

"Community Service of High School Seniors." An account of a group interview with a class of forty seniors who spent a part of their year's study of American problems actually working in various agencies in the community. Chapter 6 in *Creating a Good Environment for Learning*, 1954 yearbook of the Association for Supervision and Curriculum Development of the NEA.

Most college programs of community service are found in the junior or "community" colleges, though not all. For descriptions sampling the field of higher education, see the following articles:

"Going Beyond the Classroom in Savannah," Jeanne P. Olson. Forums, veterans guidance, a playhouse, evening classes, Red Cross service, home economics activities, and chemical research are among the ways in which a Georgia junior college relates itself to local community life. *Junior College Journal* 16:303-305; March 1946.

"How One College Serves Five Counties," L. O. Todd. A junior college stimulated development of school county coordinating councils which are themselves coordinated through a larger council, the chairman of which is the college president. Studies of land-use capability, conservation, education, religion, business, health, and so on, were made, community leadership institutes held, and many smaller group meetings arranged. *Junior College Journal* 16:295-297; March 1946.

"Preparation of Teachers for Community Service," L. P. Young. Describes the program of a teachers college which directly educates teachers for active participation in solving community problems. *Teachers College Record* 47:382-386; March 1946.

"Opportunities, Patterns of Organization, Techniques in Community Service, and a Socio-Educational Orientation," Harold R. Bottrell. Four articles presenting findings and recommendations of an investigation of community service programs in junior colleges. *Junior College Journal* 18:12-19, 57-63, 128-134, 231-237; September, October, November 1947, January 1948.

"Making Citizens out of Students," Jane E. McAllister. How Miner Teachers College makes direct community participation a major concern and activity, especially during the freshmen and sophomore years. *School Executive* 67:40-42; February 1948.

"The Community as a Laboratory in General Education," Marguerite J. Fisher. University students do political party work before elections, participate in community improvement projects, and work with civic organizations and welfare agencies. *School and Society* 73:151-153; March 1951.

CHAPTER 13

Cataloging Community Resources

Community resources must be located and made known to teachers before they can be utilized in the school program. A comprehensive inventory of such resources is thus essential, as is the systematic recording of survey findings and the diffusion of this information to all interested teachers. In this chapter we shall suggest how these things may be done effectively, and in so doing will indicate what some enterprising school systems have already accomplished in this direction.

Before we describe techniques, though, let's consider the full range of community resources and what we should mean by that term. You recall that in Chapter 3 we noted what was called the three "conceptual levels" of the community (see pp. 81-82). Adequate community study and service plans must take appropriate account of these three interrelated levels— *material, institutional,* and *psychological.* Community life, whether local, regional, national or international, cannot be understood except as all three levels are recognized and emphasized.

Suppose you are teaching about police protection as one aspect of the social process called *protecting life and health.* You will, of course, want to visit a police station to observe the complaint desk, record books, lock-up arrangements, and the like (material level: *things*). You will also need to understand court procedures such as swearing in of witnesses, rules of evi-

---

This chapter is by EDWARD G. OLSEN.

dence, roles of the prosecuting and defending attorneys, function of the bail bondsmen, and so forth (institutional level: *customs*). But even this is not enough; you must go also into the attitudes and ideals which underlie and motivate these procedures: society's desire to protect the innocent, the assumption of innocence until proved guilty beyond a reasonable doubt, the right of habeas corpus, of trial by a jury of one's peers, etc. (psychological level: *motivations*). Is it not clear that a "community experience" which involves only a field trip to the police station is a sadly unbalanced and hardly justifiable learning experience? Other illustrations of this needed "three-level" coverage are summarized on page 348.

SUGGESTED DIVISIONS OF COMMUNITY TIME STUDY *
By School Grades and "Conceptual Levels" of the Community

School Grade Levels	Conceptual Levels		
	Material (Things)	Institutional (Customs)	Psychological (Motivations)
University and College	10%	30%	60%
Junior College	20%	30%	50%
Senior High School	30%	30%	40%
Junior High School	40%	30%	30%
Intermediate Grades	50%	30%	20%
Primary Grades	60%	30%	10%

DIRECTION OF EMPHASIS IN COMMUNITY STUDY

* *Obviously the percentages shown are purely relative. They are intended to suggest a desirable direction of effort, not to divide community experiences mathematically.*

COMMUNITY RESOURCES
Illustrative Learning Activities

Economic Category	Material Level (things)	Institutional Level (customs)	Psychological Level (motivations)
NATURAL RESOURCES Forests: *Conservation*	Exhibit of commercial woods . . . *film* showing types of forests . . . *trip* to a lumber camp	Film on old and new logging operations . . . *speaker:* forester . . . *trip* to cut-over land	Book: on timber exploitation . . . *interview* a lumberjack . . . *survey* conservation legislation . . . *service project:* plant trees
HUMAN RESOURCES Working People: *Coal Miners*	Census reports on number of miners by states . . . *trip* to a mine or museum exhibit . . . *display* of coal samples	Report by government department . . . *interview* a miner, an operator . . . *film* on mining process	Survey safety measures . . . *read* social workers' reports . . . *hear* union speaker, owner . . . *discuss* problems
CAPITAL RESOURCES Industrial Plant: *Railroads*	Visit a station, roundhouse . . . *ride* on a train . . . *talk* with a conductor, engineer, porter	Survey commuters' opinions . . . *debate* "featherbedding" . . . *photograph* segregated waiting rooms	Resource people on government regulation . . . *documents* on financing . . . *film* on railroad tradition
BUSINESS ENTERPRISE Corporations: *Grocery store*	Interview grocer on stock . . . build classroom store . . . *survey* price trends . . . *tour* a warehouse	Speaker: store manager . . . *work experience:* part-time . . . *slides* on distribution techniques	Interviews on values and limitations of chain stores . . . *surveys* of consumer opinions . . . *reports* of legislative hearings
OCCUPATIONAL ORGANIZATION Business Promotion: *Chamber of Commerce*	Field trip to the office . . . *pamphlets* on local business conditions . . . *charts* showing industrial recruitment	Service project: office work . . . *survey* services offered . . . *filmstrip* on achievements	Newspaper research for editorial opinions on value to community . . . *interview* secretary
GOVERNMENTAL AGENCIES Consumer Protection: *Meat Inspection*	Display of marking equipment . . . *trip* to the stockyards . . . *photos* of laboratory experiments	Film on inspection procedures . . . *tour* his rounds with inspector . . . *read* court reports	Survey services against costs . . . *Discuss* function of government in consumer protection

Of course it is true that very young children cannot comprehend the abstractions of the psychological level, and can have only limited understanding of the institutional level. That is precisely why any justifiable program of community education will be structured according to the maturity level of the learners, as suggested by the chart on page 347. That is also why your catalog of community resources should certainly include items helpful in the understanding of community motivations and customs as well as things.

Discover Your Resources

If a survey of your community's educational opportunities has already been made by the superintendent's office, by a committee of teachers, or by some other agency, so much the better. In that case, it is only necessary to bring the file up to date and, perhaps, to arrange its contents in more useful order. But if you must start from scratch to inventory your community, there are two major approaches you may use:

The Informal Approach

Members of a committee on community resources may first record their present knowledge of the community's people, places, needs, and problems. Many committee members will probably have lived in the community for several years, and are already aware of numerous educational resources within it. Following this initial pooling of information, the committee asks other teachers, students, supervisors, administrators, and citizens to supplement the growing list. The committee may refer also to the classified section of the telephone book, to local newspaper files, to school district, and city and county legal records for additional information and other leads.

Sedro-Woolley, a small consolidated school district in upper Washington State, quickly assembled considerable community data this way: After explanation of the plan at a district teachers' meeting, all the teachers were invited to a spacious library where tables were already labeled "History," "Occupations,"

"Recreation," "Government," and the like. Each teacher sat down at the table of his major interest and on cards already there wrote suggestions for places to visit on field trips and for persons who might serve as resource people for the school. Many of the teachers wrote such suggestions at several of the tables. After all the cards were collected, the committee in charge eliminated duplications and then proceeded to seek further information concerning each suggested place and person, as well as to group the cards under useful headings and file them accordingly.

Park Ridge, Illinois, an upper-middle-class suburban community outside Chicago, approached the problem in a different manner. There a committee of the P.T.A. Council worked with the curriculum consultant and the superintendent of schools to develop a community resources inventory, stressing field trip and resource people needed as well as those known to be available. That committee first circulated to all teachers in the five schools the survey form reproduced on page 351. It also sent home to all parents a resource person inventory form somewhat like that shown on page 352. After the returns were in, the committee divided the "already used" resource people among the several lay committee members, each person taking one grade level. After eliminating grade-level duplications through group analysis, each lay person on the committee had a list of resource persons to seek out and interview to see who would be available to the school in that capacity. Meanwhile, the Curriculum Consultant interviewed all the teachers who had listed "already used" trips and people, in order to get from them essential data of the kind indicated on the inventory worksheets on pages 353-354. Similar worksheets were used by the lay committee members as they interviewed their assigned resource people. Bearing in mind the "wanted" field trip and resource person lists, the committee next sought out other possibilities of both types by canvassing the classified section of the telephone book, by asking P.T.A. members and other adults to scan the "wanted" list and to suggest other leads, and by

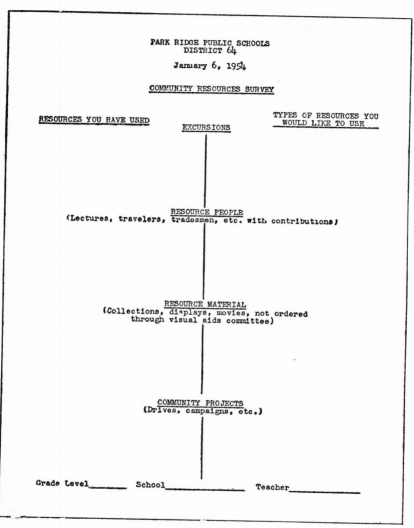

PARK RIDGE PUBLIC SCHOOLS
DISTRICT 64

January 6, 1954

COMMUNITY RESOURCES SURVEY

RESOURCES YOU HAVE USED

TYPES OF RESOURCES YOU
WOULD LIKE TO USE

EXCURSIONS

RESOURCE PEOPLE
(Lectures, travelers, tradesmen, etc. with contributions)

RESOURCE MATERIAL
(Collections, displays, movies, not ordered
through visual aids committee)

COMMUNITY PROJECTS
(Drives, campaigns, etc.)

Grade Level_____ School_____ Teacher_____

Inquiry to All Teachers—Park Ridge, Illinois

INTERESTS AND HOBBIES AS RESOURCES FOR THE MONTCLAIR PUBLIC SCHOOLS

A group of parents and school people have recognized the need for supplementing the already good educational program in the Montclair Public Schools. It would be helpful if teachers knew to whom to turn when they need further enrichment for their work. Montclair is rich (1) with people who could render real help in this connection and (2) with materials which represent interests of all sorts. This inquiry is an attempt to find both of these types of service. Would you and any other interested member of your family indicate your willingness to help by responding to the following questions?

1. Do you have articles or collections, e.g. stamps, rocks, costumes, dolls, models, kodachrome slides, etc. which you would be willing to share with some interested teacher and pupils? If so, please describe the item(s), the localities represented, etc._____

Would you be willing to take them to school to show them? Or would you prefer to have a group of pupils come to your home or place of work to see them?_____

      Once or twice a year of oftener?_____

      What age pupil preferred?_____

2. Do you have information and/or skill in some special field, such as those noted below, about which you would be willing to confer with teacher and pupils?
      Pottery, radio, pets, needlework, etc.
      Travel, art, language, literature, music, science, etc.
      Business or profession such as manufacturing, hotel service, mmed
      Medicine etc.

If so, please describe_____

      Once or twice a year or oftener?_____

      What age pupil preferred?_____

      What place preferred? School__Home__Placeoff work__Elsewhere?__

3. Any other interest of hobbies?_____

4. Do you know someone else who might be willing to offer such services?

                Signed_____

Address   Home_____   Telephone   Home_____
        Office_____   Office_____

Resource Person Questionnaire—Montclair, New Jersey

LUFKIN PUBLIC SCHOOLS COMMUNITY STUDY PROGRAM

FIELD TRIP INVENTORY WORKSHEET

Name of Place or Organization _____

Street/Address _____ Phone _____

Official to Contact _____ Title _____

NATURE OF ACTIVITY

Characterize as a learning experience, listing things to see, hear, do; speakers, audio-visual materials and publications available; pertinent topics and problems; suggested grade-level and/or subject-field use; special features and services.

LIMITING CONDITIONS

Age Group Preferred: Children____ Adolescents_____ Adults_____ Comment_____

Size of Group Acceptable: 2-10_____   10-20_____   20-30_____   30-50_____

50-100_____   Over 100_____.

Sex of Visitors: Mixed Group____ Boys Only____ Girls Only____ Comment____

Best Seasons of Year_____ Days of Week_____

Times of Day_____ Comment_____

Safety Hazards:_____

Time Required:_____

Cost Involved: _____ Comment_____

Remarks:

Investigator's Name and   Date

Field Trip Inventory Worksheet—Lufkin, Texas

Battle Creek Public Schools
Division of Instruction

Community Resource Data
1950-51

1. Are you willing to continue to permit teachers and pupils to visit your place of business? If so, will you please fill in the following form:

Place of business _____ Address _____ Tel. _____

Person who should be reached in advance of trip _____

Age level of children who would benefit from trip _____

Number of children who could be taken through plant at one time _____

Days of week on which visitors would be most welcome _____

Hours at which visitors could be received most conveniently _____

Time required to make trip through place of business _____

Pictures help a group remember much more vividly the things it has seen. Would you permit an adult to take flash pictures as the group makes its trip? _____

2. Can you provide schools with films, pamphlets, exhibits, and/or photographs that will help pupils better understand their community and your contribution to it? If so, will you please fill out the following form:

Name of Film, Pamphlet, Exhibit, or Photographs	Brief Description	Person who should be contacted to obtain material	Length of time in advance that request should be made

3. Do you have people on your staff who can talk to pupils about your industry, and its contribution to the community, and/or what it expects of the people it employs? If so, please fill out the following form:

Name of Person	Title of Person	What he can talk about	Age level of pupils to whom he can talk

Industrial Concern Questionnaire—Battle Creek, Michigan

browsing through the files of the local newspapers of the past three years.

Battle Creek, Michigan, developed its card file on community resources by sending out questionnaires and letters of inquiry. These went to people in three selected groups:

All teachers—asking them to list field trips that they had taken last year, community resource people that they had used and would recommend, and school resource people (those who had taken trips to interesting places or had similar experiences).

Selected teachers—requesting them to list several important things that their pupils had seen at a specific place visited.

Business enterprises—inquiring about field trip possibilities to their establishments, whether pictures could be taken to build up a school collection of slides, exhibits they might be willing to give to the Audio-Visual Department to become part of a collection that would be circulated to people studying Battle Creek, and resource people.

The Systematic Approach

Some committees prefer to begin instead with a more systematic approach, such as a simple classification of community life in terms of its structure, processes, and problems. For that purpose the "Community Aspects" classification of community resources shown on page 356 has been frequently used. A preliminary analysis of this nature does assure initial perspective over the whole community by directing immediate attention to every significant aspect of the community's life.

Using this systematic approach, the Community Resources Committee in Washington State's "apple capital," Wenatchee, recommended the following procedure for a local inventory of community resources:

"That each member of the committee report to the faculty of his own school on the two meetings already held to plan the survey.

"That at this time these members distribute the community resources classification list to the teachers; that each teacher make a list of places to which he would like to take trips, and also check the type of community resources in which he is particularly interested.

"That a central planning committee be set up to consist of inter-

COMMUNITY ASPECTS

1. PHYSICAL SETTING—Geography, topography, size; soil type and fertility, climate; water, mineral, and forest resources; world of nature; community spatial pattern

2. HISTORY—Pioneers, markers, monuments, sites, locations, documents, artifacts

3. POPULATION—Number, age, and sex composition; educational and occupational status; nationality pattern, racial groupings, class and caste structure

4. MINORITY GROUPS—Racial and national areas, centers, organizations, festivals and celebrations, newspapers

5. TRANSPORTATION AND COMMUNICATION—Boat, rail, bus, truck, air, and taxicab centers; postal, telegraph, telephone, radio, and television systems

6. HOME AND FAMILY LIFE—Housing, customs, budgets, food planning, decorating; welfare agencies and organizations, marriage clinics, domestic and juvenile courts; consumer protection and services; day nurseries, camps, institutions

7. INDUSTRIES AND OCCUPATIONS—Industries, business enterprises, professional services, farms, commercial opportunities, conditions of work, trade associations, labor unions, cooperative associations

8. HEALTH—Water supply, sewage and refuse disposal; milk and food safeguards; disease incidence and rates; public health facilities and medical care; private health services, promotional organizations

9. EDUCATION—Public schools, private schools, adult centers, study groups, libraries, art galleries, museums, zoos

10. RELIGION—Christian and non-Christian churches, centers, organizations, publicity agencies

11. RECREATION—Hobbies and activities; commercial and welfare organizations, agencies, centers

12. LOCAL GOVERNMENT—Offices, plants, equipment, personnel, services

13. PUBLIC SAFETY—Police, courts, prisons; traffic supervision, accident prevention, fire prevention and control, coordination of safety measures

14. PROVISIONS FOR HANDICAPPED—Public and private welfare agencies, organizations and institutions for mentally, physically, and economically handicapped persons

15. COMMUNITY PLANNING—Service clubs, private and public planning agencies, community chests, social work conferences, ministerial associations, chambers of commerce, fact-finding bodies

Suggested Classification of Community Resources

ested teachers, one from each building, appointed by the principal.
"That the central planning committee examine the lists turned in
by the teachers and (using the interests expressed there as a guide)
determine the types of community resources that will be surveyed.
Then for each type thus chosen, the central committee should set
up a sub-committee to survey that type.

"That before the end of the school year, each sub-committee
make its survey and present its findings to the central committee."

These plans were followed, and the inventory taken accordingly. Schools were dismissed early one afternoon so that
teachers might visit possible field trip centers and interview
their managers. Thus accurate information was quickly secured, and later use of community resources greatly stimulated
by the fact that nearly every teacher in the district had actively
shared in the survey program.

We must always remember that the "informal" and the "systematic" approaches are not mutually exclusive; rather, they
are two sides of the same coin. One begins by random collecting of information and then must lead to the classification of
findings into categories, a scheme, or pattern. The other starts
with a workable classification and then seeks specific community resources information within each chosen category. The
important thing is that, somehow, a *comprehensive* inventory
of *usable* resources be made.

Regardless of the initial approach, the data secured by the
investigators should first be recorded on some such worksheet
as those shown on pages 353-354. From these crude field records, essential information can later be transferred to a master
card file that is permanent.

Record Your Findings

Any inventory will prove both ephemeral and useless unless
adequate provision is made for systematic, permanent recording of its findings, and also for easy access to those findings by
busy classroom teachers. Available community resources must
be cataloged as adequately as are books, films, transcriptions,
or any other instructional tools. Not otherwise can effective use

of your community's educational resources be developed as an integrated part of your total teaching program.

Organize a Master File

Community resources data roughly noted on your inventory worksheets should be checked for accuracy and then transferred to standardized card forms which become your master file. These cards should provide space for easy recording of such essential facts as name of place or person, address, type and description of the activity or learning value, limiting conditions, and time required for the experience. Some space for cumulative evaluation is also very desirable. Several such card forms in current use are pictured on the following pages. Some are 4 by 6 inches in size, others are 5 by 8 inches. Anything smaller is not practicable.

Make Information Easily Available

A master file, however complete, will be of little actual use to teachers and students unless they can have speedy access to its information. They must be able to identify the community's resource visitors, interview and field trip possibilities, service project needs, and the like, as easily as they can locate a book or a film in the library.

Some schools solve this problem by placing duplicate master file cards in each school building, usually in the library, but sometimes in the principal's office. Snohomish County, Washington, Battle Creek, Michigan, and Denver, Colorado, are among the school systems which now use the duplicate card arrangement. Snohomish County includes mimeographed resource-person and field-trip cards as part of its comprehensive file of varied instructional materials. Different colored cards, each 4 by 6 inches in size, are used for the several kinds of teaching materials—blue for 2 by 2-inch slides, buff for motion picture films, white for filmstrips, cherry for packets of pictures and pamphlets, salmon for field trips, and green for

```
┌──────────────────────────────────────────────────────────────────┐
│ Name ............................................................ │
│ Address ................................... Phone .............. │
│ Occupation ..................................................... │
│ Collection ..................................................... │
│ ............................................................... │
│ Information .................................................... │
│ ............................................................... │
│ Age Pupil Preferred: Primary..........Up. Elem.......... Jr. H. S..........Sr. H. S....... │
│ Size of Group Preferred: ...................................... │
│ Place Preferred: School.......... Home..........Place of Work.......... Elsewhere.......... │
│ Times Per Year ............................Hours Available ...... │
│        VOLUNTEER RESOURCE FILE—THE PUBLIC SCHOOLS—MONTCLAIR, N. J.   1950 │
└──────────────────────────────────────────────────────────────────┘
```

4" x 6" card file form—Montclair, New Jersey

```
┌──────────────────────────────────────────────────────────────────┐
│                      Field Trip Preview                            │
│  Place_____ Address_____                  │
│  Activities or Objects to Observe_____                  │
│  _____                  │
│  _____                  │
│                              Best time                             │
│  Time needed at place_____ to visit_____                   │
│  Person to contact_____ Phone_____                  │
│  Grade level of interest_____                   │
│  Additional Comments_____                   │
│  _____                  │
└──────────────────────────────────────────────────────────────────┘
```

4" x 6" card file form—Snohomish County Schools, Washington

RESOURCE VISITOR.   Date _____

Subject _____

Name _____ Address _____ Phone _____

Time Available _____ Day _____ Time

Equipment Needed:

Grade Level _____

Background of Visitor _____

_____

Type of Program _____

Length of Presentation _____

Suggested Aids to Preparation _____

_____

Remarks:

Card form—University High School (front side)

TRAVEL DIRECTIONS   GENERAL COMMENTS

EVALUATION BY USERS

Teacher or Leader	School or Group	Grade or Age	Subject	Rating
1. _____	_____	_____	_____	EX G P NO
2. _____	_____	_____	_____	EX G P NO
3. _____	_____	_____	_____	EX G P NO
4. _____	_____	_____	_____	EX G P NO
5. _____	_____	_____	_____	EX G P NO
6. _____	_____	_____	_____	EX G P NO
7. _____	_____	_____	_____	EX G P NO
8. _____	_____	_____	_____	EX G P NO

(reverse side)

EX TRANSPORTATION   p-el
    Great Northern Depot
    2900 Bond Street

    Nature of activity: View lobby & route map of
    Empire Builder, telegraph office, baggage room,
    gardens.
    Take train to Marysville - 9:17 a.m.
    Take train to Snohomish   - 9:30 a.m.
    Take train from Edmonds   - 8:30 a.m.
    May watch same arrive few minutes earlier.
    Streamliner arrives 3:55 p.m.

    TIME: any time
    LENGTH: varies
    SIZE: 1 class
    USE: experience train travel & ticket purchase

    CONTACT: Mr. Pfister
    PHONE: BA 3101   MDeC/49

Card from duplicate master file—Snohomish County, Washington

Chamberlin Observatory: Dr. Albert Recht,
    University of Denver, 2930 East Warren
    Avenue   SPruce 4965

Points of observation: astronomical
instruments, astronomical observations,
organization and operation, methods of
recording data

Card from duplicate master file—Denver, Colorado

resource people. All the cards are filed together alphabetically by subject, such as Animal Life, Aircraft, City Planning, Conservation, Science, Social Studies, and so on.

Battle Creek's files of community resources are part of a 3 by 5-inch duplicate card listing of all audio-visual materials available to the school system. It includes trips, resource persons from the community, and resource teachers and students from within the schools. Names of field trips and resource people are filed under units or areas of teaching.

Denver's community resources card file is likewise found in every school building. It consists of several hundred 3 by 5-inch dittoed cards organized under printed division headings as follows:

LOCAL BUSINESS AND INDUSTRIAL ESTABLISHMENTS
  Aviation, Bakeries, Laboratories, Photography, etc.
CULTURAL INSTITUTIONS
  Churches, Libraries, Museums, Paintings, Sculpture, etc.
LOCAL AND CIVIC INSTITUTIONS
  Courts, Fire Stations, Police Department, Sewage Plant, etc.
STATE, FEDERAL, CIVIC AND POLITICAL INSTITUTIONS
  Federal Institutions, State Institutions
RECREATIONAL FACILITIES
  Parks, Theaters, Miscellaneous
EDUCATIONAL FACILITIES
  Community and Welfare Centers, Housing Projects, Observatories, etc.

Regulations governing use of busses for trips, teacher-pupil planning of the experience, request and evaluation reports, and the like are stated on cards included in the file itself.

Another and much more common way of getting community resources information to all teachers is to maintain one master card file, and from this file take essential data to publish in a community resources directory or handbook, a copy of which is then placed on every teacher's desk. Sometimes this directory is one section in a comprehensive instructional materials handbook, as in Sedro-Woolley's *Tools for Learning: A Handbook for School and Community Resources* (Washington State). This handbook has sections on "Things to See and Touch," "Pictures to See on a Screen," "Pictures to Look At," "Things to Listen To," and "Places to Go and People to Hear." This latter section states school policy for field trips and resource visitors, lists places and persons utilized and reported upon during the previous year, includes sample report forms, classifies types of resources in the town and the surrounding area, and presents an annotated directory of community resources available for use in that district. Kitsap County, Washington, also uses this instructional materials approach; its *Teaching Tools for Kitsap Schools* is a mimeographed bulletin which includes a section on "Field Trips and Community Studies" and outlines eighty possible trips in the county and the Puget Sound area.

Usually, however, the directory appears as a separate publication devoted exclusively to community resources.

El Paso, Texas, has developed a brief bulletin entitled *School Excursions and Field Trips*. This publication wisely warns that "there should be a real purpose for a school excursion. It may serve as the introduction or approach to the study of some subject or phase of a subject; it may become one of the major activities in the development of a unit; or it may be undertaken in order to verify data already collected and discussed. Whatever its purpose may be, definite preparation and plans are essential for satisfactory outcomes." Available field trip centers are then charted by general types and by items, such as name of place, person to contact, day and time to visit, time required, and best grade level.

At Your Service: Community Resources for Learning is a similar directory from Longview, Washington, except that it is organized around the "systematic" plan of community analysis mentioned on page 355. Under "Local Government," for instance, it groups four possible field trips and seven resource visitors. Eleven such categories of community life are thus presented. The manual also includes suggestions for wise use of community resources, and reproduces two sample units of work to show how community resources should be integrated with other learning experiences.

Let's Go: School Trips Having Educational Value has been issued by the Schenectady, New York, Public Schools. The Newton, Massachusetts, schools have a bulletin: *Know Your*

Newton Tour. Viewing Our City by the Louisville, Kentucky, schools and *Know Nevada* by the Nevada State Department of Education are other publications of this general kind. The examples of community resources directories just given are nearly all from small communities including rural districts and small towns. Many city and metropolitan school districts have also issued such directories for use by their teachers. These publications may also give you good ideas for planning your own catalog. Let's notice some of them briefly.

CITY, TITLE OF DIRECTORY, AND DATE OF ISSUE	CHIEF FEATURES OF THE DIRECTORY
Dearborn, Michigan *Field Trip Handbook* (1950)	Suggestions for nearly 200 trips, each described in terms of place, telephone number, address, person to contact, objective, things to see and do, observations to be made en route, teaching aids, traveling directions, etc. Some 50 resource people are listed by their fields of interest.
Des Moines, Iowa *Community Resources* (1940)	Field trips, organizations, and related speakers are listed under major areas: Health, Recreation, Government, Public Welfare, Consumer Education, Industry, Occupational Opportunity, Business, Safety, Education, Intercultural Relations, Religion, Practical and Fine Arts, and Home Membership. In each area are listed those things which can best be utilized by excursions, demonstrations, guest speakers, visual materials, pupil participation in community activity, etc. Also indicated are grade levels in which the resources can best be used.
Detroit, Michigan *Exploring Metropolitan Detroit* (1950)	Alphabetical listing of excursion centers, such as Ambassador Bridge, Board of Health, Circuit Court, Weather Bureau, Zoo.
Los Angeles, California *It's Worth a Visit* (1949, 1950)	Separate catalogs of school journeys for elementary and high schools are issued. Both include listings of trips, regulations, and procedures to be observed, and numerous ground and floor plans. The elementary school catalog also includes for every trip an extended statement of activities which may be observed upon it.

CITY, TITLE OF DIRECTORY, AND DATE OF ISSUE	CHIEF FEATURES OF THE DIRECTORY
Minneapolis, Minnesota *Field Trip Bulletins* (1948-1951)	This handbook is really a series of bulletins to teachers rather than a single directory as such. Most of the bulletins feature interpretive explanation of what will be seen on specified field trips. Bulletin #2, *Visiting the Courts*, describes the arrangement of the court room, how the jury is secured, the steps in a trial, and suggestions to visiting pupils. Bulletin #18, *Como Park Zoo*, includes drawings, vivid descriptions, and fascinating life-stories of many of the animals to be seen there.
New York City *Museums, Libraries, Parks, Zoos and Gardens as Educational Resources* (1942-43)	For each specific place which may be visited by school groups the bulletin gives the location, contact official's name and telephone number, the visiting hours, and the educational services available by arrangement.
Portland, Oregon *The Community—Our Classroom* (1950)	Field trip opportunities are cataloged under these headings: Agriculture, Communication and Transportation, Education, Food, Forestry, Government, Health, Safety, History, Mills and Manufacturing Plants, Occupations, Recreation.
St. Louis, Missouri *Educational Field Trip Handbook*	Lists about a hundred places for classroom visitation. These are divided into fifteen categories: Shops and Markets, Travel and Transportation, Communication, Public Utilities, Industries, Community Agencies, Government Agencies, Historical Points of Interest, Parks and Gardens, Museums, Public Libraries, Banks, Public Welfare Agencies, Local School and School District, Schools. Information regarding each place listed covers grade-level interest, contact person, address, and telephone number.
San Diego, California *School Excursions and Field Trips* (1946)	Trips are listed under alphabetical types: Agriculture, Brick Companies, Historic Landmarks, Welfare Agencies, and the like. For each one this information is given: address, person to contact, conditions under which the place or group prefers to cooperate with the schools, special interest centers, notes or comments. Suggestions for planning and conducting trips are featured.

Illustrative pages from several community resources directories—from both large and small school systems—are reproduced on this page and the pages following.

Who does these inventories, compiles the master files, issues the directories of community resources? Obviously these are group activities—class or workshop projects, teacher in-service education activities, committee responsibilities, administrative ventures. In each situation, specific procedures are needed which will reflect local circumstances, facilities, and personalities. Yet in nearly all communities lay people can be of immense help, especially in listing possible resource people, in

---

ARTS AND CRAFTS

1. *Ceramics, Pictures, Framing, China*

    Drees   Phone 7177
    Time—Any time
    Notice—Two weeks

2. *Tincraft*

    Ben Hamlin   Phone 7333
    Notice—Two weeks
    Will bring simple equipment and demonstrate any type of project in Tincraft. Children must furnish cans. Also prepared to talk on Plastics and their use. Will demonstrate any kind of Plastic Projects. Can talk at children's level—explanations clear.

3. *Weaving*

    Mrs. Flegenheimer   Phone 9902 Ask for Mrs. Wilder
    Prepared to talk on all types of weaving. Can explain setting up a loom. Will bring table loom and demonstrate. Excellent samples.

4. *Woodcarving*

    Carl Hollander   Phone 7410 Business phone 5543
    Woodcarving in relief. Reserves right to say "No" if he has nothing to show at the time. (Prefers Jr. high and high school.)

RESOURCE PERSONS ARE LISTED IN THIS DIRECTORY
Olympia, Washington

21. Name of firm: GRIFFITH PARK ZOO
    Address: Griffith Park, Los Angeles
    Nature of activity: Study of the animals in Griffith Park Zoo
    Of interest to: All grades, except Kindergarten
    Time of visits: 10:00 a.m. to 12:00 m. daily
    Length of visits: Unlimited
    Group size: Unlimited

22. Name of firm: HAMMOND LUMBER COMPANY
    Address: 209 Mormon Ave., Terminal Island, Calif.
    Nature of activity: Unloading of lumber from boats, distribution of lumber through the yard, and loading on trucks. Students may watch milling operations from outside of building
    Of interest to: 4th through 6th Grades
    Time of visits: 10:00 a.m. to 12:00 m. and 2.00 to 4:00 p.m. daily except Saturday and Sunday
    Length of visits: 2 hours
    Group size: 20 to 30

23. Name of firm: HELMS BAKERIES
    Address.   8800 Venice Blvd., Los Angeles 34
    Nature of activity: On this trip the students may see the flour blender and sifter, general storage room, bread mixing room, traveling ovens, laboratory, air washing and conditioning machine, slicing and bread wrapping machine, cake decorating room, and the shipping department
    Of interest to: 2nd through 5th Grades
    Time of visits: 10:00 a.m. or 10:30 a.m. latest starting time
    Length of visits: 1¼ hours
    Group size: 50

24. Name of firm: HOLLYWOOD CITIZENS-NEWS
    Address: 1545 N. Wilcox Ave., Hollywood 28
    Nature of activity: Newspaper publishing
    Of interest to: 5th and 6th Grades
    Time of visits: 1:30 to 3:00 p.m. daily except Saturday and Sunday
    Length of visits: 1 hour
    Group size: 6 to 36

25. Name of firm: HONGWANJI BUDDHIST TEMPLE OF LOS ANGELES
    Address: 119 N. Central Ave., Los Angeles 12
    Nature of activity: Buddha and shrine
    Of interest to: 5th and 6th Grades
    Time of visits: 9:00 a.m. to 12:00 m., 1:00 to 5:00 p.m., and 6:30 to 9:00 p.m. daily except Sunday
    Length of visits: 1 hour
    Group size: Unlimited

ALPHABETICAL LISTINGS IN COMMUNITY
RESOURCES DIRECTORY
Los Angeles, California

FROZEN FOODS

A. Preparation Needed by Pupils:
1. List the varieties of frozen foods on the market today.
2. Discuss with parents how food is processed for the home locker.
3. Explain the advantages of freezing food.
4. Stress safety and sanitation.

B. Benefits to Be Had from the Trip:
1. Learn that modern methods of preservation give us fresh fruits the year round.
2. Realize that cold as well as heat is a food preservative.
3. Discover that science has contributed to the welfare of people.

C. Activities Suggested by the Trip:
1. List products from home gardens that might be frozen.
2. Visit a home frozen food locker.
3. Prepare a frozen food in the classroom.
4. Make a scrap book collection of frozen food advertisements.

(1) Name of Place: Birds Eye—Snider
Address: North 2nd Avenue and C Street. Telephone, 9174.
Person with whom arrangements should be made: Mr. Ralph Sebern.
Grade or classes recommended: Grade 4, 5, and 6.
Time: Between 10:15 and noon, or 2:00 and 3:00 p.m. From April 15 to September. (Notify firm at least a week or 10 days before intended visit.)

Number of pupils: 10 or 15.

SAMPLE PAGE WITH SUGGESTED PREPARATION AND
FOLLOW-UP FOR FIELD TRIPS
Yakima, Washington

Airport
Wayne County

Dearborn Public Schools
SUGGESTION FOR A FIELD TRIP

PLACE: Wayne County Airport
ADDRESS: M-112 Expressway   TELE. NO. Lo. 2-9619
PERSON TO CONTACT: Henry Baker, airport superintendent
OBJECTIVE: To see how a large airport is constructed, arranged, and conducted to provide for the landing and taking off of huge freight and passenger planes.
THINGS TO SEE AND DO: Many kinds of freight and commercial planes use Wayne County Airport. You can see how runways are arranged and go through the hangars. Go through a plane if one is in port for some time. The group will be taken through the control tower a few at a time.
TEACHING AIDS: Films: *An Airplane Trip, Behind the Scenes at the Airport*
Filmstrips: *History of Air Transportation, Airplanes at Work*
SOME THINGS TO OBSERVE ENROUTE: Discuss the Express Highway. Why was the Expressway built? What is Wayne Airport used for mostly? What airport does Detroit bound passenger planes use? Write Wayne County Airport asking for any descriptive material they may have.
AGE OF CHILDREN PERMITTED: Six years and up.
SUITABLE FOR GRADES: Five and up.
NUMBER IN GROUP: Not limited. Group will be divided for certain departments.
DAYS AND HOURS TO VISIT: Any day and hour can be arranged between 9:30 and 4:00—Monday through Friday.
TRAVELING TIME ONE WAY: 30 minutes.
DIRECTIONS TO GET THERE: Take Expressway M-112 to the airport on the left, near road.
PARKING ACCOMMODATIONS: Ample in front of entrance to airport.
GUIDE SERVICE: Mr. Barr will make arrangements for guides. Contact Mr. Barr a week or more in advance.
EATING ACCOMMODATIONS: Restaurant available.
ADMISSION FEE: None.

MORE COMPLETE INFORMATION IS GIVEN
IN THIS DIRECTORY
Dearborn, Michigan

helping to plan for the comprehensive inventory, and in doing much of the clerical work involved.

Establish a Clearing House

However modest its initial scale, you will need some sort of central location where you can keep your community file, and where you can place together your books, bulletins, reports, clippings, exhibits and other materials relating to community study and service. In the beginning, such a "community center" may be only one drawer in a single filing cabinet, but as interest develops and community contacts increase, there will soon be need for expansion of both quarters and facilities.

Many school districts still expect the individual teacher to make his own contacts and arrangements for field trips, resource people, student interviews, community service and work experience projects, and so on. This procedure is not too bad as long as such community learning experiences are infrequent. One, two, or a half-dozen teachers can make independent arrangements for occasional field work—but ten, fifty, or a hundred teachers cannot do so without conflicts with regard to desired dates, places, and persons. Nothing will "wear out the welcome" more quickly than to permit six different teachers from four different schools to ask a local bank, for example, to receive their classes within a single week. Such anarchistic procedure almost surely produces bad public relations. "Why in the world don't they get together on these requests?" the harassed bank official will exclaim. "We're glad to welcome two or three classes a week but we can't take six—so I guess we'll have to refuse all requests from now on in order to be fair with everybody."

Lacking any centralized administration of the community resources program, that program will remain limited in effectiveness as various teachers overwork some resource people and centers while neglecting others, as they compete for dates and materials and busses, as they promote community projects independently and even in ignorance of each other's plans. And at worst, such failure to coordinate and control difficult school-community relationships will discredit the whole community emphasis because of cumulative irritations upon the community and recurrent frustrations among teachers and students.

To forestall such unhappy developments, the school system or district should establish regular administrative procedures whereby all desired community experiences are cleared and arranged by one central person. Other values of this plan are (a) convenience to busy teachers, (b) facilitation of arrangements since the community individuals or agencies can more readily contact a single, known, centrally located office, and (c) equitable use of educational resources so none are overworked and all are utilized when appropriate. The clearing house coordinator may be a full-time person in the superintendent's office, a part-time person in the principal's office, the school librarian, the curriculum director, or other suitable person. The coordinator usually serves also as chairman of a standing community resources committee which maintains the master file of community information, issues and revises the directory of community resources, and schedules needed busses, field trips, resource person visits, and the like.

How, specifically, does such a clearing house operate? Let's illustrate in terms of a small town, that of Longview, Washington, a lumber-mill community on the Columbia River. In Longview the teacher who feels that his class would profit from a field trip or a resource visitor first consults his desk directory for leads and ideas (see excerpts from typical directories on pages 368-369). After tentatively choosing two or three possible field experiences, he then consults his building's vertical card file for detailed information about them. Final choice having now been made, he next fills out a request form similar to the ones shown on page 214. This form he sends to his building principal. If the principal approves the desired activity, he forwards the request to the Elementary Supervisor who is the clearing house coordinator, and makes all field reception and travel arrangements for the teachers. After the trip, the teacher encour·

ages the children to write personal thank-you notes to the places visited, and to the Supervisor. She thanks the cooperating lay people, including the bus drivers. The whole program is coordinated by means of an 18 by 24-inch blank calendar in the Supervisor's office. As trips and resource person visits are scheduled, they are listed on stickers and posted on the calendar. There is also a cumulative record of speakers and trips for the entire year so the coordinator can see at a glance which field trip centers are being overworked or underused. Thus she can easily safeguard good public relations.

Essentially these same procedures are used in all school districts which maintain community-experience clearing houses, including the great metropolitan centers such as Los Angeles and Philadelphia. Sometimes, however, a committee rather than an individual operates the clearing house. This is usually in rural communities or very small towns when the organized program is just beginning to develop. In such cases the schedule of trips and transportation arrangements is arranged by members of the community resources committee, working with the superintendent's office. Sometimes the committee on community resources meets monthly to process the teachers' written requests for trips and resource visitors, to schedule use of the busses, and to make group evaluation of previously used community resources on the basis of teachers' ratings received. Some typical evaluation forms are reproduced on pages 226-228.

Regardless of how community experience arrangements are cleared, provision must be made for adequate administrative controls to operate under well-understood policies. It is highly important that all teachers as well as the community itself realize that educational field experiences are an integral aspect of effective instruction and, accordingly, are carefully authorized, organized, and administered. General "understandings" and oral "agreements" about field study arrangements are not enough; indeed, they may by their very generality create confusion and worsen public relations. Specific, written regulations covering field experience programs should be thoughtfully developed, officially adopted, and widely publicized—preferably by the board of education acting through appropriate channels.

A Beginning Will Be Welcomed by All

All across the country more and more schools and school systems are establishing organized, systematic community resource programs as integral aspects of their total effort toward improved education. Increasingly it is recognized that some kind of catalog of educational resources in the community is essential for every school as that school begins to expand its concept and practice of life-centered education. The beginning may be simple, the organization informal, the leadership inexperienced, yet even such leadership, organization, and beginning will be welcomed by all educators and lay people who are searching for means through which to develop more lifelike programs of education to meet today's needs and tomorrow's demands.

Learning Activities

Socio-drama

A featured speaker for American Education Week was reported in your last week's local newspaper to have criticized the schools for failing to make adequate use of many community resources. As a result, an informal, off-the-record meeting of school leaders and interested lay people has been called to discuss the matter. Here are the roles:
1. The president of the P.T.A. Council
2. The head of the teachers' association
3. The curriculum coordinator
4. The school superintendent

Discussion Topics

1. What are the philosophical assumptions underlying the pros and cons of systematically exploring the community to discover additional educational resources?

2. Should school systems develop an instructional materials center to include community materials and information for use by all teachers? What materials and data should be included?
3. Why do so many schools largely neglect the institutional and the psychological levels of community life?
4. Which is the better approach to use in taking inventory of a community, the "informal" or the "systematic" approach? Why?

Group Projects

1. Plan and carry out an illustrative survey of community resources available to teachers in your community. If your community has already been cataloged, suggest needed additions in terms of the three "community levels" described in Chapter 3.
2. Secure from various schools samples of the field experience forms they use. Compare these items with those reproduced in this chapter, and suggest needed changes in any of them.

Individual Activities

1. Draw up a detailed, step-by-step plan for developing a general field study and service program in the schools of your own home community. After criticism by the class, send this plan to that school superintendent and request his evaluation of it.
2. Evaluate the various kinds of control forms reproduced in this chapter and choose or develop those which you think will be most useful to you in your own teaching situation.
3. Prepare a talk in which you spell out for a particular school system some ways and means of cataloging that community's educational resources.

Learning Materials

Very little has been published in this field. A brief section called "Handbook on Community Resources" by Adeline Howland and Alice Myers appeared in *Community Living and the Elementary School*, the 1945 yearbook of the NEA's Department of Elementary School Principals, pages 33-38, telling how Des Moines surveyed local resources, classified them into eleven areas of living, and issued a handbook of findings. An educational resources survey in the small town of Camas, Washington, is described by Edward G. Olsen in "Co-ordinating Community Educational Services," in the *Annals of the American Academy of Political and Social Science* for September 1949. "Developing a community Resources File" in Manhasset, New York, is reported by Arthur E. Hamalainen in *The Modern Community School*, edited by Edward G.

Olsen (Appleton-Century-Crofts, 1953). *Fifty Teachers to a Classroom* by the Metropolitan School Study Council (Macmillan, 1951) reproduces file cards used in a Long Island resource person inventory system. The plan of Grosse Pointe, Michigan, for surveying and cataloging its human resources is briefly described in the *National Education Association Journal* of October 1952 by Vernon Hicks under the title "The Butcher, the Baker, the Candlestick-maker." Specific suggestions growing out of Portland, Oregon's experience with a comprehensive Instructional Materials Center are offered by Amo DeBernardis in *The School Executive*, September, 1953, "Provide the Tools but Don't Forget the Teacher." More detailed procedures in this whole general field are outlined in *Exploring the Environment* (1943), a publication of the New York State Education Department.

CHAPTER **14**

Facing Administrative Problems

It is one thing to educate students by having them quietly read prescribed textbooks at designated times within specified classroom walls; it is quite another matter if those students are to travel about the actual community in search of education through firsthand experiences. Such ventures immediately raise difficult administrative problems, among which are scheduling, transportation, expenses, and liability. Under traditional school conditions, these problems either hardly exist at all, or have long since been roughly defined and settled through official regulation. But when extensive community study and participation is undertaken, all of these matters become pressingly significant to teachers, students, and administrators alike. That is why these four major problems need to be squarely faced before any field study program is authorized by the school or undertaken by any class.

What about Scheduling?

The first problem confronting the teacher who attempts active community study (and the excuse given most often by teachers wishing to evade it!) is the school schedule. As ordinarily planned, the schedule of classes is designed to make maximal use of classrooms and teaching staff. The use of time for field study, or even for use of radio, motion pictures, and

This chapter is by JULIAN C. ALDRICH.

other such resources, has generally been of little concern in most schools. Although community study in some form is possible within the limitations of any conventional school schedule, the interested teacher should be aware of desirable administrative changes which might enhance its possibilities.

The Unplanned Schedule

Suppose we first consider the schedule which is *unplanned from the viewpoint of life-centered education,* although thoroughly planned from the book-centered point of view. Under such traditional scheduling, the teacher has classes scattered through the school day without regard to needs for visits outside the school. There will be little difficulty in arranging interviews or excursions which do not involve more than one school period, and no hindrance to the utilization of documentary materials, audio-visual aids, and resource persons in the classroom. There will be difficulty, however, in arranging field trips to last more than one class period.

Longer excursions can be planned, however, even within such traditional class schedules. The easier arrangement is to have trips lasting more than one class period scheduled for late afternoons and Saturdays. In such cases conflicts may occur with out-of-school activities of some pupils, but these are usually easier to readjust than are rigid school schedules themselves.

Many schools will allow classes to leave for several consecutive periods, even when other classes must be missed by some students. Frequently an administrator will permit trips to be scheduled upon a central office chart, and from this information, will send notice to all teachers listing students to be absent, the periods for which they are excused, and requesting for these pupils the privilege of "make-up" work. The teacher wishing such special privileges for his students will ordinarily include his own class period among those utilized. He will also be solicitous for the feelings of other teachers, especially of those who have previously demonstrated little enthusiasm for what he is trying to do. It will help to have students arrange in advance for making up the work to be missed, and to assume personal responsibility for seeing that this is done. Notes of appreciation to the cooperating teachers after the event will never be amiss.

In the unplanned schedule there may be only limited opportunity for effective field study. There will be no time barriers, however, to the use of community documents and visual aids such as reports of governmental and service agencies, specimens and models, books and periodicals, photographs and pictures of the community "then" and "now," and the raw data gathered by students as a part of their out-of-class observations.

The Partially Planned Schedule

Between such an unplanned schedule and one consciously designed for effective life-centered education lies an intermediate stage. This stage, for want of a better term, might be called a *partially planned* school schedule. In it some provisions for curricular enrichment and hence for field study are made, even though a fairly rigid class scheduling program is maintained. To illustrate: teachers are encouraged to exchange rooms in order to utilize special equipment; study periods may be used for special purposes in or outside of the school building; classes meeting during the same period may work upon common projects of mutual interest; interschool visitation may be permitted.

In most American schools, only a few classrooms are equipped to utilize films, slides, recordings, and radio programs. If such classrooms are temporarily unoccupied, or if the teachers using them for other purposes will exchange rooms, these media for community study may be more widely used. Sometimes dark rooms for photographic work may be made available to non-science classes wishing to use their facilities. Laboratories are frequently opened for experiments or research studies when not in use by science or technical classes. It is often possible for several classes meeting in one period to join for studies of consumer needs, social agencies, family welfare, human relations, and similar community problems which may properly be approached from the standpoints of various subject fields. Joint assemblies may be held by several classes to hear a speaker or to see an exhibit or a film.

In such schools, it is likely that study periods may be utilized for work on joint projects or for special studies outside of school. Thus, if the members of a given class have a good distribution of study hall time, they may find it possible to make a complete survey throughout the daytime hours.

Some school schedules are suitably arranged for teachers who wish to make occasional trips. In such cases, there is usually no general change in the total schedule, but special adjustments are made. Example: in one school the teachers desiring opportunity for excursion work were assigned classes and free periods alternating at the beginning and end of the school day. It was thus possible for these teachers to take a morning trip which could include a short time before the opening of school, the homeroom period, and the two following class periods without affecting their other classes. This plan might affect one other class taken by the pupils, but this constituted a minimum of schedule disturbance in view of the total time thus made available for field work. It was also possible to arrange joint excursions with other classes whose teachers had similar schedules.

Another plan is to limit formal examinations perhaps to the fifth, tenth, fifteenth and final weeks of the semester, and to allow excursions during other weeks. Such an arrangement prevents the necessity of giving special "make-up" examinations for a few students, one of the major sources of irritation among affected teachers.

Sometimes students are placed in permanent groups whose personnel remain together for several of their school subjects. Where two or three such subjects are scheduled at successive hours, it is possible to arrange a trip which is the joint project of the several instructors concerned with the group. Sample: the biology and the social studies teachers could arrange for the class to visit a local meat packing plant during their two class periods, and to utilize relevant findings in both subject fields. If these class hours are separated by assembly or lunch periods, the consecutive time available would be proportionately lengthened.

The Fully Planned Schedule

Here and there is a school whose time schedule is *planned to meet student needs in flexible fashion,* rather than to maintain a permanent system of time allotments for various subject fields. In such schools, vital education is considered more important than is habitual routine and the schedule, accordingly, is organized to permit the broadest possible pupil experiences with many activities and many persons. An activity program and block-scheduling of classes are the chief methods used to promote such vital education, whether it be of the older child-centered or the present life-centered type.

Block scheduling is used in both junior and senior high schools, as well as in some colleges. Arising out of the need for reducing the number of students facing the teacher at any one time, it has proved valuable for group work of all kinds, including community activities by pupils and teachers. In the junior high school, it is not unusual to have pupils assigned to a "core" teacher for three hours of class time in which are included the "subjects" of English, social studies, and mathematics or general science. In the senior high school, American history and American literature classes are often taught by the same teacher during two consecutive class periods. It is often possible to schedule a study period for such a group either before or after their "integration" class, thus providing an entire morning or afternoon for class trips or other field activities.

Another arrangement of somewhat similar nature is to schedule both science and social studies as double period laboratory courses, with the same students assigned to both courses. Such arrangements may as easily be made for other subject fields, and with the same result so far as providing consecutive hours for field work activities is concerned.

Whatever the form of block-scheduling used, the plan eliminates schedule conflicts with other subjects and other teachers. The one teacher is solely responsible for the utilization of the time assigned to his student group, and in this extended period can make excellent use of most of the community techniques described in Part III. In addition, joint assemblies, recreation, excursions, and other such activities may easily be arranged with other teachers in parallel blocks.

If block scheduling is not used, it is still possible to carry on a variety of activities which cut across time lines, providing the school operates on one of the several group study plans. The Dalton and Winnetka Plans permit individual study and group work to be so arranged that contracts or projects can be completed on a flexible time schedule. Arrangements by the teachers in conference could provide for almost any type of community study and participation. The Morrisonian Plan can be adapted to permit a wealth of community activities during the assimilation periods.

How Shall We Travel?

A second administrative difficulty is that of transportation. To be sure, resource people will usually drive their own cars or use public transport facilities; so also will individual students and small committees going into the community. But when entire classes take excursions or engage in extended field study, they may find that transportation becomes a real problem requiring special consideration. Let us therefore suggest what may be done in this connection.

The School Bus

Schools which own one or more busses and have a licensed driver can arrange transportation that is both convenient and inexpensive. If the available bus is used primarily to transport students to and from the school, the excursions will have to be scheduled with this necessity in mind; that is, the field study class will be unable to leave the school until the bus has discharged its morning load, and must return in time for the afternoon dismissal. But if a bus is assigned specifically for field trip purposes, then its use may be planned just as needed for most effective results.

ın either case, some center for traffic control should be established. This will probably be located in the superintendent's ɔffice or in that of the clearing house coordinator. Here should be kept a master list of bus assignments for the information of the office, the driver, and the teachers and student committees. Other information to be recorded at the same time should include:

> Name or number of the class
> Name of person in charge
> Number of students involved
> Outline of trip itinerary
> Starting and returning times

After transportation arrangements have been completed, the class group should be notified, the place of meeting posted, and the starting time noted. Before boarding the bus, the accepted rules for behavior on trips should be summarized and stressed as needed.

Public Carrier

When no school bus is available, transportation may have to be by public carrier. If distances are short and transfers few, the subway, suburban train, bus or trolley car may be used. In such cases, the trip itself should be chosen with due regard for the availability and convenience of the transportation facilities. Except in special cases such as Nature hikes, walking should be limited to a few blocks. If the group numbers more than a dozen, it will usually be wise to communicate in advance with the transportation officials in order that they may plan for the increased load. Should the number desiring transportation approximate the normal capacity of a bus or street-car, a special vehicle may often be arranged without extra cost. Under this arrangement, however, the regular franchised route must be followed.

Should the schedule or the route of the regular carrier be inconvenient, the group might well consider hiring a special bus. For relatively short distances in the city, where temporary crowding is not too inconvenient, several taxicabs can often be utilized to good advantage.

In the case of an extended study tour over a considerable distance, the class group will need to choose carefully among the various available forms of transportation: train, bus, boat, or plane. Considerations of time, expense, distance, and objectives of the trip will obviously determine the decision. Whatever the means chosen, it will often be possible to secure special accommodations for a sizable group: a special bus, a separate coach or Pullman car on the train, a section of a boat or ship, an entire plane. Obviously, it is essential to make travel arrangements well in advance, particularly if such special accommodations are desired.

Individual Transportation

For many trips, even some of extended duration, bicycle transportation may be desirable. While comparatively slow, travel by bicycle possesses great flexibility of itinerary, and also permits travel costs to be kept at an absolute minimum. It offers healthful exercise, recreation, and desirable social stimulation, particularly if youth hostels are utilized by the party for overnight accommodations on longer trips.

Private automobiles are convenient to use for group travel, and possess the further advantage that they do not make the group as conspicuous to the general public as does the use of bus transportation. Only experienced and fully competent adult drivers should be permitted, however, and no car should be accepted which carries less than $100,000/$300,000 public liability insurance. If this amount is not carried by the owner of the private car desired for school use, the school should request that such insurance be purchased at its own expense for the period of time necessary. Unless adequate liability insurance is carried, the legal risk of utilizing private automobiles is too great for both driver and teacher. And in any case, it is well never to use student drivers who are not of legal age; while they may be quite capable, any accident regardless of cause might bring upon the teacher and the school a charge of negligence that would be difficult to answer.

Who Will Pay the Expenses?

In most school systems, public funds are available for classroom instruction, for some documentary materials, visual and auditory aids, and for mimeographing or duplicating, as well as for limited postage and telephone calls. It is not yet common practice, however, to finance in similar fashion the school use of resource people, field interviews, excursions, surveys, extended field studies, camping, work experiences, or community service projects. Yet all of these vital educational approaches to the community involve some expense, and in this factor lies the third important obstacle confronting the community-minded teacher and class.

Free and Inexpensive Materials

The teacher who plans a community study program should thoroughly canvas all agencies and activities which might aid the program with little or no expense to the school. Some suggestions: state and local governments will usually supply official publications to schools without charge, as will numerous business corporations, advertising concerns, propaganda agencies, national committees or organizations, and the like. Senators and Representatives can often send United States government publications free. University libraries and research centers are generally open to interested students. The United States Office of Education and the National Education Association can both provide many helpful materials, either as gifts or on a loan basis. Most resource people will gladly come to the school at their own expense, and many worthwhile field activities may involve only the cost of carfare.

State universities and state Departments of Education will loan motion picture films, still pictures, filmstrips, and recordings for only postage costs; so will many federal government bureaus and large business organizations. If the school has no projector, one may probably be borrowed from a local resident or organization. Students are usually pleased to bring from home a portable radio or record player if one is needed for temporary class use.

Valuable as such materials and services may be, they are not always adequate for a satisfactory program of community study and participation. If a social research map is to be shown to the city council, for example, the students may prefer printed map symbols to homemade ones. Many films are not available except on a modest rental basis or through purchase. If speakers come from a distance or have to stay in town overnight, it is only fair to pay their expenses. Excursions and the like usually involve some extra expenses for transportation, and perhaps for food, lodging, and entrance fees. How, then, can this needed extra financing be arranged? Three policies are commonly followed to provide such funds. We shall examine the practices and merits of each.

Individual Financing

Among these three policies the least desirable is that of individual financing. Generally speaking, this policy should not be followed, although there may be some exceptions to the rule. If students are engaged in hobbies for which they habitually provide their own finances, the school might well utilize their interests and materials. For instance, pupils who make or collect photographs, pictures, books, and maps might bring them into the class for group study. Likewise, students who own motion picture equipment or belong to photography clubs might properly be encouraged to center their recreational activities upon community themes. Care must always be taken, however, not to exploit these students in the process.

Another exception would involve trips which are planned for vacation periods, or which could be enjoyed by only one or a few persons. Example: a teacher spends his vacation with some of the boys from his classes; they combine a camping trip with excursions to historic sites. Or a few students may pay all or part of their own expenses as school representatives at a national conference in a distant city. It is naturally preferable for the school to pay all such expenses as these, but it would be unfortunate if interested students, willing to finance themselves, were not allowed to be delegates simply because the school could not pay their way. Thus, students who take a camping trip during vacation, or who attend a conference during the school year, might well find their experiences the center of a class project, even though they paid their own expenses throughout.

It may also be reasonable for students to pay their own way on general class trips, service projects, work experience, and the like providing that such expenses are low in relation to their economic status as individuals, and providing further that such expenditures are planned and announced well in advance. College students, for example, can usually pay proportionately more for personal field activities than can high school students, while the latter are probably better able to finance such experiences than are elementary school pupils.

The real objection to individual financing, however, is that it is basically undemocratic. Any activity planned for a whole class should be freely available to every member of that class. Some students in almost every class find it very hard or even impossible to pay extra expenses for field activities. Teachers sometimes try to meet this problem by having a special fund, supplied by the Parent-Teacher Association or by a service club, from which the cost for needy students may be defrayed. Although the motive is commendable, the result is unfortunate. In such schools, a needy pupil will seek to protect his pride by giving every reason except the true one for not participating in the group project, or he may manage to pay his share at the cost of tremendous personal or family sacrifice.

Group Financing

A somewhat better although still unsatisfactory policy is that of group financing. Under this arrangement, the field activity in question is conceived of as a *class* project which should therefore be planned and financed by the class as a whole, rather than by its members as individuals. The financial responsibility is thus assumed by the entire group for the entire group, and all members share in carrying it, each according to his ability and each in the service of all.

When a class field activity is planned under this policy, the class convenes as a ways and means committee to consider the cost, ways of keeping it down, and methods of raising money. In considering costs, all possible corners will be cut, within the limits of safety and adequate service. Fund-raising campaigns, whatever their nature, should always be planned with due regard for the ethics of good citizenship.

In some schools, the "kitty" is begun by having each student make such contribution as he is able. If this is done, it is important that each contribution be made directly to the teacher, that it be unquestioned, and that the amount given be kept absolutely confidential. Most teachers prefer that there be no such individual payments for the reasons outlined in the previous section.

Much better practice is to divide the class into teams which compete in raising funds through group activities. Possibilities: one team might conduct a candy sale, another present a dramatic performance, another wash cars or baby-sit, and all turn in the proceeds for class use. In one school, a parking lot is maintained, manned by students during after-school hours and on week-ends. In other schools, a sum of money (ten cents to a dollar) is invested by each student, and he who makes the greatest return on the investment receives recognition and a small prize. Whatever money-raising means are used, begging ought not to be condoned. Raffles are obviously in this category.

School Financing

In a few but steadily increasing number of schools there is now official recognition of the changes which have occurred in educational philosophy and method in recent years. Not so very long ago, most schools considered instructional and maintenance costs as about the only legitimate charges against the school budget. But today free textbooks and writing materials are provided in a number of states, while in many communities, visual and auditory equipment and aids are considered a proper cost of modern school education. Sometimes such equipment and materials are paid for by Parent-Teacher Associations until school boards become willing to assume the expense. In all schools which have achieved this broader vision of educational method, it is common to find that the school will assume also the major expenses of community studies, including excursions, surveys, extended field study, service projects, work experiences, and school camping.

Teachers in such forward-looking schools will do well to plan for probable field activities well in advance, and to discuss their financial aspects with the principal, superintendent, or finance officer at the beginning of the school term. Then plans can be made to finance the projected program through appropriate measures. Such costs can be budgeted and an allotment provided, or they can be assigned to existing budgets. Funds for visual and auditory aids may be earmarked for community study materials, subsidies may be granted to the physics class or the photography club to cover community projects, extra funds may be included in provisions for public relations, speakers may be provided by the teachers' institute fund or the general assembly fund, and documentary materials may be provided by increased appropriations to the school library or the classroom library.

The school may easily provide for excursions and other field activities if their major cost is that of transportation. If the district owns a school bus or a fleet of busses, it is relatively easy to arrange a schedule of trips which will utilize these facilities during their free hours. One or more busses may even be reserved solely for such trips, as is sometimes done for athletic and musical activities. Some schools engage public carrier busses on a contract basis, and are willing to assume extra transportation cost in order to provide for desired excursions. Under these circumstances, school trips are not nearly as expensive as when special arrangements have to be made separately for each occasion.

The obvious advantage of school financing is that it assumes the educational values of an organized community program, and makes those values freely available to all interested students and teachers as a matter of course and right. With these educational and social advantages comes a financial one, since the cost of these extended school services will be at a wholesale rather than a retail rate. Thus, in the long view, the actual cost to the students and their parents is less, while at the same time they enjoy the benefits of an enriched and vitalized school program.

Is There Danger of Damage Suits for Accidents?

Legal liability on the part of teachers and school boards is not confined to the field of community study and participation. Liability exists in the case of all school activities, whether in the classroom or laboratory, on the playground or athletic field, or in the community outside. In most states, liability is based upon the rules of common law, and these rules might be summarized thus:

- All persons are liable for their own negligence, and
- A governmental division or subdivision cannot be sued for negligence in the performance of established governmental duties.

A few states have modified these rules by statute, and some others have changed them by judicial decision. It is not possible to say generally what is the law because that is specific to each state. Only the general lines of legal liability may be indicated here; reference to the school law or the Education Department of one's own state should always be made by interested teachers and administrators.

The Teacher's Liability

In all states, teachers are legally liable for their negligent acts, just as are all adults generally. It is true that there are fewer opportunities for the operation of negligence within the classroom than in the shops, on the gridiron, or in the community. Yet even the stay-at-homes run risks unless care is taken during the use of motion-picture projectors, special equipment, and during the dismissal of the class. Some greater risks are run when students are taken on excursions and when they are in the presence of natural hazards and moving machinery. But so long as the teacher acts as a prudent person, exercising as much care as a parent would, he cannot be held for negligence in the event of an accident.

The occurrence of an acident, in itself, is not proof of negligence. The fact of negligence could not be established until it was proved that the teacher exercised less care than he should have done as a reasonably prudent person in those particular circumstances, and that he should have anticipated the accident, but did not do so—neither of which is easily proved before a court of law. Since the teacher is acting with a parent's responsibility (*in locus parentis*), he must be more diligent than an ordinary bystander would be, even to the extent of protecting the child from his own acts of negligence. But, having exercised this degree of care, the teacher is not liable for accidents which involve students under his supervision.

Even where the negligence of the teacher can be proved, there are still some defenses which might be offered. Unless the negligent act of the teacher is an important factor in causing the injury, there is no liability. If the negligence of the student is greater than that of the teacher, the latter may sometimes not be held liable. Where the parent consents to the presence of the child in specific situations, the ordinary risks inherent in that activity are thereby acknowledged and assumed by the student and the parent.

In most states, teachers may not be reimbursed for damages which they may be forced to pay. New York and New Jersey, however, have changed this law so as to guarantee rather than prohibit reimbursement to their teachers. Such statutes are generally referred to as "save harmless statutes." In regard to the New Jersey law, Silvestris points out:

"The 'save harmless' statute . . . , New Jersey Revised Statutes 18:5-50.3, expressly covers 'negligence or other act resulting in accidental bodily injury to any person within or without the school building.' Yet, this is a qualified provision since the following language of the statute requires that 'such teacher or member of the supervisory or administrative staff at the time of the accident or injury was acting in the discharge of his duties within the scope of his employment and/or under the direction of said board of education.' This part of the statute, by the very language used, narrows the protection afforded to the teacher to a situation where he is acting within the scope of his employment as well as under the direction or with the permission of the board of education." [1]

The School District's Liability

In the absence of a body of judicial decisions relating to excursions and other school trips, it is impossible to speak with certainty concerning the liability of school districts in this regard. In general, the common law rule already cited applies; this has been well summarized by Punke:

"The weight of authority holds the district not liable for injury to a child in connection with school-bus transportation, unless a statute specifically provides for liability. The doctrine here, in brief, is that 'negligence cannot be imputed to the sovereign, and for this reason, in the absence of a statute, no private action for tort can be maintained against the state.' Hence, suit may not be brought against agencies performing governmental functions, and therefore exercising sovereignty within a limited sphere. Although functions necessary for maintaining schools are in general considered governmental functions, a question may arise concerning the specific aspects of a school program. In determining whether

[1] Francis N. Silvestris, *Legal Principles Underlying New Jersey Educational Law*, pp. 152-153. Unpublished doctor's thesis, New York University, 1951.

a particular activity is governmental or proprietary, an Oregon court recently said: 'The underlying test is whether the act is for the common good of all without the element of special corporate benefit or pecuniary profit.' " [2]

This doctrine of nonliability on the part of the school district has been recognized by statute in the states of New York and Washington, and should doubtless be accepted in similar manner by other states in the future.

Protecting Teacher and District from Liability

In all school situations, teachers and administrators must be sensitive to their responsibility to exercise great care. All school work, and especially all occasions for leaving the supervision and routine of the school grounds, should be planned with full regard for all physical hazards and safeguards. All possible dangers should be investigated. Areas of special hazard, such as traffic, machinery, excavations, and bodies of water should be prepared against well in advance. Thorough group discussion of such dangers, together with the development of a sound personal safety program and code, is always desirable, even with adults, under many circumstances.

Particular vigilance must be maintained when selecting travel facilities. Only reputable companies should be considered, and always the teacher or other school official should investigate the matter of insurance. In no case should student-driven automobiles be used, and considerable reserve should be maintained in the utilization of any private cars whatever.

In every case where students are to leave the school grounds, the parents should first be informed and their written permission obtained for the trip. Often a courteous letter from the school to each student's parents may serve the double purpose of securing consent and of informing the parents of the general excursion program. A useful letter of this type is reproduced on the following page.

[2] Harold H. Punke, "Liability for Injury in School-bus Transportation." *American School Board Journal,* September 1940, pp. 38 ff.

```
PARENTAL PERMISSION SLIP
(_____ Public Schools)

                                      Date _____

Dear Parents:

    The class of which your child is a member is planning a school trip to
_____ as part of their regular class
work.  The group will leave from _____ about _____, _____
                                      place           time     day
_____ and will be back at the school _____
    Date
_____.  The cost of trip will be _____
which will cover all his expenses.

        This trip is a part of the regular classroom work and will be under
the same careful teacher supervision which your child has while at school.
In order for your child to make the trip it will be necessary to have your
approval.   You can express your approval by signing the slip below and re-
turning it to the teacher.


                                   _____
                                   Teacher


                                   _____
                                   Principal
************************************************************************
    I give permission for my child _____
                                                    (Name)
to take the trip to _____, knowing that every precaution
will be taken for his safety and well being.

_____        _____
(Date)                          (Parent or Guardian)
```

Suggested Permission Form for Field Trips

St. Louis

BOARD OF EDUCATION of the CITY OF ST. LOUIS Department of Instruction	PARENTS CONSENT FOR PARTICIPATION OF PUPIL IN EDUCATIONAL FIELD TRIP

Date_____

I, the undersigned parent or legal guardian (cross out one) of

_____
(Name of Pupil)
hereby consent to his or her participation in an educational field trip to

_____on_____
(Date)
I hereby agree to assume all responsibility for physical accidents resulting from such participation without holding sponsor or any school official responsible for any accident whatsoever.

Signed_____
(Parent or Legal Guardian)

Address_____

S-14 Sept. '49 30M

DENVER PUBLIC SCH

To Parents or Guardians of_____

An excursion to_____.

is planned for (date)_____ by school bus_____
                                      street car _____
                                      walking   _____

I request that_____be allowed to take this trip and understand and agree that the School District shall not be liable in the event an accident should occur in connection with such trip.

Denver

| _____ | _____ |
| Date | Name of parent or guardian |

FORM 1100-E/S   DSP   12-46-1,500 PADS   M-672-33949

Minneapolis

_____   _____
Name of Pupil   Home Room

The above-named pupil has our consent to take the trip described below:

_____   _____
Group   Date

_____
Place

_____
Teacher who will accompany this group

       We understand the arrangements, and believe the necessary precautions and plans for the care and supervision of the pupils during the trip will be taken. Beyond this we will not hold the school or those supervising the trip responsible.

_____
Parent or Guardian

PARENT'S CONSENT—FIELD TRIP   MINNEAPOLIS PUBLIC SCHOOLS
800 (25M 9-50   Vocational School Print Shop   (Over)

Parent's Consent Forms

       It is unwise and of no legal value to have the parent sign a waiver of school responsibility, such as the card forms reproduced above require. No parent can sign away a minor's right to have suit brought in his name should occasion warrant. The value of the parental consent slip lies solely in its documentary evidence that the parent knew and approved of the activity in question, and thereby assumed with and for the child the ordinary risks inherent in such activity. Because of their possible legal significance, all parental consent slips should be preserved for some time.

As further protection for both parties, the teacher should keep his principal or other administrative official fully informed regarding his plans for student activities off the school grounds. Such advance consultation is itself presumptive evidence of prudence, and to that extent a negation of negligence.

In states having the "save harmless" statutes mentioned above, Silvestris offers these suggestions:

"As long as the statute makes provision for protection of the teacher and other school authorities for acts taking place 'within or without the school building' and actions 'in the discharge of his duties within the scope of his employment and/or under the direction of said board of education' a safer method for the protection of all concerned may be provided.

"In this respect, the best administrative procedure is to obtain some form of permission from the parent or guardian of each child in connection with such activity; this will furnish some evidence, at least, of parental knowledge and permission for the child to engage in the activity. But, more important than that is to have the school board adopt some resolution or official policy which establishes the activity as a regular part of the school program. In this manner, the teacher will be afforded protection under the provisions of the statute." [3]

Crux of the Matter

When all is said and done, these problems of legal liability, transportation, scheduling, and finance are relatively minor in significance. The school that really wants to develop a more effective program through community study and directed participation will have little difficulty with administrative details. What is all-important is the willingness of administrators and teachers to experiment together, even at the cost of a changed routine.

Learning Activities

Socio-drama

Let your class be a meeting of the Board of Education to which the school superintendent is recommending a greatly expanded

[3] Silvestris, *op. cit.*, p. 154.

community experience program. Have individual school board members react in terms of these major roles:

1. The lawyer who is concerned about legal liability by the district
2. The large property owner who is always trying to reduce taxes
3. The homemaker who believes that children should be under classroom control at all times
4. The business man who believes in learning by experience
5. The Board president who is most concerned about better public relations.

Discussion Topics

1. What, practically, can be done about the problem of scheduling students for field experiences when they are involved in a departmentalized academic program?
2. How should the administrator answer the irate parent who complains that his child is spending too much time in community study and not enough with his books?
3. What part might committees of teachers have in developing new policies for field experiences under school jurisdiction?

Group Activities

1. Develop a simple questionnaire which can be sent by each class member to his own school superintendent. This should request information about local policies concerning scheduling, transportation, and cost. Then have a committee summarize the returns in chart form.
2. Poll the class to find out how field study costs were covered in their elementary- and secondary-school experience. Evaluate the methods found.
3. In some communities the P.T.A. helps in the community study program of the school. Write to your home P.T.A. president to find out what assistance they give. Have a committee tabulate findings on the basis of which the whole class can discuss possible improvements. Send that president a copy of the class recommendations.

Individual Projects

1. Investigate your state laws and state department of education rulings regarding the use of school busses for field trips and for extended study tours, as well as for athletic and music events. Ask also for the Department's analysis of legal liability for acci-

dents to students engaged in field study activities under school supervision.

2. Local school boards often require additional safeguards in the use of school busses. Write to the superintendents of several representative school systems to ascertain local policies, and the reasons for them.

3. Find out from a liability insurance man the cost of raising private auto public liability insurance up to a $100,000-300,000 minimum.

Learning Materials

Scheduling and general administration of studies of the community are described in Margaret Koopman's pamphlet *Utilizing the Local Environment* (Hinds, Hayden, Eldredge, 1946). Other helpful accounts are found in Miller R. Collings' article "Exploring Your Community: A Direct Experience Study" in the *Journal of Educational Research* of November 1950, in Arthur Katona's "Undergraduate Social Service and Research in the Community" in *Social Education,* May 1949, and in Alan P. Mewha's "Making Use of the Community," *Social Education,* January 1952.

On the question of legal liability, you should look up your own state's laws affecting field trips. See also Harry N. Rosenfield's *Liability for School Accidents* (Harpers, 1940) and Harold H. Punke's *Law and Liability in Pupil Transportation* (University of Chicago, 1943), both of which are reasonably complete. An excellent reference book with a fine section on liability is Robert R. Hamilton and Paul R. Mort's *The Law and Public Education* (Chicago: Foundation Press, 1941). Recent court decisions are summarized by Madaline Remmlein in "Accidents Will Happen" in *Nation's Schools* of December 1948, and in Francis N. S l-vestris' *Legal Principles Underlying New Jersey Educational Law,* an unpublished doctoral thesis available through interlibrary loan from New York University. Allan Grelle's *The Statutory Basis for Conducting Field Trip (Excursion or Journey) in the United States and the Teacher Liability for Accidents Ensuing* (Ball State Teachers College, Muncie, Indiana) summarized in 1950 the statutes of the 48 states, and the states' legal interpretations of the teacher's liability.

"Using Community Service Agencies," K. J. Rehage and W. R. Sincock, states specfic items in the Philadelphia Public Schools' Policy for the Use of Services of Community Agencies in School Instruction. *Elementary Schools Journal* 54:135-36; November 1953.

ENLISTING
PUBLIC
SUPPORT

Sometimes we must wonder if we adults of today have the quality of imagination to brief our young people for the kind of world in which they have to carve out their destinies. We are the last earth-bound generation; they are the first air-borne generation. They so desperately need wise guidance—and we are so devoted to our traditional modes of thought, to our petty academic prejudices, to our compartmentalized vision of their needs. Who are we to help guide these young people through the second half of the twentieth century, into this Nuclear Age that must yet prove so wondrous or so tragic? Yet guide them we must, in the best light we can find, for that is our responsibility and likewise our opportunity. We are their teachers, their parents, their clergymen, their employers, their welfare guardians—and their education is in our hands. What resources, then, have we, all of us together, for developing youth and adult education that is at once realistic for this age, democratic in method, and effective in results?

Chapters in This Section

DEMOCRACY'S GREATEST GIFT —THE PUBLIC SCHOOL

"THE NEXT TIME you pass a public school pause a moment to think what that school means to humanity. Recall the long dark centuries when the masses were kept in ignorance—when greed and oppression ruled the world with an iron hand. From the very beginning of man's struggle for knowledge, self-respect, and the recognition of his inalienable rights, the school has been his greatest ally. We refer to the school as 'common' because it belongs to us all. It is ourselves working together to meet a universal need. But it is a most uncommon institution. It is relatively new. It is democracy's greatest gift to civilization. Throughout the world, among upward struggling peoples, wherever parents share in the aspirations of their children, the American common school is being copied. Let us keep our public schools strong and free."

The Public School

From an Annual Report of the Profession to the Public by the Executive Secretary of the National Education Association of the United States.

CHAPTER **15**

The School a Community Center

"Perhaps the most glorified and romantic institution in America's rural history is the Little Red School House. Yet its teachers were untrained and poorly paid. Their tenure was short, often lasting only through one of the three terms in the school year. Though aided by that noble persuader—the hick'ry stick—more often than not the 'teacher' failed to last out the winter term when the older boys and girls arrived, after the harvests, to learn their readin', writin', and 'rithmetic.

"Truly, the Little Red School House does not owe its present exalted position in the minds of older American citizens to its excellence as a school for children. Not only were its teachers without skills as teachers, but the frugal society they served denied them many of the books and materials necessary for learning. Such materials as were available were frequently unsuited to the interests, needs, or capacities of the children.

"Yet reverence for the Little Red School House is more than mere nostalgia—its historical position derives from another of its functions. The Little Red School House was the center of all activities of the little community it served. It was America's first community school. It was here that the citizens met to discuss the issues of the day, and to hear addresses by political office seekers; here the young folks assembled to spell, to declaim, to debate, or to present plays on the temporary stage with its sheets for curtains. Discussion, debate, literary study, recreation, romance were its customary fare. Small wonder that this typically American institution of our agrarian age had a profound influence on our people. It served them. Its hallowed position arises from its force as a community center, and not from its effectiveness as an educator of children.

This chapter is by EDWARD G. OLSEN.

401

"With the advent of the automobile and the hard surfaced road came the movie, the dance hall, the pool room, and all the other commercial places of entertainment. Inevitably the Little Red School House died as a community center. Its demise as a school soon followed." [1]

With the earlier school's decline in function as a social center came also a growing emphasis upon secular education. This happened precisely because industrialization and urbanization brought into many communities people of varied and often conflicting religious convictions. The many denominations, sects, and churches, unable to agree upon even a minimum program of religious "common learnings," could only decide that in justice to all *no* religious instruction could be permitted in the public schools. This policy progressively brought with it increasing legal restrictions against the use of public funds for sectarian purposes, and, later, widespread legislative provisions limiting the uses of public school property and appropriations strictly to "school" operation. One result was the virtual disappearance of the community-center type of school well before the end of the nineteenth century, even though the shell of the Little Red School House long remained in use by children still "in school" there.

This virtual loss of the school's social center function did not go unnoticed or unchallenged by educators of the time. In 1902, for example, John Dewey delivered his famed "School as a Social Center" address before the National Council of Education, saying in part what friendly critics of today's traditional schools must still assert with vigor:

"The school as a social center must provide at least part of that training which is necessary to keep the individual properly adjusted to a rapidly changing environment. It must interpret to him the intellectual and social meaning of the work on which he is engaged; that is, it must reveal its relations to the life and work of the world. It must make up to him in part for the decay of dogmatic and fixed methods of social discipline. It must supply him compensation for

[1] Taken by permission from Homer V. Anderson and Harold B. Gores, "The School as a Recreative Center," in the *School Executive* 67:45-56; June, 1948.

the loss of reverence and the influence of authority. And, finally, it must provide means for bringing people and their ideas and beliefs together, in such ways as will lessen friction and instability, and introduce deeper sympathy and wider understanding. . . .

"The conception of the school as a social center is born of our entire democratic movement. Everywhere we see signs of the growing recognition that the community owes to each one of its members the fullest opportunity for development. Everywhere we see the growing recognition that the community life is defective and distorted excepting as it does thus care for all its constituent parts. . . . To extend the range and the fullness of sharing in the intellectual and spiritual resources of the community is the very meaning of the community. Because the older type of education is not fully adequate to this task under changed conditions, we feel its lack and demand that the school shall become a social center." [2]

Dewey's statement greatly influenced later writers, several of whom published entire books stressing the importance and possibilities of using public school facilities for more than strictly "school" purposes. Consider, to illustrate, these statements from four subsequent volumes, all of which influenced the thinking of their times:

1910

"The school is the natural focal point of the community's social life since it centers the universal interests of children and cuts through social, religious and even racial lines. As the school plant already belongs to the people it is proper to employ it for their social activities. Making it useful for twelve instead of five hours a day would involve few administrative changes and a comparatively slight expenditure of money. Indeed, the improvement of education resulting directly from the wider use legitimatizes such action by school boards."

—Wider Use of the School Plant, by C. A. Perry.
New York: Russell Sage Foundation, 1910.

1917

"The consciousness of the evils of the wastage of material things is being succeeded by a sharp realization of the evils of the wastage

---

[2] National Education Association, *Journal of Proceedings and Addresses,* 1902, pp. 373-83.

of spiritual things. This . . . is the underlying motive of the movement to expand the school into a center for community activity."
                    —*The Social Center,* by Edward J. Ward.
                    New York: Appleton and Company, 1917.

1920

"The present movement for using the schoolhouse of a city for the
promotion of neighborhood life is one that has a long history—as
long as democracy. It is the attempt to adapt ancient usages to
modern conditions. The sense of social solidarity which gives rich
and deep meaning to the word 'neighbor' is in danger of being lost.
The neighbor is the 'nigh dweller, but what signifies this if the door
of his dwelling be shut? . . . Those who are opening our schoolhouses for the largest public services are simply carrying on the
traditions of freedom."
                    —*The Community Center,* by L. J. Hanifan,
                    quoting Samuel M. Crothers.
                    Boston: Silver Burdett, 1920.

1927

"Every school house is a potential neighborhood center. Within
its hospitable walls prejudices can be more readily abandoned; local
problems can be impartially presented, discussed, and acted upon
by 'the neighbors;' recreational expression through community
singing, pageants, clubs, and dances can contribute much to the
resolution of divisiveness, and in the meeting together of the people
of the neighborhood on common ground a true spirit of cooperation
can be developed. In the school as a focal center, an integration of
neighborhood forces can be effected."
                    —*Community Use of Schools,* by Eleanor T. Glueck.
                    Baltimore: The Williams & Wilkins Company, 1927.

Social lag is evident in education as in all other institutions.
Changed general practice always lags behind newer theory,
however convincingly presented. To be sure, the National Society for the Study of Education did in 1911 devote its yearbook to accounts of actual experiments that had been tried
in making the school a community center.[3] True, America's
schools were used during World War I as collection depots for

[3] *The City School as a Community Center* and *The Rural School as a Community Center,* Tenth Yearbook, Parts I and II. Chicago: University of Chicago
Press, 1911.

fresh peach pits to be utilized in the manufacture of gas masks. But it was not until the great depression of the early 1930's that the schools were widely used to strengthen that "sense of social solidarity which gives rich and deep meaning to the word 'neighbor.' "

The great depression was a grave psychological as well as economic emergency. People everywhere were confused, tense, frustrated, fearful, restless. All over the nation farm land lay idle, factory wheels slowed down and stopped, banks and business enterprises went bankrupt, millions of jobless walked the streets, serious predictions of rioting and revolution were common. Facing these facts, a school principal (Dr. Ross Runnels) in Maplewood, New Jersey, with the help of the local Parent-Teacher Association, turned his school into an educational center for adults and made of it an adult community school. That schoolhouse became a real community center where adults of all ages, backgrounds, and interests went to play and to learn in ways which were informal, practical, useful. They did arts and crafts work, danced and made music, discussed and debated, took vocational training and refresher courses. Watching the immediate success of Maplewood and other projects which soon developed, the federal government shortly began to promote WPA adult education and recreation programs throughout the nation on this basic pattern. Besides providing work for many unemployed teachers, these projects brought many thousands of people from all walks of life back into the schools. Whether from congested cities, suburbs or small towns, villages and rural regions, the reports were the same—people liked these good times, appreciated this new neighborly companionship, and valued the personal insights and skills developed in such adult center activities. So successful was such use of the schools as community centers that after the depression ended hundreds of communities decided to continue their adult evening and summer programs.

It was the Second World War, however, which really emphasized the physical as well as the psychological significance of the school as a community or local neighborhood center. One of President Roosevelt's first wartime acts was to call upon every public school to become a "service center for the home front." Scrap collection, agricultural service, Victory Corps activities, ration-stamp distribution, work-experience programs, inter-group relations projects, war production training, civil defense operations, and a host of other war-born necessities again made the local school the major adult learning center in many a community across the nation. Then, after the war ended, thousands of these school systems continued their after-school, evening, week-end and summer programs. Such activities as these are now commonly centered in the public schools of many rural districts, villages, towns, cities, and metropolitan areas throughout the United States:

Community Groups Which Meet in the School	Community Activities Held in the School	Community Service Functions of the School
Garden club	Choral group	Audio-visual center
4-H Club	Civil defense instruction	Arts and crafts studio
Mothers club	Concerts	Baby clinic
Parent-Teacher Association	Conservation planning	Canning equipment
Pet association	Family play nights	Community theater
Photography club	Forums	Creative writing laboratory
Boy and Girl Scouts	Hobby exhibits	Home repair shop
Service clubs	Pageants	Immunization center
Stamp club	Rhythm band	Library
Toastmaster's club	Square dancing	Science laboratory
Town athletic teams	Vacation Bible School	Youth employment center

Both cause and effect of this marked growth in community use of school facilities has been a growing popular awareness that any community has made a poor business investment when it fails to use its school buildings and equipment during the evenings, on week ends, and throughout the summer months. Traditional schools are in session 6 to 7 hours a day, 5 days a week, 36-40 weeks a year. After 4 o'clock, every Saturday and Sunday, and from June through August they are generally closed and locked, their facilities and equipment denied to community adults as well as to young people who need and could use them. Billions of dollars of useful public investment lie idle much of the time—yet the capital investment, obsolescence, and depreciation costs go right on just the same. The community school, by contrast, is open 16 hours every weekday, and often on Sundays also, throughout the entire year. *Its* plant is a comprehensive community center serving the varied interests of adults and of youth as well as educating in superior fashion the students who come there to school.

The trend of our times is markedly toward extension of school services to all the community. With this trend, as we would anticipate, has come a parallel tendency in legislation and in court decisions which together permit this wider use of public school property. Some three-fourths of the states now have specific statutory provisions which—under stated conditions—permit the use of such property and facilities for community, recreational, and civic purposes. In the remaining states the local school boards, generally speaking, have some discretion in allowing the use of school property for community events. After a comprehensive study of recent court cases, Punke concluded in 1951 that

"School may constitute an important symbol of the civilization of the nations or the communities in which they are maintained. . . . It is pertinent that at different times within recorded history the outstanding symbols of culture have varied considerably. At one time in Roman history, roads, legions, and gladiators were apparently important symbols. Perhaps medieval Europe could be characterized by feudal castles, monasteries, and serfs. Military installations, armaments, and parade uniforms have been prominent among the culture symbols of modern military dictatorships. Among the symbols which are prominent in the United States at the present time it should be possible to list public schools. . . . The community school which is equipped and available for rendering several types of service to the community generally might well become an increasingly important institution in the nation's development." [4]

[4] Harold H. Punke, *Community Uses of Public School Facilities,* pp. 216-17. New York: King's Crown Press, 1951.

How to Develop Your Community Center Program

Careful planning and effective publicity are essential aspects of any program designed to develop a school as a social center. No procedural blueprints can or should be offered, but extensive experience indicates the wisdom of following certain basic principles, among which the following seven are of major importance.

Analyze Your Legal Situation

The first step is to find out what the state and local laws permit your school to do in terms of extended public services. This may be determined, generally, by reference to your state's School Law, a compendium of statutory information usually compiled and published by each state's chief school officer— the Superintendent of Public Instruction, or the Commissioner of Education. Local school superintendents have copies of this report. From it, you may discover if your state is one of those which provides simple legislative authorization for the wider use of school property, as, to illustrate specifically, do Massachusetts and Pennsylvania.

MASSACHUSETTS

SEC. 71. "For the purpose of promoting the usefulness of public school property the school committee of any town may conduct such additional and recreational activities in or upon school property under its control, and, subject to such regulations as it may establish, and, consistently and without interference with the use of the premises for school purposes, shall allow the use thereof by individuals and associations for such educational, recreational, social, civic, philanthropic and like purposes as it deems for the interest of the community. The affiliation of any such association with a religious

PENNSYLVANIA

SEC. 627. "The board of school directors of any district may permit the use of its school grounds and buildings for social, recreation, and other proper purposes, under such rules and regulations as the board may adopt, and shall make such arrangements with any city, borough, or township authorities for the improvement, care, protection and maintenance of school buildings and grounds for school, park, play, or other recreation purposes, as it may see proper, and any board of school directors may make such arrangements as it may see proper with any officials or individuals for the temporary use of

MASSACHUSETTS

organization shall not disqualify such association from being allowed such a use for such a purpose. The use of such property as a place of assemblage for citizens to hear candidates for public office shall be considered a civic purpose within the meaning of this section."

—*General Laws Relating to Education*, Commonwealth of Massachusetts, 1940.

PENNSYLVANIA

school property for schools, playgrounds, social, recreation, or other proper educational purposes, primaries, and elections."

—*School Laws of Pennsylvania*, 1945.

Some other states—notably California, Minnesota, New York, Ohio, Oregon and Wisconsin—have enacted more specific and detailed legislation. A single illustration will indicate the general nature of such advanced authorization.

OREGON

SEC. 35-1138. "There is hereby established a civic center at each and every public schoolhouse within the state of Oregon, where the citizens of the respective public-school districts within the said state of Oregon may engage in supervised recreational activities, and where they may meet and discuss, from time to time, as they may desire, any and all subjects and questions which in their judgment may appertain to the educational, political, economic, artistic and moral interests of the citizens of the respective communities in which they may reside; provided, that such use of said public schoolhouse and grounds for such meetings shall in no wise interfere with such use and occupancy of said public schoolhouse and grounds as in now or hereafter may be required for the purposes of said public schools of the state of Oregon.

SEC. 35-1139. "Lighting, heating, janitor service and the services of a special supervising officer when needed, in connection with such use of public school buildings and grounds as set forth in section 35-1138, shall be provided for out of the county or special school funds of the respective school districts in the same manner and by the same authority as such similar services are now provided for. Such use of the said schoolhouses, property and grounds shall be granted free; provided, that in case of entertainments where an admission fee is charged, a charge may be made for the use of said schoolhouses, property and grounds.

SEC. 35-1140. "The management, direction and control of said civic center shall be vested in the board of directors of the school district. Said board of directors shall make all needful rules and regulations for conducting said civic center meetings and for such recreational activities as are provided for in section 35-1138; and said board of directors may appoint a special supervising officer who shall have charge of the grounds, preserve order, protect the school property and do all things necessary in the capacity of a peace officer to carry out the provisions and intents and purposes of this act.

SEC. 35-1141. "The provisions of this act shall not be mandatory upon the board of directors of any school district, in respect to their authority and right to exercise discretionary powers as to refusal of the use of such schoolhouse for any such purpose, or purposes; but whenever in their judgment it seems inadvisable to permit the use of such schoolhouse for the purpose requested, the board shall have the power and authority to refuse the use of such schoolhouse for any of the purposes mentioned in this act.

—*Oregon School Laws, 1937; including 1939 School Law Supplement.*

Even though some three-fourths of the states have enacted permissive legislation, there may still be practical limitations because of ambiguous statutes or strict interpretations. When state laws stipulate that school funds shall be used "solely for school purposes" it is possible to approve or to deny the use of the school as a social center—depending entirely upon the interpretation of what may be meant by "school purposes." Even when states like Oregon specify that school property may legally be used for "community" or "civic" purposes, there may still be questions concerning such use as that for dances or for public meetings to be addressed by persons alleged to be "liberals," "radicals," or "under investigation." Problems may also arise if there is no definite legislation covering such matters as cost of heat and light, custodial services, possible damages to property, and the like.

This is why the first step in developing a school as a social center is to find out just what statutory provisions exist, and the extent to which the local school board has authorization or discretion in such matters. In the absence of clear directives, two further moves should be made: (1) the school board should be asked to enact adequate rules and regulations under which school facilities may be widely used, and (2) state legislation should be sought which would authorize local boards to maintain schools as community centers, subject to specific regulation by the local boards.

Secure Lay Participation in Exploring Possibilities and in Planning

The public schools belong to the citizens of the community and are supported or attacked accordingly. It is therefore imperative that the school consult with representative and influential local people before embarking upon any school program which goes much beyond the traditionally expected limits. This necessity is considered at length in the chapter to follow, where some specific techniques for utilizing lay participation are outlined. At this point we shall merely stress the crucial importance of getting representative community leaders from the outset to help explore the local need, discover people's interests, decide governing policies, plan the program broadly, and secure widespread publicity and participation. Having thus secured initial lay cooperation, you are now ready for the third step.

Survey Community Needs and Interests

Chapter 9 has already suggested some basic techniques involved in making community surveys. Even though that chapter was oriented around school-student activities, the principles and procedures outlined there are equally sound when adapted to adult use. Advance preparation by the administrators, stimulation of professional and lay interest, identification of purposes, analysis of the problem and of data needed, decision as to survey techniques, organization of committees, reporting of findings, community publicity—all such steps are necessary, however informally followed.

The surveying group should always be conscious of the significant difference between community needs and individual interests. Although the two may coincide, this is not usual. The community's (group) needs often go unrecognized, while the personal interests of individuals are more readily identified. Personal interests, for example, may lie in such areas of desired opportunity as archery, canasta, carpentry, current affairs, dramatics, fencing, first-aid, horticulture, painting, psychology, public speaking, swimming, or tap dancing. Such personal interests can easily be discovered by the use of some such interest-inventory as that reproduced on page 413. The community's needs, on the other hand, are much more a reflection of group interaction, and as such require much more intensive analysis by the school and lay people most concerned. Engelhardt suggests that a community survey of group needs might unearth many unsolved local problems:

"Is there a suitable auditorium for group conference and discussion covering city planning and administration? Are recreational grounds sufficient to meet the needs of all age groups? Are economically underprivileged families provided with health centers, group food canning facilities, and house planning instruction? Are youth groups provided with meeting places and trained leadership in guidance and citizenship participation? Is there a survey center where the assets and potentialities of the community are under constant scrutiny? Are library and museum facilities sufficient to meet the general as well as specific needs of the citizens? Are laboratories and studios available to advance the scientific, artistic and dramatic interests of the people? Are facilities provided the physically handicapped to the end that they may become self-supporting? Are centers equipped where father and son or mother and daughter may work together in out-of-school hours on projects of common interest? Is opportunity provided for improvement in the special interests of the community, such as the breeding of animals, the forestation of its land, the character of its wheat, the potentialities of its oil deposits, the use of its soil or the variation of its crops?" [5]

A challenging list, is it not? Yet these are only a few of the typical community needs so often unmet and more often ignored. It is obvious that many personal interests of the kinds listed above cannot be satisfied unless their related community needs are first met. That is why any program designed to develop the school as a community center must begin with a community survey which will identify the group needs and resources of the community as well as the avocational and other interests of its people. Only then is the school in position to

[5] N. L. Engelhardt, "Types of Community Facilities A School Should Provide." *The School Executive* 66:42-44; December, 1946.

HOQUIAM PUBLIC SCHOOLS

Hoquiam, Washington

Questionnaire on Adult Education

There has been considerable interest shown for an Adult Night School for the Hoquiam School System. The purpose of this questionnaire is first to determine whether or not enough people are interested to organize such a school and secondly what courses people would like to have offered.

Adult Education is properly considered the top step on the public school "ladder", extending from childhood through maturity. In this state extensive Adult Education Programs are organized and administered by local school districts and by the State University and colleges. Such has been the practice since 1909 when state funds for the support of adult evening schools were first made available.

School districts are authorized by law to establish such programs of adult education as will meet local needs. Instructors must be certificated by the State Office of Public Instruction and the class must be approved by the same agency. The State Office cooperates further by financially aiding approved programs according to an established formula. Tuition and Lab fees will be held to a minimum of actual cost.

The courses and the number of courses will be limited this year because of finance, certified instructors, and facilities available. It is planned that classes will meet twice a week and for two-hour periods.

1. ARE YOU INTERESTED IN HAVING AN ADULT NIGHT SCHOOL FOR HOQUIAM SCHOOL DISTRICT #28?
   YES_____ NO_____

2. HOW MANY MEMBERS OF THE FAMILY WOULD BE INTERESTED IN ENROLLING CLASSES?_____

3. USING THE FOLLOWING LIST AS A GUIDE ONLY, PLEASE LIST TEN SUBJECTS IN THE ORDER OF YOUR PREFERENCE. REMEMBER YOU ARE INVITED TO LIST SUBJECTS OF YOUR INTEREST, MANY OF WHICH MAY NOT BE IN THE GUIDE LIST.

AUTO MECHANICS	FOREIGN LANGUAGES	1._____
PLUMBING AND HEATING	WOOD SHOP	
CARPENTRY	METAL SHOP	2._____
SHEET METAL	PHOTOGRAPHY	
PAINTING (EXTERIOR)	CREATIVE WRITING	3._____
PAINT EDUCATION	MATHEMATICS	
ART (FINE AND COMMERCIAL)	MUSIC (VOCAL & INSTR.)	4._____
CITIZENSHIP (leads to naturalization)	HOME FURNISHING	
MEN AND WOMEN'S PHYSICAL EDUCATION	HOME CONSTRUCTION	5._____
ADULT DRIVER TRAINING	OFFICE MACHINES	
RETAIL SELLING	INTERIOR DECORATING	6._____
FOOD HANDLE..S	KNITTING	
TYPEWRITING	PLASTICS	7._____
SHORTHAND	HOME ECON. (FOOD)	
BOOKKEEPING	HOME ECON. (SEWING)	8._____
FURNITURE RENOVATION	OLD TIME DANCING	
ENGLISH COMPOSITION	KITCHEN PLANNING	9._____
EMOTIONAL GROWTH OF CHILDREN	PARLIAMENTARY LAW	
CIVICS	PUBLIC SPEAKING	10._____
LANDSCAPE GARDENING	BIOLOGY	
MECHANICAL DRAWING	PHYSICS	
CARD GAMES	CHEMISTRY	
SALESMANSHIP	ANY OTHER INTEREST	

Adult Interest Inventory

know to what extent and in which directions it should extend its present offerings to the community as a whole. With this information at hand, however, the planning committee can now move on to step four.

Decide Basic Policies

The central committee of lay and school people is now in position to plan a program which, in the light of the survey findings, can best meet the needs and serve the interests of the community. But first there are basic policies to consider. Shall the school building be open for community use during the evenings? On week ends? During school vacations, including summers? For what general purposes? For what kinds of activities? Under what controlling regulations? With what provisions for financing? For supervision? For administration? These are some of the fundamental questions which must be decided even before specific program-planning can begin.

The general answer, of course, is to adopt whatever policies will most effectively meet the community needs and interests already discovered, and will at the same time not thwart the prior responsibility of the school to its established child and youth education program. Controlling regulations must obviously be framed in terms of the local situation. Such regulations generally provide that community groups desiring to use school facilities shall apply to the school superintendent or principal, whose decision in each case shall be governed by whatever legislative and school board policies are in effect. The group agrees to be responsible for any damage done by members, and to see that lights are out and doors are locked after the event in question. There is usually no charge for using the building and equipment unless tickets are sold on a commercial basis, or unless funds are otherwise provided for custodial care, light, and heat, instruction and supplies, and the like.

Some state departments of education are authorized by law to make state financial aid available to local school districts which utilize their schools as adult centers. In some communities it may be necessary to pass local tax legislation to secure essential funds as Chicago, for example, did recently when the citizens were persuaded to increase the previous public school playground tax levy from .0125 per cent to .025 per cent of assessed valuation—an increase of only $1.00 per year on a house assessed at $8,000, but sufficient to open up "Lighted School Houses" in many neighborhoods in the city which had no suitable recreational facilities.

Secure Competent Leadership

The school must do more than merely make its buildings and equipment available to adults who wish to use them. If it is to serve its larger function as a center for adult learning activities, it must actually help community groups to identify, define, and solve community problems of the kinds suggested in step 3 above. The school, in short, must realize and accept its twin responsibility for helping meet community needs as well as serving individual interests.

This requires competent leadership. Perhaps we should begin to think in terms of superintendents of education, rather than of superintendents of schools—as Norris, Tennessee, did years ago when it first developed its community school program. Possibly a new professional career area may become prominent in the years ahead: that of Director of Community Education. In any event, the school board's present responsibility is to find qualified leadership to organize, promote, supervise, and administer this expanded aspect of the school's community service.

Certainly the minimum essential is to engage the school superintendent and the building principals, as well as the custodial staff, on a twelve-months basis, with adequate salary. Although this is almost commonplace with respect to superintendents, it is by no means universal. In many communities, small as well as large, such specialists as the teachers of vocational agriculture, music, homemaking, and physical education already work with community adults as part of their regular year-round jobs. The next step, greatly needed, is to extend the list of twelve-month contracts until all teachers are so employed. Under this arrangement, each one is available for community service as well as for curriculum building, extended professional training, and the like.

But what about evening work during the regular school year? Should teachers teach young people all day, and then be expected—or allowed—to work with adults in the evenings? Aren't teachers entitled to have their evenings free after strenuous days in their classrooms?

All such queries rest upon a single presupposition of which we are often quite unconscious: that the teacher's *proper* role and *main* job is that of instructing children in school classrooms between the hours of eight and four o'clock five days a week, nine months a year. This, of course, is the obvious assumption of the traditional school, and within that frame of reference it is surely valid. But the *community* school is something different, since it seeks to improve the quality of living in the community as a whole—of adults as well as of children— at whatever times or seasons are most feasible. That is why in the community school some teachers' main jobs may involve working with adults in the evenings, on week-ends, and during the summer months as well as in the "school year." That is why in this school some teachers may give half days to children and evenings to adults; others may teach all summer and take December as their vacation month. The same flexibility is necessary with regard to janitors and the custodial staff; they must be hired in sufficient numbers to service buildings and equipment whenever they are needed. We had better not make a fetish of the old eight to four o'clock, Monday through Friday, September to June schedule, just because it happens to have been traditional in our rural past. Today the hours of the teacher, as well as those of the service staff, in a community school must range the clock.

The important thing, of course, is to develop flexible schedules to meet program needs, and to see to it that individual teachers and others involved are not exploited as the school program thus expands. The possibilities and advantages of utilizing community lay people as resource persons in part-time service are obvious, and have already been suggested in Chapter 7.

Plan New School Plants for Community Use

However great the community's need for a social center, or however fine our professional intentions, the hard fact remains that most of our elementary school houses were built for the single purpose of seating groups of children in custodial classrooms. The same is true of most high school plants, except that these often include also a small library, a large gymnasium, a dark auditorium, a small science laboratory, a crowded homemaking room, and some inadequately equipped shops. All such buildings likewise reflect the traditional school orientation for which they were originally designed.

But schools still to be built are a different matter. They can be designed and constructed for dual use by children and adults throughout the year. No new school should be built unless it has, or can later incorporate, adequate facilities for all-around use. It is tragic that even today billions of dollars are being spent upon new construction that is already obsolescent in terms of best current thinking about what schools should do in their communities.

A recent doctoral study has identified the facilities which a jury of specialists agreed are now considered desirable in the school plant which is to house a community as well as a day-school program.[6] Their nature and scope indicates something of what is meant by the "school as a community center" concept. Since the standards listed include over sixty major headings, many with sub-headings, it is not possible here to show them all. The following selection will give you a general idea of the total group of standards:

1. Facilities to be used by adults, such as the auditorium, gymnasium, cafeteria, library, shops, community room, and so forth, should be grouped together to provide accessibility and economy in heating.
6. Parking areas should be near the buildings.

[6] Kullman, Nathan E., Jr., *School Plant Facilities Desirable for Community Use in a Community-School Program.* Ithaca, New York: Cornell University.

11. Arts and crafts rooms should be near a shop and home economics rooms.
14. Guidance office space should be provided near the central office and include provision for private counseling space.
28. The adult area should be remote from the building, partially shaded, and should include an open shelter with chairs or benches and provision for games such as horseshoes and checkers.
30. The picnic or park area should include benches and facilities such as fireplaces, water, garbage disposal, and shelter.
47. Shops should have space for storing materials and projects of adult users.
48. All shops, arts, and crafts rooms should contain sufficient equipment to meet adult needs in addition to regular pupil needs.
53. The principal's private office should be large enough to hold a small group of people.

In our democratic society, the schools which belong to the people should be responsible for the education of all interested persons, without reference to age limitations. Old school plants and facilities may have to be re-designed toward that end; new ones must certainly be planned accordingly from the outset.

Get the Community into the Planning

Whether the building be new or old, it is still wise to involve as many community people as possible in the planning of the expanded program, and to do so from the very outset. Teachers and students, parents and other lay persons, the board of education, the superintendent and the architect (if a building is under consideration) should all consider carefully the factors outlined in this chapter. As practical psychologists, we all know the first principle of successful public relations: If you want somebody to support your program, be sure that he fully understands its needs and values, and shares with personal satisfaction in its development. Thus do we build both passive consent and active support for that program. It will not be too difficult to raise the tax rate or pass the bond issue if the community as a whole has become familiar with the proposed expansion, and convinced of its wider importance through some such process of lay participation as that outlined in the chapter to follow.

A Central Resource

As the population grows older and as leisure time increases, the need and demand for a well-rounded, community-wide educational and recreational program will markedly increase. We must never forget that in a democratic society the educational system is responsible for offering educational opportunities to adults as well as to children. In that process, the public school plant is and must become a central resource for full-time community use.

Learning Activities

Socio-drama

At the next election the voters of your community will decide whether or not to increase local property taxes ¼ of 1 per cent in order to finance a proposed "Lighted School House" adult education and social center plan. A number of prominent community organizations have already pledged their support. Chief opposition comes from one newspaper which says frankly that it is championing the interests of the "down-trodden taxpayer." Public interest in the election outcome is mounting daily. Suppose you stage two confidential strategy meetings, one by the supporters and the other by the opponents of the measure, in which each group argues within itself about how best to make its appeal in the final two weeks before the election. After the drama, identify the fundamental assumptions about community psychology each side was using.

Discussion Topics

1. Should any groups be barred from using public school facilities, under accepted regulations for such use. because of their beliefs or purposes? Stage a symposium or panel discussion to bring out various views on this question.
2. Did your elementary or high school operate as a community center? In what respects, and under what conditions?

3. Should teachers be expected to give additional time to school operations in the evening, on week ends, and during the summers?

Group Projects

1. Plan a promotional campaign for a specific community designed to convince the majority of the electorate that they should vote to increase taxes somewhat in order to make possible wider use of school plants and facilities.
2. Send out interviewers to ask several score of lay people their opinions on community use of school buildings. Let follow-up questions seek to sample their individual interests and needs which the public school might serve through adult programs of a kind it does not now offer.
3. Make an extensive list of the specific services which the schools of your community should offer to the community.

Individual Activities

1. Consult your state school law to discover what provisions have been made to authorize the community use of public school buildings. Check with local boards of education for additional rulings.
2. After scanning the literature, draw up a model statement of the rules and regulations which a school board might adopt to govern community use of school plant and facilities.
3. Draw simple floor plans showing your ideas of a school building construction that would make it suitable for both youth education and as an after-school community center.
4. Review earlier thinking about the community center idea as expressed in the publications mentioned below, then write out your own comparison of those views with the ones suggested in this chapter.

Learning Materials

Earlier thinking about the school as a community center is as sound today as it was then. If you want to scan the ideas in this field you will find these publications surprisingly up-to-date in their argument and their appeal: National Education Association, *Journal of Proceedings and Addresses* 1902, pp. 373-383 (John Dewey's famed address on "The School As a Social Center"); C. A. Perry's *Wider Use of the School Plant* (New York Charities Publication Committee, 1910); The Tenth Yearbook of the National Society for the Study of Education, Parts I and II,

The City School As a Community Center and *The Rural School As a Community Center* (1911); E. J. Ward's *The Social Center* (Appleton, 1917); L. J. Hanifan's *The Community Center* (Silver Burdett, 1920); Eleanor T. Glueck's *The Community Use of Schools* (Williams & Wilkins, 1927).

More recently a flood of magazine articles have continued the argument for making community centers of our public schools. Among the best of such statements are these:

"Schools Should Be Community Centers," Agnes E. Benedict. In many communities adults use school shops, laboratories, and other facilities freely during the evening. Some typical programs are described. *Parents' Magazine* 14:24-25; October 1939.

"Extending the School as a Community Center," Albert R. Renwick. Emphasis is placed upon adult use of the school for recreation and health, and upon the thesis that teachers should be community leaders. *Education* 65:113-123; October 1944.

"The School as the Community's Meeting Place," Orin G. Graff. Develops the viewpoint that "the school is a community center only to the degree that it assists town groups in cooperatively defining and solving problems in terms of long-range benefits to the community." *School Executive* 64:65-68; November 1944; also in *Education Digest* 10:58-60; December 1944.

"Extending the Use of School Plants," William E. Arnold. Outlines theory, history, programs, and costs involved. *School Executive* 66:11-13; June 1947.

"Let's Keep Schools Open in Summer," H. M. Lafferty. Pleads for year-round use of plant and personnel, discusses historic reasons for non-use, cites reasons for full utilization, and offers three plans for different degrees of summer use. *Nation's Schools* 48:41-42; July 1951.

"Should We Run Our Schools on a 12-Month Basis?", Myron Stearns. Schools are over-crowded, billions of dollars are needed for new buildings, yet every year from June to September our present school buildings stand idle. Offers a solution for providing pupil space and saving tax dollars. *Better Homes and Gardens*, pp. 6, 9-10; June 1952.

"Community Recreation Programs and Their Relation to Schools," Raymond H. Ostrander. Urges cooperative efforts, outlines the needed role of the school, and stresses the important part played by the teacher. *School Executive* 71:19-22; July 1952.

"The School as a Community Center," Robert E. Alexander. "The strength of our country has depended in the past on the strength of the family. It may depend to an equal degree in the future on the design and use of the school as a community center." *School Executive* 72:62-63; November 1952.

Dramatic descriptions of school as community centers in action are found in the recent literature also. *The Modern Community School* (Appleton-Century-Crofts, 1953) edited by Edward G. Olsen, includes the story of how a metropolis went about the business of developing two "pilot" schools as community centers (in chapter 4). Olsen's *School and Community Programs* (Prentice-Hall, 1949) reproduces four vital accounts of community center operations in rural, town, and city schools. For other stimulating accounts, browse through several of these magazine reports:

"Central School Serves Its Community," Lois Clark. Relates numerous ways in which a rural school is used by community adult groups and explains the simple administrative arrangements in force. *National Education Association Journal* 37:276-277; May 1948.

"Use of School Plant by Adults of the Community," O. C. Aderhold and Joe A. Williams. Specific suggestions for adult use of cafeteria, auditorium, gymnasium, library, homemaking department, industrial arts shop, agricultural shop, commercial department, science department, athletic field, and so on. *School Executive* 67:49-50; June 1948.

"How Schools Can Function in Summer Months," Zeno B. Katterle. Suggests a community recreation program using school buildings, school farms, schools as employment headquarters for youth work experience, well-baby clinics, social dances, arts and crafts activities, pre-school play programs, dramatics, pet parades, hiking, concerts, and athletic programs. *School Executive* 67:40-42; June 1948.

"Lights on Nightly in Wilmington Schools," Vivienne Anderson. Describes many activities carried on every night of the week by educational, recreational, civic, business, labor, cultural, and athletic groups in the community. Leadership administrative policies are outlined. *Clearing House* 24:331-334; February 1950.

"Rural School: A Face-Lifting for Community Service," Clara Evans and Hazel Davis. Explains how a rural school was dressed up and given more adequate equipment as first step in making it a community center. Planning and work were cooperatively done by school and community, and a group of students and teachers from a neighboring teachers college. *Clearing House* 24:495-96; April 1950.

"Summertime Was a Busy Time in Indianapolis' Schools," W. S. Barhart. The total program touched the lives of 16,000 pupils and required the services of 342 classroom teachers. Interest-activities such as music, food preparation, shop and gardening were featured in part-time sessions. High school pupils earned academic credits. *American School Board Journal*, 121:33-34; September 1950.

"Community Headquarters," Hazel Moss Duncan. Tells how a country school teacher helps parents and children plan the school program to meet the everyday needs of children at school and families at home. *National Education Association Journal* 40:12-14; January 1951.

"When Schools Reach Out," C. O. Fitzwater. The story of a small, village-centered community where school and community affairs have come to be considered inseparable parts of a total enterprise in good living for all. *Educational Leadership* 8:262-66; February 1951; also in *Education Digest* 26:37-39; May 1951.

Legal bases for the wider use of school property have been examined by Harold H. Punke in his *Community Uses of Public School Facilities* (King's Crown, 1951), a carefully documented study of pertinent court cases. Includes a thoughtful statement of the social implications of such community use. Keesecker's "State Laws Permitting Wider Use of School Property," in *School Life* for March 1948 illustrates the need for clarifying present laws, and cites typical state statutes of two chief kinds: simple authorization and specific, detailed authorization.

Planning school plants for community use involves architectural planning of a high order if the buildings and facilities are to be equally suitable for child and adult use. Engelhardt's books stand almost alone in this field. *Planning the Community School* by N. L. Engelhardt and N. L. Engelhardt, Jr. (American Book, 1940) discusses architectural planning for the building which is designed to operate as a community center for adults as well as a community school for young people. *Planning Elementary School Buildings* by N. L. Engelhardt, N. L. Engelhardt, Jr., and Stanton Leggett (Dodge, 1953) and *Planning Secondary School Buildings* by N. L. Engelhardt and S. F. Leggett (Reinhold, 1949) are comprehensive manuals for architects, schoolmen, and the lay public. Nathan E. Kullman's Cornell University doctoral study *School Plant Facilities Desirable for Community Use in a Community-School Program* reports the kinds of programs in operation and suggests standards for desirable facilities permitting community use of school plants. The *American School and University* annual volumes carry many worthwhile articles on school plant planning for community use. See also some of these magazine articles:

"Neighborhood Schools: Home Base for Teaching Children; Headquarters for Adult Education," Ernest O. Melby. Concise statement of the community education philosophy and program, with emphasis upon the major characteristics of a suitable school plant. *Nation's Schools* 36:34; July 1945.

"Designing and Creating Tomorrow's Schools," Virginia F. Matson and E. J. Matson. Vivid argument for community-wide planning of new buildings to meet modern conceptions of good educational programs. *American School Board Journal* 112:27-28; January 1946.

"Plant Facilities for the Community School," New York City Conference on School Building. Reports group discussions on three basic questions: what makes a community school, community services which a school should consider, and building modifications for a community school. *School Executive* 65:7-72; January 1946.

"School and Community Join Forces in School Plant Planning," T. C. Holy and J. H. Herrick. Step-by-step description of a successful program which produced favorable public relations. *Nation's Schools* 37:28-30; March 1946.

"Community School Facilities." Series of articles on kinds and character of building facilities needed to serve all the people of the community.

Topics treated include community survey and land needed, rooms for community meetings, for working and repairing things, for reading and research, food service and preservation, and all-year recreation. *School Executive* 66:41-58; December 1946.

"The Community School," Stanton Leggett. Detailed descriptions with diagrams showing desirable features of the school designed to operate as a community center for adults as well as a community school for children. *School Executive* 68:44-45; January, 1949.

"Planning the High School for Tomorrow's Curriculum," Lawrence B. Perkins. An outstanding school architect says that his profession's main function "is in surveying existing plant in terms of future curriculum, and relating future building programs to the educational program." *Educational Leadership* 9:409-412; April 1952.

"A New Theoretical Approach to Secondary School Planning," G. Robert Koopman. Outlines and diagrams essential purposes and designs for the community-planned school. *Nation's Schools* 52:50-57; December 1953.

"Reactions from the Field on G. R. Koopman's Approach to Secondary School Planning." Several good analyses of the suggested plan. *Nation's Schools* 53:66-69; January 1954.

"Built for Community Use and Lifelong Economy," H. D. Crull and others. Detailed plans and diagrams, explained in dialog narrative. *Nation's Schools* 53:60-65; January 1954.

CHAPTER **16**

Lay Participation

"Keep Out" . . . "Come and See" . . . "Let's Plan Together" . . . such has been the trend in attitude of typical
school people toward the participation of laymen in school
affairs during the past two generations. Years ago the prevalent
view was that lay people had no business "interfering" with
school matters unless they were members of the board of education. That board existed to manage the schools, and any
direct participation on the part of parents or any other adults
was looked upon as an intrusion into matters of no proper
concern to them. The Parent-Teacher Association from its very
beginning in 1897 has been careful to assure school personnel
that its activities would always be supportive and never direc-
tive. Even today there are occasional school administrators
who growl about "interference with my business" if lay people
show any real concern for the improvement of the school program in their own communities.

After World War I, however, it became apparent that closer,
more cordial relationships between school and community
people were essential if the schools were to receive needed
public support, especially financial. One result of this new
awareness was the establishment of American Education
Week, sponsored since 1920 by the American Legion, the

This chapter is by EDWARD G. OLSEN.

National Congress of Parents and Teachers, the National Education Association, and the United States Office of Education. Another effect was the acceptance of a merchandising concept of "selling" the schools to the public through discrete advertising, including such techniques as Visit-Your-School days, Open-House nights, memberships by administrators in prestige service clubs, distribution of school bulletins, and other avenues of "school interpretation." Implicit in all such "come and see what we are doing" measures was the accepted assumption that lay people ought to be informed about school affairs so their support could more easily be secured for the programs which the school in its wisdom had planned.

Then out of the community organization experience of the Second War and the community school philosophy which won widening acclaim after that war came a new and more significant concept of our professional-lay relations: that of constructive participation by lay people, including students, in many areas of school policy and program planning, execution, and evaluation. This in no way relegates the board of education to a secondary position; on the contrary it fully recognizes the board's legal responsibility and simply seeks to help the board through fact-finding and recommendive services. Thus has been the typical change of our professional frame of reference during the first half of this twentieth century:

ATTITUDE:	FROM ⟶	THROUGH ⟶	INTO
Toward the Public:	KEEP OUT ("This is *my* school")	COME AND SEE ("This is *our* school")	LET'S PLAN TOGETHER ("This is *your* school")
Toward the School:	TRADITIONAL (Book-centered)	PROGRESSIVE (Child-centered)	COMMUNITY (Life-centered)
Toward the Job:	IMPART KNOWLEDGE ("I teach Civics")	HELP CHILDREN GROW ("I teach John")	IMPROVE LIVING ("I help John become a better citizen")

What Is Lay Participation?

"Lay participation" means the constructive involvement of non-school people in school policy and program planning, execution, and evaluation. It is a "working together with" process, an interaction of professional and lay people in fact-finding and policy recommendations based on objective analysis of needs and resources in the light of chosen purposes. Lay participation may involve one individual acting as a resource person to a school class, or it may include several hundred people organized in a community-wide citizens' advisory council.

So new is this third stage in school public relations—even in theory—that Lay Participation is not mentioned in the 1943 *Encyclopedia of Modern Education* or in the 1950 edition of the *Encyclopedia of Educational Research*. Actually, of course, our public schools have always belonged to the people, been locally controlled, and so subject to lay influences of various kinds. What is now new is the recognition of the social and educational importance of conscious, sustained, widespread, representative lay support for the school and for the improvement of its program. Perhaps it is significant that the Educational Policies Commission's first 1952 recommendation to the National Education Association was that "Teachers, school administrators, and professional education associations make deliberate efforts to encourage and utilize the participation of lay citizens in policy-making for public education; and that, toward this end, they study and carry out the EPC recommendations contained in *Citizens and Educational Policies*." [1]

Why Such Interest in Lay Participation?

Two major trends in school-community relations have been apparent in recent years. The first is the general public's increasing concern about school education. People in all walks

[1] National Education Association, *Addresses and Proceedings* 1952, p. 335. Washington, the Association, 1952.

of life make something of a fetish of organized book-learning, even while they may condemn it for not overcoming many of the weaknesses and evils inherent in the community and in society as a whole. William Graham Sumner pointed out in 1906 this very tendency:

"Popular education and certain faiths about popular education are in the morés of our time. We regard illiteracy as an abomination. We ascribe to elementary book learning power to form character, make good citizens, keep family morés pure, elevate morals, establish individual character, civilize barbarians, and cure social vice and disease. We apply schooling as a remedy for every social phenomenon we do not like." [2]

Far more today do many people feel and fear the weakened moral influence of home and church, and the growing influences of various disintegrative forces in society. How easy it then becomes to turn to the public school to criticize its curriculum, to attack its methods, to malign its fundamental role in our democratic life! Yet fortunately a constructive effect is also a direct result of our popular concern for better education. Citizens also know that schools cannot provide adequate education by themselves, that they need and merit the full cooperation of other agencies and of many lay individuals, that when schools are subjected to unwarranted attacks their own children and the whole community, even democracy itself, suffers. As people generally become more aware of their civic responsibility for better education, they do seek ways to help.

The second important trend is in the thinking of school people themselves. Educators now generally recognize that lay people may be immensely valuable to their school programs in the role of resource persons, that community groups may serve as important two-way channels of communication between school and community, that education is a community-wide as well as a school function, and that people "care when they share." As practical psychologists, teachers and administrators

[2] William G. Sumner, *The Folkways*. Boston: Ginn and Company, 1906, p. 628.

have come to realize the first principle of successful public relations: If you want somebody to support a program, be sure that he understands its values and has shared with personal satisfaction in the planning and development of that program.

How Do Lay People Participate?

Paying school taxes might be considered a minimum form of lay participation in school affairs. So might the mother's coming to the school for a conference with the teacher, or to act as room mother in an elementary school. So also would be the visit of parents to the school during American Education Week or on Open House night. More direct lay participation, however, usually comes through one or more of at least six channels:

• **Through membership in the Parent-Teacher Association** or other parents' group organized solely to aid the school. These Associations include as members millions of parents and teachers, professional school people as well as laymen. Besides its sponsorship or support of hot lunch programs, audio-visual education, guidance services and the like, the P.T.A. is usually glad to cooperate in efforts to make the school a real community center, to locate and list resource visitors to the classroom, to assist with field trips and surveys, and to develop the community school program generally. The following statement of recommendations by the Washington State Congress of Parents and Teachers (1949) to its local associations indicates the P.T.A. interest in the community education outlook:

"Community improvement through joint school-community action is now widely accepted as one essential aspect of democratic education for the atomic age. This requires that all students, future citizens, understand their local community's problems, resources and processes for orderly improvement. To this end, school systems throughout our state are now developing organized programs of local community study and service. Here is one important area of education action in which our schools need and must have P.T.A. help if effective work is to be done.

"Every local association is urged to undertake a study of the ways in which it can best assist the school in developing such a program of community study and service. Each P.T.A. might well:

1. "Secure official authorization for general community use of school facilities—buildings, cafeteria, gymnasium, library, audio-visual materials, athletic equipment, etc.—under proper safe-guards and arrangements. Every school should be an active community center.
2. "Urge school officials to promote wider use of community resources through carefully planned field trips, resource visitors, student interviews, local surveys, extended field studies, civic service projects, work experiences and school camping. Any school program can be greatly vitalized as pupils experience such direct contact with the realities of their environment.
3. "Offer the school officials assistance in making a systematic and cooperative survey of local community needs and resources. Such a survey is essential to a community resources program.
4. "Help individual teachers plan and conduct field trips for their classes. The aid of fathers as well as mothers is often needed at such times.
5. "Compile for school use a list of local adults who possess special abilities, interests, backgrounds, hobbies, collections, etc., which they would be willing to share with pupils in the classroom. Many P.T.A. members would themselves prove excellent resource visitors.
6. "With the school, enlist the aid of the State Office of Public Instruction in planning, organizing and evaluating a comprehensive community resources program for the better education of youth and the democratic improvement of your community living."

• **Through service as resource people** to the classroom, laboratory, shop, assembly, guidance office, school library, curriculum committee, administrative staff, or board of education. As we have seen in Chapter 7, every community is rich with potentially valuable lay people who can in their special areas of competence make important contributions to the school program. Other chapters have suggested the fine service lay people can render as they help the schools develop successful field trips, surveys, school camping, work experiences, and community improvement projects—all of which require lay participation for success.

• **As members of community groups** which support specific school activities. These groups include the service clubs which may provide band uniforms, the Dads Clubs organized to follow the teams, the business organizations which buy advertising space in the school paper or yearbook, the chambers of commerce which help find living quarters for new teachers, and the like.

• **As members of boards of education** of the local district, county, or state. More than 300,000 lay people across the nation thus participate officially in school affairs through their membership in thousands of school boards and associations of school boards.

• **Through community councils,** either as individual members or as members of constitutent organizations which make up the councils. There are about 11,000 such coordinating councils in the United States today, each composed of agencies, organizations, and individuals willing to work together for community improvement. These councils are nearly always interested in public schools; some of them give practically all their attention to school needs and problems.

• **Through school-initiated citizens' committees,** organized by and of lay representative people to study schools and make recommendations to boards of education, administrators, and teachers. Such committees may be temporary or permanent; concerned with specific matters like financial measures or curriculum development, or with over-all policy; they may operate on neighborhood, community, county, state, or national levels; they may merely study situations or they may lead in social action. The common denominator of them all is that they seek to examine school problems objectively and to develop long-time workable plans as recommendations for meeting those needs. Citizens committees are also a new invention. Hull reports that only 10 per cent of the several hundred lay advisory committees he studied in 1949 had been operating ten years or longer, but that over 70 per cent had been formed during the preceding five years.[3]

Many states now have some kind of state-level citizens' educational council, the better known including Alabama, Connecticut, Delaware, Florida, Georgia, Illinois, Iowa, Kentucky, Louisiana, Maryland, Massachusetts, Minnesota, Mississippi, New Hampshire, Ohio, South Dakota and Washington. Such councils, whether local, state, or national, strengthen the grass roots of American democracy even as they serve to improve public school education.

[3] J. H. Hull, *Lay Advisory Committees to Boards of Education in the United States.*

In this connection, the work of the National Citizens Commission for the Public Schools is especially noteworthy. Founded in 1949 with the financial support of the Carnegie Corporation and the General Education Board, it is composed of prominent laymen, none of whom are professionally connected with education, religion, or politics. They live in many sections of the nation and reflect many different kinds of experience and varied views on education. They seek to strengthen the public schools by enlisting widespread community study of the schools by lay people. Not posing as experts on school affairs, the members of the National Commission seek to present or impose no program of their own; the Commission is simply a clearing house for local experience and a fact-finding body which undertakes intensive studies of current educational problems. Its Executive Director has stated the Commission's objective in these words:

"The Commission hopes that committees of businessmen, housewives, newspapermen, labor leaders, and farmers—in short, committees of citizens working with their boards of education—will be formed in every community to decide what kind of education is needed there and to help the educators provide it. Because many of the most successful of these committees have been started by school superintendents and school boards, the Commission realizes that the initiative of school executives is one of the most important ingredients in the recipe it is writing for better schools. Throughout the nation there are countless laymen of great ability who have never shown any interest in the schools—but who are just waiting to be asked. If these people must be asked, the logical people to approach them, the Commission believes, are school board members and school administrators in their own communities.

"The whole program and organization of the Commission is aimed toward one target—a resurgence of popular interest in the public schools. Just as both educators and laymen must play a part in the creation and maintenance of any good school, so must both educators and laymen take part in encouraging the broad public interest which must precede any large-scale improvement. Therefore, the Commission addresses to both educators and laymen the one key statement which lies at the heart of its plans. 'The problems of public education concern all of us, and it is time for all of us to do something about them.' " [4]

What Principles Should Be Followed?

Specific procedures will obviously depend upon local situations, but certain principles around which to organize constructive lay participation of many kinds appear to be sound. Seven of these will be outlined briefly.

Don't "Use" Lay People Exploitively

Even folks helping as resource persons in the classroom or in the community need to feel that they are making a constructive contribution in their own creative way; that they are not merely instructional puppets being manipulated by the school for its own, perhaps undisclosed, purposes. True, the line between cooperative assistance and veiled exploitation, however kindly, is not easy to draw; it is perhaps largely a matter of the basic spirit in which the whole lay participation program is sought, developed, and evaluated. The vitally important aspect of the whole thing is that the school be willing to trust the lay helper's personal integrity and basic competence as a mature adult who is genuinely interested in educational welfare. Mutual regard is initially required, and mutual trust will be built up only through sustained, tested experience in mutual effort.

Stress Reciprocal Values

Most people are willing, even anxious, to help the school develop a better program for children and youth if they think they can actually help to do so. It is always wise, however, to stress also the fact that the participating adults may benefit personally from the experience, and that the general community life will likewise be improved. Cooperating adults may

[4] Henry Toy, Jr., "The Program of the National Citizens Commission for the Public Schools." *School Executive* 69:11-14; February 1950.

find deep personal satisfaction in working with devoted teachers, interested students, and able administrators toward solutions of genuine school and community problems of common concern. Communities find that the educational process becomes more vital, more meaningful and challenging to students, more closely related to community needs, and hence more effective in improving the quality of local living here and now. Lay participation is not only something generous adults do *for* schools; it is also an intrinsically rewarding process to the adults themselves.

Involve Students Also

Even small children may be resource people to their classmates, or to the pupils in another room. A child who has lived in a foreign country, or who spent a summer in reconstructed Colonial Williamsburg, or who can show how to preserve leaves—or who has any other kind of special knowledge or skill needed by a group, can be a valuable resource person to it. In this sense, students themselves are excellent lay participants in the community school program, both as resource people and as official student representatives on curriculum committees, community councils, and even on citizens' school commissions.

Begin with Felt Problems

What school matters are the people in your community concerned about? The three R's? Lunchroom manners? Adolescent rebellion? Sex education? Charges of subversive textbooks? Whatever the items, the point of lay concern is the point of lay interest, and the point of interest is the place at which lay people will most likely be willing to work with the school to improve its program. To determine such concerns and interests, you might informally sample individual opinions, or you may wish to conduct some kind of community survey. The important thing is to start with the basic concerns and go on from them into extended, objective, cooperative study of the situation.

Work with and Through School Authorities

Teachers are citizens, and in all matters of civic concern should exercise their civic rights accordingly. Nevertheless, they are also professional workers who are therefore bound by a code of professional ethics which should govern their professional activities. This means among other things that teachers will be gracious and tactful in their community relationships, and will want to secure administrative consent before seeking lay participation if such has not been local practice heretofor. The same goes for the administrator's responsibility to the school board. When new policy is involved, the appropriate school authorities should always be asked to approve and support it before possible lay participants are invited.

Keep a Balance

In commercial and controversial areas it is well to maintain something of a balance between opposing interests. If you ask Mr. Smith, salesman for the Alpha Insurance Company, to explain insurance to your class this year, be sure to invite Mr. Jones from the Beta Company to do the same next year. This fundamental principle holds true when making up possible membership lists for lay members of curriculum committees, of community councils, or of citizens' commissions. Good public relations as well as sound education and effective administration require that lay people brought into policy-advising cooperation with the school be representative of the entire community, not of some segment, faction, interest, or viewpoint alone, however respected. It is sometimes good strategy to invite outside critics of the schools to serve on fact-finding committees. Where this has been done, such critics have often come to support the school program as they learned the true facts about it and themselves discovered its major needs.

Face the Obstacles

Both school and community people are apt to be somewhat unsure of each other, possibly suspicious, even fearful. "Professionals" may consider lay people as intruding, possessive, pressure-minded busy-bodies, intent on "gettting into our schools" in order to "grind their own axes." "Practical-minded citizens" may perhaps look down on teachers as frustrated neurotics, irritable drillmasters, condescending crackpots, or even as naive subversives. Stereotypes like these are far more common on both sides than we like to admit. Such notions can be dispelled only through a sustained process of cooperative, successful, personally satisfying experiences with numerous persons of the mistrusted group. The lay participation process, if soundly developed, is the best means of securing this very result. Throughout such an experience process, however, these possible prejudices should be kept in mind.

A more specific point of confusion may be differing ideas about the proper roles of the "experts" and the lay advisers. "Why do you ask us to help?" the lay person may ask. "You're supposed to know your business; I don't. That's why we pay you. You're a trained educator, aren't you?"

Certainly lay people have the right to expect that competent educators will have tested answers to technical questions— matters of teaching method, evaluation, reporting, and the like. It is usually a mistake for teachers to sit down with a group of parents, for example, and ask breezily, "What shall be put on the new report card? How do you want us to teach the consumer education course? What books about the United Nations do you want us to use?" All such *hows* and *whats* are really technical matters, beyond the proper province of lay people as such, but presumably within the professional competence of the educator. But *whether or not* to include behavior statements as well as academic grades on the report card, *whether or not* to stress intelligent buying, *whether or not* to teach about the UN are matters of basic school policy, and hence are appropriate items for joint school-community decision. If the "what are we going to do" decisions are made in cooperation with representative lay people, the "how are we going to do it" decisions are properly up to the educators alone. If this division of function is clearly understood by all parties from the beginning, perhaps the crucial obstacle to successful lay participation will have been avoided.

No Other Choice

Whether we like it or not, the public school has no real alternative to working with the community and reflecting the will of the people. Local control of the schools is our established tradition and our democratic strength. This does not mean that schools should descend to the level of bowing to every community pressure group which comes along; quite the contrary, for only in enlightened public support won through widespread public participation is the school likely to find strength to resist those very groups. As the American Association of School Administrators has well said, "Active lay participation in developing school policies is undoubtedly one of the most effective ways to bring the whole community to the realization that it has a stake in the whole educational enterprise." [5]

Learning Activities

Socio-drama

Hold a meeting of the Citizens Commission for the Public Schools in your town. Sitting as a committee of the whole, develop an agenda for next year's program.

Discussion Topics

1. Does lay participation encourage pressure groups and individuals to make unfortunate demands upon the school?

[5] Twenty-third Yearbook, *Paths to Better Schools,* p. 245. Washington: National Education Association, 1945.

2. Do you think lay people are competent to help plan a curriculum?
3. What are the proper roles of educators and lay persons acting cooperatively for school and community improvement?

Group Activities

1. Have committees report to the class on recent lay participation articles in both professional and popular magazines.
2. Investigate the extent, kind, and probable values of lay participation in several school systems which could be visited by class committees.
3. Invite several superintendents to discuss with your group the extent to which their teaching staffs and interested lay people actually participate in planning new school buildings. Phrase your questions to the superintendents so as to bring out what seems to be their individual philosophies of community relations and education.
4. Visit one or more meetings in which lay people are constructively dealing with school affairs, and afterwards analyze their probable contributions.

Individual Projects

1. Find out if there is a citizens commission for the public schools in your community. If so, invite the chairman to address the class. If not, write to the National Citizens Commission for literature which you may use as a bulletin board and library display.
2. Read critically several of the basic references listed for this chapter. Prepare an analysis of each, indicating its major assumptions and your own reactions to them.
3. Are not professional educators supposed to know best how to plan and organize a school program? Then why this desire for lay participation? Write out a one-page response to these fundamental queries.
4. Become familiar with the kinds of articles featured in the *National Parent-Teacher Magazine*.
5. Develop a small "handbook for parents" which stresses and explains several ways in which their active participation in school affairs is wanted.

Learning Materials

General treatments of lay participation are still few. The Educational Policies Commission has a report, *Citizens and Educational Policies*

(1951), which is an excellent general analysis of values and principles. Herbert M. Hamlin's *Citizens' Committees in the Public Schools* (Illinois Interstate Printers & Publishers, 1952) samples the literature of lay participation, and suggests basic procedures in organizing citizens' committees. *How to Conduct a Citizens' School Survey* by Merle R. Sumption (Prentice-Hall, 1952) shows in detail how a community can organize and conduct a school survey which will give the board of education a long-range plan for meeting the educational needs of the community. Richard W. Poston's *Democracy Is You* (Harper, 1953) is a practical guide to co-operative community study, showing how citizens can identify local problems, collect pertinent information and develop a sound, coordinated program of community improvement.

A brief analysis of the values to be achieved through lay participation is *Lay Advisory Committees,* published by the American Association of School Administrators (1951). New York State has issued two manuals designed to foster more intelligent lay participation: *Stimulating Educational Change Through Lay Participation in Planning* (1947) and *An Education Program for Our Schools* (1950). *The School Executive* devoted its January 1952 issue to "Citizens Organize for Better Schools," while *Educational Leadership*'s theme the following month was "Citizens Participate." *Public Action for Powerful Schools,* published by the Metropolitan School Study Council (Teachers College, Columbia, 1949), explores the skills that can be used to better schools through lay participation in educational planning. In Connecticut, the Governor's Fact-Finding Commission on Education presented in its *Do Citizens and Education Mix?* the findings of a study of 85 school-community study groups in that state. An historical statement tracing causal developments in the field of lay participation is Truman M. Pierce's "The Growing Trend Toward Lay Participation in Education" in the *Peabody Journal of Education,* November 1950. Other significant journal articles well worth your attention are these:

"Formula for Merging School and Community," Robert G. Koopman. Education is too narrowly defined, the school is too separatistic, teacher-education largely ignores school-community relations, and the idea of "selling" the school to the public is abominable. Needed is a merger of school and community through widespread lay participation in education. *Nation's Schools* 42:22-24; August 1943.

"Florida Plans Its Educational Future," Edgar L. Morphet. The story of a fighting campaign cooperatively organized and managed by educators and laymen, which stirred the citizens of an entire state and brought about some far-reaching results. *School Executive* 67:41-43; September 1947.

"Community Leaders As School Advisers," Emery Stoops. Describes the organization and activities of an advisory committee which meets monthly for the purpose of "studying educational problems as a means of enlisting community support for a better instructional program." *School Executive* 67:38; May 1948.

"Study Councils," Nine articles, reporting lay study council philosophy, programs, procedures, and problems. *School Executive* 69:57-72; February 1950.

"A Community Looks at Its Schools," C. C. Loew and M. R. Sumption. Tells how lay citizens, students, public school teachers and administrators and university professors joined to make a cooperative school survey as a basis for immediate improvement in school practices. *Nation's Schools* 46:40-43; December 1950.

"Citizens Committees—A Report to the People from the Director of the NCCPS," Henry Toy, Jr. The Director of the National Citizens Commission for the Public Schools summarizes the achievements of the more than 1500 local groups now organized. Analyzes the Pasadena and Denver situations. *School Executive* 71:41-43; January 1952.

"When Recommendations Gather Dust, It's Time for Lay Participation," Edward J. Russell. The story of how a New England community developed an effective program for making practical use of a professional school survey. The essential element was local involvement—sustained and constructive. *Nation's Schools* 50:35-37; July 1952.

"Community Participation in Building Educational Programs," Ernest O. Melby. Dynamic analysis of the problem of freedom in our time, with the educator's obligation to maintain a strong democratic faith brought into focus. This faith is both cause and effect of effective lay participation in policy planning. *North Central Association Quarterly* 27:267-72; January 1953.

"Michigan Area Study Act Helps Local Groups Evaluate Local Programs," Roland S. Strolle. Reports how a state legislative act provides machinery for lay and professional groups with which to analyze and evaluate their total educational programs. *School Executive* 72:64-66; April 1953.

"Citizens Committees and Boards of Education," Henry Toy, Jr. Clarifies the question of what should be the proper relationship between citizens committees and boards of education. *School Executive* 72:19-21; May 1953.

Lay participation in curriculum planning has been analyzed by Helen Storen in her *Laymen Help Plan the Curriculum* (NEA, 1947), a small volume which summarizes basic principles of effective participation and answers some of the usual objections to it. For other discussions, see these articles:

"Evaluation of Rural Community Planning in Relation to the Curriculum of Rural Education," C. E. Ragsdale. Describes how lay citizens cooperate with school for community planning in rural schools. Seven major values for pupils are listed. *Journal of Educational Research* 38:286-290; December 1944.

"Tailored to Fit: How Norwood, Ohio, Revised Its School Curriculum to Meet Specific Community Needs," Harold S. Bates. How a city of

40,000 surveyed itself four ways to determine how better to build a functional education program. Findings led to school program improvements. *Progressive Education* 22:8-10; January 1945.

"How an Urban Community Proceeded to Decide What Its Schools Should Do," A. K. Loomis and R. B. Raup and B. O. Smith. Describes techniques used to shape public opinion concerning some aspects of modern education. Parents and teachers met in conference to discuss findings and decide desired school policies. Edited by B. O. Smith. *Teachers College Record* 46:236-240; January 1945.

"Cooperative Venture in Rural Planning," Clara O. Wilson. Tells how community members cooperated with teachers and students from the nearby University, and with the State Department of Education, to convert their typical rural school into a center of activity for children and adults alike. *Educational Leadership* 3:220-221; February 1946.

"Curriculum Improvement Means Planning and Effort," Cecil J. Parker. Presents a basic frame of reference for successful effort in working with both professional and lay people. *California Journal of Secondary Education* 25:393-396; November 1950.

"A Community Plans for Better Schools," Paul E. Johnson. Reports operating principles, basic beliefs, fundamental conditions, leadership responsibilities and action projects in a community where citizens generally help to plan school programs. *Educational Leadership* 9:501-507; May 1952.

"Parents Are a Valuable Resource," Mary Norris Lloyd. If curriculum is conceived to be what is done for children under the influence of the school, parents and other citizens can and should take an important role in developing it. *Educational Leadership* 11:354-58; March 1954.

"Parents and Staff Cooperate in System-Wide Improvement," Maurice R. Ahrens. How one school system has secured effective coordination between the Curriculum Council and the Parents Council. *Educational Leadership* 11:337-42; March 1954.

Lay help in school plant planning is stressed in books by Engelhardt and others: N. L. Engelhardt and N. L. Engelhardt, Jr. *Planning the Community School* (American Book, 1940), and N. L. Engelhardt and S. F. Leggett, *Planning Secondary School Buildings* (Reinhold, 1949). Glance also at these articles:

"A Community Plans Its School Facilities," Chester F. Miller. How school authorities established a program to get the active intelligent cooperation of many school and community people in planning a new school building. The successive steps taken are described and charted. *Nation's Schools* 24:16-20; December 1939.

"Designing and Creating Tomorrow's Schools," Virginia F. Matson and E. J. Matson. Vivid argument for community-wide planning of new buildings to meet modern conceptions of good educational programs. *American School Board Journal* 112:27-28; January 1946.

"Community Plans Its School Buildings," Cleve O. Westby. Creative
leadership in getting laymen and school people to plan together is the
key to development of school buildings well located, designed and
equipped. *Educational Leadership*, 6:285-289; February 1949.
"Together They Built," Earl M. Hughes and Lawrence B. Perkins. Community planning for two new schools started long before the foundations were laid. *National Education Association Journal* 43:141-43;
March 1954.

**Emphasis upon techniques, procedures, and principles of successful
lay participation** is found in *How Can We Help Get Better Schools?* by
the National Citizens' Commission for the Public Schools. J. H. Hull's
Lay Advisory Committees to Boards of Education in the United States
(California Association of School Administrators, 1949) summarizes a
doctoral study of 44 lay committees throughout the nation. Factors
analyzed include organization and structure, methods of operation, activities, functions, accomplishments, and evaluation. *Public Action for Powerful Schools* (Teachers College, Columbia, 1949) summarizes fundamental principles of policy-making as seen by the Metropolitan School
Study Council. *Working Together for Better Schools* by J. Wilmer Menge
and Roland C. Faunce (American Book, 1953) is a handbook for lay participation in school-community planning, stressing valid purposes and
techniques. The story of a three-year experiment in lay participation in
the Bronx, New York, is told by John W. Polley, Joseph O. Loretan, and
Clara F. Blitzer in *Community Action for Education* (Bureau of Publications, Teachers College, Columbia University, 1953). These selected
magazine references will be valuable also:

"Lay Advisory Commission Puts Into Effect the Partnership Between
School and Community," Leslie W. Kindred. Purposes, membership,
size, policies, programs, limitations and values are presented. *Nation's
Schools* 43:43-44; March 1949.
"A Cooperative Study at Indian Knoll," Elizabeth M. Bailey and Nell W.
McClothlin. Tells what happened when a community organized a co-
operative project to improve its schools. Five basic principles of school-
community cooperation are listed. *Educational Leadership* 7:398-401;
March 1950.
"How to Organize Local Citizens Committees," Henry Toy, Jr. Some
suggestions by the Director of the National Citizens Commission for
the Public Schools. *Nation's Schools* 46:26-28; July 1950.
"How to Organize Lay Advisory Committees," J. H. Hull. Suggest steps
to take and procedures to follow. *School Executive* 20:49; December
1950.
"Cooperative Planning Through the School-Community Council,"
Stephen Romine. Lists essential principles, needs and values of the
school-community advisory council. *Educational Administration and
Supervision* 36:485-489; December 1950.

"Local Citizens Solve an Acute School Shortage Problem," S. P. Marland, Jr. Illustrates and defines basic principles in using lay leaders successfully. *School Executive* 70:54-56; August 1951. Also in *Education Digest* 17:22-24; November 1951.

"Technics of Setting Up a Citizens' Advisory Group," M. R. Sumption. Concise account of basic steps and procedures. *Nation's Schools* 48:71-72; October 1951.

"Let's Clarify the Relationship of Administrator and Citizens' Committee," Grant Venn and Zeno B. Katterle. Discusses common misunderstandings of proper functions, and suggests the specific role as that of permanent coordinator. *Nation's Schools* 49:51-54; June 1952.

Home-school and parent-teacher relationships are the active concern in every issue of the *National Parent-Teacher Magazine.* Excellent articles in this field are also found in *Parents' Magazine.* The best book in this field is *Effective Home-School Relations* by James L. Hymes (Prentice-Hall, 1953). The National Congress of Parents and Teachers published *Community Life in a Democracy* (1942) suggesting in it many practical possibilities for parent-teacher-school cooperation. Muriel W. Brown's *Partners in Education* (Association for Childhood Education, 1950) is a pamphlet guide to better home-school relationships, with examples in developing the curriculum, working out policies, finding community leaders, and the like. *Working With Parents,* a handbook issued by the United States Office of Education (1948), suggests many ways of securing wider development of parent participation programs. Arndt and Bowles' *Parents, Teachers and Youth Build Together* and Eva H. Grant's *Parents and Teachers as Partners* (Science Research Associates, 1952) are two more bulletins which show how home and school can work together toward their mutual goal—well-adjusted and well-educated children. Wilbur A. Yauch's *How Good Is Your School?* (Harper, 1951) is a book directed primarily at parents to help them be intelligent in evaluating the schools. "Home-School Relations" is the theme of *Educational Leadership* for February 1950, where 11 articles charting various phases of the field appear.

The National Citizens' Commission for the Public Schools maintains an office at 2 West 45th St., New York 19, N. Y., and will gladly send literature upon request. *What Do You Know About Your Schools?* is one of its guides to the study of local needs and problems.

Motion Pictures

Pop Rings the Bell. A dramatized story of a typical school which is meeting the new demands on education. School taxes are shown to be an investment in a better future, not merely a present burden. National School Service, 23 minutes, 1944.

Schoolhouse in the Red. Deals with the sociological and psychological factors involved when small communities face up to the problems of joining their school districts onto a larger unit. It contrasts the activities of a typical one-room school with those of a consolidated school, and shows how one community group went about solving the question. Agrafilms, 42 minutes, color, 1948.

The Sixth Chair. Contrasts dark, crowded schools with lighted, cheerful industrial plants in the community, and dramatically shows how we may fight public complacency about such obsolete school conditions. National School Service, 1949, 18 minutes.

Fight for Better Schools. Shows in detail how the citizens of Arlington County, Virginia, brought about complete reorganization of their school administration and facilities, and briefly how other groups operate. March of Time, 19 minutes, 1949.

CHAPTER **17**

Community Coordination

For generations we maintained the book-centered school in its social isolation. Then we discovered the community and eagerly sought to use its varied resources to enrich and vitalize our academic programs. In recent years teachers have done much to bring the community into the school and to take the children into the community. But in that very process of *academically* bridging the gulf between community and school we have discovered that community conflicts and disorganizations are reflected in our students' behavior, that mere information about the community is insufficient to influence personal living or community improvement, that active student participation in community processes is both educationally and civically inadequate as long as dominant community influences oppose the work of the school or even remain indifferent toward it. Thus, we have been driven to recognize the inescapable truth: that *the education of the whole child in his total environment is and must remain a community function* despite the existence and development of the school. Education cannot be identified solely with schooling, nor learning with formal instruction. That is why "education for democracy" cannot be much more than a delusive verbalism unless it is everywhere *grounded in appropriate, community-wide, and community-guided action.* Such action may and should be

This chapter is by EDWARD G. OLSEN.

stimulated by the school, but never confined within it. For in the classic words of Joseph K. Hart:

"The democratic problem in education is not primarily a problem of training children; it is the problem of *making a community* within which children cannot help growing up to be democratic, intelligent, disciplined to freedom, reverent of the goods of life, and eager to share in the tasks of the age. A school cannot produce this result; nothing but a community can do so." [1]

In recent years, educational psychology has disclosed the essential unity of personality as it develops through interaction of mind and body, beliefs and emotions, thinking and doing. We know now that a student's mind cannot be abstracted and educated apart from these other vital aspects of his total existence. Educational sociology, meanwhile, has revealed the essential unity of one's life experience, showing that all influences which impinge upon the individual educate him in some manner and some degree, for better or for worse. Quoting again from Hart:

"No child can escape his community. He may not like his parents, or the neighbors or the ways of the world. He may groan under the processes of living, and wish he were dead. But he goes on living, and he goes on living in the community.

"The life of the community flows about him, foul or pure: he swims in it, drinks it, goes to sleep in it, and wakes to the new day to find it still about him. He belongs to it: it nourishes him, or starves him, or poisons him: it gives him the substance of his life. And in the long run it takes its toll of him, and all he is." [2]

Whether we realize it or not, whether we like it or not, we all learn what we live, not just what we study. Thus we are compelled to recognize this truth: that when the school seeks to promote the constructive education of the child it can do so adequately only with reference to his total environment. This being so, the community school is fully committed to the idea that education is—and ought much more to be—a posi-

[1] *The Discovery of Intelligence*, p. 383. New York: Century Co., 1924.
[2] *Adult Education*, pp. 82-83. New York: Thomas Y. Crowell, 1927.

tive, community-building enterprise which can never be confined to the school and certainly not concentrated within school walls. Some practical expressions of this education-as-a-community-function conception were suggested by Goodwin Watson when he wrote that "The community health officials should also be the teachers of health . . . . If the community is ready for better household arts, what is needed is not a set of special school equipment but visitors who can demonstrate in the homes . . . A consumer's cooperative can serve as the town's method of consumer education . . . . The music leader will be not primarily a school person but an addition to the community life. The introduction to literature can best be handled by the staff of the public library . . . . The factory will be the gateway of contact with economic life . . . .

"All of this varied program should be the concern of an educational director, whose business it will be to keep all of life as educative as possible . . . . School will go in homes, the library, the hospital, the cooperative store, the dairy barns, the little theatre, and in all the museums, shops and studios which can be set up to facilitate the pursuit of worthy interests." [3]

The school is society's chief formal agency for the education of children, youth, and adults. What, then, is its special responsibility as one among many other educative agencies in the community? The answer is clear: the school's proper role within the total educative process is both residual and coordinative. In its residual role it is obligated to teach all those ideas, skills, appreciations, abilities, attitudes, and ideals which are essential to people's effective living and which they do not acquire through non-school channels. In its coordinative role, the school will lead other community agencies to develop consciously cooperative programs for the more effective and economical education of all people.

Stating the same principle even more specifically, we may say that the community school's function is to identify the

[3] Unpublished manuscript. Used by permission.

basic life-needs of those whom it serves, analyze the community to discover to what extent and degree those needs are already being met through non-school experiences, provide a sound school program to meet the remaining needs, and lead the community in more effectively coordinating its total educative resources for the increased benefit of all its members, adults as well as children.

All this implies that a school will neither duplicate the desirable educational offerings generally available through other community agencies, nor fail to utilize them to the fullest extent through leadership in coordinated community educational programs. Surely it is clear that effective education for our times requires continuous and cooperative planning on the part of homes, churches, welfare agencies, service clubs, clinics, professional groups, veterans organizations, business associations, labor unions, women's clubs, youth agencies, etc., *and schools.*

The local agency through which such joint planning can best be developed is commonly called the community council. As a social invention this is nothing new; nearly all of our larger cities have had councils of social agencies for many years. The first true coordinating council, however, was formally organized in Berkeley, California, in 1919. It was developed by the superintendent of schools and the chief of police in order to secure community-wide participation in more effectively meeting the problems of youth in that city. By 1940, over three hundred local coordinating councils had been organized in 26 states. Today they number several thousand, listed under a variety of names—"community council," "neighborhood council," "youth council," "social welfare council," "human relations council," and the like.

World War II, the Korean War, and the many local needs in the home effort gave tremendous impetus to the whole coordinating council idea. Nearly every American community has now had intensive experience in cooperatively developing and administering its local Office of Civilian Defense, its War Council, its United Service Organization center, and other similar community-wide agencies occasioned by war. Councils on community defense, committees on the care of children for working mothers, citizens unity associations, youth councils, adult education councils, religious instruction councils—many such agencies as these are now personally familiar to Americans in every section of our nation.

Most of the pre-war councils originated in the essentially negative, though highly commendable, purpose of ameliorating poverty or of preventing juvenile delinquency. The war years focused attention upon problems of home defense, of providing recreational facilities for service men and women, of caring for the children of employed mothers, and of combatting wartime delinquency. In pursuing these essential ends, local citizens, agencies, and organizations of many kinds learned to work together as they had never done before. It is essential that this war-born community cooperation be maintained and greatly extended in the future, no matter when hot or cold hostilities cease. Improving racial, religious, ethnic and other intergroup relationships is one obvious problem with which practically every American community must seriously grapple. Providing educative work opportunities for youth is another that is fundamental to American democracy. So are problems of housing, efficient local government, health, recreation, and welfare matters. Such as these will demand the best thinking and cooperative planning of every community in the years ahead.

Another, and perhaps more significant, conception of community coordination is now emerging. This view holds that the community council should be an agency through which school personnel and community citizens may maintain active and continuing cooperation in the planning of basic school policy itself. As indicated in the previous chapter, educational cooperation of this nature is highly desirable in a nation which prides itself upon local control of its schools, and is particularly important when the school's program involves widespread use of resource people, field trips, surveys, community service projects, work experiences, and other activities outside the classroom.

In all such programs—whether for the prevention of delinquency, the promotion of better human relations, the provision of work experience, the planning of community educative opportunities or any other—the fundamental key to success is community *coordination*. Neither the school alone, nor any other agency alone, can do these things to best advantage. But when all plan and work together, much can be accomplished. When education is conceived as examined, living experience, when the community is recognized as the matrix of that experience, when the community's responsibility for promoting better experience for its youth is widely affirmed, and when the school actually develops a residual and a coordinating function, then, but not until then, will education for life begin to be truly functional.

What Is a Community Council?

Community organizations express both the genius and the frustrations of many an American city, town, and even rural region. Studies show that in communities of five to ten thousand people, there are typically from fifty to seventy-five different organized groups of some importance. In larger cities, such organizations are numbered in the hundreds or even the thousands.[4] No matter how large or how small the community, the common cry is likely to be: "We have too many organizations already! Why should we start another?"

Reaction like that is certainly understandable. Every community, almost regardless of size and location, has a multitude of organizations. Each of these groups seeks to meet rather

[4] Gordon W. Blackwell, "Community Structure and Community Organization." *Journal of Educational Sociology* 23:176-182; November 1949.

specialized needs in the community. All of them are in competition with each other in one way or another—especially for the people's attention, time, money, and leadership abilities. Thus it is these very factors of specialized concern and group competition which together make adequate coordination of planning so essential. The very multiplicity of *vertical* organizations makes some *horizontal* coordination of effort imperative for community welfare.

A community council is a cooperative organization of groups and individuals having some measure of community status, who work together to attack problems of common concern in their community. In the 38,000 communities of the United States there are about 11,000 community councils. Of these, some 1,000 are general community councils; the others are specialized in terms of particular aspects of community life.[5] The kinds of membership in a general community council have been well summarized by the Wisconsin Community Organization Committee in its excellent little pamphlet, *Teamwork in the Community:*[6]

"The membership of a community council usually includes (1) delegates or representatives of civic, professional, educational, religious, agricultural, labor, and business organizations; (2) delegates or representatives of public and voluntary community service agencies; and (3) individual members chosen for their interest, knowledge, or competence in civic affairs and not representing any particular organization.

"All economic and social groups, as well as geographic areas, should be urged to participate. A community council cannot get results if it leaves out groups which have a genuine interest in community improvement and direct lines of communication to citizens. The main idea, when it comes to membership, is to *get* participation, not to *limit* it.

"The following is a suggested list of agencies and organizations for a community council:

[5] American Council for the Community, *The Training of Community Counselors. Reports of Conference on Training for Community Service.* New York: The Council (119 East 19th Street), 1949.

[6] Used by special permission of the Committee.

Agricultural organizations
Business and professional organizations
Educational institutions and services
Fraternal and service clubs
Governmental agencies and departments
Health and welfare agencies
Human relations groups
Industry
Labor organizations
Patriotic organizations
Racial and nationality groups
Religious organizations
Women's groups
Youth organizations

"A community council needs youth for its own sake and for the sake of youth. In return for receiving new ideas and fresh enthusiasm it will give youth a training ground for future responsible leadership.

"While it is important to include professional staff of member agencies, the success of a community council in winning community support will depend most upon strong citizen participation."

What Does a Community Council Do?

A coordinating council is chiefly a fact-finding, advisory, and catalytic influence, not a super-administrative agency. Its purpose is to improve the quality of living in the community by getting people to study problems and needs in relation to resources and possible plans for actively meeting them. The more specific purposes sought by practically all councils today have been outlined in the Wisconsin bulletin just quoted:

"No two community councils will be exactly alike in program, but they share the general purpose of improving all phases of community life. The most vital part of a community council's job is to study problems and needs and to plan cooperatively to meet them. It does this by:

1. Encouraging informed citizen participation
2. Fact-finding
3. Developing public understanding and support
4. Coordinating community activities and services
5. Cooperative action"

Each of these five functions is then described briefly as follows.

1. **Encouraging Informed Citizen Participation.** Citizen participation in community life is the foundation of a strong democracy. But an active citizen must be a well-informed citizen. A truly representative community council educates for civic leadership.

Illustrations:

—Through a fact-finding committee to study needs and resources of a community.

—Through a radio panel about recreational services.

—Through directing a poll of youth and adult employment opportunities.

2. **Fact-Finding.** One of the most valuable things a community council can do is continually and carefully to gather facts about its community—its health, human relations, education, recreation, religious, economic and welfare needs—and to agree on how these needs can best be met. If a council does nothing more than to study such facts and present them fairly and completely, it has proved its worth.

A council will find it advantageous to call in consultants from outside the community to direct or assist in making fact-finding studies.

Illustrations:

—A study to find out how widely boys and girls are participating in the program of youth agencies. Such a study might result in the discovery that certain age or racial groups are not being served, or that some areas have more than enough youth agencies, while others have too few.

—A study of the public health nursing activities carried on by a private agency, the health department and the schools. This might reveal a duplication of services for control of communicable disease and a neglect of bedside care. In this case, the community might agree to establish one central nursing service or otherwise plan for total service coverage.

—A study of the zoning problems in relation to adequate housing. This might result in improved living conditions for families.

3. **Developing Public Understanding and Support.** A community council stimulates public awareness of community problems, develops an understanding of how the community deals with these problems, and gains support for the necessary services and programs. How? By sponsoring public meetings and forums; maintaining speakers' bureaus; distributing studies and reports; and

getting publicity through the press and radio. Community understanding of needs and services develops through council delegates'
reports to their own organizations.

Illustrations:

—Publishing a directory of the community's health, welfare, education and recreation resources.
—Issuing a report on health and other community needs.
—Sponsoring a family life institute or conferences of community improvement.
—Arranging for newspaper articles or radio programs of an informational or educational nature.
—Providing up-to-date information on business, industry and
employment opportunities.

4. **Coordinating Community Activities and Services.** Community
councils provide a meeting ground for people from different public
or voluntary agencies or organizations to come together, share their
experiences, understand each other's viewpoints, and agree on
some definite plans. By working voluntarily on joint projects, community leaders learn to lift their eyes from their own specialized
interests and take a look at the whole community. When advisable,
they assign parts of the total job to suitable organizations so that
people will receive the best possible services with the least duplication of effort, time, and money.

A community council also coordinates by bringing old and new
services into proper balance. By its understanding of all the facts
it is more likely to reflect the best judgment of all concerned.

Councils often provide some common service to member organizations unable to achieve it alone.

Illustrations:

—Arranging meetings at which each organization can describe its
purpose and program to other organizations.
—Creating a Christmas Bureau to coordinate the flood of spon-
taneous giving.
—Getting out a calendar of future events and meetings to help
individual organizations avoid conflicts in dates.
—Developing a cooperative training program for volunteer leaders of all leisure-time organizations.

5. **Cooperative Action.** After considering the facts and agreeing
upon a logical course of action, the council takes steps to carry out

its plans. This may require modifying an existing service or developing an entirely new one. In any case, interested citizens and organizations arrive at a joint decision.

Council action may mean conference and negotiation with officials administering the services. It may mean consultation with the group which appropriates funds such as Community Chest, or county, village or town boards or the city council.

Councils should not generally operate community services directly, though they may do so occasionally on a temporary demonstration basis.

Illustrations:

—Negotiating with two existing agencies or organizations for a merger of their services or projects.

—Holding conferences with school authorities to work out plans for use of school buildings for summer recreation.

—Presenting to the city council recommendations for improvement of a swimming beach or pool.

Where Does the School Fit in? [7]

In any community, the public school is likely to be the only permanent agency which is supported by all the people and which already serves most of the children. As such, the school has—or should deserve to have—the confidence of the community. The school is thus in a strategic position to initiate proposals for community coordination, and to carry a major share of the responsibility for developing proposals into plans, plans into policies, and policies into action.

It is inconceivable that a community council should be organized without the school being represented. Most school people recognize the council as a force having great educational potentialities, and hence are eager to support it. School people can clearly see the deep significance to democratic living inherent in the work of a good council. Here, people of divergent background and outlook meet together with common purposes to work for the common good. Thus does the educator see in the coordinating council a new area in which

[7] This section was written for this book by Anne Wright, Superintendent of District #3, Philadelphia Public Schools.

he may serve by giving a definitely educational direction to its activities.

School people who participate in a coordinating council would do well to keep in mind their particular responsibility as professional educators. Among those special obligations which are also opportunities are these:

- To provide leadership and to act with others in making and keeping the Council a potent educational force in the community.
- To maintain the democratic values of group discussion, group planning, group decision, and the scientific values of objective thinking about controversial issues.
- To guide the Council in the use of evaluative procedures so that results may be reliably appraised, and purposes adjusted to changing needs.
- To aid in sensitizing the Council's membership to youth needs, youth interests, and youth problems.
- To endeavor to widen the base of Council membership so that young people are included in the deliberations and are encouraged to participate actively in both planning and executing of policies.

The last two of these five responsibilities merit more extended analysis. Young people now in school need to participate actively in community affairs, and the community itself benefits when they do so. A radio program once featured four high school students from different parts of the country. These young people discussed their problems of the future with a great deal of intelligence and feeling. During the question period, the adult chairman of the program inquired of these youth representatives, "What do you want of us older folks? What can we do to help you solve your problems, to face your future?" The reply came without hesitation. It was forceful, honest, almost pleading in its sincerity: "*Let us work with you now in the solution of your problems.* Your present problems are part of our future problems. Don't make us wait to be of use. We can think. We can plan. Don't push us to one side with the comment, 'They're only kids.'" What a picture of youth's energy, enthusiasm, vision of service—being patronized by adults with the smiling comment, "They're only kids." We must not forget how other countries have seized upon the energies of youth and rallied them to their national purposes while we have often forced our young people into civic stagnation while waiting for the day when they will be considered "old enough" to work with adults on projects affecting the common welfare.

If the young people are to fulfil their proper role as active, participating citizens they must have every opportunity to study, to evaluate, and to contribute to the constructive life of their local communities. Such opportunities are a challenge to the initiative and the creative thinking of young people, for they require youth to work on equal basis with adults in the development of intelligent programs for community action. In some cases, the schools will initiate such action—as in the form of service projects and work experiences—but in others the schools will cooperate with other community agencies, enlisting youth in the coordinated program. The source of stimulation to action is not important. What is important is that communities become deeply aware of their problems, their responsibilities, and their resources for meeting both. To that awareness the school can contribute much.

How Is a Community Council Started?

Just how do you go about starting a community council? To answer this practical question in concrete terms, let's read part of the "log" of the Columbia Community Council in upstate New York—a true story of one small community's adventure in developing the skills of adult cooperation, both in education and in planned community action for the common good. Within it, let's interpolate as titles some basic principles which were observed and which thereby helped to assure success. Here is that dramatic story.[8]

[8] *Adventure in Cooperation: Community Building in a Central School District*. Albany, N. Y.: Bureau of Adult Education, State Education Department, 1949.

Study the Problem Situation

Three years ago our Central School P.T.A. asked a question: "What's happening to our 1700 kids when school doesn't keep?" This led to another question: "What's happening to our big, gangling, loose-jointed Central School community?"

We reasoned that our kids are the product of the whole community. We can't look young Jimmie in the eye unless we provide the kind of ideal community that children and parents thrive in, body, mind, spirit . . . in work, hope, citizenship, education, fun and friendship.

Get Some Key People to Face the Facts

Anything we should be doing? "Yes," said the P.T.A., and named a committee of twelve to take stock of community needs and propose an action program. The committee proposed a Columbia Community Council devoted to the whole welfare.

But "thundering Jehosophat," said a skeptic, "whole welfare . . . that means everything: health, welfare, planning, safety, libraries, adult education, recreation, conservation . . ."

"Yep" said a village sage, "Exactly!" And that was exactly the contract that the newborn Columbia Community Council took on.

Organize a Community Team

Here's what we said: "Let's call all the hands together, farmer, suburbanite, Catholic, Protestant, and Jew, lawyer, Negro, typesetter, and housewife. Let's organize a community team. Then let's take a good look at the whole welfare of the whole district and start building, step by step and stone by stone."

Here's the team: 410 paid members, 21 directors and officers, 19 committees, and staff. Quite a team: Note the members:

architect	telephone official	librarian
druggist	office holder	rabbi
housewife	preacher	gladiolus raiser
teacher	editor	student
garage man	general store manager	bacteriologist
general farmer	historian	feed store owner
stenographer	chemist	hardware owner
government officer	reporter	grocer
printer	chicken raiser	builder
scientific breeder of	doctor	real estate man
dairy cattle	dentist	blanket maker
insurance salesman	welfare worker	

Size Up the Job

You might say we used this formula: stop and look, listen, analyze, act.

We stopped and looked:
First we used a blackboard in a "town meeting." "What's on your mind?" asked the chairman. And he wrote down what we said: adult education, safety, choral society, playgrounds, ball league, town meetings, swimming places, planning, libraries, homes of veterans, a district directory, etc. . . . thirty some suggestions.

Then we listened:
We listened to a lot of people in all parts of the districts . . . in committees . . . in town meetings . . . and here and there.

And analyzed:
What are the really big needs? The priorities? What's the nature of the difficulties to be overcome? What are the best ways to tackle the job?

And we acted:
Beginning with a few projects . . . veterans housing, a directory, town meetings, etc. . . . we steadily expanded to 19 projects under 19 committees.

Decide Specific Objectives

In all this bustle of activity what are the BIG THINGS we're after? Good community? Sure thing . . . but what IS a good community? Here's our thinking:

- We want a community of friendly neighbors.
- We want a community that practices cooperation by everybody in getting important things done.
- We want a community that is alive to its local, state, national, and world responsibilities.
- We want a community where education is everybody's continuing business from cradle to grave . . . because this is America and because education is the life line of democracy.
- We want a community good to look at, healthful and prosperous to live in, well planned for tomorrow, well governed.
- We want a community rich in the arts and in the fun of living.
- We want a community soil that grows good homes.
- We want community roots that produce great Americans.

Determine Strategy

Every political campaign, every battle needs a strategy. So does a community program. Experience tells us that a community program without a strategy goes swiftly on the rocks. To plan our strategy we looked first at the problem:

We live in a big, queerly shaped tract embracing city workers, farmers, villagers. The only strong bond is our school. But many others of our problems should be shared: adult education, highways, planning, recreation, welfare. Our hamlets and village are too small to do everything alone. Result: scores of community services are missing.

Second, we asked what human resources, organizations, skills, and projects are necessary if we're to lick our problems.

Third, we set down (in the rough) some of the strategy lines we'd follow. Briefly, these lines are:

- Continuous adult education.
- Communications . . . "talking to each other."
- Taking care of our simple, close-up "doorstep" needs.
- Community wide participation . . . "getting everybody on the team" . . . fullest use of volunteers.
- Playing ball with our many groups, clubs, etc.
- A free but cooperative relation to schools, town boards, state departments, and other agencies.
- An efficient central staff and a headquarters.
- Constant attention to the skills of cooperation.
- Decentralization by means of village and hamlet associations.
- Continuous training of new leaders and workers.
- Keeping a whole view of the whole community.

[The Columbia Council report now spells out each of these eleven "strategy lines" in some detail. Suppose we notice two of them here: *community-wide participation* and *cooperation with public services.*]

Get Community-Wide Participation

Out our way the neighbors had gotten into the bad habit of saying "they." We knew the Columbia Council idea wouldn't get far until the neighbors learned to say "we." When do people say "we?" The answer was simple. People say "we" when they have a finger in the pie. But it's not so simple to get 12,000 fingers in the pie.

We'd seen a dozen people control a Town Board . . . a handful ran the P.T.A. in the old days . . . and we had plenty of skeptics to tell us that "the best committee is two men, one of them off fishing." But we said "let's take this 100 per cent participation business seriously. We won't get 100 per cent participation, but let's try."

Here's the story of our try . . . put to arithmetic:

Canvass every section systematically for paid voting members. We got	410
19 communities. Each on the average puts about 25 people to work. 19 times 25 is	475
Lend a hand to a local or neighborhood association. 6 times 200 is	1200
A goal of 500 in adult education	500
Work with clubs, Grange, fire companies, etc., on lighting, safety, conservation and other projects. X agencies times X members is	a lot of people
Work with schools on recreation, playgrounds, student projects	hundreds
Put a library depot in reach of every citizen	thousands
Our "Town Meeting on Wheels" . . . each meeting in a different church or hall in the area	hundreds

TOTAL: A first-class ground swell of interest . . . community-wide.

Get Help from Public Agencies

A live community can call on a lot of helping agencies. Most citizens and groups have no idea of what public services are available. Columbia Council finds out. Here are some of the public and semi-public bodies we've called on in three years:

Schools	State Police
State Youth Commission	Public Service Commission
County Political Committees	State Comptroller
Cornell Rural Extension	State Housing Division
N. Y. State Citizens Council	Conservation Department
County Health Department	Veterans Administration
National Municipal League	Department of Public Works
Federal Bureau of Investigation	N. Y. Regional Plan
State Education Department	State Department of Commerce
State Teachers College	Town Boards

Constantly Appraise Results

You know, we didn't honestly feel too sure when we started that things weren't too complicated nowadays for the citizens to take a "whole look at the whole community." But we tried just that. And Columbia Council experience tells us not only that people are amazingly good at the broad look when given a chance and a challenge—but that by stiff and urgent logic we've got to take the whole look or the modern community will continue to fall apart at the seams at a time when man needs community as he never needed it before. Looking back, we see that things are much clearer when we study them (and tackle them) in relation to each other . . . that we can't hope to use a score of state and other services intelligently unless we fit things together at home . . . and, most of all, that the only way we can really mobilize all our people and their many talents is through good community organization.

This is the way we see it now:

—If we can use education, planning and social skills to make democracy work in American communities . . .

—We can make it work in America as a nation.

—If democracy works in the nations . . .

—It will work in the world.

MOBILIZING THE WHOLE PEOPLE BEHIND A WHOLE VIEW AND A WHOLE PROGRAM FOR THE WHOLE COMMUNITY IS A BIG GOAL, A LONG TASK, AND A THRILLING ADVENTURE IN DEMOCRACY.

Such is the dramatic story of three small communities. What a demonstration of the power and the potentialities inherent in constructive community coordination!

Education at its Best

Education, properly considered, is a function of the entire community, not merely of the schools alone.

Education, truly understood, must provide much guided, first-hand experience with community affairs and problems.

Education, adequately conceived, must be organized around the moral purpose of building a better community, state, nation, and world.

Students and teachers and laymen—cooperatively attacking real problems of personal interest and social concern! Here is modern education at its best, and here too is epitomized that emerging educational institution of the next generation, the life-centered, community school. For clearly it is that school which can most easily bridge the historic gulf between learning and living, and which can thereby best serve the common cause of democracy and education in our time.

Learning Activities

Socio-drama

Stage a mock coordinating council meeting, with teams of class members representing each of several local organization members. Bearing in mind the probable viewpoints of each organization, discuss the application of a political or a religious group for the use of a public school building as a meeting place. As a climax of this discussion, draw up a model statement of policy and procedure to cover all applications in the future.

Discussion Topics

1. Do you see any dangers to a school which participates in a coordinating council? If so, spell them out and examine.
2. If a school joins a coordinating council, is the responsibility of the school board altered? What about its legal obligations?
3. Should high school students serve as members of a community council, officially representing their school on it?
4. Could something like the community adult development program be tailor-made for your own community? What might this class do to start it?

Group Projects

1. Divide the labor and scan recent literature for descriptions of community council programs, then compare their essential operating principles with those presented in this chapter.
2. Attend a session of a community council and discuss your reactions.

3. View the listed motion pictures and sample some of *The People Act* transcriptions, then decide the feasibility of such projects generally.

Individual Activities

1. Outline in some detail a 20-minute talk to be given before a local service club on the community coordination movement and its local possibilities.
2. Draft a script for a possible *The People Act* story of a community improvement program known to you personally.
3. Set up a display of community council literature.

Learning Materials

Basic principles and procedures of community coordination are discussed in Arthur Hillman's *Community Organization and Planning* (Macmillan, 1950). Clarence King's *Organizing for Community Action* (Harper, 1948) summarizes successful techniques, and illustrates with many brief case studies. Numerous vivid accounts of cooperative citizens' programs designed to handle urgent local problems are presented by Jean and Jess Ogden in *Small Communities in Action* (Harper, 1946) and also in *These Things We Tried* (University of Virginia, 1948). Coordinated community efforts led by various schools are described in chapter 12 of Olsen's *School and Community Programs*. The ways in which the Southern States Work-Conference, made up of educational leaders from 14 states, sought to view education in terms of its relation to regional resources are described in *Building a Better Southern Region Through Education* (1945). Although designed for rural Iowa, *Strong Communities Build Strong Democracy: Guides for Studying and Developing Community Action* (Iowa State College, 1951) is an excellent general treatment of values and techniques. The relationships between community cooperative planning and personal mental health are explored in a publication of the Hogg Foundation: *Family, Community and Mental Health* (University of Texas, 1950). Paul L. Essert and R. W. Howard's *Educational Planning by Neighborhoods in Centralized Districts* (Teachers College, Columbia, 1952) is a dramatic historical picture of the ways in which local citizens reorganized rural school districts into centralized districts. *Informal Groups and the Community* by Hurley H. Doddy (Teachers College, Columbia, 1952) outlines techniques for identifying and discovering those inconspicuous community groups which are so influential in the development of attitudes, opinions, and personality. It also presents implications for institution-community relationships, and describes various roles of informal groups in community development. *A Community Youth Development Program* by Robert J. Havighurst and others (University of Chicago, 1952) reports an experiment designed to test the hypothesis that the community, through local persons appropriately trained, can increase the production of unusually able, creative young people and can reduce its production of socially and personally maladjusted young people.

Descriptions and activities of community councils at work are easily sampled in the magazines:

"When Neighbors Get Together," William Bacon. Describes two community council programs in action; one concerned about youth recreation and the other racial harmony. *Educational Leadership* 2:111-114; December 1944.

"Town That Found Itself," Leslie Kindred and Bernard G. Kelner. Dramatic account of how a deteriorating town of mixed racial and religious population was led by local teachers to found a school and community associations—which established a branch library, health clinic, baby ward, etc., and greatly reduced tensions as it built community morale. *Parents' Magazine* 21:28-29; September 1946.

"Community Program for Child Development," Miriam E. Lowenberg. The Child Health Institute functions as a coordinating agency for health services, teaching, and research by all community health agencies, including the schools. *Childhood Education* 25:22-27; September 1948.

"Helping New York Communities to Help Themselves," H. Curtis Mial. Describes the history, program, services, and future plans of the New York State Citizens' Council. This is a private organization carrying on ⌐ community development and education program aimed at helping citizens build better communities. *Adult Education Journal* 9:6-12; January 1950.

"A Community Organizes to Help Itself," Joseph B. Gucky and Herbert Corey. Tells the story of an experimental program of community improvement through a coordinating council. Seven committees and their projects are described. *Educational Leadership* 7:388-392; March 1950.

"How Minneapolis Beat the Bigots," Clive Howard. Excellent example of how key people and groups in a single community banded together to fight undemocratic forces. *Woman's Home Companion,* November 1951.

"School-Community Liason—A New Approach," J. D. Mezirow. Describes the effective work done by the Minnesota Youth Conservation Commission, a new public agency designed to assist local communities to organize community councils. *The Community Organizes for Youth* is the title of its manual presenting aims, organization, and techniques. *School & Society* 75:65-68; February 2, 1952.

The role of the school in community coordination is illustrated by several case studies in Chapter 12 of *School and Community Programs* edited by Edward G. Olsen. Other interesting examples of what has been done by the school appear in the following articles:

"School Participation in the Organization and Work of a Coordinating Council," Robert E. Gibson and Aubrey E. Haan. In a town of 4,000 people there were fifty-five social and fraternal organizations working independently until the school principal led the organization of a Community Council. Its problems, procedures, and values for in-service teacher education are outlined. *National Elementary Principal* 21:382-386; July 1942.

"Co-ordinated School-Community Health Program," Marjorie Easta-brooks. Describes an experimental school-community health program carried on by the schools of forty-four districts in thirty counties of Washington State. *National Association of Secondary School Principals Bulletin* 29:57-66; December 1945.

"Participation in Community Coordination and Planning," Harold C. Hunt and J. Paul Leonard. Discusses the school administrator's re-sponsibility for surveying community needs and leading the process of organizing a community council for youth. In National Society for Study of Education, *Changing Conceptions in Educational Adminis-tration*, Forty-fifth Yearbook, Part II, Chapter V. Chicago: University of Chicago Press, 1946.

"How One College Serves Five Counties," L. O. Todd. A junior college stimulated development of school county coordinating councils which are themselves coordinated through a larger council, the chairman of which is the college president. *Junior College Journal* 16:295-297; March 1946.

"Schools Can Create Democracy's Communities," W. Joe Scott. The com-munity council is the best agency through which local communities can solve their problems and improve themselves. The public school, as the foremost institution for developing and promoting democratic living in its area, should lead in establishing such a council. *National Association of Secondary School Principals Bulletin* 30:73-84; May 1946.

"Community Cooperates," Victor Leonard. Well-timed efforts by the school superintendent produced a chain of events which changed a stagnating community into a progressive one. Community coordination has benefited both community living and school curriculum. *School Executive* 66:40; December 1946.

"Role of the Superintendent of Schools in Community Planning," William C. Reavis. Describes the historic role of the superintendent in com-munity planning and discusses four present responsibilities in that area. *Elementary School Journal* 47:434-441; April 1947; *American School Board Journal* 114:45-46; May 1947.

"Education and Community Organization," John W. Herring. Analyzes the present community movement and then lists 6 suggestions. *School and Society*, 68:273-276; October 23, 1948.

"Co-ordinating Community Educational Services," Edward G. Olsen. Suggests the role of the school in community coordination and illus-trates with case-studies on local, state, and regional levels. *Annals of the American Academy of Political and Social Science* 265:130-135; September 1949.

"School As An Integrating Agency in Community Life," L. H. Carstin. Considers disintegrative agencies of community life, concludes that the school can help develop a local espirit de corps, and lists both obstacles and possibilities. *Journal of Educational Sociology*, 21:409-416; March 1948.

"Wagon Mound Builds a Health Center," Charles H. Wood. Tells how all the people of a small rural community worked together to meet their problem of inadequate medical services. The school led the campaign. *National Education Association Journal* 40:185-186; March 1951.

"A Community Youth Development Plan," Robert J. Havighurst. Outlines a long-term plan set up in a midwestern city to help children make a satisfactory life adjustment by early discovery of, and assistance to, those with special talents or problems. *School Review* 51:457-466; November 1951.

Descriptions of community council operations in Cedar City, Utah, New York City, Allegan, Michigan and Weimar, Texas are presented by Ianthus Wright, Simon Beagle, Arthur A. Kaechele and Clay Doyle, respectively. *School Executive* 72:58-65; January 1953.

Special issues of professional magazines are excellent sources. The *Journal of Educational Sociology* frequently devotes entire issues to varied aspects of community coordination. See especially February, April, and September 1936; March and October 1937; January and April 1938; May 1940; March 1945; December 1946; March 1948; November 1949. "Coordinating Forces in the Community" for health, conservation, vocational efficiency, and citizenship development are the respective themes of three special issues of *Educational Outlook:* November 1950, January 1951, and March 1951.

Organizations specifically concerned with community development are gaining strength. Two especially are important: The American Council for the Community (119 East 19th Street, New York 3, N. Y.) and Community Service, Inc. (Yellow Springs, Ohio). The former publishes a quarterly journal of community development called *Communities, USA* and also a series of Community Handbooks. Each *Handbook* summarizes the body of experiences and principles that have grown out of specific situations in local communities. The latter agency devotes its efforts to "strengthening two weak links in the chain of our democracy: the small community and education for community." Its *Community Service News* appears bimonthly.

Motion Pictures

Playtown, U.S.A. Designed to show how a community can develop a year-round, all-age recreation program if a few citizens want it and organize their efforts to that end. Association Films, 23 minutes, 1946.

Make Way for Youth. A community combats inter-group prejudice by organizing a youth council through which young people work together for common concerns. Association Films, 22 minutes, 1947.

The Lambertville Story. The true story of a community program to establish a Saturday night, teen-age recreation center. A motor accident involving adolescents shocks the citizens into a realization of their responsibility to provide wholesome recreational activities. Teaching Film Custodians, 20 minutes, 1949.

Board of Education. Shows how residents of a rural community organized into a cooperative group to obtain a modern, consolidated school. United World, 23 minutes, 1951.

Transcriptions

The People Act. A series of 26 half-hour broadcasts about men and women in ordinary situations who are working together to solve crucial everyday problems of community living such as crime and corruption, intergroup and labor-management strife, soil erosion, mentally retarded children, housing, alcoholism, and the like. For sale from The People Act Center, State College, Pennsylvania; free on loan from the Federal Radio Education Committee, United States Office of Education, Washington 25, D. C.

TOWARD THE COMMUNITY SCHOOL

It is never enough to honor the past, to worship at the shrines of pioneering educators who have led us into the present. Our job now is to follow their guiding stars into new lands, not to sit content by the ashes of old campfires. To accept this challenge is to stand with the stalwart, facing the future with courage, devotion, and skill. To fail would be the unthinkable betrayal of democratic youth in this generation. That is why the traditional school of yesterday, respected as it is, must now be transformed and rebuilt as the community school of today and tomorrow. Perhaps this is the major trend and the great unfinished educational task of our profession in the second half of the twentieth century.

Chapters in This Section

Examine Your Thinking

(Check this chart after reading pages 473-476.)

? TRADITIONAL SCHOOL ? PROGRESSIVE SCHOOL ? COMMUNITY SCHOOL ?

Which basic philosophy and program do I *favor*? Which do I usually *practice*?
What do I really *think*, and what do I typically *do*? Is there a *contrast*?
Why? What can I do *now*? How shall I proceed to *plan for the future*?

LEVELS OF SCHOOL PRACTICE

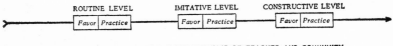

ROUTINE LEVEL — Favor | Practice
IMITATIVE LEVEL — Favor | Practice
CONSTRUCTIVE LEVEL — Favor | Practice

LEVELS OF INSIGHT INTO THE RELATIONSHIP OF TEACHER AND COMMUNITY

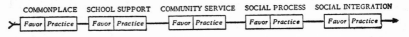

COMMONPLACE — Favor | Practice
SCHOOL SUPPORT — Favor | Practice
COMMUNITY SERVICE — Favor | Practice
SOCIAL PROCESS — Favor | Practice
SOCIAL INTEGRATION — Favor | Practice

BASIC CURRICULUM ORIENTATION

CONVENTIONAL SUBJECTS — Favor | Practice
CHILD INTERESTS — Favor | Practice
LIFE NEEDS — Favor | Practice

SCHOOL'S RELATIONSHIP TO ITS COMMUNITY

STUDY ABOUT — Favor | Practice
PARTICIPATE IN — Favor | Practice
CONTRIBUTE TO — Favor | Practice

CHAPTER **18**

Getting Started

How, then, will you begin? What kind of community study and service program will you seek to develop in your school or school system? Through what steps might you go about starting or developing a genuine community school? These are among the immediate, down-to-earth questions which arise as soon as we begin to consider personally the professional implications of the life-centered school concept. So let us think together about certain simple and practicable steps which can be taken by any teacher, group of teachers, faculty, or school system desiring to investigate techniques for developing a more community-related school program.

No specific blueprint can or should be presented. The special needs and resources of each school and community will differ too much from those of others to make such blueprinting possible, even if it were considered desirable. Furthermore, any program that will truly meet the needs of a particular school and also enlist the wholehearted support of its faculty, students, administrators, and community at large must be a program that is locally devised by local people.

There is both responsibility and challenge in this democratic process of program-planning—not by outside experts, not by administrators or supervisors or teachers alone, not by laymen imposing their will as a pressure group upon a school, but

This chapter is by EDWARD G. OLSEN.

rather by all these people working cooperatively together to design and evaluate a program that is genuinely tailor-made to meet specific local desires and needs.

Now let's assume that you want to explore the possibilities of a community resources program, and that you are in position not only to explore but also to plan and to experiment. What might you do? Suppose we proceed to consider that question. We shall do so by suggesting some basic techniques of approach through which you may successfully develop as much or as little of an organized community resources program as you or your group may feel to be desirable or possible in your particular situation. We shall examine some approaches which may be practically useful to the individual teacher working alone, as well as to a faculty or staff thinking together about the problems of relating school learnings more closely to community needs and resources.

What, then, might you do—as a teacher, a supervisor or administrator, a guidance counselor, a faculty committee, a class of prospective teachers—to plan, develop, or expand a practical community resources program? Two major steps are immediately obvious: you will need to think clearly about the desirable role of the school in community life today, and you may want to examine seriously the possibilities of transforming your school into a genuine community school.

Thinking It Through

Where are you now in your thinking about the desirable role of the school in community life today? Here is the first and most fundamental question you should answer to your own satisfaction, for upon that answer will hinge all your further thinking about planning and program-making. To stimulate and clarify thinking on this point, three challenging queries are presented: How does your school now relate to your community? What do you say is a teacher's responsibility to his community? Which curriculum pattern will you follow?

How Does Your School Now Relate to Your Community?

The Educational Policies Commission has presented some excellent criteria by which you may appraise your school's present program with respect to community living. The Commission identifies three qualitative levels of school practice, as follows:[1]

- **Routine level.** Is your school insulated by ignorance and indifference from the surrounding community? Does your school consider that the effect of community life on the students is none of its affair? Do you accept with resignation the evil effects which some community contacts may have on your students? Is your faculty only vaguely aware of students' home conditions? Do you know little about the libraries, settlement houses, health clinics, housing projects, playgrounds, and other agencies which serve your students? Do you direct the attention of your students inward toward books and papers, rather than outward toward human needs and problems? If so, however excellent the job your school is doing in a narrow field, it is missing a glorious opportunity for wider service. It is functioning at the routine level in community activities. To rise above that level will require that you do some things that are different and difficult.

- **Imitative level.** Do you have frequent excursions into the community for the students in your school? Do the students regard these excusions merely as a lark? Does the faculty regard them as a necessary but unpleasant interference with "regular" duties? Are such activities only vaguely related to the classroom instruction? Do the students on these excursions admire or deplore what they see, as the case may be, but fail to draw conclusions or to develop programs of action? Is your school very busy with good deeds for charity's sake, but little concerned with the conditions which make charity necessary, or with possible remedies for these conditions? If so, your school is at the imitative level. You have the community activities but not the community action. You have only the scaffolding, within which a genuine use of the community for civic education is yet unbuilt.

- **Constructive level.** Are the students in your school learning at firsthand about the social and economic conditions of their com-

[1] *Learning the Ways of Democracy,* Chapter 9. Washington: National Education Association, 1940.

munity? Do they have opportunity and encouragement to do something about these conditions? Are they guided in their appraisal of community needs by applying accepted and valid standards of democracy? Does the community profit by the study and work of these young citizens? Do your community studies seek to penetrate beyond surface conditions to the deeper issues of cause and cure? Do your students themselves initiate, plan, and carry out many projects of value to their community? If so, you have a school at the constructive level. You are in the vanguard of a forward moving democracy. Your school is not likely to lack public support, because its relation to the public welfare will be visible on every hand.

Routine, imitative, constructive—on which of these levels does your school now relate itself to its community? Are you satisfied with your present level of performance? If not, what can you do about it?

What Do You Say Is a Teacher's Responsibility to His Community?

In its first Yearbook, the John Dewey Society identified five successive types or levels of insight into the relationship of teacher and community.[2] On which of these five levels do you think you now stand as an educational worker?

• **Commonplace level**—conform to the community. Live in the community, visit homes of pupils, go to church, respect community conventions, and the like.

• **School support level**—do community work for the school. Enlist parental and public support for the school's program, strive for increased financial aid, resist pressure-group attacks, and so on.

• **Community service level**—carry on service projects. Allow use of school buildings and equipment for community functions, participate in local clean-up campaigns, health drives, music weeks, housing projects, crime prevention, city beautification, etc.

• **Social process level**—work with progressive community groups. Discover the most basic, profound, far-reaching needs of the community, locate those genuinely progressive forces which are creatively seeking to meet those needs, and ally yourself with those groups to work cooperatively with them, even against reactionary opposition.

[2] *The Teacher and Society*, Chapter 9. New York: Appleton-Century, 1937.

• **Social integration level**—make community life itself educative. Strive to make the entire life of the community educative in the best and highest sense of that term. Recognize that schools alone can do little to improve youth behavior if their best efforts are constantly frustrated by inadequate, unwholesome, or even vicious community conditions of living. Work always to make the entire community consciously and deeply aware of its direct educational responsibility, and constantly more adept in meeting it.

Five successive levels! Which one do you and your school favor? And what holds you back from promoting in practice the ideal you accept in theory?

Which Curriculum Pattern Will You Follow?

Why do we maintain schools in a democracy? What a naive question! But is it, really? Hard thinking needs to be done upon it! Is it, fundamentally considered, because we wish to help our children:

• **Master subject matter**—grammar, geography, literature, algebra, history, and so on—making them proficient in largely verbalistic book knowledge, meanwhile keeping them out of mischief through an extensive program of "extracurricular" activities?
• **Follow individual interests**—bird flights, sunsets, the Incas, electronics, and the like—meanwhile giving them a good time, developing their personalities, and essentially sheltering them in a socially indifferent curriculum?
• **Attain competence in living**—as members and future founders of healthy families, efficient producers and consumers of economic goods and services, intelligently participating citizens in our democratic society, ethical builders of world civilization—through extensive and carefully guided personal experience with the persistent processes and problems of living during the second half of the critical twentieth century?

Why do we have schools? Better yet, why *should* we have schools? What is your real philosophy of modern education— is it basically book-centered, child-centered, or life-centered?

It is quite possible, of course, to make extensive use of community resources under any of these curriculum orientations, but the primary purposes sought and the community approaches utilized will differ considerably between them. You may, for example:

• **Retain the conventional subjects.** Then you will use community resources to illustrate, enrich, and vitalize the subject matter taught. In studying about the community you will utilize local documentary materials, audio-visual aids, resource people, interviews, field trips and school camping. But perhaps you have a program in which you . . .

• **Follow child interests** in previously unplanned sequence. Here you will doubtless utilize many community resources of varied types as stimulants to aesthetic, intellectual, and socializing pupil experiences and interests. In this approach you will develop community experiences chiefly as springboards to greater individual growth. To the six techniques listed above you will doubtless add local surveys and extended field studies. But if you are dissatisfied with both the subject-centered and the child-centered patterns, then you will surely want to . . .

• **Develop a core-curriculum** centering directly in the basic social processes and persisting life-problems. If this is your curriculum plan, you will go beyond community study and experience into community participation and service. Then you will add work experiences and community service projects to the eight learning techniques listed in the above sections.

Conventional subjects . . . activity program . . . core-curriculum . . . with which do you work, and through which would you like to organize educational experiences in your community? Just *why* do you answer as you do?

Owing to the fragmentary character of most community school programs, little real progress has yet been made in determining the scope and sequence, or even the basic nature, of the community school program. Although its curriculum is generally of the "core" variety, no two community schools are alike—as you will know if you are acquainted with such volumes as the Association for Supervision and Curriculum Development's *The Community School,* edited by Samuel Everett, and the Association's more recent report *The Modern Community School,* edited by Edward G. Olsen; Elsie Clapp's *Community Schools in Action* and *The Use of Resources in*

Education; the National Society for the Study of Education's 1953 Yearbook *The Community School;* and Olsen's *School and Community Programs.* Much more actual experimentation will have to be carried on before we can expect to reach any general agreement on basic operating principles for the community school program.

Yet it is true that recent experience and present thinking do now suggest that the life-centered community school of the future may be based upon a number of practical basic principles which are already discernible. Suppose we list several such principles as suggestions, remembering as we proceed that the term "principle" here means not some permanent, established, universally valid "truth," but only a reasonable hypothesis with which to experiment further. Throughout this summary, as in the entire volume, we take for granted a fundamentally *democratic* purpose and procedure. We had better not forget that education in Fascist Italy, in Nazi Germany, in totalitarian Japan, and in Communist Russia has all been definitely "life-centered"—each within its own, anti-democratic scheme of social values. Our conscious concern must ever be that of developing more functional school programs grounded firmly in the democratic faith and process.

1. Analyze the improvement-of-living aim into its functional elements. At least three such elements are apparent: *social understanding*—developing growing comprehension of our changing culture; *social motivation*—establishing incentives to democratic social improvement; and *social skills*—increasing personal competence in community participation and leadership. Such differentiation (even though it cannot actually be maintained in a functional learning situation) serves to forestall a prevalent belief that community experiences are primarily a device for stimulating intellectual understanding. Knowledge is needed, but without adequate motivation it is sterile. Both knowledge and motivation are futile, even dangerous, unless they are utilized and directed by democratic group skills and values.

2. Define the community as the service area of the school, but relate it directly and constantly with the larger areas of region, nation, world. Such definition eliminates the ever-present danger of fostering those provincial attitudes which sometimes arise when community studies and activities are confined to the immediate locality alone. Since the community is essentially a set of social relationships rather than a geographic area, we must today study the locality more intensively, and the world more extensively, than we have done in the past.

3. Recognize three levels of culture to be studied in every community. Whether the community under analysis is local or distant, contemporary or historic, we need to examine its three interrelated aspects: the *material culture*—geographic factors together with the things people have made or used; the *institutional culture*—the mass habits or customs of the people; and the *psychological culture*—the motivating beliefs of the people. Such recognition safeguards against the common practice of relating community study to the material culture alone, with consequent disregard for the institutional and especially the psychological level which ultimately shapes both of the others.

4. Stress the interrelationships between such factors as community setting, social statuses, social processes, and social problems. The community must be perceived in its wholeness as well as in its elements; in its virtues as in its vices. It is therefore well to concentrate upon setting, processes, and structure, rather than upon problems, until at least the senior high school level. Young children are intensely interested in the physical environment and in ways of living, but they do not become deeply concerned with larger social issues until later adolescence has brought both wider social interests and full intellectual maturity. Such concentration provides initial perspective upon normal social processes, and thereby avoids that "rotten-spot" preoccupation which often seems to result in cynicism rather than citizenship among high school students suddenly plunged into "social problems" courses.

5. Plan for sequential development of community experiences throughout each year of the school program. Such planning lessens the possibility of purely sporadic delvings into limited segments of community life, of repeating community activities unnecessarily, and of giving undue attention to superficial or transitory matters. Comprehensive planning enables each community experience to be functionally related with both prior and subsequent experiences, and thereby contributes to the child's developing sense of at-homeness in his world, to his improving techniques of getting vital information, and to his growing ability to generalize abstractly from concrete experiences.

6. Begin this sequence with consideration of material culture in the local community. Such beginning takes a proper account of the young child's dominant interests as well as of his natural difficulty in thinking abstractly about the institutional and psychological levels of human culture. Abstractions will remain mere verbalisms unless each new experience is made meaningful in terms of significant past experience.

7. Expand this initial study into other related dimensions. Move progressively into three always-related dimensions of community life: *space*—in other areas, geographically; *time*—in other communities and areas, historically; and *scope*—in institutional and psychological culture levels. Such expansion stimulates the child to think increasingly in terms of symbols as his developing ability to do so progressively permits.

8. Use all appropriate techniques for relating the school with the community. At different times, for particular purposes, under specific arrangements you will want to utilize many or most of the school-community interaction possibilities: *first-hand experiences* with reality—resource people, field trips, surveys, work experiences, service projects, school camping, school as social center, lay participation, coordination in the local community, and, as far as feasible, in the larger areas as well; *expressive activities* permitting creative re-enactment of community situations through drawing, painting, dramatizing, dancing, displaying, and so on; *audio-visual aids* in the study of communities remote in space or time or both; and *words written and spoken*—documentary materials and discussions to help with intensive analysis of the local community as well as in the study of other community areas through all three community levels. Such varied use of relevant approaches avoids the common imbalance of learning resulting from limited use of one or two techniques alone, and also emphasizes the fact that highly worthwhile learning does not always require direct community experience on the part of the learner.

9. Focus attention upon the needs, problems, and social contributions of young people. Such focusing stresses the organic relationship between each individual student's life and the operation of the social processes, thus stimulating a psychological identification of youth interests with adult concerns. Indeed it is true that problem-solving is central to the thinking process itself—and that often we evade the curriculum implications of that fact.

10. Direct personal loyalties toward our finest traditions, ethical ideals, and moral and spiritual values. Sometimes patriotism is limited to geographic territory, to political structure, or to some other segment of the material or institutional culture. The crying necessity is to expand provincial loyalties—political, social, economic, religious—into a broader and deeper devotion to genuine human welfare everywhere. Such direction of fundamental loyalties provides the only assurance of individual and national stability in our world of rapid material and institutional change.

Planning Together

Here, then, is your first vital question: *What do you really believe* about the desirable function of education in our democracy, and about the school's and the teacher's proper relationship with the supporting community? As you ponder this very real problem you will naturally be much interested in discovering what other schools most like your own have thought and done in somewhat similar communities—small elementary schools in rural regions of homogeneous population; large high schools in cities of mixed racial composition; liberal arts or teachers colleges serving industrial regions, and similar situations. But how can you find out what has been done elsewhere? There are at least four good sources of information you can use:

• **Personal visits** to other schools where worthwhile community resources programs are under way. This is obviously the best of all approaches, insofar as it is possible on a wide scale.

• **Resource people** from such schools, to discuss their programs and perhaps show pictures, display exhibits, demonstrate achievements, and the like.

• **Educational consultants** who have specialized in school-community programs and who can present a realistic overview of developments throughout the state and nation. Such consultants may be secured from university schools of education, from neighboring teachers' colleges, from state departments of public instruction, and from private planning and human relations organizations.

• **Professional literature** such as books, bulletins, magazine articles, courses of study, and units of work.

Now then: What do you actually think—as an individual, a class, a school faculty, or a lay citizens' group—about the kind and scope and extent of the community resources program you desire? Three suggestions that may help you determine what you really do think may be helpful at this point:

• **Get down on paper** a brief statement of your present ideas about the desirable interrelations between your school and your community. Be honest and frank. Think about the things you were taught in school, the methods your teachers used, the content and the ways you may be teaching others now, the pupils you really know and their vital life-needs today. Record both your *thinking* and your *practice* on the adjoining check list. Then ask yourself how satisfied you really are with your present school-community situation. You may be surprised if you are candid!

IS YOUR SCHOOL A COMMUNITY SCHOOL?
SHOULD IT BE A COMMUNITY SCHOOL?

This Check List Will Tell You Your Answer!

Here are seven characteristics of the community school. Beside each one are four numerals representing a range of practice (and thinking) from "nothing done" to "largely achieved." To contrast your school practice with your own thinking, put *circles* around numbers which most nearly indicate actual school practice, and *boxes* around numbers which most nearly reflect your own thinking of what should be.

COMMUNITY SCHOOL CHARACTERISTICS	PRACTICE AND THINKING IN SCHOOL X			
	Nothing Done	*A Little Accomplished*	*Well On Our Way*	*Largely Achieved*
1. Improves the quality of living here and now.	0	1	2	3
2. Uses the community as a laboratory for learning.	0	1	2	3
3. Makes the school plant a community center.	0	1	2	3
4. Organizes the core-curriculum around the processes and problems of living.	0	1	2	3
5. Includes lay people in school policy and program planning.	0	1	2	3
6. Leads in community co-ordination.	0	1	2	3
7. Practices and promotes democracy in all human relationships.	0	1	2	3

Scoring Directions: Add together the encircled figures to get the score for your school practice. Then add the boxed figures to get the score for your own thinking. Contrast the scores and consider the implications.

A score of 21 denotes a genuine community school.
A score of 14 shows excellent progress toward a community school.
A score of 7 indicates that a beginning has been made.
A score of less than 7 suggests a complacent traditional school.

• **Write out these statements anonymously** if you are a school staff, a class of prospective or in-service teachers, or a citizens' group. Turn the statements in to a small committee of your own choice for summarizing. Let that committee report your varied opinions to the entire group, identifying for you all the chief viewpoints, issues, agreements, and conflicts thus expressed.

• **Discuss these statements and their implications** in staff, class, or other group meetings. Exchange ideas, and criticize positions taken. Clarify both majority and minority opinion. Be sure that you discuss principles rather than personalities, and try to reach group concensus with full respect for minority views.

• Plan your program in terms of immediate and long-range needs and objectives, in view of your particular resources and obstacles, and in the light of over-all possibilities and probabilities realistically appraised. Remember that educational aims must be defined in behavior terms if they are to prove practical guides to school activities. In what respects, then, do you want your students (and yourself!) to be different people as a result of their guided participation in community life? More specifically, what do you want pupils to *know* about the community? How do you want pupils to *feel* and act in the community? What do you want pupils to be able to *do* about what they know and feel? Then the question becomes that of ways and means. This is where you build curricula, courses of study, units of work, vitalized lesson plans. This is where you really begin to develop community cooperation.

• Constantly evaluate your plans and program, being sure to determine with some validity how you are going to know how well you have done what you set out to do. There is need for continuous, careful appraisal of principles, plans, and procedures in the light of chosen orientation and specific objectives sought. Think always of how you can solve your problems in ways that are constructive, cooperative, democratic.

Zest for Living

These are some definite and practical procedures that are recommended to those who seek to develop genuine community schools. Perhaps they sound too ambitious, but that is more a matter of appearance than of fact. To be sure, the development of any new plan or program is always difficult, which should not be minimized. Re-thinking our philosophy, re-planning our policy, re-designing our efforts—difficult, yes, but what a fine challenge to interest and effort! What an opportunity to find new professional outlooks, new zest for living—and, above all, the great personal satisfaction of being on the right side of history, of doing our part now to build a better world through humane and democratic education.

Learning Activities

Discussion Topics

1. In the light of what we know about basic purposes in modern education, our present curriculum, the community, the pupils, and plant facilities and staff, what changes ought to be made in our public school program?
2. Although we often speak of "the community" as though it is an entity of public feeling, we know that it is actually made up of many "publics." How, then, should and can the school seek to meet "community needs"?
3. If a "traditional" school were to attempt to become a "community" school, what changes would need to be made in its fundamental aims? Curriculum? Teaching methods? Materials of instruction? Personnel relationships?

Group Activities

1. Using the chart on page 482, have each member report his own school experience. Then summarize the findings in graphic form. Note modes and extremes of experience.
2. Follow the steps in thinking suggested on page 470 and finally summarize majority and minority opinions of classmates concerning the community school philosophy and practice.
3. Examine some of the more forward-looking curriculums and courses of study, and evaluate them in terms of the seven community-school characteristics set forth in Chapter 1.

4. Poll the class to discover the school experiences of its members in terms of the three "levels of practice" reported on page 475. Discuss implications for future practice.

Individual Projects

1. Write out, with reasons, your answer to the question on page 475: "On which of these five levels do you think you now stand as an educational worker?"
2. What other basic principles can you add to those suggested in this chapter?
3. Outline in detail your personal plan for helping your school associates move toward the development of a school program which better meets real needs.

Learning Materials

Books which report successful programs can provide varied and tested suggestions for your own situation—providing that you use them as "leads" and not as blueprints. *The Modern Community School* (Appleton-Century-Crofts, 1953), edited by Edward G. Olsen, describes valid community school programs in rural, town and city areas and in terms of three operational levels: "Getting Started," "Going Forward," and "Taking Stock." An older publication, similar in purpose and challenge is *The Community School,* edited by Samuel Everett (Appleton-Century, 1938). This volume reports the philosophy, programs and principles of nine community schools in both rural and urban situations. Olsen's *School and Community Programs* includes over 150 concrete illustrations of community study and service projects in many fields and at all academic levels (Prentice-Hall, 1949). The National Society for the Study of Education's 1953 Yearbook, *The Community School,* was edited by Maurice Seay (University of Chicago Press) to report, analyze and evaluate research findings in this field. Detailed descriptions of numerous community school programs are provided by William K. McCharen's *Selected Community School Programs in the South* (George Peabody College for Teachers). Elsie R. Clapp's *The Use of Resources in Education* tells in vivid, personalized narrative what was done in two rural schools to develop the personal and community resources which children and their families use in daily living. *Education for All American Children* and *Education for All American Youth: A Further Look,* both by the Educational Policies Commission (National Education Association, 1948, 1952), describe in some detail the kinds of schools whose programs are oriented around the community concept.

The current professional periodicals are rich sources of contemporary reporting. An hour's browsing through recent issues of such journals as *Childhood Education, Clearing House, Education Digest, Educational*

Leadership, Journal of Educational Sociology, Nation's Schools, National Education Association Journal, School Executive, School Review and *Social Education* can be most rewarding. Selective utilization of current reporting is always evidence of true professional effort. But if you would pinpoint your scrutiny of the magazine literature, then check the *Education Index* under such headings as these:

Community and School	Community Life	Community Schools
Community Centers	Community Planning	Community Service
Community Councils	Community Resources	Teachers and Community

CHAPTER 19

Freedom to Learn

Ours is an era of stress and strife, of tension and upheaval, of political, economic, and social changes unparalled in history. Yet the Damoclean menace of our Nuclear Air Age is human, not technological. Security and freedom in our century are threatened, not by the forces of Nature, but simply by the results of man's failure to establish his human relations upon a stable, world-wide foundation of justice and peaceful cooperation.

In technology, the human race is in the jet-propelled Nuclear Air Age, but in human relationships—especially between people of different races, nations, and religions—its development lags far behind. As a human race we are both supermen and apemen; while technical inventions have brought our culture to a high peak of material advance, we can also utilize our technology to destroy civilization.

As Toynbee has observed:

"The heart of our difficulty is the difference in pace between the hare-swift movement of the scientific intellect, which can revolutionize our technology within the span of a single lifetime, and the tortoise-slow movement of the subconscious underbelly of the human psyche. . . . The inability of the subconscious to fly at the intellect's pace is apt to drive the subconscious, in blind panic, into an irrational, obstinate, anachronistic conservatism that may land us in disaster unless we can contrive to buy from Fate the time that

This chapter is by EDWARD G. OLSEN.

the subconscious psyche requires for accomplishing the slow and painful task of adapting itself to the inevitable human consequences of a revolutionary change of technological circumstances." [1]

There is the great challenge to democratic education in our time! Somehow we must inflame youth with a burning conviction that human relations is their great frontier; that the challenge and responsibility of their generation is to improve the quality of living, both for the individual and for the group. Around us all is the stark menace of "social lag"—the lag of human relations behind technical advance . . . of ethics behind machines . . . of world cooperation behind technology . . . of education behind science . . . of school programs behind human needs . . . of social lag!

The high stakes at issue in our world today are the minds and the hearts and the loyalties of men and women everywhere. Our historic democratic ideals, our republican traditions, our practice and promise of liberty are all driven into mortal combat with the organized forces of communism. Perhaps the supreme civic lesson of this fact is that human freedom is indivisible: that intellectual, artistic, religious, social, economic, and political freedoms are and must be inseparable if any of them are long to endure. Of course the necessities of civilized living require that we distinguish between liberty and license, between free speech and libel, between personal freedom and group security. But let's not forget that the great foe of democracy is totalitarianism, regardless of its form, guise or name. When the minds of some are enslaved by ignorance and prejudice, by fears and hatreds, by cynicism, indifference, and habits of tabloid thinking, then the freedom of all is surely in danger.

Perhaps never in modern times has there been so much general concern for moral and spiritual values as now—so much unrest, so deep-seated a feeling that unless we get our grip on basic values, all is lost. And it is precisely this "parched-ground hunger for certainty" that underlies and partly moti-

[1] Arnold J. Toynbee, "Men Must Choose." *The Atlantic Monthly* 191:27-30; January 1953. Used by permission of the author and *The Atlantic Monthly*.

vates current attacks upon our public schools and their programs.

Yet substantial "certainty" in the political-social-economic realm of life is not to be found in the past, however revered; it is something that must be built in the future, however hazardous and difficult that process. This means that no school can build a realistic program closely related to community processes and problems unless there is adequate freedom of thought and discussion, freedom of inquiry, freedom to depart from traditional teaching methods, freedom to deal frankly with controversial issues, and freedom to utilize the community as a laboratory for learning. Yet in most communities there are groups and individuals who will seriously interfere with these freedoms if they see any possibility of success in doing so. Every school has therefore the professional and civic responsibility of dealing with all issues and problems of community life which are of vital importance to the pupils at their maturity level, and of protecting its basic right to make fair-minded study of such problems without interference. All classroom teachers, as well as all administrators, are involved in this social obligation, since an attack upon any one curriculum area is essentially an attack upon the democratic educational process itself.

How Can We Preserve Freedom to Learn?

Realistically considered, academic freedom is an earned privilege rather than an automatic right. Ideally, wishfully, desirably we think of freedom to learn and to teach as a democratic *right* to which we are entitled regardless of power politics and pressure group influence. But actually, it is a right which exists by sufferance.

Those who are concerned about the prevalent widespread attacks on freedom to learn would do well to analyze this vital distinction in terms of their personal situations in their own communities.[2] Perchance they will then realize that the

[2] The suggestions which follow are adapted from the author's "Preserving Academic Freedom" in the *National Education Association Journal* 26:3-4; January 1937.

degree of academic freedom permitted the teacher is usually proportional to a complex of three factors: (1) The extent to which the teacher's expressed convictions upon controversial issues agree with those of the community's dominant groups; (2) the actual defensive power of the professional organizations with which the teacher is affiliated; and (3) the amount of personal respect which the teacher has earned for himself in his community.

Every school administrator knows that the person who has made himself generally respected as a well-informed, judicially-minded, and courteously considerate person has freedom to express opinions and engage in activities which would draw instant fire upon the heads of less respected people. If a community likes a teacher *as a person* it tends to be tolerant of his ideas. And if we assent to the proposition that the socially sensitive and professionally competent teacher has a moral obligation to keep his job, then it becomes clear that he has the obligation to make himself personally liked in his community. Here are some ways to work at that.

Know Your Own Prejudices

All one's thinking is inevitably colored by his emotional conditioning. It is therefore your first obligation to dig out and to understand your own underlying "frame of reference" —your personal complex of attitudes and prejudices which has developed in reaction to past experiences and which now strongly influences or even dominates your thinking. Unless the teacher of controversial subject matter is careful to recognize and then honestly analyze his own prejudgments and rationalizations he can hardly expect to avoid being tripped up by them. Let him constantly inquire: Do I show an air of superiority as psychological compensation for felt feelings of inferiority? Do I project my personal failures in life upon society and blame it for all my misfortunes? Do I unconsciously seek to find some personal devil upon whom to fix all responsibility for my own fears and misfortunes—the politicians, the unions, the internationalists, the corporations, the "eggheads," and the like? Do I naively indoctrinate my own particular social values in the guise of legitimate "education" while I strenuously oppose differing viewpoints as insidious "propaganda"?

Be Objective at All Times

Emotional maturity is almost a *sine qua non* of academic freedom. We all need to cultivate habits of emotional stability which will permit us to discuss and to analyze nationalism or religious traditions with the same lack of emotion with which we speak of tomorrow's weather. This does not mean that we must assert no emphases or possess no deep personal convictions, but simply that we must give all sides a fair hearing. The teacher who wants to win and preserve his privileges of uncensored instruction must remain calm in his approach, balanced in his judgments, sincere in motive, and judicious in treatment of his subject. He should surely develop a wholesome sense of personal responsibility for improving and reconstructing the civilization of which he is a part, but above all he must retain his full intellectual and professional integrity, having sold out his mind to no man and no party.

Analyze Your Community

Before beginning to teach in a new community, the astute teacher will survey that community in terms of its dominant interests and its present and possible tensions. He will discover so far as he can what the general spirit and the popular attitudes of that community seem to be, who its leading citizens and powerful figures are, what its industries are and by whom they are owned, who the schoolboard members are and what their occupations and prejudices may be, who are the liberal ministers and what is the extent of their influence, what causes of friction between teachers and town have arisen in the past, and so on. He will endeavor, in short, to take account of all factors which have or might have a bearing upon his own position as teacher in that community. This is certainly not to suggest that he ought to compromise his convictions upon fundamental issues, but only that by thus analyzing the local situation in advance he is better able to foresee and so to avoid small indiscretions which may offend community sensibilities and so become points of irritation against him.

Participate in Community Activities

Remember always that people tend to give or to withhold their allegiance because of emotional sympathies, and not after a rational balancing of the facts. Popular acceptance or rejection of your ideas will depend far more upon the total impression which you make in the community than it will upon your sayings alone, however wise they may be. Studies have shown that there is a high correlation between the average man's *feeling-tone* and his personal *judgment*. It is therefore essential that the teacher deliberately set out to build up "status" for himself by becoming an integral part of the community as quickly as possible. Most people have the "outside agitator" complex, and will quickly resent advice or criticism, no matter how friendly and valid, which comes from someone who is not yet "accepted." If he is wise, the teacher will therefore enter fully into community activities and will make whatever personal contributions to the community life his own talents and time permit. He will be constructive in all his suggestions, and will emphasize always the necessity of preserving the American traditions of democratic government, full civil liberties, and equal opportunity for all.

Know Your Facts

The wise person will never express an opinion upon controversial issues unless he is prepared to substantiate his statements with chapter and verse from recognized sources. Unless he is sure of his facts and is able to name and defend his sources of information upon demand, he will inevitably lose prestige when challenged, and suspicion of exaggeration or even of fabrication will fall upon him. The effective educator will therefore remember that facts are both shield and sword, and will arm himself accordingly. He will discriminate carefully between sources of information, and will be especially critical of statements which tend to substantiate his own point of view.

Recognize Stereotyped Language

Walter Lippmann's classic analysis of the "stereotype" and its role in blocking the thought-process deserves careful study by every teacher. Lippmann pointed out that the use of such words or phrases as "agitator," "Harvard man," "international banker," "100 per cent American," "bureaucracy," "regimentation," "drive the communists out of Washington," and the like arouse violent emotional reactions in the hearer and thereby effectively block further critical reasoning in that area of discussion. Such emotionalized slogans are the natural weapons of the demagog, but they will be carefully avoided by the educator who wants to cultivate in his students habits of thorough-going appraisal. This does not mean that he may not discuss the *concepts* involved, for that he must do if he is to be an effective teacher. It simply suggests that "almost anything can be said on any subject on any occasion if appropriate language is chosen," as Charles A. Beard once put it

Expose Fallacies; Don't Suppress Them

Well-informed educators are keenly aware of the extent to which many people attempt to distort or to suppress their opponents' opinions, statements, and viewpoints. The teacher, however, has the clear obligation to present all sides of controversial issues to his classes, and to assure each side of a fair hearing. Thus his students will gain invaluable practice in learning to challenge constructively all dogmatic statements whatever their source of origin, and to accept no opinion except upon the basis of the best evidence available.

Support Your Professional Organizations

Let the individual teacher become ever so discreet in his community relationships; let him consciously build up whatever personal status he can achieve—and he may still be easy prey for any determined attack. But let him ally himself with those professional organizations which are already struggling against widespread teacher intimidation, and he will find his own chances for intellectual freedom enormously increased thereby. For true strength lies only in unity, and in the long run it is united strength which can protect the individual teacher from the enemies of realistic education.

Professional measures such as these can do much to secure and increase freedom to learn and to teach. Yet there may still be times when the teacher must take a resolute stand against unwarranted interference from pressure groups. At such times, he will be far better equipped to give battle if he has also developed an enduring faith in those freedoms which underly our whole system of democracy and public education—freedom of thought and of speech, freedom to learn and to teach the truth, freedom to attack undemocratic policies and practices, freedom to ally one's self with any group supporting democratic purposes. Even then, of course, personal sacrifices may sometimes be demanded if principles like these are persistently upheld. Yet sacrifices to preserve intellectual integrity are often individually, and always socially, preferable to acquiescent acceptance of intellectual tyranny. Martyrdom may enlighten a people as slavery never can.

For democracy is more than a system of government, necessary as democratic government is to human liberty. Democracy is more than a pattern of ways for group living, essential as democratic relationships are to individual dignity and opportunity. Democracy is above all else a dynamic social faith in the ability of enlightened people to manage their own affairs with justice and intelligence. Self-government and equality of opportunity are but practical expressions of this heroic faith bred in the struggles of many centuries.

Hallmarks of Democracy

Respect for the worth of the individual person regardless of race, nationality, religion or social status . . . belief that the human mind can be trusted if it is free . . . confidence in the methods of cooperation, tolerance and peace . . . individual and group practice of these convictions . . . these are among the hallmarks of democracy today. And that is why democracy must depend for its very existence upon enlightened education of all people everywhere—the very kind of education that the *community school* is best equipped to provide and produce.

Learning Activities

Socio-drama

The editor of your local newspaper has been approached by a representative of a national group organized to spread mistrust of modern public education. He has shown the editor some of his literature, speaks guardedly of having powerful local support for these views, and hints at advertising losses unless the paper publishes a series of prepared items "exposing" the schools. The editor listens carefully, then invites him back for a later appointment. At that time, the editor confronts the agitator with the superintendent of schools, the president of the board of education, the chairman of the parent-teacher council, the secretary of the chamber of commerce, and the president of the council of churches. Now dramatize the ensuing discussion and its possible results.

Discussion Topics

1. What kinds of pressures operate on public schools in your community? On non-public schools? Can the school ever be free from pressures? Should it be?
2. Should students study public problems or issues which are current matters of controversy in the community?
3. What can school people actually do to safeguard freedom to learn?
4. How can they secure lay help?

Group Activities

1. Have a committee read about attacks on public schools as reported in the literature, then sketch a number of such cases for the class and lead group discussion of their probable causes, apparent effects, and basic significance.
2. Secure from the National Education Association its kit of materials dealing with attacks on the schools and what to do about them. Arrange items as a display, and give committee reports on each item in the kit.
3. Study the effect of pressure groups on textbooks, in your own areas as well as nationally.
4. Through committees review the history of previous periods of attack on public schools, especially during the 1930's. Compare the extent, nature, and significance of those times with today.

Individual Projects

1. Illustrate the concept of "social lag" through the medium of an original cartoon, a poem, a chart, or a scrapbook of clippings annotated with your comments.
2. Write to the executive secretary of your state teachers' association for a summary of any of your state's laws which bear upon freedom to learn and to teach.
3. Find out if any serious tensions over educational policies are present in your community now. Report to the class their history, nature, and current status, with your own considered recommendations for resolving them.
4. In not more than three sentences for each, state (a) your position on the central problem explained in this chapter, (b) the major opposition positions you reject, (c) the educational significance of your own view, and (d) your real reasons for the position you take.

Learning Materials

Public relations' problems and approaches generally are discussed in a number of recent volumes. The American Association of School Administrators' 1950 Yearbook, *Public Relations for America's Schools*, explores the broad field, indicates essential landmarks, and suggests specific procedures while stressing purposes, principles, relationships, and values. The NEA's Association for Supervision and Curriculum Development, in its *Building Public Confidence in Our Schools*, gives timely illustrations of how schools work with community groups to improve instructional programs. The NEA's Department of Elementary School

Principals devoted its 1949 Yearbook to *The Public and the Elementary School,* an analysis of the public relations program of the school in terms of the principal, the curriculum, the children, the teachers, the parents, community agencies, the public, and the administration. Two pamphlets of special interest are *It Starts in the Classroom,* published by the National School Public Relations Association (NEA, 1951) and *Public Relations for Rural and Village Teachers,* issued by the United States Office of Education (1946). Wm. A. Yeager's *School-Community Relations* (Dryden, 1951) is an encyclopedic treatment with chapters on such general topics as pupils, finance, and the board of education as well as on specific problems, such as concepts of school-community relations and the community school. George H. Holmes' *Public Relations for Teacher Education* (American Association of Colleges of Teacher Education, 1950) is intended to help colleges develop better programs of public relations. Benjamin Fine's *Educational Publicity* (Harper, 1951) stresses public relations policies and procedures, especially through the newspaper. *Social Interpretation* by Arthur B. Moehlman (Appleton-Century, 1938) is an older, comprehensive treatment of the principles and practices of community and school interpretation. Dorman G. Stout's *Teacher and Community* (World Book, 1941) emphasizes the techniques of leadership whereby teachers may promote better understanding and cooperation between school and community. A monumental general volume of considerable value to educators is Philip Lesly's *Public Relations Handbook* (Prentice-Hall, 1950), 900 pages long and illustrated.

The problem of educational freedom today is analyzed in the John Dewey Society's yearbook *Educational Freedom in an Age of Anxiety* (Harper, 1953) which discusses our critical age in the light of general social anxiety, the meaning and place of freedom, power, and the law, the need for shared experience, secular and religious education, community pressures, and other factors. Waves of attacks on the public schools and ways to overcome them are described by 30 leaders in American education, government, and community life in *Freedom and Public Education,* edited by Ernest O. Melby and Morton Puner (Harper, 1953). Melby's pamphlet *American Education Under Fire* (Anti-Defamation League of B'nai B'rith, 1951) describes the "phony Three-R fight" on the schools, asserts that good education is dynamic and spiritual in nature, answers the typical charges made, and sketches suggestions. *This Happened in Pasadena* is David Hulburd's documented account of the chain of events through which a determined minority forced the superintendent of schools to resign because they objected to his policies (Macmillan, 1951). The distinguished news broadcaster, Elmer Davis, presents in *But We Were Born Free* (Bobbs-Merrill, 1954) a challenging collection of essays on man and intellectual freedom.

Recent and current magazines should be scanned for further background on this whole problem of freedom to learn and to teach. Among them you might well look at these:

"The Nation Reaches a Verdict in the Case of the People vs. Today's Schools," Otis A. Brosby. Reports a public-opinion study of 97,000 people in 371 cities in over a third of the 48 states. Some 70% felt children today read as well as the previous generation, 77% favored general education in contrast to specific vocational instruction, only 16% objected to sex education in the elementary school, nearly all wanted "an understanding of religion" taught. *Nation's Schools* 47:34-37; January 1951.

"The Attack on Modern Education," Louis Kaplan. It is a mistake to assume that an informed public is a supporting public. We must also develop effective lay participation in policy-making. *Phi Delta Kappen* 32:223-226; January 1951; *Education Digest* 16:1-3; March 1951.

"Right-Wing 'Front' Organizations: They Sow Distrust," Robert A. Skaife. Lists eight organizations now attacking the schools, and illustrates the nature of their efforts. *Nation's Schools* 47:27-30; January 1951: *Education Digest* 16:1-4; April 1951.

"Academic Freedom," Willard B. Spalding. Explores problems involved in the interrelation of academic with other freedoms, and frankly faces the dilemma confronting those who seek to preserve freedom of inquiry in an age characterized by conflicts between great value-systems. *Progressive Education* 28:111-117; February 1951.

"What Can School Board Members Do to Answer Criticisms of Public Education?" Irving R. Melbo. Outlines sources of criticisms, how to receive criticisms, basic board responsibility, techniques for channeling and treating criticisms. *American School Board Journal* 122:27-28 ff; May 1951.

"They Want Tailored Schools," Robert A. Skaife. Documents some current attacks on school textbooks and curricula. *Nations Schools* 47:35-37; May 1951.

"Who's Trying to Ruin Our Schools," Arthur Morse. A documented exposé of organizations and individuals who attack the schools. *McCall's Magazine*, September 1951.

"What Are They Calling You Today?", Richard B. Kennan. Specific suggestions for meeting criticism of and attacks on the schools. *Childhood Education* 28:53-57; October 1951.

"Symposium on Textbooks." Presents the views of a publisher, two authors, a school superintendent, a parent and two outspoken critics of present-day textbooks. *Saturday Review,* April 19, 1952.

"Why Scapegoat the Schools?", Jean D. Grambs and Franklin Patterson. A sociological analysis of the current attacks on public education. *School Executive* 71:48-50; August 1952.

"The Battle of the Books," John H. Haefner. Offers calm, constructive, courageous suggestions for meeting attacks on textbooks. *National Education Association Journal* 42:227-228; April 1953.

"Freedom of the Mind," Agnes E. Meyer. Calls for a powerful counter-offensive against forces that undermine freedom to learn. *National Education Association Journal* 42:207-210; April 1953; *Education Digest* 18:1-5; April 1953.

"What Is Behind the Attacks on Education?", Ernest O. Melby. Vicious criticisms of public education share three striking characteristics: anti-intellectualism, isolationism, and character assassination. *Educational Leadership* 10:451-453; April 1953.

"How Much Academic Freedom?", Howard Mumford Jones; "What Is Academic Freedom?", Joseph Alsop; "The Present Danger, a report from the University Presidents." Three incisive articles examining many facets of the problem on the college and university level. *The Atlantic,* June 1953, pp. 36-46.

How to safeguard and strengthen our schools in the public eye is explored in *Forces Affecting American Education,* the 1953 Yearbook of the ASCD, which analyzes the cultural currents, pressure groups, and communication agencies influencing our society, and in the light of these factors points up the educator's responsibilities. *New Challenges to Our Schools,* edited by S. F. Cary (Wilson, 1953), is a compilation of pro and con opinion in such fields as school costs, civic education, "frills or fundamentals," and public versus private schools. *What People Think About Their Schools* by Harold C. Hand (World Book, 1948) describes a workable procedure for gaining reliable information on teacher, parent, and pupil opinion on any school matter. Paul R. Mort and W. S. Vincent's *A Look at Our Schools* (Jacques Cattell Press, 1946) helps parents and others understand recent changes in school programs and the reasons therefore, including such items as the three R's, character and discipline, and what really makes a good school. So also does H. M. Lafferty's *Sense and Nonsense in Education* (Macmillan, 1947), a refreshing and penetrating discussion. *How Good Is Your School?* by Wilbur A. Yauch (Harper, 1951) should be examined again in this connection. Olsen's *School and Community Programs* devotes Chapter 11 to eight dynamic case studies of different public relations techniques and approaches. In *The American School Superintendency* (1952), the American Association of School Administrators offers in Chapter 6 many concrete suggestions for developing a philosophy of school-community relations, helping school-board and staff to work with the community, organizing a diversified program, informing the community, rendering community services, developing school-community cooperation in planning, and in being a coordinator of group effort. See also the Association's 1950 Yearbook, *Public Relations for America's Schools,* for extensive treatment of this whole field. *The School Administrator and Subversive Activities* by E. Edmund Reutter, Jr., discusses loyalty oaths, communism, academic freedom, and so on, and offers constructive proposals (Bureau of Publications, Teachers College, Columbia University, 1951).

As for magazine articles, you might well examine several of these:

"Nothing too Good for the Schoolhouse," Frances B. Chase. First-prize winner in a national essay contest "How to Gain Public Support for Schools." *Nation's Schools* 37:22-24: February 1946.

"Make Them Like It and They'll Support It," Earl C. Kelley. Second-prize winner in a national essay contest "How to Gain Public Support for Schools." *Nation's Schools* 37:22-24; March 1946.

"Learning How the Schools Stand with Local Groups," O. H. Heckathorne. Educators who seek more community support for school programs would do well to find out which local groups are friends, which are indifferent, and which are potential allies. A questionnaire which secured such information in a Pennsylvania school is here explained. *Clearing House* 20:482-485; April 1946.

"Public Relations—Modern Design," Worth McClure. Unless the superintendent assumes his rightful place as a leader of community planning, all the usual school publicity devices will be virtually worthless. *Education* 66:614-617; June 1946.

"Public Relations in a School System," Howard W. Hightower. Points out real significance of public relations and the role of the principal therein; lists 20 ways of knowing the community and suggests 17 ways of informing the public about the school. *Educational Administration and Supervision* 32:44-9-457; November 1946.

"Small Community's Program of Public Relations," J. W. Edgar. Asserts that special problems and situations in the small community make its school public relations a completely different program from that in larger communities. Five basic principles of good public relations are explained. *School Executive* 66:67-68; March 1947.

"Planning School Public Relations." Series of articles on planning, organizing, and operating successful public relations programs. Topics treated include public understanding of school objectives and potentialities, the annual report and public opinion poll, laymen as resource visitors and consultants, current publicity, large and small community problems. *School Executive* 66:55-68; March 1947.

"We Make the High School Annual Interpret Our School," M. Helen Connor. How one school photographed its complete curricular and extra-curricular program, wrote non-technical captions for each picture, and thus presented a comprehensive portrayal of itself to its community. *Nation's Schools* 40:30-32; October 1947.

"Freeways to Friendships," Harry A. Fosdick. Caveman Gigg-nu, the first public-relations expert, lays down some simple principles for school public-relations committees. *National Education Association Journal* 38:582-583; November 1949.

"What U. S. Thinks about Its Schools." Summarizes the findings of Elmo Roper on attitudes of Americans toward many aspects of the schools. *Life Magazine* 29:11; October 16, 1950; *Education Digest* 16:40-42; December 1950.

"Community Participation in Building Educational Programs," Ernest O. Melby. Analyzes the crisis in education as but a facet of the crisis in our common life, and challenges educators to develop a great democratic faith as the only basis for creative education, and even for the preservation of freedom itself. *North Central Association Quarterly* 27:267-272; January 1953.

as an end in itself. It is clear also that child interests and self-expressions are splendid educational springboards to be used as such, but that they must never be mistaken for educational goals in themselves. Today we know that *practical school methods* must be evolved out of the psychological study of child nature—but we are also aware that *valid school purposes* can be discovered only through sociological analysis of culture patterns, as judged in terms of their demands upon the individual and in the light of the highest ethical values we know.

In a sharp break with the academic orientation of previous pronouncements on school aims, the famous "Seven Cardinal Principles" were enunciated to American schoolmen in 1918 by the Commission on the Reorganization of Secondary Education of the National Education Association. The essential purpose of public education, said this statement in effect, is to help induct the young into the ongoing life of society, to help them master the tools and develop the insights and abilities necessary in individual and group living. Schools do not exist to teach subject matter as such. They are (or should be) designed for a direct attack upon the problem of learning to live successfully, wholesomely, creatively. Although the Seven Cardinal Principles were initially suggested as guidelines to the reorganization of secondary education, they were soon generalized as effective statements of the chief life areas in which all persons must become as competent as possible:

1. Health
2. Command of fundamental processes
3. Worthy home membership
4. Vocational efficiency
5. Civic participation
6. Worthy use of leisure
7. Ethical character

The emphasis is upon individual development through acquisition of more useful knowledge.

By the early 1930's it was evident that the Seven Aims left much to be desired. America and most of the world had experienced a business depression unparalleled in depth and duration. "Rugged individualism" as a social philosophy was giving

way to a rising popular demand for economic security and
equality of opportunity. If the schools were to meet the new
needs of the new times, they would have to broaden their
basic orientation. Social welfare as well as individual development (the two being always inextricable, whether recognized
as such or not) would have to become part of our guiding
star. Accordingly, in 1934, a committee of the National Education Association listed ten desirable "Social-Economic Goals
of America" which, by implication, would also be considered
purposes of school education:

1.	Hereditary strength	*Now concern shifted*
2.	Physical security	*to the fundamental*
3.	Participation in an evolving culture	*life needs of people*
4.	An active, flexible personality	*growing up in a*
5.	Suitable occupations	*rapidly changing*
6.	Economic security	*culture which some-*
7.	Mental security	*times seemed to*
8.	Equality of opportunity	*threaten personal*
9.	Freedom	*security.*
10.	Fair play	

This "Ten Goals" concept of the individual as always living
in and being influenced by his society was a milestone in the
development of educational aims. Yet it was obviously dated
too soon by passing events to serve as a lasting guide toward
the future. Greatly needed was a more enduring and inherently
authoritative presentation of basic aims.

The Educational Policies Commission of the National Education Association and the American Association of School
Administrators presented such a statement in 1938 in its *Purposes of Education in American Democracy*. Here is described
"what we think the schools of the United States ought to try
to accomplish," and "some of the things we think need to be
done if these purposes are to be realized." The adjoining page
lists the four-fold grouping of purposes which the Commission
spelled out of its conviction that "the democratic way of life
establishes the purpose of American education. And the demo-

THE PURPOSES OF EDUCATION IN AMERICAN DEMOCRACY

SELF-REALIZATION

The educated person has an appetite for learning . . can speak the mother tongue clearly . . . read efficiently . . . write effectively . . . solve problems of counting and calculating . . . is skilled in listening and observing . . . understands the basic facts concerning health and disease . . . protects his own health and that of his dependents . . . works to improve the health of the community . . . is participant and spectator in many sports and other pastimes . . . has mental resources for the use of leisure . . . appreciates beauty . . . gives responsible direction to his own life.

ECONOMIC EFFICIENCY

The educated producer knows the satisfaction of good workmanship . . . understands the requirements and opportunities of various jobs . . . has *selected* his occupation . . . succeeds in his chosen vocation . . . maintains and improves his efficiency . . . appreciates the social value of his work. The educated consumer plans the economics of his own life . . . develops standards for guiding his expenditures . . . is an informed and skillful buyer . . . takes appropriate measures to safeguard his interests.

HUMAN RELATIONSHIP

The educated person puts human relationships first . . . enjoys a rich, sincere, and varied social life . . . can work and play with others . . . observes the amenities of social behavior . . . appreciates the family as a social institution . . . conserves family ideas . . . is skilled in home-making . . . maintains democratic family relationships.

CIVIC RESPONSIBILITY

The educated citizen is sensitive to the disparities of human circumstance . . . acts to correct unsatisfactory conditions . . . seeks to understand social structures and social processes . . . has defenses against propaganda . . . respects honest differences of opinion . . . has a regard for the nation's resources . . . measures scientific advance by its contribution to the general welfare . . . is a cooperating member of the world community . . . respects the law . . . is economically literate . . . accepts his civic duties . . . acts upon an unswerving loyalty to democratic ideals.

THE IMPERATIVE NEEDS OF ALL AMERICAN YOUTH

1. All youth need to develop saleable skills and those understandings and attitudes that make the worker an intelligent and productive participant in economic life. To this end, most youth need supervised work experience as well as education in the skills and knowledge of their occupations.

2. All youth need to develop and maintain good health and physical fitness.

3. All youth need to understand the rights and duties of the citizens of a democratic society, and to be diligent and competent in the performance of their duties as members of the community and citizens of the state and nation.

4. All youth need to understand the significance of the family for the individual and society and the conditions conducive to the successful family life.

5. All youth need to know how to purchase and use goods and services intelligently, understanding both the values received by the consumer and the economic consequences of their act.

6. All youth need to understand the methods of science, the influence of science on human life, and the main scientific facts concerning the nature of the world and men.

7. All youth need to be able to use their leisure time well, and to budget it wisely, balancing activities that yield satisfactions to the individual with those that are socially useful.

8. All youth need opportunities to develop their capacities to appreciate the beauty in literature, art, music, and nature.

9. All youth need to develop respect for other persons, to grow in their insight into ethical values and principles, and to be able to live and work cooperatively with others.

10. All youth need to grow in their ability to think rationally, to express their thoughts clearly, and to read and listen with understanding.

cratic way is being sharply and sometimes successfully challenged at home and abroad. These hard facts make the achievement of democracy through education the most urgent and the most intensely practical problem facing our profession."

Nearly a decade later, the National Association of Secondary-School Principals, an NEA department, summarized the basic life needs of young people today as the "Imperative Needs of Youth" which the curriculum and the entire educational program of the secondary school should be designed to meet adequately.

Highly significant is the fact that both these latter statements encompass the wide range of basic life needs, and that both present those needs as educational purposes expressed in terms of individual behavior in a democratic society. Improving the actual quality of living is generally now conceived to be the fundamental goal of American school education—so far as formal, widely accepted statements of aims go, at least.

Thus has the historic struggle for realism in education found widespread philosophic acceptance in our time. Now it is generally agreed [3] that the primary function of education is to transmit, clarify, create, interpret, and evaluate experience. This requires that our schools at all levels find their guiding purposes in the enduring life-needs of people within their own communities—communities that are never abstracted from their regional, national, and world-wide relationships. If education is to be realistic, it must be closely articulated with the problems and resources of modern life.

What Milestones Mark the Road?

Are school leaders actually promoting and developing life-centered education? Indeed they are, many of them. Across the nation and through the years of this twentieth century our professional practice has been coming ever closer to our newer thinking. Suppose we glance at some evidences of this major trend toward closer integration of school and community in American life during the past two generations. The major direction of developments is indeed clear.

[3] Except by neo-scholastics, such as Mortimer J. Adler, Arthur E. Bestor, Mark Van Doren, Stringfellow Barr, Scott Buchanan, and Robert M. Hutchins, all of whom are oriented chiefly in terms of university and adult education.

1897 . . . National Congress of Parents and Teachers Founded

Beginning as the National Congress of Mothers, the P.T.A. soon involved in addition both fathers and teachers in its organization and took on the purposes and program familiar today in most American communities. Through the years its purposes have remained these:

● To promote the welfare of children and youth in home, school, church, and community.
● To raise the standards of home life.
● To secure adequate laws for the care and protection of children and youth.
● To bring into closer relation the home and the school so that parents and teachers may cooperate intelligently in the training of the child.
● To develop between educators and the general public such united efforts as will secure for every child the highest advantages in physical, mental, social, and spiritual education.

From its beginning, the National Congress has been strictly educational, non-commercial, non-sectarian, and non-partisan in program and activities.

1899 . . . School and Society Published

John Dewey's *School and Society* was the first book to stress the social responsibility of the school to improve the community as well as to educate the child. He began by saying that "we are apt to look at the school from an individualistic standpoint, as something between teacher and pupil, or between teacher and parent. That which interests us most is naturally the progress made by the individual child of our acquaintance, his normal physical development, his advance in ability to read, write, and figure, his growth in the knowledge of geography and history, improvement in manners, habits of promptness, order and industry—it is from such standards as these that we judge the work of the school. And rightly so. Yet the range of the outlook needs to be enlarged. What the best and wisest parent wants for his own child, that must the community want for all its children. Any other ideal for our schools is narrow and unlovely; acted upon, it destroys our democracy."

1911 . . . First Professional Yearbook Devoted to School-Community Relations

The National Society for the Study of Education published *The City School as a Community Center,* and *The Rural School as a Community Center.* These slender volumes presented accounts of adult lectures in school buildings, vacation use of school playgrounds, evening use of school facilities for recreation, home and school associations, and extension courses. The yearbook concluded that "the secret of success of the work described seems to have been in bringing the school into touch with the community at as many points as possible, and by having the school relate itself to some form of helpful work that may be appreciated by the community.[4]

1913 . . . First Book on Community Resources and Education

Joseph K. Hart's *Eductional Resources of Village and Rural Communities*[5] is still most timely in its conception of the community as the true educational influence: "Within the community there is work that educates and provides for life; within the community are the roots of the cosmopolitanism that marks the truly educated man; within the community there is room for a noble and dignified culture and leisure for all. Let us become aware of our community resources, physical, social, moral. Let us recognize the part they play and will always play in the actual education of our boys and girls. Let us consciously extend their powers within legitimate bounds until our modern education within the community shall be, as completely as possible, natural, immediate, and free. Let us

[4] National Society for the Study of Education, Tenth Yearbook, 1911, Part II, p. 66.
[5] New York: The Macmillan Co., 1913.

organize our socially supplementary institution—the school—until it shall adequately reinforce the work of education where it is weak and supply it where it is wanting. So, and only so, will the child become really educated, the community find education genuine, practical, thorough, and vitally moral, and the school become in our times what it was originally intended to be—the social instrument for doing those things of an educational nature which are not already being done more effectively by the primitive and unconscious influences of the community's common life." In later years, Hart produced other notable volumes, such as *The Discovery of Intelligence* (1924), *A Social Interpretation of Education* (1929), and *Education in the Humane Community* (1951), all of which established him as the father of the community school concept in the United States.

1923 . . . Project Curriculum in Community Study

In his book, *An Experiment with a Project Curriculum,* Ellsworth Collings told how he organized the life of a rural school around the problems of the community, and demonstrated in the process that a project curriculum was more effective than the traditional subject-centered pattern of learning, even for the so-called fundamentals.[6] In addition, it enriched the living of the community as well as of the pupils by relating the local community to wider affairs. This experiment did much to stimulate professional interest in further experimentation with curriculum patterns centering in community needs.

1927 . . . First State Education Department Monograph on Field Trips

Published in the centennial year of Pestalozzi's death, the foreword to Pennsylvania's *Visual Education and the School Journey* stated that "just as Pestalozzi enriched teaching and facilitated learning through practical methods, so can the

---

[6] New York: The Macmillan Co., 1923.

teachers of Pennsylvania make their work more effective by bringing pupils into direct contact with objects and phenomena about which they wish to learn, and by directing them into situations where they can see, handle, and meditate upon the things with which their study is concerned. School Journeys make available a wealth of material that can be used to visualize and vitalize instruction." This influential 95-page bulletin emphasized the role of sensory aids in the learning process, then explained, illustrated, and urged the technique of the field trip as a major way of making school education meaningful.

1931 . . . Virginia's Curriculum Program

The first attempt to build a comprehensive, sequential core-curriculum on a statewide basis was the Virginia Curriculum Program, begun in 1931. The "core" was a series of basic themes or topics, around each of which was organized much of the school program in that particular year:

Grade	Theme for the Year
1	Home and School Life
2	Community Life
3	Adaptation of Life to Environmental Forces of Nature
4	Adaptation of Life to Advancing Physical Frontiers
5	Effects of Inventions and Discoveries upon Our Living
6	Effects of Machine Production upon Our Living
7	Social Provision for Cooperative Living
8	Adaptation of Our Living through Nature, Social and Mechanical Inventions, and Discoveries
9	Agrarianism and Industrialism and Their Effects upon Our Living
10	Effects of Changing Culture and Changing Social Institutions upon Our Living
11	Effects of a Continuously Planning Social Order upon Our Living

This pioneering effort soon influenced other states, notably Georgia, Mississippi, and Kansas, to develop similar core-curricula. These latter programs improved upon Virginia's by centering their major themes more directly around the fundamental social processes. Georgia, for example, called these processes the "persistent problems, or basic aspects of living," and urged that all seven life-problems identified as such be studied in every grade from pre-school through adult education: (1) Maintaining physical, mental, and emotional health, (2) Earning a living, (3) Performing the responsibilities of citizenship, (4) Utilizing and controlling the natural environment for individual and social needs, (5) Receiving and transmitting ideas, and transporting persons and commodities, (6) Expressing aesthetic and spiritual impulses, (7) Utilizing education as a means of acquiring and transmitting the social heritage, and as an agency for conserving and improving human and material resources.

1932 . . . First Yearbook Devoted to School-Community Administrative Contacts

Issued by the Department of Elementary School Principals of the National Education Association, *The Principal and His Community* treated such topics as the principal's community relationships, findings of a national survey of elementary schools, "outside contacts," community surveys, home contacts, the P.T.A. movement, schools as community centers, school publicity, service clubs, social and welfare agencies, field trips and exhibits, government agencies. Thirteen years later the Department published its second yearbook devoted to community education: *Community Living and the Elementary School.*[7] Many descriptions of actual practice in both rural and urban situations were presented. The underlying philosophy was stressed, as were tested procedures in utilizing community resources in the curriculum, building community understanding of the school, meeting new community needs, and adventuring in school-community coordination.

[7] Twenty-fourth Yearbook, 1945.

1933 . . . Field Study Courses for Teachers and Arkansas Program for Improvement of Instruction

A series of fully-accredited field study courses specifically for teachers was launched by the New Jersey State Teachers College at Montclair. For the first time, an outstanding teachers college made field studies of local, regional, and national communities an integral part of its professional program, and gave full academic credit for it. These travel courses included Field Studies in the Metropolitan Community, New England and French Canada, Eastern United States, and Continental United States. A Bureau of Field Studies was established in the College to plan, promote and conduct these courses, and to do the needed research. The Bureau's first publication, *Field Studies in a Teachers College,* announced that "the purpose of the field studies courses is to demonstrate to teachers and administrators that the true subject matter of education consists not merely of words in textbooks, but of first-hand, directed experience with real things and real people, and, furthermore, to train them in the use of community resources, both local and national, for educational purposes."

Also in 1933 the Arkansas Program for the Improvement of Instruction was begun—a community school development project instituted by the State Board of Education in cooperation with the teacher education institutions, professional organizations of teachers and parents, and other interested groups. Oriented about the community school idea, the specific purposes were to improve teaching procedures, to promote wider and better use of community resources, and to emphasize the necessity of active cooperation between all community agencies interested educationally in community welfare. Community surveys were made to determine need, interest, and resources; community-school programs developed under the direction of an expert coordinator; teachers' field workshop courses were conducted in selected counties; and summer workshops were organized in each of the six state senior colleges. Financed in part by the General Education Board, the project was originally scheduled to cover five years but actually went several years beyond that time.

1934 . . . First Yearbook on Community Leadership

The first yearbook devoted to the meaning, value, and function of community leadership and methods for community cooperation was published by the Michigan Education Association as its seventh yearbook, *Cooperative Community Leadership*.

1938 . . . First Book on the Community School and First Yearbook on Techniques of Community Study

Edited by Samuel Everett for the Society for Curriculum Study, *The Community School* was first to deal with the concept and practice of the community school as such. It described in detail the programs and operating principles of nine community schools, and analyzed them in terms of basic contrasts between the "traditional" and the "community" types of school program.

That same year, the National Council for the Social Studies published *The Utilization of Community Resources in the Social Studies*. Despite its social studies' orientation, this volume aroused wide professional interest in the whole community-resources idea because it stressed teacher-education for community understanding, education through community participation, and the building of better human relations through community activity.

1939 . . . The Sloan Project in Applied Economics

"What would happen if the schools, serving low-income groups where unrealized opportunities exist, built the major part of their programs around the three economic necessities of food, housing, and clothing? What would be the result if somehow the old-time subjects were geared to present realities, if community needs were pointed out, latent possibilities demonstrated, and every glimmer of effort made to translate learning into practice, tactfully encouraged?" Such were the fundamental questions which the state universities of Kentucky, Florida, and Vermont, in cooperation with their respective state departments of education, sought to answer through long-time controlled experimentation beginning in 1939. This "Applied Economics Project" was financed by the Alfred P. Sloan Foundation and is often called the "Sloan Project." Exploratory surveys were made, new curriculum materials produced for every grade level, specific programs developed in selected schools, and results measured in terms of specific improvement in the material standard of living in the communities.

Four years later the American Association of Colleges for Teacher Education began active participation in the project. Member colleges in various parts of the nation, in cooperation with local school systems, sought to help pupils and their families improve home conditions by centering school learning activities around better ways of living. Everywhere the conclusion was the same: material standards of living were often significantly improved through what was taught in the classroom, and that when standardized achievement tests were given, more than normal progress was usually shown.

1940 . . . Southern States Work Conference on School Administrative Problems

This was the first attempt by a large group of educational leaders from an entire region to study the relation of education to natural resources and human resources. The state departments of education and the state education associations of fouteen states formed the work conference. Through conferences, research, and publications it helped to gear child, youth, and adult education to the basic problem: that of using all actual and potential resources of the region for the benefit of the people. Over 150 persons, organized into 28 committees, prepared materials dealing with the need for Southern development and planned the building of an educational program to meet that need directly, ways of organizing and administering schools accordingly, and techniques for evaluating achievements continuously.

1942 . . . New York State Teacher-Education Standard

The New York State Board of Regents adopted four major criteria as standards to be used by the State Department of Education in appraising college and university programs of teacher education within the state. One criterion required, in part, that future teachers of the academic subjects in New York State high schools should have developed "an appreciation of the nature of contemporary society and the role of the schools in the sound promotion of the enduring interests of this society. This implies a much larger measure of actual participation in community life than has been characteristic of either teachers or young people attending school. . . . Such a study of society cannot be realistic if it is confined to the reading of books. It calls for active participation by the student in community or regional life and close contact with various representative public and private agencies. The resources and institutions of the local community or region should be used as a laboratory for the study of society." [8]

1943 . . . Progressive Education Association Becomes Community-Minded and Committee on Southern Regional Studies and Education Formed

The Board of the American Education Fellowship (formerly the Progressive Education Association) announced its new and basic orientation: that of educating the whole child in and through his community as well as in his school.

For years we have been inviting all who would to come to us, into

[8] Committee on Teacher Education of the Association of Colleges and Universities of the State of New York. *Criteria for Teacher Education*. p. 4. State Board of Regents, Albany, New York, September 1, 1942.

the schools, to see what we were doing there and to help us do it. The *new job* calls for us to cooperate outside as well as inside the schools, to go out into the communities in which schools stand, and in which our children live. We must see what the forces are that affect the lives of our children outside of school; we must take a militant part in seeing that our towns provide all the necessary services for children, and that these services operate efficiently. We must put ourselves back of every effort by established agencies to do a good job.

Your Board unanimously proposes a broadening of the interests and program of this Association to include the communities in which children live.[9]

Thus was abandoned that older, almost anarchistic emphasis which progressive education had placed upon the individual as such. Here was progressive education's official recognition that individual human beings, unique as each one is in personality and potentiality, nevertheless are influenced, even moulded, in behavior by community values and patterns.

In the same year the American Council on Education appointed the Committee on Southern Regional Studies and Education. Its purpose was to assist existing agencies in the South develop methods and materials to close the gap between research findings and their educational use. The purpose was to help the 38 regional agencies and more than 650 state institutions and organizations to translate scientific knowledge into improved living for all people of the South. The Committee sponsored regional conferences, published two books, *Channeling Research Into Education* and *Education for Use of Regional Resources,* issues a newsletter, *Resource-Use Education,* and provides a regional consultation and clearinghouse service in resource-use education.

1944 . . . Educational Policies Commission Urges Community Schools

Disclaiming "blueprints" but presenting "samples," the Educational Policies Commission boldly described in *Education for All American Youth* the kinds of life-centered, community

[9] "Your Board Reports." *Progressive Education* 20:368-70; December 1943.

high schools which must everywhere be developed if youth needs are to be met, and if federal control of education is to be avoided. This was a detailed and comprehensive plan showing how America's 30,000 high schools and junior colleges could be transformed in purpose and program to provide adequate educational services which will actually meet the basic needs and capitalize the varied abilities of *all* American youth. In succeeding years, the Commission published similar volumes dealing with pre-school education (*The Educational Services for Younger Children*, 1945) and with the elementary school (*Education for All American Children*, 1948). In 1952 the Commission issued *Education for All American Youth: A Further Look* written in terms of current national and international developments and of local progress in secondary education. Again, and even more emphatically, the emphasis was placed upon school-community relations and the community school.

1945 . . . State Department Division of School and Community Relations

The first Division of School and Community Relations of its kind was established in the Washington State Office of Public Instruction. Its immediate function was to provide consultant service to school districts, administrators, curriculum committees, parent-teacher associations, colleges and universities, and others interested in relating school programs more closely with community life needs and resources. The basic purpose was twofold: (a) To help schools develop systematic programs of community study and service so that students might know better their own community's varied needs, problems, and resources, and might feel a growing sense of personal responsibility for improving the quality of living; and (b) to stimulate improved school and community relations, lay participation in school policy and program planning, and community coordination of educational services.[10]

[10] For a fuller description see Edward G. Olsen, *School and Community Programs*, pp. 486-490. New York: Prentice-Hall, 1949.

1946 . . . The Montana Study Started

The Montana Study was established for a three-year period —a research project in community needs and human resources carried on by the Greater University of Montana, and financed initially by one of the foundations. Its overall purpose was to study ways to improve the quality of living in small communities. More immediate objectives were "to get the university off the campus," "find ways to stabilize the small community and family in Montana," and "find ways to raise the appreciative and spiritual standards of living of the people of the state." Under guidance by a state-wide advisory committee, the Montana Study engaged in fundamental research, in community field work, and in promotion of teacher education for the community-centered conception which was basic to the whole project. Under its leadership, many communities engaged in a ten-week, self-study project through which they examined themselves socially, culturally, economically, reported on their own problems, and made recommendations to themselves for their own futures. In cooperation with the University's School of Education, in-service programs were developed through which teachers could learn to serve as community and educational leaders for people of all ages and economic backgrounds. Similar projects for teacher-leadership in local cultural development were undertaken through cooperation of members of the State Teachers' Association.

1947 . . . National Commission on Life Adjustment Education for Youth

Appointed by the United States Office of Education, this Commission was established to encourage the development of functional programs for high school students. The directing purpose was to gear instruction to modern living, so that the imperative needs of all youth may be met through secondary education that is realistic. In many states, State departments of education found local schools which would cooperate in planned efforts to achieve the goals of an improved curriculum program. Focusing upon home membership, work, and citizenship as major life-needs of youth, these experimental programs stress also such other common problems as developing an effective personality, living healthfully and safely, spending leisure wholesomely, and managing personal finances wisely. Specific curriculum improvement projects undertaken were concerned with invigorating existing courses, with the enrichment of broad fields, with the building of common learnings courses, and with programs that cut across subject lines. Community lay participation in school planning for better education has been sought and secured from the beginning.

1948 . . . Cooperative Program in Educational Administration

At its national convention, the American Association of School Administrators approved and adopted a nation-wide, intensive, cooperative, action-research program in the improvement of school administration. Motivating this vast project was the growing recognition that the school administrator now has a new and highly significant role: that of managing a community-type school and hence of working closely in and with his community as a social service agent. The basic question was, "What are the practical implications of this community concept of educational leadership for patterns of pre-service education, in-service experience, and advanced professional training?" Co-sponsoring the study with the AASA are the National Association of Chief State School Officers and the National Conference of County and Rural Superintendents. Financed by the W. K. Kellogg Foundation, the CPEA was begun with a series of five regional conferences which identified 130 areas of concern.

These were then grouped into nine major areas as the scope of the study: the role of the superintendent; the superintendent and his job; the superintendent and his relations with the public, the board, and his staff; administrative personnel; teacher personnel; the superintendent and the curriculum;

the board of education; reorganization; and finance. To answer the basic question of the superintendent's leadership role and community as well as school responsibilities in each of these areas, eight key universities were chosen as regional centers: Teachers College, Columbia University; Harvard University; the University of Chicago; George Peabody College for Teachers; the University of Texas; the University of Oregon; Ohio State University; and Leland Stanford University. Each institution secured continuing cooperation from other colleges and from many school systems in its region for a three to five year project. Through careful, cooperative action-research they examine both the content and the procedures of effective school administration. It is expected that when the final reports are completed they will have as great significance for the upgrading and future training of school administrators as the famous Flexner Report of 1910 had on the medical profession of its day.

1949 . . . National Citizens Commission for the Public Schools

"The problems of public education concern all of us, and it is time for *all* of us to do something about them" said a group of influential laymen as they founded this national lay participation organization. Its purpose is to stimulate a resurgence of popular interest in the public schools and to help local committees of citizens working with their boards of education to decide intelligently what kind of public education they really want, and how to help the educators provide it. To this end, the Commission operates as a national clearing house for information between local and state organizations of community citizens committees. Its program is basically threefold:

- Promotion of a series of projects to encourage active interest in the public schools
- Assistance to community citizen committees for school improvement
- Far-reaching studies designed to help answer some of the

most frequently asked and fundamentally important questions
about the schools.

1953 . . . Two Progress Reports

The Community School, a comprehensive yearbook summarizing much of what is established in this field, was published by the National Society for the Study of Education.
Reporting both theory and current practice, the volume identifies the community school "as one which offers suitable educational opportunities to all age groups and which fashions
learning experiences for both adults and young people out of
the unsolved problems of community life." Assuming this to
be a major goal of school education, the book explains the
nature of community organization in relation to educational
procedures, and reports numerous case-studies of community
improvement through community-school programs.

The Modern Community School edited by Edward G. Olsen was written by the Committee on the Community School
of the Association for Supervision and Curriculum Development of the National Education Association. It sought to provide a fresh analysis of community school programs, current
best practice, tested principles for developing a community
school, and a value frame of reference that is educationally
sound and dynamic as well as thoroughly democratic.

Signposts of Progress

Are all these events mere straws in the onrushing
stream of things? Perhaps so—but in them is sure
direction toward the future. It is now widely agreed
that the school's responsible function is to improve
the quality of human living, both individual and
group, and that such improvement requires a far
closer cooperation between school and community
than has been typical in even the immediate past.
If our school instruction is to become truly effective,
we must organize much of it around fundamental

human needs, we must directly relate school programs with community life processes and problems, and we must provide extensive community study and service opportunities for children, youth, and adults alike. Within a rigorously democratic frame of reference we must help citizens of all age groups to attain realistic understanding of our precarious civilization, to develop higher moral standards with feelings of personal responsibility for improving human welfare, and also to learn the essential skills of democratic group enterprise for the common good. Not otherwise will the schools and colleges of our Nuclear Air Age justify their cost or even their continued existence. Such is the general concept of school-community relations now winning acceptance by teachers, school administrators, school board members, and many other lay people throughout the nation.

Some may assert that this community school philosophy and procedure threatens liberal education. To such critics we would simply suggest that true liberal education is that which liberates a person from blind subservience to the morés of his group as these have been defined by the traditions of a particular people, place, and period in history. Liberal education means a freeing of the mind from provincial pettiness in every field. It is perspective at its best. It is to "see life steadily and see it whole" as Matthew Arnold wisely said. *To see life steadily and to see it whole* is also a major value and purpose of life-centered education.

There is more even than that to the educational viewpoint we have outlined. The intellect does not operate in an emotional vacuum. Almost above all else, youth today needs a sense of *belonging*—of being *wanted by society* in times of peace as well as during years of war. If only for psychological maturation and emotional stability, each youth must develop his personal conception of *individual worth* through his achievement of genuine *social recognition*. Particularly in these times of strain and confusion, we must somehow succeed in giving all our children and young people a realistic understanding of their world, extensive opportunity to participate with personal satisfaction and social recognition in its ongoing processes of living, and consequent possibility of developing those feelings of true achievement, personal worth, and social sensitivity which are essential to emotional adjustment and to democratic citizenship. If we cannot, then there is grave danger that the new generation, disillusioned with the social unreality of the traditional and progressive schools, may express their accumulated frustration in movements destructive of democracy itself.

These years hold promise as well as hazard for youth and education. If we can succeed in developing widespread educational programs that are psychologically satisfying and socially creative, and which function in all teaching areas at all school levels, we may hope to witness during the second half of this century a vital expansion of democratically effective living, both personal and social. This requires that we increasingly relate education to life experience, school instruction to individual and community needs, teaching to living at its highest and best. Whatever the specific nature of such future educational programs, we may even now assert with confidence that their primary purpose must be to channel the splendid energies of youth toward the progressive, cooperative improvement of community life in its local, regional, national, and international aspects. Here looms the supreme educational and civic opportunity of our times. What a challenge to peaceful reconstruction of this war-weary world!

Learning Activities

Socio-Drama

Have class members assume the roles of the following, evaluate educational trends each in terms of his own orientation, and state the reasons for his views:

1. A classical humanist
2. Comenius
3. Pestalozzi
4. Spencer
5. Dewey
6. Hart

Discussion Topics

1. The community school is sometimes criticized on the ground that children are too immature to tackle the real problems involved in improving the quality of living. Is this objection justified? In what sense can you defend the community-school idea against this charge?
2. Looking back upon your own (a) elementary school, (b) secondary school, (c) college experiences, would you say that your teachers were fundamentally

    book-centered,
    child-centered,
    life-centered

    in their teaching purposes? Which orientation do you think was favored by your parents and why?
3. What other "milestones" do you think should be added to this list? Why?
4. Debate this proposition: Resolved: That the Great Books plan for the liberal arts curriculum on the college level is superior to the social process and problem core of the community school.

Group Projects

1. Develop and circulate a questionnaire to determine student and faculty opinion upon the questions:
    (a) Should institutions of higher education bring their influence to bear directly upon current social, economic, and political community problems?
    (b) What factors limit their efforts in these directions?

2. Arrange an attractive display of the "milestone" publications mentioned in this chapter. Add others which you feel worthy of inclusion and tell the class your reasons.
3. Invite the president of your Parent-Teacher Association to speak to the class on the community responsibilities of the schools and the work of the Parent-Teacher Association in this connection.
4. Devise a chart presentation of the major advances in school practice resulting from the "milestones" listed in this chapter.

Individual Activities

1. Write a paper on the "sense" and "social" realism movement in education since the Middle Ages.
2. Review the literature on the Sloan Project in Applied Economics, and summarize its conclusions.
3. Report to the class on the Montana Study and lead group discussion of this study's implications for other community situations.
4. Review the program and recommendations of the National Commission on Life Adjustment Education for Youth. Compare these recommendations with the Seven Characteristics of the Community School sketched in Chapter 1.
5. Write to the nearest university acting as a regional center for the Cooperative Project in Educational Administration. Request progress reports and summaries of findings with special reference to the community responsibilities of school administrators.

Learning Materials

The historic struggle for realism in school education can be traced in any comprehensive history of education textbook such as Paul Monroe's classic *Textbook in the History of Education* (Macmillan, 1919), Chapter 8. Chapters 15 and 16 in the National Society for the Study of Education's yearbook *The Community School* (University of Chicago Press, 1952) provides excellent perspective also. A provocative, popularly written treatment is Everett Dean Martin's *The Meaning of a Liberal Education* (Garden City, 1926), especially Chapters 4, 5, 12, and 13. For an objective sketch of the whole school-community integration movement during the first forty years of this century, see Fannie Dunn's Chapter 8 in *Community Resources in Rural Schools*, the 1939 Yearbook of the NEA's Department of Rural Education. The expansion of the community school concept in recent years is documented in Chapter 6 of *The Modern Community School* (Appleton-Century-Crofts, 1953), edited by Edward G. Olsen for the Association for Supervision and Curriculum Development of the NEA.

The "Sloan Project in Applied Economics" is described through charts.

pictures, and text in Clara M. Olson and Norman D. Fletcher's *Learn and Live* (Alfred P. Sloan Foundation, 1946). Some of the work done in the "Sloan schools" is described in the May, 1946, *Bulletin of the National Association of Secondary-School Principals* which presents a series of articles stressing the need to improve the quality of living through education, and suggests the core-curriculum as a vehicle. A later *Bulletin* (May 1948) reports basic philosophy, typical school activities, units of work, and development of instructional materials, all reflecting this Sloan experiment. The American Association of Colleges for Teacher Education participated extensively in this project, as described in Stewart B. Hamblen and Richmond Page's *Improvement of Living Through the Schools*. Examples of what some community schools are doing to improve their community's food habits, housing, and clothing selection and care are given in *Schools Count in Country Life*, issued by the United States Office of Education (1947). Emphasis is given to total faculty planning to discover and meet economic and health needs, and to suggested pupil problems and activities in solving these problems.

The Montana Study story is dramatically told by Richard W. Poston in *Small Town Renaissance* (Harper, 1950), which shows how small communities improved their own quality of living through self-study groups which eventuated in creative community action in such areas as industry, art, recreation, and education. The Study's director, Baker Brownell, summarized his conclusions in *The Human Community, Its Philosophy and Practice for a Time of Crisis* (Harper, 1950), a lucid, charming, and disturbing statement about community living today. The problem is how men can achieve community status which will support aspirational life in the face of the disintegrative impact of technology on outmoded cultural inheritances. "An Evaluation of the Montana Study" by Bert Hansen reviews the history and philosophy of the Study, and evaluates the community work actually done as a result of it (*Journal of Higher Education* 20:18-27; January 1949).

The Life Adjustment Education program has thus far been reported chiefly in several bulletins issued by the United States Office of Education, and in the professional journals. Harl Douglass' *Education for Life Adjustment* (Ronald, 1950) is one important book in this area.

Office of Education

Life Adjustment Education, 1949.
Life Adjustment Education in the American Culture, 1951.
Vitalizing Secondary Education, 1951.

Magazines

National Association of Secondary School Principals Bulletin, issues of April 1949, April 1951, April 1953.
North Central Association Quarterly, issue of April 1950.

The **Cooperative Program in Educational Administration** may be followed through various progress reports in the periodicals. See especially these and others you can locate through the *Education Index:*

"AASA-Kellogg Project Promises a Better Life for the Superintendent," A. H. Rice. *Nation's Schools* 46:31-35; November 1950.

"CPEA in New England," C. G. Sargent and G. E. Flower. *Nation's Schools* 48:43-46; December 1951.

"Cooperative Program in Educational Administration in the Middle Atlantic Region," D. R. Davies. *School Executive* 71:73-74; May 1952.

"Cooperative Program in Educational Administration and How it Grew," John S. Carroll. *Journal of Teacher Education* 3:105-112; June 1952.

"School-Community Development Study: Ohio Center of the Co-operative Program in School Administration." *Educational Research Bulletin* 31:169-196; October 1952.

"Educational Administration at Mid-Century," D. R. Davies. *Teachers College Record* 54:125-130; December 1952. Same, *Educational Outlook* 27:56-62; January 1953.

"Results of Action Research in Educational Administration," *School Executive* 73:67-79; November 1953.

"The CPEA in 1953," Hugh B. Masters. *School Executive* 73:62-64; January 1954.

"The Importance of Human Relations in Educational Administration." *Nation's Schools* 53:43-54; January 1954.

Index*

* Each item that is the subject of a chapter is followed by the chapter number; the number of the page on which the chapter starts is given in *italics*.

531